Answering Their Country's Call

Answering
Their Country's Call
Marylanders in World War II

. . . .

Edited by Michael H. Rogers

The Johns Hopkins University Press

Baltimore and London

© 2002 The Johns Hopkins University Press
All rights reserved. Published 2002
Printed in the United States of America
on acid-free paper

9 8 7 6 5 4 3 2 1

The Johns Hopkins University Press
2715 North Charles Street
Baltimore, Maryland 21218-4363
www.press.jhu.edu

Library of Congress Cataloging-in-Publication Data

Answering their country's call : Marylanders in World
War II / edited by Michael H. Rogers ; foreword by
William Donald Schaefer.

    p. cm.

  ISBN 0-8018-7126-3 (alk. paper)

  1. Soldiers—Maryland—Biography. 2. World War,
1939–1945—Maryland. 3. United States—Armed
Forces—Biography. 4. African-American soldiers—
Maryland—History—20th century. 5. Maryland—
Biography. I. Rogers, Michael H.

  D769.85.M3 M37 2002

  940.54'12752—dc21

                             2002003289

A catalog record for this book is available from the
British Library.

To MY HEROES, Nolan, Barbara, Suzie, and Bobby; to the memory of Florence A. Rogers; and to the memory of those men and women, of all nations, who gave their lives in the cause of a better world from 1939 to 1945, this book is fondly and reverently dedicated.

CONTENTS

FOREWORD

As a native and lifelong resident of the great State of Maryland, I am proud to contribute to a book that captures a sampling of some of her finest citizens. On the following pages you will read about Maryland citizens of tremendous character and courage who served in the Second World War. Some were credited with performing heroic acts in the face of the enemy, while others performed duties that were perhaps less glamorous but no less important in achieving total victory in the war. Whether on the front lines or on the many Maryland assembly lines that rolled during the war, the contributions of Maryland's citizens proved vital to the overall war effort and helped preserve freedom and peace throughout the world.

The generation of Americans who fought in World War II is slipping away. Monuments and memorials mark their valor, but many of their individual stories of personal struggle, courage, and bravery have not been told. I have chosen to participate in this documentary project because of its unique approach. The stories of Maryland's World War II veterans are told in their own voices. You have an opportunity to learn about this war from the men and women who experienced it firsthand and see it through their eyes. You will read about the joys, fears, triumphs, and tragedies of the Second World War told with the detail and accuracy that only those who lived through the war could express.

I am proud to have been one of the many Marylanders who served my country in the Second World War. I continue to have tremendous respect and admiration for all of Maryland's citizens who helped lead our nation to victory and for those Marylanders who have been called upon once again to defend the freedom for which we are thankful.

—William Donald Schaefer

ACKNOWLEDGMENTS

SPECIAL THANKS to George Rich, for helping make this book possible. Many thanks as well to Governor William Donald Schaefer, Delegate Clarence Davis, Mary Yates, Dorothy Hoover, Ralph Lewis, Scott Stevens, Robert J. Brugger and the Johns Hopkins University Press, Col. Erwin A. Burtnick, Erin O'Connor, and Kristen Saunders.

INTRODUCTION

I NEVER HAD ANY INTENTION of writing this book. It started as a project to explore my interest in the Second World War and to answer questions I had about how a man can leave his home, say goodbye to everyone he has ever known, and go off to war and fight in combat knowing that he may never come back. My curiosity had never been satisfied by books or documentaries, which seemed to me never to ask the right questions. I remember once watching a documentary about the Marine invasion of Iwo Jima. The film showed Marines loading into a landing craft, and then the commentary switched to detailing what happened after they had landed. "Wait a minute," I thought. "What did those Marines think about, talk about, and do while in those landing craft preparing to go into combat?" I wanted to know. I am fortunate enough never to have experienced combat for myself, and even now, despite having asked many veterans to describe it, I can't say that I truly understand what it must have felt like.

The events that compelled me to start collecting the experiences of our World War II veterans began on Election Day 2000 while I was waiting in line to vote. The line was long, and when I turned around to see how much it had grown, I noticed an elderly man and his wife standing quietly behind me. There was nothing remarkable about the couple, other than the fact that the gentleman wore a baseball cap with the words "I am a World War II veteran." Perhaps it was the boredom of waiting in line, perhaps it was my interest in combat, but something made me say hello to the man in the cap, and we struck up a conversation.

"So, you're a veteran of World War II?" I said, extending my hand to introduce myself. The man took my hand, shook it, nodded his head, and said, "Yeah, it was a long time ago." I felt the eyes of the people standing in line nearby turn towards me. They had heard my question, and they too seemed curious about what this veteran might have to say. "Where did you serve?" I asked. He cleared his throat and adjusted his cap and tugged on his jacket sleeves. "I was in the 2nd Infantry Division. In Europe, you know." "The 2nd Infantry?" I said. "Wow, you were at the Bulge, then." I knew that the 2nd Infantry Division had played a pivotal role in stopping the Nazi advance through the Ardennes in December 1944. I also knew that they had suffered tremendous casualties in the process. "The 2nd was hit pretty hard, wasn't it?" I asked. He cast his eyes towards the floor and said, "Yup, I lost my whole darn company. I slept in the snow for almost a week." We talked for about ten minutes. I don't recall exactly what we spoke about, but I was careful not to ask too many questions for fear of awakening perhaps painful memories.

The line began moving, my turn to vote was quickly approaching, and I had every intention of just saying goodbye to the man and wishing him and his wife a pleasant day. As a way of ending the conversation I blurted out that his family must be very proud of his wartime service. At this he threw his hands up in the air and said, "Nah, no one in my family cares about what happened except my wife, and we never talk about it anymore. My kids never asked. No one cares what we did back then." I couldn't believe what I was hearing. "That's not true," I said. "I care, and a lot of other people care, too. I appreciate what you and the rest of you did." Then I said, "Thanks. Perhaps no one has ever said that to you." He gave me a smile and seemed content to leave the conversation at that, but I asked if he had ever considered recording his experiences. His grandchildren or great-grandchildren, I argued, might one day come across his words and develop an appreciation for his services that his own children may not have felt. He answered, "I don't have the energy, and my hands hurt all the time."

I don't know why I said what I said next, but it changed my life forever. "I will do it. I'll meet you, and you can tell me what happened, and I'll write it down for you." I had never thought of doing such a thing before. "Look, here's my number," I said. "Please call me so we can meet somewhere. I mean it." The man took the piece of paper with my number, looked at it and glanced at his wife, and then tucked it into his jacket. "OK, we'll see," he said. "I am busy now, but maybe in a few weeks."

Those were the last words I ever heard him speak. I don't recall his name, and he never called. I wonder what he did with my number. I wonder if he ever thought of calling. I wonder what fantastic stories he might have had about himself and the men he served with. Whatever those stories were, they are now probably lost.

My encounter with the man from the 2nd Infantry Division and the words we exchanged resounded in my mind for days. I could not get over the fact that his family had shown no interest in his wartime experiences and that he had never talked about them in all the years since. It got me thinking about other World War II veterans

I knew. One of them was a man named Guy Cicone, a Howard County circuit court judge in Ellicott City. When I was young, my father and I would go the Colts games, and we would sit next to Guy and his wife, Marie. He always called me "Little Buddy." Guy and Marie did not have kids of their own, and I liked to think that maybe they thought of me as the son they never had.

Guy smoked a pipe, and as much as the smoke annoyed me, it wouldn't have been a Colts game without the smoke. It was always a struggle for Guy to fill his pipe with tobacco because he was missing two or three fingers from his right hand, and one day I asked my father what had happened to them. He told me that Guy had been a tank commander during the Second World War, and his tank encountered a German roadblock in Italy. The tank was hit by machine-gun fire, and when he reached up to close the turret hatch, he was hit in the hand. That's how Guy lost his fingers. He spent years in an Army hospital recovering, but he had saved himself and his crew.

I had spent countless hours sitting next to Guy at the Colts games, but I never had the courage to ask him what had happened to his hand. I recall my father or Marie saying that Guy didn't like talking about his wartime experiences. Guy is gone now. He died before I could talk with him about those experiences, and as far as I know the little details of what happened on the day he lost his fingers are also gone, lost into history, forever.

Remembering my buddy Guy, I vowed to find people like him, people I could interview and ask the questions I had been afraid to ask him. I was determined to record the little details about their wartime experiences that would otherwise be lost. Every time I picked up the paper or watched the news I became acutely aware of how many World War II veterans were passing away each day, and it motivated me to get started right away.

I sat down and made a list of the kinds of veterans I hoped to interview. The list was short: a bomber pilot, a fighter pilot, a Marine, and an Army infantryman. The only prerequisite I had was that the veteran must have served in combat. There were many aspects of the war I could have focused on, but I wanted to speak to the men who had put their lives on the line. Only they could answer my questions about what combat was like, what it felt like to get shot at, to kill, to see themselves or their buddies wounded, to see others killed.

My search for the veterans who would eventually appear in this book began in the first week of December 2000. In some cases I used Internet resources to search public records, which allowed me to find the few veterans who appear in this book who served in public office in Maryland. But mostly I found these individuals by chance. I began by going up to men on the street who looked old enough to have served in the war and asking if they were combat veterans. I sometimes made embarrassing errors of judgment; there are many fifty-year-old men who look eighty, and quite a few eighty-year-old men who look fifty. To my surprise, most of the World War II veterans I met were healthy, active, young-looking people. Most of the people I approached had not served in the war or in combat but had a co-worker, neighbor, or friend who had, and they were kind enough to provide a name and sometimes a number for me to call.

Calling a perfect stranger to ask to be allowed into his home can be tricky. Fortunately, the Maryland Veterans Commission and Col. Erwin Burtnick unofficially recognized my project as an important research endeavor, which provided me with some legitimacy and assured the veterans that I was an honest student of history. I needed this because many veterans have grown suspicious of people asking about their wartime experiences because a few unscrupulous people have befriended veterans and then offered to "polish" their war medals, only to take them and never be heard from again. I made it a point never to ask on the phone if the person had been awarded medals, and never asked to see them unless he volunteered to bring them out.

The greatest surprise to me during my search was just how much interest others showed in talking and learning about our veterans. Finding time and energy for the interviewing, the research, and the writing was often difficult. The positive energy I received from family, friends, and complete strangers kept me going when the daily pressures of my job and personal life threatened to extinguish my enthusiasm for the project.

I arranged my first interview during a visit to a local delicatessen where there were always some old-timers hanging out. I nervously approached a group assembled around a large table. They stopped talking when I walked up and introduced myself and asked if any of them had served in the Second World War. The man closest to me said he had been in the Navy during the war. He then said, "You need to talk to that guy over there, he's a real hero. He's got some stories." One of the other men at the table asked, "What's all this for, anyway?" I didn't have an easy answer. My questions about the experience of combat seemed too complicated to explain, and I didn't want to bore this group of men who were attentively waiting for my response. Then I thought of a simple explanation: "It's for a book I'm writing." Until that instant I had never had any intention of writing a book, but now I knew: I was going to write a book about World War II combat veterans from Maryland. I left the deli with a few phone numbers and an appointment for my first interview that same evening. I visit that deli often, and now there are tables full of old-timers whom I am proud to call my friends.

My interview technique was admittedly amateurish. In fact, that first interview was such a disaster that I couldn't use it for the book and didn't have the guts to go back and relive the horrible experience. In the interviews, I would spend about three hours, sometimes more, with each person at his or her home—enough time for both of us to feel that we had covered all we could. I would tape-record the conversation, then go home and transcribe it. This was the most time-consuming aspect of the project for me, a helpless hunt-and-peck typist. I learned the hard way the importance of taking a few extra minutes during the interview to confirm the spelling of names and places, to avoid massive confusion later on. I would then arrange the material in chronological order, polish the paragraphs as best I could, and mail a draft copy of the text to the interviewee with the request that he or she correct any blatant factual errors (as well as my misspellings of names and places) and to insert any additional words he or she felt would add flavor to the profile.

It took weeks of sending revisions back and forth to complete each profile. In almost every case I was astonished at the attention each interviewee paid to the project. Quite often I would receive numerous additional pages in return, detailing thoughts or experiences the person had remembered since our meeting. The patience of the men and women I interviewed and their eagerness to help me get the facts right were truly amazing, and greatly appreciated. On occasion the returned draft would have some sentences scratched out. When I called to ask why, the response would often be, "I can't say that in print." But I insisted that the words they had spoken during the interview be included in their profile, and I fought, sometimes tooth and nail, to ensure that their stories were presented in the same raw vocabulary they had instinctively used during our meeting. There is no political correctness in war, as I once heard someone say.

I have numerous stories—stories I think funny now, but not then—of failing to bring enough tape to an interview, of forgetting the tape recorder altogether, and, on one occasion, of actually drowning my recorder in my bag when a bottle of water spilled and I had to drive in a heavy rain to a nearby mall to buy another (Dorothy Steinbis Davis remembers this, too). My travels all across our great State of Maryland to interview the men and women who appear in this book will provide me with fond memories for as long as I live.

. . .

I opened the interviews by telling the participants that this was their opportunity to tell the world about themselves, their generation, the war, and perhaps someone they knew who did not survive but whom they wished the world to remember. I wanted them to speak about the war in the way they wanted, without my forcing anything on them.

The questions I asked generally came up spontaneously as the interview progressed, giving a unique quality to each profile. There was a general set of questions that I asked all the participants—

where they had grown up, how they got into the service, what they did while in uniform—but from there on it was a fairly informal discussion conducted across the kitchen table or sitting on the living room couch. During the process I had to develop tactful ways of asking that the barking dog be put outside, that the ringer on the phone be turned off, and that the spouse watch television in another room.

From the outset of the project I wanted to record as much "user information" as possible: detail about the planes, tanks, weapons, food, and other equipment these veterans had used during the war. While the machines and tools they used will sit in museums for a thousand years, we may never know how they operated in combat unless we hear about it from the men and women who used them. At the outset of each interview I explained that I hoped to record as much information as possible related to the senses of touch, smell, taste, sight, and sound. I asked questions like "What does combat sound like?" "What did your C rations look and taste like?" and "What did the dead look like?" More important, I wanted to record the emotions these veterans had experienced in war, so I asked questions like "How would you describe combat to someone who has never been in it?" "What did it feel like to see dead and dying men?" "How did it feel to kill?" and "Did you hate the enemy?" I also asked if they remembered anything humorous (not many had an answer to this one) or something that made their lives a bit more bearable. The amount of detail I was able to get with these questions was startling. Hearing these men and women recall so many details from sixty years ago told me just how profoundly their wartime experiences were etched into their brains.

During the interviews I often heard, "I never told anyone this before." Sometimes the spouse would sit in the room with us during the interview and before I left would pull me aside to say, "He's never talked about the war before. Thank you for getting him to open up. I had no idea." I was amazed at how many of them had never until now shared their thoughts about the war, not even with their spouses. I wonder why so many aging war veterans feel compelled to share their thoughts only in the later stages of their lives. Perhaps they just need finally to let go of some of the things they have been carrying with them all these years.

At the conclusion of the interview I asked each person exactly the same question: "Who do you think are the real heroes of the Second World War?" Of all the questions I asked, this one produced the greatest emotional response. Some cried, and some sat silent for a time before answering. Most began their answer by stating that they were not, by any definition of the word, a "hero." (In these cases I responded by saying that I reserved the right to call them heroes whether they liked it or not.) The question was intentionally loaded so as to elicit an emotional response. Perhaps it was not fair, but I think the most poignant aspect of what these veterans wish to share with the world can be read in the final paragraph of each profile, in which they answer this question.

. . .

The profiles assembled here are intended to present the uniqueness of the individual's intimate experience of combat and to capture the human quality of war that is often overlooked when history is recalled in terms of armies, battles, and campaigns. I had hoped to include representatives of all the branches of military service and of as many of the theaters of operation as possible but in the end was not able to find all the men and women I would have needed to talk to. The fact that the Navy and Coast Guard are relatively underrepresented in this book does not indicate any lack of appreciation on my part for the significant contributions both organizations made in achieving victory in the war.

At the onset of the project I had no intention of including women, I must admit. I had no idea of the vital role women played during the war until I read an article in the *Baltimore Sun* featuring four Army nurses that captivated me. The article revealed to me how close women were to the front lines all across the globe during the Second World War. The author of the article helped me contact two of those nurses, and I now feel that this book would not have been complete without the profiles of these two women detailing the contributions and sacrifices made by women during the war.

I also had little understanding of the role African Americans played in the Second World War. I had seen movies and read books about the Tuskegee Airmen, but beyond that I had never heard of any experiences of black enlisted men. I was fortunate enough to meet State Delegate Clarence Davis, who I discovered was dedicated to preserving the history of African Americans in the military, and he provided me with the names of four or five black World War II veterans for my project. The experience of meeting and listening to the stories of these men gave me a profound new perspective.

Unless noted otherwise, all the photographs appearing in this book are from the personal collections of the participants. These photographs have been hidden away in drawers and closets since the end of the war, and very few of them have been seen by the public until now. Almost every participant is shown in a photograph taken during the war. I considered including recent pictures as well but decided that it would detract from the message that the war was fought and won primarily by very young men and women.

. . .

These are just some of the Marylanders who between 1941 and 1945 answered the call to preserve the freedoms we enjoy today. Some of them performed exceptionally heroic deeds but shy away when the word "hero" is mentioned; that title they reverently reserve for those who sacrificed their lives. Their stories add to the growing body of knowledge about Marylanders who served in conflict to defend our country. Only by recounting these stories can we ensure that their sacrifices are documented for future generations.

In this book I hope to honor not only the men and women I had the privilege of meeting but also the millions of others who served our nation bravely during the Second World War.

H Company, 115th Infantry Regiment, 29th Division, Maryland National Guard

The following brief unit history was written by the late Sterling Wilmer Hoover. Hoover was born in Manchester, Maryland, on March 25, 1918, and enlisted in the Army in 1941. He was assigned to the heavy-weapons platoon of H Company, 115th Infantry, and landed on Easy Red Beach, Normandy, at 10:40 A.M. on the morning of June 6, 1944. He served thirty-seven consecutive days in combat until being wounded on July 12 a few miles from Saint-Lô when an artillery shell landed in the trees above him, killing one man and wounding another and himself. The piece of shrapnel that was removed from his hip was identified as part of the rotary band from an American 155-mm. artillery shell. Hoover expressed just one wish during his last discussions of the war before his death in 1996, and it was that the people of Carroll County, Maryland, remember and be proud of the boys of H Company who had come from Westminster.

Of the 130 men shown in this photograph, twenty-eight participated in the initial landings in Normandy, France. Twelve were killed in action or died of wounds; twenty-one were wounded in action; three were prisoners of war; and one reportedly deserted. Sadly, five were victims of suicide in the years following the war. Five hundred seventy-one men served with H Company between February 1941 and January 1946. Fifty-four of these men were killed in action, 145 wounded, and 31 taken prisoner. Men of H Company were awarded eleven Silver Stars and thirty Bronze Stars, and for its performance on D-Day, June 6, 1944, the 115th Infantry Regiment, which included H Company, was cited for "gallantry and outstanding performance of duty in action in the vicinity of St. Laurent sur Mer, Normandy, France."

The three regiments of the 29th Infantry Division trace their beginnings to before the American Revolution. The 175th Infantry was organized in Baltimore in 1774 as the Corps of Cadets. It became the "Dandy 5th" Regiment of the Maryland Line, supporting George Washington at Brooklyn Heights and saving the Continental Army as it retreated from the battle of Long Island. The 115th Infantry Regiment, drawn from the various counties of Maryland, was organized in 1783 as a rifle company whose job it was to protect the city of Baltimore. The 116th claimed descent from Captain John Smith's company of musketeers in Jamestown, Virginia, in 1620, and later, during the

Civil War, formed the nucleus of Stonewall Jackson's troops, earning the nickname "the Stonewall Brigade." When the 29th Division was formed in 1917 during World War I, there was concern that troops from Virginia and Maryland might not get along. But the excellent combat record of the "Blue and Gray Division," symbolic of the North and South having come together, was proof of their cohesiveness.

The 115th Infantry Regiment was demobilized after participating in the last three months of fighting in the First World War and was reactivated in February 1941 as one of two all-Maryland regiments in the 29th Division.

When formed as part of the 29th Division in 1917, it was composed of parts of three Maryland National Guard infantry regiments: the 1st, 4th, and 5th. The 115th Infantry Regiment suffered a total of 1,846 casualties, slightly more than 50 percent. Seventy-seven of its members were recommended for Distinguished Service Crosses for their work during the Argonne encounter, nearly double the number of the next nearest competitor. The regiment was dissolved on June 7, 1919, when the 1st and 5th Maryland National Guard Regiments were reorganized, and it remained inactive until 1941.

In February of 1941, H Company of the 115th Infantry Regiment was designated as a heavy-weapons company. Under its new configuration the company increased in size from 123 to 205 men. The company exchanged its full machine-gun equipment for eight .30-cal. and two .50-cal. machine guns, four 81-mm. mortars, and ten M1 Garand rifles. Each man was equipped with an automatic pistol. Additional equipment for transportation included two motorcycles with sidecars, five one-and-one-half-ton trucks for command and reconnaissance, and seventeen half-ton trucks as weapon carriers.

The 29th hit the worst spot on D-Day, where the "Fighting 1st" Division and elements of the 29th smashed head on into a reinforced German division waiting on the beach. The assault troops of the 29th Division overcame every obstacle the enemy could put in their way. During the European campaign—June 6, 1944, to May 7, 1945—the 29th Infantry Division suffered in excess of twenty thousand casualties, including thirty-five hundred killed, the second highest casualty total of the sixty U.S. divisions that participated in the war.

Answering Their Country's Call

ROBERT R. AYRES

Chestertown, Maryland

VMSB-234 Bomber Squadron, USMC

Robert Randolph Ayres Jr. was born in Chestertown, Maryland, on November 4, 1919. He graduated from City College in 1938 and attended the University of Maryland until 1942, his junior year, when he enlisted in the Marine Corps. He was selected to fly the Dauntless SBD dive bomber, completing eighty combat missions, and is a recipient of the Purple Heart, two Air Medals with seven gold stars (in lieu of the Air Medal), and the Distinguished Flying Cross. He graduated from the University of Maryland in 1960 and retired from active duty in 1963 with the rank of lieutenant colonel. In retirement, he became a supporter of the University of Maryland's athletic department, helping to solicit funding for scholarships. He is survived by his wife, Catherine, whom he married in 1957, and by their two daughters, son, and three grandchildren.

Special thanks to Lt. Col. Ralph H. Lewis of Gainesville, Florida, for his generous assistance in providing historical information regarding VMSB-234 and his recollections of the late Robert Ayres.

My name is Robert Randolph Ayres Jr. and I was a United States Marine, and proud to be one. I remember the first time I saw my father in his uniform, and I knew then I wanted to be a soldier, too. I grew up in Chestertown, Maryland, and lived at 111 High Street. Growing up in Chestertown was a great experience. Like any small town, everyone knew one another, and it was a peaceful and quiet place to live. My father was the clerk of the court in Kent County, but when times became tough during the depression he jumped at a job opportunity with A&P Grocery in Baltimore. I graduated from City College, and I enrolled at the University of Maryland, where I began civilian flight school training in a Piper Cub.

After my junior year at Maryland I played with the idea of joining the military service—which branch, I was not yet sure. I eventually

1

joined the Marine Corps because a friend of mine from UM had joined six months earlier, and when he called me up one day to say he was enjoying the experience I think I was sold. Before I left UM I had accumulated over sixty hours of flight training, and the Marines needed pilots at the onset of the war, so they readily granted my wishes to become an aviation cadet.

After enlisting I was sent to flight school to a base called an E-base, or elimination base, at Anacostia Naval Air Station just outside of Washington, D.C. Candidates had to successfully perform eighty hours of solo flying and learn basic Morse code to continue training. Following Anacostia, I was sent to Fort Jackson, South Carolina, where I was taught a little more about flying. In August of 1942 I completed my flight training and received my commission in the Marine Corps. I was sent to San Diego, California, to await transfer overseas, and although we had scored some big victories in the Pacific, losses in pilots were high and I thought I was being thrown into the war as cannon fodder. On August 23 I boarded the merchant ship *Day Star* and began my voyage into the Pacific.

A week later we arrived at Oahu, then just a territory of the Hawaiian Islands. I was sent to the Marine Corps air station at Ewa, and I learned I had been assigned to Dive-Bomber Squadron VMSB-234 and would fly the SBD Douglas Dauntless aircraft. When I first saw the SBD I climbed into the cockpit, took ten minutes to figure out where everything was, and I was up and flying a few minutes later. The SBD was a very stable aircraft. When you got it up in the air, you felt like you were the master of it. It was a durable plane and could sustain a lot of damage. I thought it was a pretty plane too, and I loved it. The basic principle of the SBD was to get over a target, nose over into a steep dive, and direct a 1,000-, 500-, or 250-pound bomb onto the target. Of the original twenty-five pilots in the squadron, twenty-two had little or no operational experience in the Dauntless, so we immediately initiated a hectic training program.

The Pacific war was still a new experience for all of us, and things were often being figured out as we went along. Most of the credit for getting our squadron into gear was owed to Maj. William Robertson and Sgt. Maj. Albert Gordon, who were busy processing us new recruits and organizing our training. On one occasion the sergeant major lined up a newly arrived group of enlisted Marines to issue assignments. The sergeant major asked, "Has anyone had any experience working on motors, cars, motorcycles, or lawn mowers?" Several men raised their hands. "OK, you guys fall out. You're going for two weeks of aircraft mechanics school. Now, anyone here ever build or work on radios?" Again, several men raised their hands, and the sergeant major motioned for the men to step forward. "You'll be assigned to radio repair school. Does anyone know how to type?" One man stepped forward. "Son, you'll work for me." So it went until everyone had been assigned to fill a needed position.

A 1944 photo of Robert Ayres *(right)* and his tail gunner, James Entwistle. When they met, Bob said to Jim, "Don't worry, boy, I am going to get back home, and you'll be 5 feet right behind me." They flew nearly eighty combat missions together, building a close bond of friendship that they maintained throughout their lives.

On September 28, 1942, I was briefly assigned to VMSB-141, a land-based squadron on American Samoa. The base there was used to train and outfit new squadrons before heading into combat, and it was also a place for experienced squadrons to rest, receive replacements, and prepare for their next tour. It was not an ideal assignment for anyone anxious to fight the Japs. All I did was fly an SBC-4 on submarine patrol and count whales. It was here I put a plane in the ocean and earned the nickname "Salty" from the guys who pulled me to dry land, and the name stuck with me during my entire career. In January of 1943 I was assigned back to VMSB-234, and not a minute too soon.

We learned the squadron was to be based on Guadalcanal Island in the Solomon Island chain. On the evening before heading to Guadalcanal I was introduced to my tail gunner, Corp. James Entwistle. Jim was from Marietta, Georgia, and one of the finest men I have ever met. We began to get to know one another over a dinner of steak and eggs, and I remember telling Jim, "Don't worry, boy, I am going to get back home, and you'll be five feet right behind me." We should have known the good meal was a precursor to something happening the next day. We began to learn that whenever the Marines gave us a good meal, it meant we were going to get shot at soon.

The next morning, January 28, 1943, the men in the squadron were loaded onto an R4D transport aircraft, and we began our trip to

Guadalcanal for our first tour of duty. I was very excited when we broke through the clouds above Guadalcanal and I saw my first glimpse of this exotic tropical island surrounded by an azure blue ocean. The lush foliage below was formed in an endless variety of hues of green interspersed between a majestic mountain range that ran down its length. Large groves of coconut palm plantations could easily be seen on the northeast coastal plain. It was hard to imagine just a few months before the island had been the site of fierce fighting, and the crew of the transport told us some Japanese forces still controlled parts of the island. We passed over an airstrip, circling once, and landed on Henderson Field, our new home.

After landing we were instructed to report to the Command Center to report for duty. As we walked across the field, five Japanese Mitsubishi fighters came in low from the east. I watched all five get shot down in a hail of antiaircraft fire, and we cheered their destruction. I don't think the Marines could have planned a warmer welcoming for us to the war.

After reporting in, we were loaded onto trucks and driven to a bivouac area in the midst of a large coconut grove about a mile from the airstrip. Our tents were neatly lined up between rows of palm trees, each tent containing four Army cots complete with a blanket and mosquito net. The sides of the tents were drawn up, otherwise the heat inside would be suffocating. A rough network of drainage ditches surrounded the tents to divert rainwater from flooding the dirt floors and turning them to mud, and foxholes had been dug nearby for protection during air raids. Our outhouse was at one end of our camp, and the mess tent was located far away at the other. (It is arguable as to which facility had the more delicate scent.) Our water supply was distributed throughout the area within several large canvas bags, called "Lister bags," which were supported on tripods with spigots near the bottom.

Like most pilots, I carried and stored my personal items in a standard-issue green handbag. Though I am sure the exact content of each pilot's bag varied, I suspect most were similar to mine. In it I carried my toilet articles, a towel, extra pairs of underwear and socks, my flight gear (helmet, goggles, gloves, "Mae West" life jacket, K-Bar knife, and flashlight), writing paper, and photographs. My entire inventory of other worldly possessions consisted of what I had on my back, a flight suit, casual shoes, an overseas or baseball cap, and an extra khaki shirt and pants. We all had our .45-cal. automatic, ammunition, and water canteen. To say the least, it was bare-bones living, but I suppose adequate for where we were and what we had come to do. Life on Guadalcanal was tolerable, but no picnic.

We couldn't forget Japanese forces still occupied portions of the island, but it didn't take long before I realized the Japanese were not our only enemies on Guadalcanal. The jungle that had looked so beautiful and inviting as we approached the island was actually a dark, damp, humid, and malaria-infested hell. The Marines and Army men who fought on Guadalcanal must have endured unimaginable horrors while fighting in its jungles. Mosquitoes and other unidentified flying and crawling insects plagued our daily lives. Every activity invited potential infection from the slightest wound or bite. Annoyances abounded throughout our daily lives, including an all-encompassing mildew, sweltering heat, and ankle-deep mud during the rain or choking dust when dry. There was no escape from these simultaneously occurring plagues, and they were our constant companions.

The jungle had its small wonders, though, as we discovered a friendly green lizard that loved to eat mosquitoes. We threw as many as we could catch into our tents so they would eat any mosquitoes that were persistent enough to sneak through the netting. The mosquitoes didn't stand a chance with all these hungry lizards standing guard over us. Mornings began with a check of your sheets to make sure you didn't accidentally squash some lizards that had crawled into your bed during the night. Our other friends were the exotic birds that inhabited the island. These loud and beautiful birds were easily spooked by the unique high-pitched sound of the Japanese bombers. When the birds became upset, it was a good indication trouble was on its way towards us. The birds were better than any radar, and when the Japs arrived we were always ready and waiting and shot most of them down. Those birds were one of our best-kept secrets of the war.

The outcome of the battle for the Solomon Island chain was still in question when my squadron arrived at Guadalcanal. We were briefed on the buildup of enemy troops, supplies, and facilities in the northern and central Solomon Islands, and on the increased destroyer activity heading for Guadalcanal. The Navy made the assumption that the destroyers were bringing fresh troops and equipment to reinforce the remaining beleaguered forces on Guadalcanal, when in actuality they were trying to rescue their stranded troops to use elsewhere. In any event, our mission was to attack and sink or damage as much enemy shipping as possible in order to disrupt the Japanese activities.

A typical day began with breakfast, then we headed over to the operation tent and sat around and waited for something to happen. A call would come through from a scout plane or a ground station reporting of a target, and we would go out and get it. Missions were not limited to naval targets, and we struck enemy airfields and other facilities within range of our aircraft.

I flew my first combat mission in the afternoon of February 1, 1943. We got up early in the morning and had breakfast, which usually consisted of Spam or Vienna sausages and coffee. We were briefed on our missions, and then Jim and I went out and checked the plane. At one in the afternoon a message was received from the La Vella coast watch station. A "Tokyo Express" consisting of twenty

Dauntless dive bombers of VMSB-234 line the muddy field of the Marine naval air station on Guadalcanal in June 1943. Under constant air attack during the early stages of the war, the Marines on Guadalcanal also faced the dangers and discomforts of living in a rain-soaked, disease-infested tropical jungle. (Official USMC photo)

Ayres in the cockpit of his Douglas Dauntless SBD dive bomber in 1944.

Japanese destroyers 200 miles from Guadalcanal was headed our way. The term "Tokyo Express" was given to the seemingly endless number of Japanese ships carrying reinforcements to and from Guadalcanal and the other islands in the Solomon chain. It was essential for us to sink as many as we could so our ground forces could defeat the Japanese troops on the islands. Within minutes we were in our planes, and off we went.

I was one of sixteen SBD dive bombers that took off from Henderson Field to attack the Japanese destroyers heading for Guadalcanal. We were accompanied by sixteen fighters (four each of Marine F4Fs, Army P-38s and P-39s, and New Zealand P-40s). It wasn't long before the squadron leader came over the intercom and said, "Look below, boys, there's those sons of bitches." I looked down and saw the huge wake in the water created by the twenty Japanese destroyers sailing in two columns of ten each.

The attack dive was always an exhilarating experience. The enemy fired at us, but I never heard anything going on around the aircraft because my ears were covered with earphones and the sound

Dauntless bombers of VMSB-234 loaded with 500-pound bombs on their way to attack the Japanese airfield at Munda Point, New Georgia, Solomon Islands, in February 1943. The SBD's perforated air brake flaps *(foreground)* when deployed slowed the aircraft during its steep attack dives. Although considered "obsolete" by the time the United States entered the war, the Dauntless was admired by the men who flew it for its stability and durability, and it was a workhorse for the U.S. Navy in the Pacific war. These bombers participated in every major engagement in the Pacific and contributed to the sinking of all six Japanese carriers lost in 1942 plus many other enemy ships. Armed with forward-firing twin .50-cal. machine guns and rear twin .30-cal. machine guns, and with a total payload capacity of 2,250 pounds in bombs (1,600 on the fuselage mount and 650 on underwing mounts), the Dauntless could deliver a hefty punch. Nearly six thousand Dauntless bombers were built before production was ended in late 1944.

of the engine drowned out any other noises. Being fired on looked like little red balls coming at me, which were actually the tracer rounds between the other rounds I couldn't see. The plane had a bombing sight in the front of the cockpit, but it wasn't worth a damn, so I just lined up on the target and dropped the bomb before I pulled out of the dive. There was an electrical switch on the stick to drop our bomb, but most of us never used it. Instead, we used the manual release just to the right of the seat to make sure we got it off. No pilot wanted to make a dive just to have it wasted by a faulty electrical switch.

We were warned that thirty Japanese fighters were flying cover over the destroyers, but when we arrived we were surprised at their absence. We received a distress call from one of our destroyers, and we deduced the missing fighters had forgone their escort mission to attack the destroyer. The commander of the fighter flight asked permission to lend the destroyer a hand, and our flight commander gladly agreed. We later learned they did not arrive in time to save our destroyer from sinking, but our fighters caught up with the Japanese planes, and the resulting aerial battle resulted in a little payback, with our planes recording twenty-one enemy aircraft destroyed.

We didn't dwell on the ongoing sideshow too long, and I was relieved we would not have to contend with both enemy fighters and antiaircraft while attacking the destroyers. There was no possibility our sixteen SBDs could sink the twenty ships, so the objective was to concentrate our initial attack on the lead destroyer and then sink and damage as many others as possible. Capt. Hoyle Barr was my three-plane section leader, and I was flying on his left wing and Lt. Donald Russell was on his right wing. We climbed to 11,000 feet and increased speed in preparation for a high-speed descending approach to penetrate the initial antiaircraft barrage as rapidly as possible. We began our descent, and when we passed through 8,000 feet Captain Barr wiggled his wings, which was our signal to nose over and begin our attack dive. I called out to Jim before tipping the nose over for our dive, "Jim, hold on tight, here we go."

I was in my attack dive, and I was looking down on the destroyers, and I noticed what appeared to be lights blinking on the decks of the destroyers. Long streams of tracers flowed past the aircraft, and flak bursts exploded nearby, making me aware of the fact that those lights were flashes from their antiaircraft guns. The destroyers started a left turn, which was their standard defensive maneuver, and their defensive fire intensified but was inaccurate. Captain Barr lost his target, regained it too late, and his bomb hit the water 25 feet in front of the second ship. I weaved and skidded to avoid enemy fire while firing my machine guns until at 1,000 feet I pulled out of my dive (any lower than 1,000 feet earned a pilot the nickname "Eager Beaver") just after releasing my bomb. The bomb missed the lead destroyer, exploding about 10 feet off its starboard bow, but close enough, I hoped, to cause damage. The concussion from our bomb hit our plane in the rear as Jim gave me a play-by-play of the action behind me while spraying the destroyer's deck with three hundred rounds from his .30-cal. machine gun. I dipped to the left and back to the right to give Jim a broad area of fire and so he wouldn't shoot through the tail surfaces of our aircraft. Behind us, Lieutenant Russell lined up on the lead destroyer, and his bomb disappeared into the smoke, but the following members of the squadron scored direct hits. I upped my flaps and rejoined the flight, and we high-tailed it back to Guadalcanal. Our first mission had scored several hits on the destroyers, and the lead destroyer was left dead in the water and burning. The after-action intelligence report stated that we had probably sunk two destroyers and damaged two others. When we landed I found a hole in my right wing caused by an unexploded 40-mm. shell, but Jim and I had survived our baptism of fire.

Our damaged planes were repaired, and we struck another force of twenty-six destroyers six days later on February 7. Captain Barr was leading our flight at 11,000 feet when we encountered heavy antiaircraft fire from the destroyers below. My aircraft was hit again, and it was thrown onto its back and into a spin that I was able to recover from at 4,000 feet. To my surprise, when I regained control I was directly over a Jap destroyer, so I nosed over into a dive while I readied our bomb. I was in perfect position for the attack, and all I had to do was just reach down and rack it off. The bomb struck squarely on the bow of the ship, and the concussion of the explosion jolted our plane. Jim fired his gun as we regained altitude, and he yelled, "You hit it! You hit it!" I veered to the right so I could get a better look, and I'll never forget the satisfaction of seeing that destroyer break into two pieces and sink before my eyes. It was the thrill of my life to that point.

Subsequent missions were run on alternating days over the next few months. We struck any shipping we found and attacked the Japanese air base on Munda Point on New Georgia Island in the Solomon Islands. The mission took on a daily routine, and the press referred to our missions as "milk runs over Munda." It was anything but a milk run, as heavy antiaircraft guns protected the base, and it seemed we always had a Jap Zero on our tail. Jim kept the fighters at bay long enough to allow our fighters time to scare them off. Our fighter pilot friends always got a good laugh by calling us lumbering bombers "bait" when they went trawling for Japanese fighters. I think they were right.

The squadron lost four planes during our first tour. We lost four pilots and gunners during our first mission to Munda Point, sadly, two by accident. Lieutenant Moss was hit by flak and died instantly. Sergeant Henze, his gunner, bailed out but severed his leg on the stabilizer and died in a hospital soon after. Captain Moore, distracted by enemy fire, inadvertently led his second division under

Ayres and Entwistle pose for a publicity photo in February 1943 during press coverage of the "milk runs over Munda": daily missions against the Japanese airfield at Munda Point. As the handwritten commentary at the top attests, most men who flew in combat understood and accepted the inherent dangers of their responsibilities.

the diving planes of the first division and was run down by Lieutenant Murphy's diving plane. Captain Moore's left wing was sheared off, but he and his gunner, Pfc. Reed, parachuted to safety. Or so we thought. We discovered later the Japanese had captured Moore and Reed and beheaded them. I guess I felt lucky it wasn't me, and I always said my prayers of thanks I was still alive. I hated the Japanese. I wanted to kill them all, and I hope I got as many as I could during the war. We lost seven more planes to enemy fire during the next two tours, but luckily in each case all the pilots and gunners were rescued.

Flying in combat was stressful. I considered the job dangerous as hell, and there was always lots of stuff fired at us every mission to remind us of this fact. Being in combat was just a job we had to do. It was a matter of getting them before they got you. I never had a fear of flying in combat, and we all accepted the fact that our aircraft were instruments of war, and as such were inherently dangerous to operate even under ideal conditions. We all had friends killed in training, and this perhaps preconditioned me, to some degree, to cope with fear and tragedy during combat. The youthful confidence of all the men in the squadron perhaps verged on a sense of invincibility, and thoughts to the contrary were never present, or at least never revealed.

After returning to base our missions were "officially" concluded with a debriefing to ascertain their effectiveness. Doc Allis, our squadron doctor, then subjected us to a cursory medical exam. He presented each of us with a small bottle of Lejun brandy with a label that read, "U.S. Navy Medical Department." The amount in each bottle was small, perhaps an ounce, just enough to "soothe

the nerves," as Doc Allis would say. Jim didn't drink, so he gave me his bottle, and he also collected for me any bottles from others in the squadron who didn't drink. By the time I polished off all these bottles of brandy, I was happily more than just "soothed."

Except for two trips to Sydney, Australia, for a little R&R, neither of which I can remember getting very much of during the war, our time out of combat was spent at Turtle Bay on Espíritu Santo Island in the New Hebrides. Living conditions there were measurably improved over Guadalcanal. We lived in "Dallas huts," prefabricated plywood buildings with screened window openings and blinds that could be closed to keep the rain out. Our hut was actually two huts put together making a room about 10 by 12 feet, easily enough room for six or seven cots. Although we still had no electric lights we did have the added luxury of a wood floor. We were well fed, dry, and therefore comfortable.

Baltimore Flier Wins DFC For Sinking Jap Destroyer

Ayres receives the Distinguished Flying Cross in recognition of his outstanding combat performance, which included the sinking of a Japanese destroyer. "For heroism and extraordinary achievement as a pilot of a dive bomber in Marine Scout Bombing Squadron Two-Three-Four, during action against enemy Japanese forces in the Solomon Islands area from February 1 to September 8, 1943. Skillfully maneuvering his plane during two attacks against Japanese Task Forces consisting of twenty destroyers each, Captain Ayres courageously dove through shattering enemy anti-aircraft fire to a perilously low altitude before releasing his bombs, scoring a near miss and a direct hit." (Press headline from the *Baltimore Sun*)

During the day we took care of our squadron duties and occasionally flew to keep sharp. Evenings were spent at "the Club," this again being two Dallas huts put together. In it we had wood benches along the walls and cases of beer stacked in the center of the floor. For those who smoked, there were cigarettes. The cigarettes were unique in that no one had ever heard of the brand Chelsey. They came fifty to a sealed tin that when opened was always moldy inside. The beer brand was Golden Gate, so I suppose it came from somewhere near San Francisco. I have never heard of it since, so I presume it didn't survive the war, which was a good thing because although we drank it, warm no less, it had only a slight resemblance to the taste of beer, and a distasteful one at that. More troubling to us wannabe rowdy pilots was that we doubted it had any alcoholic content. So the evenings were spent sipping our warm Golden Gate beer, smoking our moldy Chelsey cigarettes, singing war songs, and sharing stories of sweethearts back home. We complained a lot, but we all had to agree: this, after all, was the good life.

I was wounded and earned a Purple Heart on a mission against a Japanese supply depot. As I zeroed in on a building I saw this little guy emerge from the jungle and aim his rifle at me, and the SOB hit me squarely in the left cheek. The only satisfaction was that I dropped canisters of napalm on his head and I incinerated him. After being wounded, I returned home to form a new squadron, but after a year stateside I was sent back to the Pacific to rejoin my old squadron as a replacement. A lot of things had changed since my first mission, when only a handful of planes were launched on a mission. By this time a typical mission included over a hundred SBDs and sixty torpedo bombers. It was an awesome feeling to be part of such a massive force, and it wasn't a matter of if we would win the war, but when.

Today I sit here thinking of my gunner, Jim, who stayed a close friend all these years. Now that he is gone I miss him dearly. I think I am pretty tough, but on Memorial Day I sit here thinking of the friends I lost back then, and I find myself crying my eyes out. There were so many heroes during the war, but if a group of men deserves respect, it is the Marines who made bloody assault after bloody assault on the beaches throughout the Pacific. I worry that some people today either don't remember or don't give a damn about what sacrifices were made to preserve our freedom. I hope all the men who gave their lives during the war are never forgotten.

SIDNEY BLUM

Owings Mills, Maryland
76th Infantry Division, U.S. Army Medical Corps

Sidney Blum

Sidney Blum was born in New York City on January 6, 1924. He enlisted in the Army before completing his senior year in high school. He was assigned as a Corpsman serving with the infantry and is a recipient of the Purple Heart. After the war, Blum moved to Baltimore and worked for the Veterans Administration as a dental technician for thirty-five years until his retirement in 1979. He married his late wife, Thelma, in June 1946 and has one daughter and one grandson.

I was in high school and working a part-time job as a dental assistant when one day I realized everyone I knew had either enlisted or been drafted in the service. I figured I had better enlist before I was drafted, and by enlisting I could pick the branch of service I would join. I had doubts about flying, and I got seasick easily, so I decided on the Army.

I was sent to Camp Grant in Illinois for basic training and then Fort Meade, Maryland, for advanced training. We practiced endlessly dressing wounds, applying splints, administering morphine and penicillin, and filling out EMT tags (emergency medical tags) for the wounded. Our training was excellent, and we worked on volunteers who pretended to be wounded, but they never screamed and yelled like the men I later saw wounded in combat.

I was assigned to the 76th Infantry Division, and we were shipped overseas in November of 1944. The division landed in Hampshire, England, on December 21, and on January 17, 1945, the division landed in Le Havre, France. Le Havre was wrecked, but the countryside was beautiful. I remember seeing a lot of young Frenchmen in civilian clothes and wondered why we were the only ones fighting to free their homeland. The division was on its way to Sedan in northern France when we changed directions to help stop the German breakthrough in the Ardennes. I remember it was snowing heavily, and it was really cold, with temperatures twenty to thirty degrees below zero. We managed to stay reasonably warm by wearing many layers of clothes, blankets, or anything else we could scrounge.

We eventually got in a position backing up the 17th Airborne, which had been reduced to 50 percent fighting strength from the beating they had received during the German Bulge offensive. We didn't stay long, as we were sent to Luxembourg to relieve the 87th Infantry, which had received a similar mauling. By this time the German attack had stalled, and we found numerous German tanks abandoned because they had run out of fuel. The attack had caused mass confusion among our troops, and in some instances the Germans were disguised as American GIs, creating panic and suspicion everywhere. We were careful to give passwords and counter-passwords, and there were a few nervous moments with all those trigger-happy GIs shouting back and forth.

As a combat medical aide, my primary responsibility was to follow the platoon during an advance and watch for GIs who were wounded. As soon as a GI went down, the other GIs would shout out for help. In most instances I was close enough to the action to know that the incoming fire had probably hit some of our men. My first response was to assess the amount of damage done to the wounded. If the GI had received a leg or arm wound, I would put a tourniquet around the wound and give him a shot of morphine to ease the pain. If the wound was serious, the most important thing was to get the litter bearers to carry the wounded back to an aid station where doctors could repair the damage. I didn't bother to write down instructions or how the man was hurt; all I could do was throw on a compress and shoot them up with morphine and penicillin and hope they made it back alive.

I tried to comfort the wounded as best I could, but during an advance I had to keep pace with the platoon, and I often had to leave the wounded behind. I worried a lot about wounded screaming too much, as I felt this would hurt the morale of the other men, so I spent as much effort as I could trying to quiet the wounded. Most wounded men felt better as soon as someone arrived to help, and I imagine it was still a very scary time for a wounded man, but there was just so much I could do.

If a GI were killed, I would cover him up with his poncho and put his helmet on top so it wouldn't blow off. I would take a dog tag from around his neck and remove any personal effects and hold on to them until I could give them to the platoon sergeant or lieutenant. There was no stopping to mourn or think about the dead; we had to keep going forward and hope the killed were buried. At the end of the day I reported how many guys were wounded and killed and handed over personal effects.

We didn't treat just combat wounds. There were so many ailments the men suffered from because of exposure, poor hygiene, and lousy diets. A man had to be really sick to be allowed off the front lines, and just having a headache or a general sense of not

During his company's advance through a captured airfield near Plauen, Germany, in April 1945, Sidney Blum paused for a moment to pose at the controls of a grounded German ME-109 fighter.

feeling well was not enough. Given our stress levels and living situations, I think not feeling well was a more common condition than uncommon. We had great soldiers in the 76th, and I had very little problem with men faking injury or illness or otherwise unable to deal with their injuries.

I think most people can get used to anything if exposed to it long enough, and after seeing so much death and carnage I think I dealt with it by not getting close to anyone. I knew each man as far as working together, but I didn't want to know anything about his personal life. I became this way after watching a buddy named Bauer advance on a house and witnessing a shell land in front of him that blew his head off. I will never forget watching his headless body stand there for a few seconds before it just slumped backwards onto the ground. There is no way I could adequately describe the effect of watching something like happen, and the effect it had on me and the rest of the platoon. Bauer was a twenty-year-old kid from Iowa, and I didn't hear anyone mention his name again. It was a terrible feeling to see a young man killed like that.

Sometimes men just couldn't cope with combat, and I had to keep an eye out for men who began showing signs of cracking under the stress of battle. Men would shut down, shake uncontrollably, or just act in peculiar ways if they were having a rough time. It was important to get these men to the rear as quickly as possible, because a soldier in this state was completely ineffective in combat, and his inability to react could put him and the men around him at greater risk of injury. In one case I had to smack a guy in the mouth because he was hollering so much, I felt he was having a bad effect on the morale of the other men. I felt sorry for the guy, and I didn't want him to embarrass himself any further, because I knew he was a good soldier. He just needed a few hours to regain his composure, and he returned back as good a soldier as we knew he was.

In the infantry the worst things were artillery and mortars. A lot of guys just couldn't take the sound and effects of these weapons and would just go nuts. Nobody in their right mind can take being under artillery fire for long, and some guys had just a little less fortitude, and they would crack first. We spent 110 continuous days in heavy fighting, and I am amazed more men didn't fall apart.

The Germans were tough soldiers, but we were a lot tougher. The Germans were scared of Patton's Third Army, and our 76th Division was nicknamed "Roosevelt's Butchers" by the Germans. There were certain unspoken laws of the battlefield, and one was that if one of our guys were taken prisoner and roughed up or killed, we would return the favor by not taking any German prisoners. History books do not like to mention that on some days our American GIs just didn't take prisoners. It happened on both sides, and people should understand that in war men are transformed; they lose all resemblance to the kind of men they were before the war. I witnessed a few well-educated men referred to as "gentlemen" back home become the most ruthless and bloodthirsty natural-born killers. If a German SS soldier made it back to the detention camps in our sector, he was pretty lucky to still be alive. After we liberated the concentration camps I don't think I ever saw an SS soldier taken prisoner again. That's the way the game was played, and we won.

We treated wounded Germans on occasion, but never before treating our wounded first. As a medic, I wore large red and white crosses on my uniform, and this was intended to designate us as noncombatants. Germans frequently shot at and killed medics, and in response many of our medics refused to help the wounded Germans. I remember walking past wounded Germans on numerous occasions, but I had to keep pace with the platoon and could not stop to help.

The day I earned my Purple Heart our platoon was readying for an attack on the town of Badsuden when a mortar round landed between me and two other men. The other two guys were killed instantly, and I received wounds to my arms and rear. I felt able to continue, but the lieutenant asked me to get some attention back at our aid station. By the time I returned, our outfit had captured half the town, and fortunately none of our guys were hurt too bad.

One of my most memorable moments of the war was watching our forces cross the Rhine River. It was a rainy day, and the 417th Infantry Regiment spearheaded the assault across the river. I stood on the bank of the Rhine and watched as German mines floated down the river and artillery blew all but four of the boats to pieces. It was sort of hard to watch the destruction of so many men, and I hope we never forget men like those who died in the river that day. The heroic efforts of the 417th established a foothold on the opposite bank, opening the door the next morning for another battalion to cross with only slight casualties. The Rhine crossing opened the floodgates for our forces to begin the invasion of Germany.

When the German Army began their retreat, we picked up so many of their abandoned vehicles our column began to look more German than American. We could radio our planes circling above us that were trying to figure out if we were friend or foe. But the German fighters that thought we were German had no chance once they realized we were Americans, and we laughed like hell imagining the look on the faces of those German pilots when our antiaircraft opened up on them and shot them down.

When the war finally ended we found time to unwind and relax. We uncovered huge stores of champagne and Portuguese sardines, and I remember washing my clothes in champagne when the water was too filthy to use. We came across a bank that had millions of dollars in reichmarks, and for a few minutes I must have been the richest guy in the division. Within moments my fortune was lost, as the paper money had all but disappeared. I recall there was a real shortage of toilet paper at the time.

The funny thing was that no matter what town we entered, we failed to find a single Nazi. We had been fighting the Nazis for the past four years, and now there was not a single Nazi to be found in Germany, anywhere. We questioned the townspeople if they or anyone they knew were a member of the Nazi Party. All we ever heard was, *"Nein, ich weis nicht,"* translated to mean "I don't know." Who the heck had we been fighting? We eventually found some Nazis in the prison camps. The real Nazis were arrogant sons of bitches and proud to let us know who they were and, I think, what they had done. There was a complete disbelief among our troops in what we saw at the Nazi death camps. There were piles of dead bodies in some cases 10 feet high. It was just horrible.

The whole country seemed crowded with Ukrainians. These people had been brought to Germany as slave laborers during the war, and after the war we had trouble keeping them from trying to kill the Germans. The Germans wanted our cigarettes, so we traded our rations for cameras and film so we could take pictures to send home. The funny thing was that after they walked away with our cigarettes, we called the checkpoint guards to stop the Germans we had just traded with to confiscate them back. They got quite upset, but it was just our way of having fun. Overall, the German people were in a worse condition than I had imagined, and I felt bad for the children. There wasn't much food around, and they were starving. We always had hungry kids trying to get into our camps looking for food.

We ran into the Russians, and I thought they were terrific guys. Most of them were Mongolians, and they wanted our watches more than anything else. I had picked up a few Mickey Mouse watches, and the Russians got really excited when I pulled those out. They had lots of money, and we sold whatever we could, even our soap.

We were loaded onto forty-and-eight trains (named so because in the old days they held forty men or eight mules) and began our trip back to France and home. As we rolled through the German countryside the German civilians lined both sides of the tracks begging for food or whatever we could give them. The only ones we allowed on the train were the attractive women, and they were quickly booted off if they refused to "perform" for the GIs. In a short period the train had as many girls as soldiers, and we were packed tight in the cars. Some guys fired their guns and mortars at buildings we passed to kill the time and to get a laugh. It was the longest, most crowded and memorable train trip I ever took.

The real heroes of the Second World War were the infantrymen who carried the heaviest burden of the war. The infantryman was a special breed of man. Within a few hours of combat you saw the span of your entire life pass before you, and would witness the outer layers of others peel away to reveal what kind of man they were inside, good or bad. The bonds between combat infantrymen were stronger than I could ever explain. The life of every man depended on the men around him, and the only way to escape was to be wounded, killed, or captured. You retain images from the war you just can't let go. I remember walking past an aid station and seeing German prisoners casually trying to match dog tags and severed heads, arms, and legs with the bodies of dead GIs and Germans. It was a horrible sight. I still don't think people here have any idea of just how costly the war was, on all sides.

I think about the men who joined our unit who had already earned multiple battle stars from previous campaigns. It was a crime to watch these men who had served their country for so long die face down in the mud along the side of the road, or in the middle of nowhere. Any man who fought with the possibility that it could have been him lying there dead in the mud is my hero.

DANIEL B. BREWSTER

Glyndon, Maryland
6th Marine Division

Daniel Baugh Brewster was born in Brooklandville, Maryland, on November 23, 1923. A 1942 graduate of Saint Paul's School, he attended Princeton University before enlisting in the Marine Corps in the fall of 1942. He was wounded in combat on seven occasions and is a recipient of the Purple Heart with two gold stars and the Bronze Star for valor in recognition of his actions fighting on Okinawa. After the war he graduated from Princeton and received a law degree from the University of Maryland in 1949. He was elected to the Maryland House of Delegates in 1950, the U.S. House of Representatives in 1958, and the U.S. Senate in 1962. Senator Brewster retired from the Marine Corps Reserves in 1972 with the rank of colonel. He and his wife, Judy, have three children.

I remember December 7th of 1941 like it was yesterday. I couldn't believe it when we heard what had happened. Overnight the sentiment of the country turned against the Japanese and Germans. I remember hanging on to every word of President Roosevelt's address to the country the following day, and I think we were all committed to the war from the very first day.

I was attending Princeton in 1942 and playing football when one day I ran into my roommates who were heading to join the Navy because they wanted to be aviation pilots. I went along, and I thought for sure they would want a tough football player, but to my dismay I flunked the physical exam because I was color-blind. The others teased me relentlessly that I was a dreaded "4-F," which meant you were unacceptable for military service. I turned right around and entered the Marine Corps recruiting office around the corner and inquired about enlisting in the Marines. The Marine Corps was happy to take my application.

On the day I left for basic training my parents drove me to the old Camden Yards Station where the baseball stadium is now located. I said goodbye and boarded the train, and I rode for two days until we arrived in South Carolina. I was thinking about nothing in particular at the time, just that I was going to war. I was a bit curious as to what awaited me around the corner. It was unthinkable that we would lose the war, but I knew it might be difficult and costly at times. I was certain we would prevail. Throughout the war our collective thoughts centered on how quickly we could get the job done and get home.

Basic training at Parris Island was pretty tough in those days. We had an excellent drill sergeant who had served with the 4th Marine Regiment in Asia, and within a few months we had received what I thought was excellent training. After basic training I thought I was headed somewhere else, but I was ordered to become a drill sergeant. Before I knew what had happened to me, I was enrolled in an officers training course and shipped to Quantico, Virginia, to become an officer. I received my commission on June 3rd of 1943. I suppose I was the youngest officer in the Marine Corps at nineteen years and six months.

I was assigned to the Marine Corps school at Quantico and became a lecturer on combat tactics, of all things. I thought this was odd because I had never served in combat, and I felt I was in way over my head, so I managed to get released from my duties and was shipped off to Pearl Harbor. My new assignment was the headquarters company commander of the 1st Marine Brigade. I thought this was the worst assignment I could have had. It was basically a housekeeping job for a lot of higher brass. I was very glad when our outfit was ordered to Guadalcanal to prepare for our invasion of Guam.

My first contact with the Japanese was on the second day after arriving on Guam. The initial invasion forces had suffered heavy losses, so when the call went out for replacements I quickly stepped forward. My commanding officer knew I was anxious to get a combat assignment, so he sent me to the 4th Marine Regiment and put me in command of a rifle platoon. I remained a platoon leader throughout the Guam campaign, primarily mopping up the remaining forces of Japanese on the island. This was my introduction to combat and the killing of enemy soldiers. My fondest memory while on Guam was when we found a warehouse full of Japanese beer. We waited anxiously for our allotment to be tested, to make sure the Japanese had not poisoned it. I found out later that it was tested by an impatient gunnery sergeant that grabbed a bottle, took a big drink, and said it was OK.

We didn't really see the Japanese as human beings. We looked at them as some lesser form of life. We had pure hatred for every single one of them, and I thought nothing of killing them. Both sides rarely took prisoners, especially after we learned about what the Japs had done to our men on Bataan. We captured them only when ordered. The Japanese were dedicated, semireligious fighters, and they fought to the very last man. They were tenacious, brave, and I

Members of L Company, 3rd Battalion, 4th Marine Regiment, 6th Marine Division, on Okinawa in June 1945. *Seated, from left:* Lieutenants Marvin Plock, Marvin Perskie, unknown. *Back row, from left:* Lieutenants Hanson, Daniel Brewster, Hugh Semple (a pro football player before the war), Bill Allison. The 3rd Marine Amphibious Corps and the 24th Army Corps, which participated in the invasion of Okinawa (Operation Iceberg), together suffered more than seven thousand killed and thirty thousand wounded in fighting that raged from April 1 to June 21, 1945. The nature of the combat and the loss of life on Okinawa were a grim forecast of what an invasion of the Japanese homeland would have entailed for the Allies.

think foolish in that they fought on even when any semieducated military commander could know their situation was hopeless. Instead of surrendering, they would blow themselves up with hand grenades or shoot themselves in the heart by using their toes to pull the triggers of their rifles. Towards the end of the Okinawa campaign we watched in amazement as groups of men, women, and children dove from cliffs to their deaths rather than surrender.

Feelings of hatred are easy to keep when you see so many of your fellow Marines killed. The most difficult thing I had to deal with was the constant loss of my men. We took terrible casualties and suffered nearly 100 percent casualties on Okinawa. The Japs were very tricky and often feigned death to let you pass in order to shoot you in the back. We quickly learned that when you passed a Jap corpse, you often stuck it with your bayonet or put a rifle round into it.

On one occasion while I was on Okinawa a call went down the line for Japanese prisoners for intelligence purposes. I instructed my men to round up any if possible, and we found two Japanese that would surrender. They were in pretty rough condition, but they were able to walk. I informed headquarters I had a couple of prisoners and to expect their arrival shortly. I called for a sergeant and instructed him to walk the prisoners back to headquarters. A minute or so later I heard shots from a BAR (Browning automatic rifle). I turned to where the sound came from, and I saw the sergeant walking slowly back up the hill to where I was. I asked the sergeant where his prisoners were, and he replied that they tried to escape and he had to shoot them. I called him a liar and just shook my head. I had to call back to headquarters and tell them we had no prisoners coming. Some men just could not accept having even just a few Japanese survive.

Okinawa is the largest island in the Ryukyu Islands chain, measuring 25 miles in length and 4 to 10 miles in width. Its close proximity to the Japanese mainland ensured that the Japanese would put up a bitter struggle. The northern part of the island was full of ravines and paddies and was very difficult to cross. The native Japanese people, who suffered horribly during the war, inhabited the southern part of Okinawa that was primarily farmland with some hills and an occasional steep cliff the Japanese used effectively to mount artillery and set fortifications. The weather was always warm and wet, and the terrain was muddy.

Across a front line that measured only a few miles, we had four to five entire divisions deployed abreast with massive artillery support. The capital city of Naha was literally leveled, and the civilian population suffered grievous losses. Perhaps more tragic was the Japanese practice of using the helpless native population as shields. At night we would set up our machine guns, and when we saw movement we would send up flares to illuminate the figures and we would fire. It wasn't until the next morning we would realize that a majority of the dead were in fact natives with just a few Japanese soldiers intermingled in the heaps of dead bodies.

The 6th Marine Division along with the 1st Marine and 7th and 96th Army Divisions landed on the island of Okinawa on April 1, 1945, relatively unopposed. The following day I experienced the worst day of my life. I was in command of sixty-five men of a reinforced 2nd Platoon, Company L, 3rd Battalion. Our company was ordered to secure a portion of the 6th Division's left flank. We entered a ravine that had a small stream winding down its center between the sheer ridges of the ravine. At some points the ravine narrowed to a tight squeeze but then widened out into a rice paddy surrounded by hills. I think we all felt a little uneasy about our limited mobility within the ravine, but my superior, Capt. Nelson C. Dale, ordered us to push forward to find the Japs' main line of resistance. We had barely cleared the ravine when the whole hillside above the rice paddy erupted with fire from camouflaged caves and bunkers. Captain Dale was standing next to me, and he was fatally wounded. Our runner, who was also next to me, was hit in the neck and killed as well. I hit the deck and ordered our machine-gun unit to return fire on the caves above, but they were all struck within seconds. I don't think they managed to get a shot off before all six men of the gun crew were killed.

We had no option but to get up and run for cover. I ran and crawled through small ditches in the rice paddy and stuck my head up to look around when a bullet struck my helmet from behind. The bullet split my scalp, showering my face with blood, but it fortunately went through my helmet and out the other side without causing major injury. I managed to assemble fifteen men and found a small hump in the ground that protected us from the incoming fire. For the next twelve hours we fought off one frontal assault after another with just hand grenades and our small hand-held weapons. Twice I sent a runner to find help, but only the third managed to escape alive. Our relief finally arrived late in the afternoon with tank support, and they overran the Japanese. We counted 250 to 300 Japanese dead within 100 yards of our defensive position. At the end of the day, seventeen of my men and I walked out of that ravine. We left behind sixty men who were either dead or so badly wounded they needed to be carried out. We had been completely suckered by the Japanese and were half a mile behind enemy lines when they opened up on us. We were like ducks in a barrel, and we were slaughtered. We had done our jobs and made contact with the enemy.

My experiences on Okinawa were just one bitter day after another. We fought for every stinking yard, and the casualties were just staggering. The Japanese resistance stiffened the further we advanced into the island. Their plan in the south of the island was to use the natural barriers created by the Asa River near the capital of Naha. In early May the Japanese launched massive counterattacks, and we repulsed every one in ferocious fighting. The Japanese defenses were so tough and deep they were dubbed the "Siegfried Line of the Pacific." They massed artillery to protect their installations of log bunkers and concrete pillboxes. The Japs burrowed into deep caves with connecting tunnels far beneath the surface, and it was difficult, and costly, to root them out.

Sugar Loaf Hill was a heavily defended position guarding the approaches to Naha, and it took a dozen assaults and the lives of many Marines to capture it. As my platoon approached Sugar Loaf Hill there was already a terrific firefight going on, and everyone we came across was dead, dying, or wounded. We dug in on the flank of Sugar Loaf Hill, and our company was ordered to hold our positions through the night. We expected a counterattack, so I ordered my men to dig in and find what cover they could. I had a fantastic platoon sergeant named Patty Doyle, and Patty and I were walking among the men placing them when a mortar shell must have landed squarely on his shoulder. The mortar blew Patty's head off and sent shrapnel that put holes in my legs and knocked me to the

Brewster Wounded 7 Times But Missed No Combat Day

From the day after First Lieutenant Daniel B. Brewster, Jr., USMC, of Brooklandville, landed on Okinawa until the final day of the battle for Oroku peninsula, he was wounded seven times—but he never missed a day with his unit in combat.

Lieutenant Brewster received his first wounds second day ashore on the island, according to an Associated Press dispatch from Okinawa.

While his platoon was pinned down by enemy fire for seven hours in a narrow wooded ravine, a bullet pierced his helmet, furrowed through his hair and scratched his scalp. In the same action his foot was cut slightly when a bullet tore through his shoe.

Wounded Twice Again

He was wounded twice again on Sugar Loaf Hill overlooking Naha city—this time by shell fragments—during one of the heaviest artillery barrages ever experienced by the Marines in the Pacific. Refusing to be evacuated, however, he remained with his men and led them to the assault across the Asato River into Naha.

During the crossing of the river—pushing through chest-deep water under intense enemy fire—he was hit in the finger.

Then, in fighting in the residential district of Naha's northern suburbs, a shell fragment wounded him in the neck.

Returns After Treatment

After Naha had been taken, Lieutenant Brewster left his platoon—part of the 3d Battalion of the 4th Marines—to undergo treatment at a rear aid station, but he returned to his unit the following morning.

Later, twelve days after the amphibious assault on Oroku Peninsula, on the last day of that battle, he was wounded for the seventh time, nicked by a sniper's bullet during the mopping-up action.

The son of Mrs. William F. Cochran, Jr., of Brooklandville, Lieutenant Brewster was graduated from St. Paul's School for boys here. He left Princeton University to enlist in the Marine Corps as a private.

For the wounds he sustained in combat, Brewster was awarded the Purple Heart with two gold stars in lieu of an additional Purple Heart. His leadership of his platoon and their accomplishments on Okinawa are detailed in an article that appeared in the *Baltimore Sun* in 1945.

ground. I called out for my other sergeant, Lane Lackey. Lackey was Doyle's best friend, and when he arrived he took one look at Sergeant Doyle's headless body and just lost all composure. He went into shock and was completely unable to function. That was a long night.

Unless a person lives through such horror, I don't think you can understand what it is like to experience the trauma of seeing men you know killed and sometimes blown into little pieces. The battlefield puts tremendous stress on an individual, but most of my men were able to cope with being under fire, deal with the loss of friends, sometimes in horrific conditions. It amazes me how we could endure this hell and continue about our business. The few men who were not able to handle it were sent to the rear to work supply units. There were no "cowards." I think that word is inapplicable when in combat. Anyone who has not been in combat cannot know the true horrors one has to endure, and it is quite natural to want to run away from this type of situation. The noise, the blood, the sorrow, and the complete destruction of life one can witness could make the hardest of men crack up.

We lost about half our men that night on Sugar Loaf Hill, but the next morning we were ordered to cross the Asato River to assault the Okinawan capital of Naha. We spotted an old broken-down bridge that would be a good point to cross the river, so I gathered a fire team and started for the bridge. A photographer with our outfit asked if he could go with us because he wanted to photograph the Marines entering Naha, and I agreed. We made our way to the bridge, and before we crossed we came under fire. We were hit with high-velocity shells and had no time to react, so we jumped in the water and started wading back to shore. As we made it to dry land a mortar shell landed in the middle of our team, killing the photographer instantly. They later collected his remains, and they amounted to what we could fit into a small C ration box. Another explosion killed more of my men, and I was hit in the finger and neck. I withdrew the rest of my men, and as we crawled to safety I felt a sting in my neck. I reached to feel my neck, and when I looked at my hand it was just soaked in blood. I thought that I had had it, but I was relieved to discover the blood was gushing from my finger and not from the neck.

I was put out of action for a few days, and upon my return a week later I participated in one of the last actions of the campaign against the remaining Jap forces on Yaejudake, an escarpment 3,000 yards long and 600 feet high. We made an amphibious landing behind the main line of Japanese resistance and caught the Japs totally unprepared. We advanced through their main lines and reached a large cave that held the last defenders. As always, we threw in a 20-pound satchel of explosives and brought fire on the cave until all the Japanese guns were silenced. We didn't know it at the time, but the Japanese admiral and his staff had all committed suicide in the cave before we had even arrived.

I think it is worth noting that President Roosevelt died while we were on Okinawa. We were stunned to hear of his death. We had no idea he was even sick, and we all took a moment of silence in his honor when the word was passed to us that he was no longer our leader.

When the fighting stopped on Okinawa, I hoped to be sent home. However, my outfit was shipped back to Guam, where we began preparing for the invasion of the Japanese home island of Kyūshū. President Truman had the good sense to drop the atomic bomb on Japan, which ended the war. Truman saved hundreds of thousands of lives by using the atomic bombs. I hear people say that it was a horrible thing that we dropped the bombs, but they weren't the ones responsible for leading the invasion of the Japanese homeland. Our 6th Division was slated to lead the assault on the Jap mainland, and if that had happened there is no doubt in my mind that I, and all of my men, would have been killed. We would all have died on the beaches of Japan. The Japs would have naturally fought us even harder on their homeland, and our forces would have sustained tens if not hundreds of thousands of dead and wounded. The Japanese homeland would have been decimated, and millions of Japanese would have perished.

When the war ended, I once again had hopes of being sent home. I was called into the colonel's office, and he told me the news that I was being sent to Japan. I remember he said, "Brewster, get your company ready, we're going to Japan." I said, "But Colonel, I have multiple wounds received in battle, I think I am entitled to go home." The colonel looked up from his desk and said, "Brewster, you didn't hear me, did you?" Well, the next day I was on a ship and headed for Japan. Our ship sailed up Tokyo Bay and landed at the Yokosuka naval base. Looking back, I am very glad I went. It was the last great symbolic step a Marine from the 4th Marine Regiment could make. Our regiment had been wiped out on Bataan at the start of the war and was chosen to be the first to land on the Japanese homeland. General MacArthur wanted his 11th Airborne Army boys to land first, but I think we beat them to the punch. I spent a few weeks there and was home in time for Christmas in 1945.

Years later I passed through Japan when President Johnson asked me to represent him at a conference and to dedicate a war memorial in Korea. I had the opportunity to stop in Okinawa, and I went looking for Sugar Loaf Hill. I remembered it as a torn, bloody, pockmarked, cratered, barren, and deadly fought-over piece of land. Today there is a housing development with a water tank on it. There were no signs or memorials to remember all the Marines who fought and died on that very spot.

I had no feelings of hostility towards the Japanese I met after the war. The anger I had during the war had finally subsided. But through all these years, I cannot help but feel a sense of prejudice towards the Japanese. I don't buy Japanese products; I buy only American.

There were a few lighter moments I remember fondly, and I guess it wasn't all that bad. We had a few occasions when we could have a beer, talk about booze, girls, and the good times we had back home. Above all, we talked about how the hell we were going to end the war and when we were going to get home.

My generation lost so many members in the war. Of my Saint Paul's class of 1942, we had eight men killed in the war. I lost almost half of the men who served in my platoon, and I miss them all dearly. I wish they were still here.

EDWARD D. BUROW

Baltimore, Maryland
2nd and 4th Marine Divisions

Edward Dale Burow was born in the mining town of Beachley, Pennsylvania, on May 30, 1921. After moving to Baltimore in 1941 in search of employment, he enlisted in the Marine Corps and served in combat on Guadalcanal and Iwo Jima, receiving the Purple Heart and the Bronze Star for valor. He is one of three Burow brothers who served during the war. After the war, he returned to Baltimore to continue working with the B&O Railroad, where he was employed as a freight handler for forty-two years until his retirement in 1983. He and his wife, Virginia, have two children and two grandchildren.

In 1941 I was living on Cross Street in Baltimore working for the B&O Railroad as a freight mover at the old Camden Station making twenty-seven dollars a week. A few weeks after Pearl Harbor, my boss came over to me and started bad-mouthing the Japs for the attack, and he told me I should enlist in the service to go after the bastards. I shrugged off the suggestion, but that night I went to the movie *Shores of Tripoli,* and I became so fascinated with the Marines I woke up the next morning and decided to enlist. Before I knew what had happened I was on my way to Parris Island, South Carolina, where I was trained to be a Marine.

I was trained by a tough group of guys, and they really got me into shape. But no matter how much you train, you can never be fully prepared for war. I was continuously told how rotten the Japs were and what monsters they had become and the Marines were suppose to rid the world of them. I was being brainwashed, and because I was young and naive, it worked. We were trained to fight a traditional war, but we never fought that way because the Japanese fought like Indians, and we had to adapt ourselves to fight just like them.

After basic training I was assigned to the 2nd Marine Division. My outfit was loaded onto trains, and we traveled across the continent to San Diego, where we boarded ships to take us to American Samoa. The troopship was an awful place with little ventilation, and it was always hot and it smelled foul. We couldn't sit down even when we ate, and if the seas were rough you really had to hold on tight or you would be tossed around. Some guys would grab chow and within a minute their food was all over the floor, and I don't think some guys ate at all during the trip, they were so sick. The ship smelled so bad I would sneak out onto the ship's deck and slip into a lifeboat so I could sleep.

Then came the day we were told we were going to Guadalcanal. I had never heard of Guadalcanal, and it was something like a mystery. We were given little information on what to expect, and we had no idea of what the Japanese were going to be like. The night before we landed we listened to a speech about how this was our chance to hit back at the Japs and how we were going to wipe them up real fast. The Marines were always real positive, and they never told us just how bad it was really going to be. We landed on Guadalcanal with little opposition, and I remember the birds were singing as we came ashore.

Guadalcanal was a hot, rainy, steamy, smelly place plagued by swarms of flies and mosquitoes. The jungle was thick and so dark in places that when you walked through it you would think it was the dead of night. The Japs rarely buried their dead, and it added to an overall stench of rottenness across the island. The native population was very helpful, and I think they hated the Japanese more than we did. The Japs treated the natives poorly, and those who could fight back did so by attacking the Japs at night armed with just machetes. When we woke on some mornings the natives would have a pile of Japanese heads sitting in the middle of our camp. I'm glad they were on our side.

On our second day we were moving forward into the jungle when we were ambushed. It was dark and we couldn't see the Japs, and everyone started to run back the way we came. This was exactly the opposite of what we were trained to do, but we had never trained getting ambushed before, either. It was an awful scene, and guys were getting shot all around me. I turned and ran too, and I passed over the body of our lieutenant, a tough ex-FBI man named Dressler. My heart sank when I saw him lying there dead with his pearl-handled revolver by his side. We ran towards a clearing, and the sergeant stopped us so he could begin to count heads to determine who was missing. One guy named Bendricks came sprinting out of the jungle covered in blood. We grabbed him, thinking he was wounded, but he threw us aside. He sat down and asked for a cigarette, which was an odd request because we all knew Bendricks didn't smoke. He sat there and smoked like I never saw a man smoke before. He must have downed a dozen cigarettes while he told us how he jumped into a machine-gun nest by accident and had clubbed a few Japs to death with his BAR (Browning automatic

Guadalcanal natives armed with knives and machetes would sometimes attack Japanese soldiers at night in retaliation for the bitter treatment they had received. By daybreak they would have accumulated a pile of heads from their Japanese victims to show the Americans. The Marines were happy to receive their assistance.

rifle). I sat there listening to Bendricks, thinking about the rotten situation we had gotten ourselves into.

We retreated from the jungle and didn't move back into the area of the ambush for a few days. When we returned we found the Japs had mutilated our men by repeatedly stabbing their bodies or cutting off body parts and by pulling out their entrails. It was just unbelievable. Later we discovered the Japs would dig up the bodies of our buried dead and mutilate them, too. Only by experiencing these types of things can anyone really understand why the war with the Japs became so violent and merciless. I was determined to give back to the Japs everything they gave us, and more.

When we lost a fellow Marine, it made us fight harder; we were all close, and it was like losing a brother. The Japanese defenders on Guadalcanal were the most brutal and cunning soldiers possible, and our time on Guadalcanal was the most brutal of all our time during the war. If a Jap cut off the head of one of our guys, we cut the heads off ten of theirs. One of my most memorable images from Guadalcanal was during Christmas. Instead of Christmas trees, the tank and truck drivers got a real chuckle by decorating their vehicles with the heads of dead Japanese. Our colonel, after reading a notice from intelligence requesting prisoners for interrogation, said that if he caught any Marine taking a prisoner he would shoot the son of a bitch himself. We got the message, and I don't think we ever took a single prisoner. The Guadalcanal experience helped prepare us for other battles, but it was a difficult time because we had little excess to work with. But we learned what type of fighters the Japs would be, and we learned how to defeat them.

The 2nd Division was relieved and sent to Wellington, New Zealand, for further training. I soon discovered (as did a good percentage of our division) I had contracted malaria on Guadalcanal. I became so sick my weight dropped from 185 to 140 pounds. I was examined by a doctor, and he determined I was "unfit for combat," and I was sent back to the States for better treatment under the stipulation I would remain inactive for three months.

In October of 1944 I was still recovering at the naval base in Key West, Florida, when I received a letter from my mother telling me my brother Fred had been killed at Anzio, Italy, while fighting with the 36th Infantry Division. I was so upset I went to the commanding officer, a Major Blyner, to ask if I could return to Pennsylvania so I could be with my mother. He refused and said, "Son, don't you know there's a war going on?" Boy, did I ever.

I eventually recovered from my illness, and although I didn't have to, I volunteered to return to the Pacific. I really wanted to go to Europe to fight the Germans so I could pay them back for killing my brother, but the next best thing was to fight the Japs.

When I was reactivated I was assigned to the 4th Marine Division, which was assigned a portion of the job of assaulting Iwo Jima. I first saw Iwo Jima from the deck of our ship, and the island looked like it was the most desolate place on earth. Before our invasion the Navy battleships and planes had shelled the heck out of the island until there were no trees or anything of significance to be found. The Japs were dug in deep, and the bombing had little effect. When we arrived they still had a huge gun on top of Mount Suribachi, and the Japs dueled it out with our battleships. I thought our boys had hit that gun on several occasions, but within a few minutes it would rise up out of the ground on an elevator and fire again. On the morning of February 19, 1945, Sergeant Geddings and I were standing topside watching a bombardment when he leaned over to me and said, "Ed, this looks bad. I think this island will kill every one of us." Geddings was a dear friend of mine who had been wounded on Saipan, and I had to endure watching him die a few days later when we assaulted Charlie Dog Ridge.

It wasn't long until Geddings and I were geared up and ready to go over the sides to load the landing craft. As we did, all the guns from every ship began to fire on Iwo. Tracers and shells of all sizes were whipping by, making it seem like the Fourth of July a hundred times over. The sound was just a continuous rolling thunder. The water was rough, and we were tossed and slammed against the side of the ship while climbing down the nets to the landing craft. Many men were injured trying to jump down into the landing craft. I remember most of the Marines were violently sick from the motion of the landing craft bouncing in the rough sea, and the black, noxious fumes from the engines just made matters worse. I remember thinking that this was a hell of a way for some of us to spend the last moments of our lives, throwing up and violently ill.

As we made our way to the beach I could see all kinds of tracers flying over our heads. Every so often a big 16-inch shell from a battleship would pass over our heads, and it would actually lift our little craft up a bit from the change in pressure it caused. I could feel the heat from the big shells on the back of my neck as they flew over.

The Japanese artillery began to land all around, and several landing craft were blown up, which sent pieces of men and boats up into the air. The first wave lost so many boats that we were called back to the original line of departure to try a second approach. We circled towards the beach once more before we were able to make it onto land. As we headed towards the beach, I don't remember hearing much talking. I was scared to death, and I just hoped we would get through all the shelling and at least have a chance to fight. I remember a guy next to me tugged on my sleeve and pointed to the guy driving the landing craft. The driver was above us and could see everything happening on the beach, and his eyes must have been as big as headlights. Just looking at him scared me even more.

We were given the get-ready signal, and before we hit bottom the driver cut the engines like that was where he wanted us to get off. Lieutenant Sheffield turned and yelled for him to step on it until we hit the beach. Having to wade through deep water would have made us big, slow targets for the Jap guns, and I am glad the lieutenant had the good sense to get us closer to the beach. The driver must have been just scared to death, because he hit the throttle so hard he beached the boat about 10 yards on land. I don't think the poor bastard ever got off the beach, and I guess it's because we yelled at him so much.

When that ramp went down we ran like hell, because the first thing to do was to get as far off the beach as possible. My first sight was machine-gun tracer fire crossing in front of us, and I thought at that second not a single man would live for more than a minute under such fire. We followed Lieutenant Sheffield forward, but we got only a few steps before his head was blown off and his brains flew back onto all of us running just behind him. I didn't stop to pause for reflection; I just wanted to get off that beach and find cover. The lieutenant's best friend was Platoon Sergeant Lucas. The last image I have of Sergeant Lucas was of him kneeling over Lieutenant Sheffield's body, and I never saw either man again.

There was no way to run on the beaches; the sand was too soft. We slowly made our way onto the bluff, and when I dropped down for cover I felt something hard under my leg, and I looked down to see I was sitting on a mine. It must have been for a vehicle, and my little weight didn't cause it to explode. We were caught in a merciless crossfire, and it was a slaughter. It seemed to me that every second someone else was getting hit. All reality appeared lost, and I thought I had been thrown right into hell. Never in a million years could anyone believe what I saw unless they were there. It is indescribable, the hell the Marines endured on the beaches of Iwo Jima.

Iwo Jima (Sulphur Island) viewed from SSW toward NNE in an aerial photograph taken before the invasion. The island is dominated by Mount Suribachi, on which the Japanese defenders had established hidden bunkers and gun emplacements that commanded the beaches below. Despite weeks of constant bombardment by the Navy prior to the Marines' amphibious landing on February 19, 1945, Japanese artillery, mortar, and machine-gun fire on and around Mount Suribachi rained down in a murderous barrage upon the Marines when they landed. The lives of nearly seven thousand Americans, including six thousand Marines, were sacrificed in capturing the island. (U.S. Navy photo)

There were pieces of landing craft, pieces of bodies, and dead men everywhere. Somehow we managed to make it off the beach, but at a huge cost in lives.

As night fell we were assembled into a column and started to advance inland. The lieutenant leading our column, who I had never seen before, pushed further and further inland until our Sergeant Atkins, a fifty-year-old Marine with a handlebar mustache who refused a rear-echelon position, came running back to our position motioning for us to turn back. He pointed out several small mounds of earth we couldn't have seen, and it was then we realized each was a Jap machine-gun position. I owe my life to Sergeant Atkins, because we would have been cut to pieces if we had continued any further. Atkins was later wounded by shrapnel, and he died while on the same ship I was on when the wounded were evacuated to Guam, and I witnessed his burial at sea.

The Japanese had a very elaborate defense system on Iwo Jima, and fighting was done for every foot of land. A tunnel system extended deep underground that connected every Japanese position.

The Japs seldom came out of their holes during the day, and we had to burn them out one by one. Systematically, we set up crossfire on a bunker while a Marine ran up as close to the opening of the bunker as possible to toss in a 20-pound satchel charge. We had a little guy named Corporal Alwine who did this dozens of times. After each explosion he would be sent flying, and we thought he had died every time, but he always got up and came running back. If any man deserved a medal it would have been Alwine. A sniper later killed him.

The flamethrower was the greatest weapon we had. There was no way the Japs could outrun the flamethrowers, and I don't think we could have taken the island without them. If a Jap ran from a hole, we shot him dead, or the flamethrowers on our tanks could shoot 75 yards or more, and they crisped the Japs up until they looked like burnt wood.

When the flag was hoisted above Mount Suribachi we had just crossed airfield number 1. During the taking of the field we lost many men from heavy artillery fire, and I watched a couple tanks get blown up when they hit mines. The Japs placed tank mines in the runway, and I saw a tank hit one and get blown straight up in the air, and its turret separated from the tank and landed a distance away. When we watched our flag go up we all went a little crazy for a few minutes to celebrate. Most of the island was still in Japanese hands, but it gave us a great boost to see our flag on top of that mountain. It meant the Americans were there to stay, and to this day when I see the American flag I think of Mount Suribachi, and when I see people not respecting our flag I think about the men who died trying to put it up there.

The Japs liked to come out as darkness approached, and we used rocket launchers to catch them trying to assemble for an attack. One time we caught three hundred or so Japs in the open, and the rockets blew them all up. The Japs made our nights difficult, and we always slept two men to a foxhole with one man sleeping while the

Marines dig in under Japanese bombardment of the beaches of Iwo Jima, waiting for the order to move forward. In the background, men unload landing craft in the shadow of Mount Suribachi. Bogged down in the soft black volcanic ash, the Marines were exposed to withering fire from Japanese artillery. (AP News Feature photo)

other kept watch. We were always on alert at daybreak because the Japs attacked like clockwork in the morning. We ate when we could and never had a chance to take a bath except to wash our faces with a little water we poured in our helmets to act as a bowl. In addition to my rifle, I carried two belts of extra clips, a canteen for water, and two toothbrushes, one to keep the sand out of my rifle and the other for my teeth. I was on Iwo Jima for seven days before I was wounded, so I didn't wash for a week. Some guys on Iwo didn't wash for a month or longer.

On the 26th of February I was given lead of a squad of thirteen men during our assault on Hill 382. Half of the men in the squad I had never seen before, and I didn't bother with learning any new names. Hill 382 was heavily defended, and the rugged terrain made our assault difficult. Until our assault on that day, I had seen plenty of dead Japs but never more than two alive. On Hill 382 we encountered over two hundred Japanese, and my squad killed at least fifty of them. We had to advance through narrow pathways in the rock, which made it impossible to know if there were Japs above you or around the corner. Jap snipers were hidden in every crevice, and I thought I was going to die a hundred times, and I feel lucky to have gotten away with just the wounds I received.

The squad encountered a Japanese machine-gun position midway up the hill, and we managed to infiltrate behind it and establish a fire position. The machine gun was centered in a horseshoe-shaped trench overlooking the Marines advancing up the hill on our left flank. I knew it was going to be a turkey shoot, and I instructed the squad to pull out all their extra clips and keep them handy so they could reload quickly. On my signal the entire squad fired. I leveled my rifle on the ground and aimed at the back of the machine gunner and hit him square in the neck, and he slumped forward. We were so close I could hear the Japs shout back and forth to each other, and they had no idea we were in their rear. I started on the left side and went down the line of Japs until we had shot them all dead. Two Japs that had been hidden tried to run, but not realizing we were behind them they ran right at us. When they finally saw us they tried to lift their rifles to fire but got hung up on one another, and the entire squad cut them to pieces as they desperately tried to pull free. I didn't want to press our luck, so I motioned for the squad to back off as yet another Jap poked his head up from the trench. I just couldn't let this one get away, so I motioned to a few members in the squad as to where he was. We waited for a minute for him to poke his head up once more, and when he did we all drilled him. The last I saw of him was his leg up in the air, kicking like a mule. As we moved out, a guy with a flamethrower came along, and we motioned towards the trench. He gave us a thumbs-up, and he cremated whatever we had missed.

We resumed our advance another 30 yards until we heard some Japanese voices, so we stopped and hit the dirt. I told the squad to sit tight as Pvt. Joe Juliano and I edged forward to get a better look ahead. We peered over a small rise and saw a camouflaged gun position and some Japs who were bobbing up and down firing their rifles. Joe and I gathered our incendiary and fragmentation grenades and threw as many as we could into the Jap position before running for cover. There were several explosions and then screams. We were spotted by another group of Japs and came under rifle fire. We couldn't run back, so Joe and I ran forward to find better cover while the rest of the squad returned fire. We jumped into a small depression, and Joe noticed some Japs trying to come around our position. They were running towards us through a narrow passage, which ended in a sharp drop-off of about 4 feet. Instead of running and jumping down, the Japs were sitting on the ledge to slide down the rock face. I raised my rifle to fire, but Joe grabbed my arm and said if I did we would be trapped. I told him to just sit down and to keep handing me clips because I knew this would be another turkey shoot. The first few Japs made it, but as the next one stopped to sit down I nailed him right in the chest. Joe kept passing me clips as I fired round after round into the next ten Japs until they wised up and turned back. I sent Joe back to bring up the squad while I scouted forward. As I got up I spotted two Japs running up the hill, so I fired but missed. I followed them to the top of the hill, where I came across an antiaircraft position surrounded by a large circle of sandbags. All I could see were the hands of the gunner, so I fired, and I must have hit them because the gun went flying upright. A few helmets appeared over the edge of the sandbag wall, and I fired, and I think I hit a couple more. I emptied five clips into the gun position and decided to move closer for a better angle to shoot.

I was making my way around a large boulder when I ran into two Japs coming from the other side. We literally ran into one another, and my rifle stuck into the stomach of the first Jap. I unconsciously fired as fast as I could and foolishly emptied my entire clip into his belly. It was a horrible feeling seeing my empty clip spring from my M1, knowing another Jap was right behind him. Before I could move, the other Jap shot me at point-blank range, hitting me in the upper portion of my right arm. I fell backwards and tripped over a boulder, and was fully expecting the Jap to bayonet me. To my surprise, he had ducked back behind the boulder. I had a .45-cal. in my right pants pocket, and I struggled with my left arm to get it free. I had to cock it using my knees because my right arm was useless. The Jap started tossing grenade after grenade at me, but he either misjudged my position or was so nervous he threw them too far from where I was. He eventually got lucky, and he threw a grenade close enough that the explosion shredded the back of my pants. I yelled in pain, and I guess he thought he had gotten me. I just knew he was going to come finish me off, and I waited with my .45 until he poked his head around the boulder, and he was so close I was able to put a round right between his eyes. He fell backwards, and when I crawled over to where he was I remember seeing his tongue had come all the way out of his mouth, and I thought it was the longest tongue I would ever see.

I had lost the squad, so I limped back down the hill as fast as I could until I fell into a bomb crater filled with other wounded and dead Marines. A Corpsman grabbed me, and I had begun showing him my arm when he asked what had happened to my ass. I didn't think I was hurt too bad, but when I reached back I felt the blood dripping from my body. The Corpsman helped me to an aid station, and that was the end of my fighting days.

I fully recovered from my wounds and was released from the hospital to return to duty and was assigned as an acting sergeant by Lt. Red Bays. I had served with Red on Iwo Jima, and we were preparing for the inevitable invasion of Japan. We were very concerned about our chances of surviving again in combat, and when I heard Truman decided to drop the atomic bombs, I could have kissed Truman. We all partied for a few days, and Lieutenant Bays saw me off. He cried when he told me I probably would never get my promotion because the war had ended. I think I felt like crying, too.

I returned to the States and headed up to Pennsylvania to visit my mother. By law, I had ninety days of free time before I had to report back to my old job, and I spent most of it working on a dam construction job on the Youghiogheny River. I had seen an advertisement on the side of the road for laborers, so I inquired with the foreman. He asked what skills I had, and I said I didn't have any except that I knew how to kill Japs. He patted me on the shoulder and hired me on the spot. I worked there for eighty-nine days and returned to the B&O Railroad on the ninetieth day.

The real heroes of the Second World War were the mothers of the men who died far from home. I think they probably suffered the most, thinking of their lost sons. They claim the dead are the heroes, but you have the living heroes that have to live all these years thinking about the dead. I will remember my buddies that were killed until the day I die. I hope their families received the honor due them. I miss them. I can't forget the war and will never forget that war is hell. War is compounded hell. We should do everything we can to avoid any more of it.

JOHN V. CHAMBERLAIN

Towson, Maryland

96th Infantry Division, U.S. Army

John Victor Chamberlain was born in Lakeland, Florida, on August 26, 1926. He enlisted in the Army after graduating from high school in 1944 and was called to duty on his eighteenth birthday. He was assigned to the 96th Infantry Division on May 1, 1945, as a replacement in a platoon that had been decimated during the first month of combat on Okinawa. He participated in the fighting for Okinawa and is a recipient of the Purple Heart and the Bronze Star for valor. In 1955 Chamberlain moved to Maryland and began a career at Goucher College, where he taught religion for thirty-six years until his retirement in 1991. He married his first wife, Elaine, in 1950 and has two children and seven grandchildren.

I was in high school during the early stages of the war, and I followed the events very carefully and read about all the heroes who were fighting all over the world. As I got older and closer to eligibility for entering the service, I decided I wanted to be one of those heroes, too. I clearly remember seeing the gold stars in the windows in my neighborhood representing boys who had been killed in the war, but I still thought of the war as a big game of cowboys-and-Indians. I first tried to volunteer for the Navy, but my eyesight was not up to their requirements, so I walked over to the Army enlistment desk, and they took my application. They wouldn't call me to duty until after my eighteenth birthday, but I was excited to be part of a war we all knew had to be fought and won.

When I was called to service in the fall of 1944, I was sent to Fort McClelland in Alabama. I remember my mother standing on the train platform crying as I was leaving. I didn't understand what she was crying for at the time, but I learned later. I was homesick during my first few days, and it took some time to get accustomed to the basic living conditions at the camp. We were repeatedly shown propaganda films about the villainous Germans and Japanese and how

37

in the end the American soldier always came to the rescue. During my sixteen weeks of training I eagerly accepted all of what I was taught, and I had little thought of what lay ahead of me. At the onset of my training it appeared to me that the war in Europe was close to ending, but just about at the end of my training we were surprised to hear about the German counterattack at the Bulge, and we all knew there was still some hard fighting ahead of us. I had no preference of where I fought, and as it turned out I was sent to the Pacific to fight the Japanese.

I completed my training in the early part of 1945 and was issued a nine-day pass to come home for a few days before having to report to Fort Lewis in Seattle. I wore my complete uniform while back home, and I paraded around town like a real big shot. I was having fun, but it was not fun for my mother, who continuously had a worried expression on her face during my leave. I eventually made my way to Seattle, where I joined a group of replacements loaded onto a Liberty ship headed for the Hawaiian Islands. We were packed in tight on the ship. Daily life was getting in line for breakfast, and as soon as you completed that meal you got right back in line for lunch and repeated this again for dinner. The only break was a movie in the evening. The fact that most of the soldiers were extremely ill from seasickness made the month-long voyage a memorable time.

After landing in Hawaii we began training again to ready us for our entry into combat. We trained in the jungles on the northern shore of Oahu, and I later thought this was ironic because Okinawa has no jungle forest. In mid-April my group was again moved further west to a staging area on Saipan. It was on Saipan I learned I was to be assigned to the 383rd Infantry Regiment of the 96th Infantry Division as a replacement for a soldier who had been killed or wounded on Okinawa. We were told the battle had been raging on Okinawa since the 1st of April. I didn't even know how to pronounce the name Okinawa when I first read it, and for me it was a meaningless place on the map. We were briefed on Okinawa's size, terrain, and how the battle had progressed so far.

As we approached Okinawa I could see that the Navy was shelling parts of the island. I had never seen such a sight or heard such a noise as I did when the battleships fired a full broadside towards the island. It was absolutely stunning to watch the big ships slide sideways from the recoil of firing their big guns. I recall feeling a great sense of anticipation as I headed towards the beaches on Okinawa, and I was anxious to finally see what combat was like. Our LCI (landing craft, infantry) landed on the beach, and we filed into a line and marched off to the front.

During my first few days on Okinawa we set up camp and were allowed to walk around a bit to explore our new surroundings. By this time the northern two-thirds of the island had been secured, and the battle for the southern portion of Okinawa was just develop-

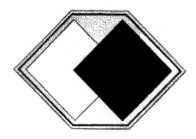

ing. I was assigned to a rifle squad that had been reduced from eight men to four men. I was appointed as a first scout, which was the most dangerous position in the squad because it was responsible for leading the squad forward. It was typical for new recruits to be assigned the most dangerous duties because the guys who had already been through the fighting reserved the right to hang back a little.

We didn't carry much extra equipment into battle and left our packs in camp. I carried an M1 rifle, extra ammunition, and a bayonet on my belt, a canteen of water, packets of Atabrine tablets to ward off malaria, and since this was a time before antibiotics we each carried six sulfa tablets that we were instructed to swallow if wounded to prevent infection. I was under the command of a platoon lieutenant who gave us orders when to move forward or when to rest. My platoon spent a few days as a forward unit then pulled back and let another unit move ahead. It was wonderful when we were relieved. We slept in tents instead of foxholes, ate C rations that were a little better than the K rations we ate while on the line, and collected as much candy and cigarettes as we could. Best of all, I had a sense of relief from the constant fear I experienced while up on the front lines.

My first experience in combat was while on sniper duty, which was to engage the enemy at long range and kill enemy soldiers we spotted. But the first Japanese soldier I killed had taken me totally by surprise at close range. I was walking down a path, and a Japanese soldier came running full speed right towards me. I didn't realize he wasn't armed, and in hindsight I could have easily captured him, but I picked up my rifle and shot him. It was unnecessary, but I was trained to kill, and I did what I was trained to do and shot him dead. I was elated: I had faced the enemy and survived my first encounter. I went around bragging to the other men in the platoon that I had killed my first Jap soldier and even put a notch on my rifle stock. It was a great relief for me to know I had overcome my fear of the enemy and I had done my job.

Our typical day was comprised of a steady advance against the Japanese line, digging in, calling for artillery support, then resuming the advance and hoping there wasn't anyone out there waiting in hiding for us. Okinawa was a battle against ridge after ridge made of coral, and each successive one was higher than the last. One of the hardest things to overcome on Okinawa was the thought of fighting up an endless succession of ridges as far as the eye could see. Perhaps the only advantage the Japanese had over us was how they utilized these ridges for excellent defensive positions. There were times we had to cross open areas under heavy enemy fire. The platoon would advance one at a time, and the next man wouldn't leave until the other was safely across. Each time a man moved I heard the crack of a Japanese rifle, and after a daily regimen of such conditions my attitude about combat being an adventure quickly changed. I was scared, and my blood was pumping hard most of the time, but the training I had received and the good leadership in the field enabled me to overcome the fear long enough each time to do what needed to be done. It is no coincidence that young eighteen-year-old boys are sent into combat, because they are the ones who follow directions without hesitation and still have a little bit of cowboy left in their bodies to get the job done. I never had an opportunity to do much independent thinking with the platoon lieutenant and sergeant leading us with great precision into combat. I did what I was told to do, and I hope they realized I did it as well as I could.

The first person I knew who was wounded on Okinawa was a guy named Ray Gilpen who was hit by a rifle bullet that entered the back of his neck and exited through his chin. Fortunately for Ray, it was a small bullet, and his jaw was not blown away. I remember he turned to me, and I saw his eyes were open wide, and all he said was "Uh-oh" before collapsing on the ground. As I watched the medics carry his body away, the fear inside me of being wounded or killed deepened considerably. Watching my fellow soldiers get wounded or killed never aroused a sense of wanting revenge against the Japanese. While I reacted with anger, I witnessed some men who just couldn't handle the stress of battle. None of us ever had any contemptuous feelings against these men because everyone shared these same fears to some degree.

One of the most frightening experiences I encountered was while bedding down on the crest of a hill during the night. Our artillery began shelling a Japanese position just a few hundred yards forward of us. The guns were miles behind our position, and I listened to the shells flying overhead. The most frightening sound was listening to the rounds that sounded like they were going to fall short onto our position. The destructive power of those shells was enormous, and the night sky was illuminated with the glare from the explosions. Phosphorous flares were hung in the air on small parachutes so the Army, Marines, and Navy artillery could pinpoint their fire against the Japanese. The unnatural light of the flares flickered across the landscape, creating a surreal silvery-white atmosphere until the last light burned out and we were once again in total darkness, alone with our fears and the sound of the shells passing overhead and exploding nearby.

The advantage we had over the Japanese was just incredible. We rarely received incoming Japanese artillery, and it was a tremendous advantage for our side. The Japanese were model soldiers who fought ferociously and were very determined to fight to the death and even committed suicide before surrendering. I never saw a Japanese soldier taken prisoner on Okinawa, but I knew somewhere on the island some had surrendered.

I was awarded a minor award for participating in the destruction of a machine-gun nest, just one of many we had to overcome on Okinawa. Advancing on a machine-gun position was always done delicately, and on this occasion I crawled forward under friendly ri-

John Chamberlain *(back row, left)* with members of his platoon on Mindoro Island following their time on Okinawa training for the invasion of Japan. To Chamberlain's left is Pfc. Ray Gilpen, who was shot through the chin on Okinawa but survived. Pfc. Steve Carter appears in the middle row, left, and to his left is Pfc. Tony Byrne. The others are unidentified. Carter is holding an M1918A2 Browning automatic rifle. The BAR was adopted for use by the military in 1940 and widely used by the Army and Marines during the Second World War. The BAR fired a box magazine of twenty rounds in two automatic modes, slow (300–450 rounds per minute) and fast (500–650 rounds per minute). The Army infantry squad of nine men was tactically organized around a single BAR, whereas a Marine squad of thirteen men was organized around three BAR firing teams, which gave the Marines a great combat advantage in terms of firepower. The BAR was a very reliable weapon that offered an excellent combination of portability, rapid fire, range (600 yards), and penetrating power.

fle cover until I was close enough to throw a grenade into the opening of the enemy bunker. The lieutenant wrote up the incident in an embellished fashion to ensure I would receive the Bronze Star, when in fact my actions on that day were no different from any other day or any other soldier.

On June 16 the platoon began to receive rifle fire from Japanese fortified in the entrance of a cave. I was holding a BAR (Browning automatic rifle), and along with two other riflemen I fired continually into the cave until we managed to force the Japanese back from its entrance. One of the riflemen then ran forward and threw a satchel charge containing 22 pounds of plastic explosives into the mouth of the cave to demolish it and kill or entomb any surviving Japanese in the cave. The detonation cap exploded, but the charge didn't, and this usually meant the Japanese had managed to pull the cap out from the explosives before it could detonate. The soldier threw another charge into the cave, and this time all 44 pounds of explosives detonated, and it was quite an explosion and the cave was sealed shut. Fragments of rock and coral were thrown during the explosion, and I was superficially wounded across my knee.

I was sent to a field hospital on Guam, and during my recovery I was put in charge of a small detail of Japanese prisoners of war who had been instructed to inventory a warehouse of supplies. The prisoners had been noncombatant service troops on the island of Rota before their capture. They all were very cooperative and peaceful, and there were times I left my rifle within their reach to help them move boxes. One of them took a white handkerchief and drew a traditional Japanese picture on it and gave it to me as a gift. A major gave me hell for fraternizing with the Japanese, but this was a very poignant moment for me because for the first time, I saw these Japanese men as human beings. This experience led to the profound feeling of remorse I was to experience after the war.

I sometimes recall the images of the many dead Japanese we came across as we moved forward. Despite the smell of the dead Japanese soldiers who were in the later stages of putrefaction, we still rifled through their pockets and packs to get pictures or other souvenirs. One of the terrible things in the history of warfare is the plundering of the vanquished by the victors, and at the time the emotions of battle didn't allow any of us to hesitate from ransacking the destroyed homes of Japanese and taking their personal belongings for trophies. We never did anything nearly as horrible as raping and murdering, but looking back I realize it was a violation of the privacy of those innocent civilians. Some would rationalize that the violation committed against the United States by the Japanese would permit us to act the same in return, but I still cannot believe I did such things, even if it was just to steal a few lacquered trays.

There were many Japanese civilians on Okinawa, and they were told the Americans would rape and torture Okinawan civilians, so many killed themselves before being captured. There were instances when dozens of Japanese women and children jumped to their deaths from fear of what the Americans would do to them. It was extremely saddening to hear such tales.

As we fought our way down Okinawa we often came upon peculiar Okinawan family tombs with their plastered domes, walled courtyards, and 2-foot by 3-foot openings. We routinely destroyed these with explosives because the Japanese soldiers routinely used them as sniper nests. The Japanese soldiers would use tombs even if they held a significant number of civilians with the hope we would not fire on civilians. On one occasion our platoon came upon a tomb with a plywood barrier over the opening. The lieutenant had a Japanese phrase book, and he tried to induce whoever might be inside to come out. Eventually an old lady did come out, frightened out of her wits. We deduced from her incomprehensible and panic-stricken responses that there were soldiers in the tomb along with members of her family, but no one else could be coaxed out. The lieutenant ordered me to fire my rifle through the opening. I did, and I heard a baby scream. We could not leave the tomb untouched with the possibility of Japanese soldiers at our rear, so the lieutenant ordered me to push down the plywood doorway and throw a 22-pound explosive charge in the tomb. I did, and I know I killed innocent civilians.

During my time in combat I felt that nothing had adversely affected my spirit. But when I came home from the war I began having many nightmares about the cave I destroyed and other such events. I never remembered the nightmares, but my mother said I often woke in the middle of the night screaming. I began to accept the truth that I had deeper trauma than I was willing to admit, and I felt guilt for what I had done on Okinawa. My Christian teaching allowed me to resolve the conflict inside me. "Your life is not your own, it was bought with a price," the Apostle Paul says. So my life is not my own to live for my own ends; it was bought with the price of the Okinawans I killed. I cannot repay them directly, but I can live for the well-being of the human family.

I am very proud of my service during the war and keep my decorations nearby as a reminder of the service I performed for my country. Someone once told me that the difference between a hero and a coward is a coward just thinks faster. I think the real heroes of the Second World War were the medics. They were conscientious objectors who stood alongside the fighting men, without weapons, tended to the wounded, and were shot and killed just like the rest of us. They were incredibly brave men who perhaps performed more bravely than any man who carried a gun.

MERRITT O. CHANCE

Brookeville, Maryland

VMF-312 Fighter Squadron, USMC

Merritt Ogle Chance was born in Washington, D.C., on August 18, 1923. He was raised in Brookeville, Maryland, by his grandparents, who adopted him when he was six years old. He enlisted in the Marine Corps after his graduation from Sherwood High School in Sandy Spring, Maryland, in 1942. Fulfilling a boyhood dream of becoming a fighter pilot, he flew fifty-three combat missions in the F4U Vought Corsair and is a recipient of the Distinguished Flying Cross. Near the conclusion of the war, Chance was assigned stateside as a combat flight instructor. In 1951 he graduated from the University of Maryland and returned to active duty in 1952 as a flight instructor until the conclusion of the Korean War. After separation from the reserves in 1957 with the rank of major, he began a career designing commercial airports and highways, which led to a position working for the Federal Aviation Administration developing standards for airport design and safety until his retirement in 1983. He and his wife, Nancy, were married in 1945 and have one son.

My father was a career Marine and a veteran of the First World War, so we talked on numerous occasions about my dreams of being in the military and of becoming a fighter pilot. I planned on attending college just so I could complete the mandatory two years of college that would make me eligible to apply to the Army Air Corps. When I learned the Navy had eliminated the requirement for pilot candidates to have college experience, I immediately forgot my plans to attend college and enlisted in the Marine Corps. I traveled to the Navy recruiting office in Washington, D.C., a few weeks before my high school graduation and expressed my interest of becoming a pilot. I was given a physical examination and a written test, which lasted three hours. I passed both and was accepted as a naval aviation cadet. Two days after my high school graduation my girlfriend (and future wife), Nancy, dropped me off at the train station to re-

44

port for duty. I was very excited to begin my training, and I had no hesitation about going off to war.

The train took me to the University of Virginia, where I began a course in civilian pilot training. I was taught U.S. Navy history and the proper etiquette of becoming a naval officer. I studied the basics of flight and began to learn how to fly in a Piper Cub airplane. I completed my first solo flight in August of 1942 and then departed for preflight school in Athens, Georgia. Preflight was the Navy's version of boot camp for aviation cadets, and we didn't do any flying, but we did a lot of parade-ground drills and other physical endurance exercises. After preflight I was sent to Dallas, Texas, for elementary flight training and began flying again in a Stearman two-passenger plane. I remember the Stearman had an intercom system in which the instructor could talk but I could only listen to his instructions and commands. I perfected my basic flying techniques and was introduced to the art of formation flying. I wasn't taught combat flying techniques until I began intermediate and then advanced flight school in Pensacola, Florida. When my graduation approached in July of 1943, I was asked if I had a preference in what type of aircraft and what branch I would like to fly. I chose to fly alone because I still had the dream of becoming a fighter pilot. The thought of being responsible for the lives of others was just too much for me to accept. I figured I had a good chance of getting myself killed, and I didn't want to get anyone else killed, too.

Merritt Chance *(back row, eighth from right)* and his VMF-312 Marine Fighter Squadron at Parris Island in December 1943. Of the men shown in this photo, 90 percent were eventually stationed on Okinawa flying ground support during the ground battle, and all survived their time in combat.

Following my graduation and receiving my commission in the Marine Corps, I was sent to preoperational school at Miami Naval Air Station. I continued to improve my flying skills by performing more formation flying and began to practice air gunnery and flying using only my instruments. On occasion I flew the Brewster Buffalo. The Buffalo was a much faster and more powerful plane, and I thought it was superior to the Navy's workhorse F4F that I flew later in my training—that is, if it was working. Sometimes the landing gear jammed and I had to use a pair of pliers to lower the gear down manually. Of the twelve Buffalos on the base, I don't recall more than two ever working properly at one time.

In August of 1943, a few days after my twentieth birthday, I arrived at Parris Island, South Carolina, and was assigned to Marine Fighter Squadron VMF-312. The squadron had been slowly assembled with pilots of various flying backgrounds, including multi-engine bombers and observation planes, and only a few men in the squadron had graduated from advanced fighter school. We soon became friends and became comfortably dependent on each other.

The squadron spent a lot of time performing formation flying and acrobatics, and we practiced aerial gunnery by firing at a 2-foot by 25-foot banner trailed behind another plane. When practicing gunnery, each plane fired a different color round so we could determine who hit the target and who missed. I was not as good a shot as some of the other pilots, but not as bad as one guy who ran into the target towline. We all kidded one another about our failures, but we were also very supportive when we felt it was needed.

The squadron was formed in an age when fighter pilots were given latitude to be aggressive and flamboyant, and I think we had been selected as fighters because we all demonstrated this attitude. We did things no pilot would ever get away with today, and we really got away with murder. We never missed an opportunity to fly under bridges, buzz buildings at high speeds, or chase people off sailboats. We fired so many tracer rounds into the woods surrounding Parris Island I think we were responsible for hundreds of fires. We performed so many formation acrobatics it was amazing none of us were ever killed.

We were all young; the average age was twenty-three, and our oldest member was twenty-eight. The squadron was made up of some interesting people, including guys who were always on the hunt for booze, girls, and a good time. Jimmy "Zoomie" Webb was the son of a Baptist minister, and he could pick any lock ever made, and with Zoomie around we had access to anything we had the desire to get. Later, while stationed on Espíritu Santo Island, Zoomie disappeared during a practice exercise, but when the squadron landed there wasn't a man among us who didn't think Jimmy was coming back. Two weeks later we saw a light flashing on the upper part of the island, so we called a PT boat to check it out, and sure enough, there was Zoomie. Luckily he suffered no injuries during his emergency parachuting after his horizontal stabilizer separated, causing him to lose control of his plane. Zoomie was in good spirits when he was found walking down the beach with a bunch of bananas over one shoulder and a bow and arrow over the other.

When we were first introduced to the Vought Corsair, very few of us had ever seen the plane before. The one person with the most flying experience in the Corsair had only ten hours in the plane. Our commanding officer, Major Day (who was later killed in combat), assembled the squadron in a room and handed each of us an operating manual for the Corsair. He said, "Read this manual. When you think you are ready to fly, go fly." The Army Air Corps had rejected the original Corsair, so it was graciously given to the Navy. The Navy couldn't get it onto their carriers, so they graciously gave it to us Marines. I think the Marines were the only ones who said, "Thanks."

The early F4U1A Corsair was first introduced into combat by VMF-114 on Guadalcanal in 1942. It was a great improvement in speed and maneuverability over the F4F the Marines had been using, but the early Corsair was a less than perfect plane. I would describe it as "unusual," for lack of a better term. The plane had a very distinctive nose extending 13 feet forward of the cockpit. This greatly reduced the pilot's visibility forward and of the ground, so someone had the bright idea of installing a piece of clear Plexiglas on the floor of the cockpit so the pilot could see the runway by looking down between his legs. What had seemed like a good idea was in practice a poor one, because the radial engine leaked so much oil the Plexiglas became obscured under a thick layer of oil shortly after takeoff. Visibility was especially poor for the pilots who were short in stature. We had one small guy in our squadron named Jim Reese, and no other pilot dared do a head-on pass with Jim because we weren't sure he could see us over the nose of his plane. In the early version of the Corsair, the lever used to raise and lower the landing gear was inconveniently located near the ankle, and once again the smaller pilots were handicapped by having to reach far below the control panel to operate the lever. It was not uncommon to see a Corsair dip down slightly after takeoff as the pilot leaned forward to reach the lever. To overcome this, some pilots found they could use the edge of the shoe sole to raise the lever.

The Corsair was started using an explosive charge resembling the type of shell used in a shotgun. It didn't always start on the first or second try, and the breech firing the charge had to be replaced often. The early canopy resembled a birdcage because it had so many metal frames holding the glass in place, but the installation of a single Plexiglas dome improved visibility. Visibility over the nose while on the ground was improved when 8 inches were added to the rear wheel and the cockpit was moved forward. A design fault caused the left wing to stall before the right, which caused the plane to flip during landings or very slow flight. This problem was re-

This photograph of three Chance Vought F4U Corsairs depicts the number 530 Corsair flown by Merritt Chance during the war. A close look at plastic model-airplane kits on the shelves of hobby stores reveals that a number of model manufacturers around the world used this famous photograph as the basis for the decals that accompany their kits. (Official USMC photo)

duced when an 8-inch piece of wood was taped to the right wing, which caused that wing to stall more like the left wing. The first experimental Corsair was armed with two .30-cal. guns in the nose and one .50-cal. gun in each wing. The latter versions had the nose guns removed, and three .50-cal. guns were placed in each wing.

The Corsair was fast, and it was the first radial engine aircraft to exceed 400 mph. The air-cooled engine could take a punishing as compared to other aircraft, whose water-cooled engines would overheat and stall when even slightly damaged. There were times when I saw a Corsair return from a mission with one or two of its engine cylinders missing. Its 2,000-horsepower engine turned a large 13 1/2-foot propeller requiring a large clearance above the ground. This posed a problem for the designers, who needed to get the wheels on the ground without adding substantial weight to the aircraft. The solution was the gull-wing shape, which adequately lowered the gear to the ground and created a profile that has since become one of the most recognizable and admired in aviation history.

The early Corsair was not a forgiving airplane, and it took your full concentration to fly it from the moment you started its engine until the time you turned it off. The plane was difficult to fly, and many inexperienced pilots were killed, earning the Corsair the nickname of "Ensign and Second Lieutenant Killer." Between the time I joined the squadron and my last mission in combat, twelve pilots I knew were killed while flying the Corsair, and only two of them were killed by enemy fire. Despite some of its early growing pains, the later-model Corsair was an excellent airplane. It was a fast plane with a great payload capacity. It had good control at high speeds, and it performed rolls and loops with little effort. I loved flying the Corsair. It was a powerful and graceful aircraft once you learned how to handle it.

The squadron left Parris Island on January 1st of 1944. Some of the guys flew their planes out to San Diego, and the rest of us, including me, went by train. While in San Diego we did just a little flying in Piper Cubs to stay sharp, because our Corsairs had been taken and assigned to other squadrons. We stayed put until the end of February but kept busy learning plane recognition techniques and accompanied the enlisted men down to the rifle range, where I became a pretty good shot with a rifle. The squadron was shipped out on the carrier USS *Hornet* on February 28th of 1944, and five days later we arrived in Hawaii, at Ewa Marine Air Station. We received new Corsairs and practiced more gunnery and bombing and began flying with bomber squadrons to practice escort formation flying.

On June 25th of 1944 we were shipped out on the USS *Nassau* to Turtle Bay on the island of Espíritu Santo in the New Hebrides about 500 miles south of Guadalcanal. We continued our training and perfected our water navigation skills, which were critical for flying in the open waters of the Pacific. We also spent some time shuttling replacement planes to Guadalcanal. When we were shipped out to Manus Island in the Admiralty Islands in Papua New Guinea, we all thought we were finally going to get our shot in combat, but we were soon sent back to Espíritu Santo. We all felt very disappointed. We were given yet another round of training, learning how to employ the rockets our Corsairs were equipped to fire. Frustration concerning our inactivity was mounting until the end of March of 1945, when the squadron flew back to the Admiralty Islands and we were told we were headed to Okinawa, and the war. Our planes were loaded onto a baby carrier that was loaded with so many planes there was little room for planes to be loaded onto the catapults for takeoff. If the carrier had been attacked, any pilot taking off to defend the ship would have had no chance of returning for a landing.

In just a few days the squadron was catapulted off the carrier, and I was fortunate to be the last plane in line, because the Navy guys had given us the wrong tab setting for our flaps, and the first guys who flew off the deck shot into the air like a rocket. It took the rest of the squadron to gradually adjust the tab settings, until I had it just right by the time it was my turn.

The squadron landed on Kadena Field, Okinawa, which was located in the central part of the island. This airfield was only 65 feet wide by 2,800 feet long, which made our takeoffs and landings a little hairy. Later this field was expanded to handle B-29 bombers, especially those that had emergencies after returning from missions over Japan. From first glance the field appeared to be in good shape, but it rained very hard shortly after we arrived, creating large holes in the runway. The holes were poorly repaired, and when our Corsairs hit these holes, our landing gear went so far into the ground our propeller hit the ground and both the propeller and engine were damaged. Collisions with the construction equipment that littered the airfield also cost the squadron a few of our planes. An executive officer from another squadron on the base was killed when he ran into a bulldozer during a landing at night. The Navy Seabees came to our rescue and corrected all the problems. We quickly discovered life was always better near the Seabees because they could make or invent anything we needed from scratch. A number of the Seabees had great artistic talent, and they created authentic-looking replicas of Japanese battle flags that they sold to unsuspecting rear-echelon guys passing through.

The Marines and Army were engaged in fierce fighting south of our position near the Okinawan capital of Naha. The Japanese artillery had our field sighted with their guns, and we lost seventeen airplanes to artillery fire during our tour on Okinawa. When we heard the first boom of the Japanese shells exploding, we all dove into our foxholes and waited for the coming barrage. We dug our foxholes in the center of our tents and covered them with spent casings from 105-mm. artillery shells so we could sleep a little more relaxed under cover at night. We were shelled at least twice a week during the first few weeks, and we lost our Corpsman one night when we were shelled. Twice I witnessed Japanese planes attack the base, but the Japanese planes didn't pose as great a threat to our lives as our own antiaircraft arsenal.

The Army had stationed a number of 20-mm. and quad .50-cal. antiaircraft guns around the airfield, and anytime a Japanese plane was spotted, even if well out of range, every gun erupted into action. I believe the antiaircraft crews were less concerned about their aim than about how fast they could fire, and our base quickly became awash with a hail of friendly cannon and bullet fire. Tracer fire could be seen wildly traversing back and forth into the sky, and shells crossed the airfield at dangerously low trajectories. The best thing to do was lay low until the Japanese planes passed harmlessly overhead and our guns fell silent. The comic irony was lost when one of our Navy F6F planes was shot down while chasing a Japanese Zero over the base. The Zero escaped unharmed. Our communications officer, Lieutenant Stevenson, was badly injured when an unexploded 20-mm. shell landed in his back while he was crouching in his foxhole.

Our daily living on Okinawa was relatively comfortable, and I couldn't complain about the food too much. We had a savvy ground technician who was very adept at diverting certain trucks full of some of our favorite foodstuffs from the beach areas to our direction. Our squadron was a self-sustained unit in that we had our own cooks, bakers, and support staff. The only time the squadron received additional assistance was during times of extensive maintenance and overhauling of our aircraft.

In addition to my squadron, the 322nd and 323rd Marine Fighter Squadron and one torpedo-bomber squadron were stationed at Kadena. Each squadron consisted of twenty-four planes divided into six divisions, with four planes in each division. During typical operating periods, four divisions in each squadron flew each day while the other two divisions rested on a rotating schedule. Pilots with the rank of captain and major generally flew the same plane all the time, but after the squadron lost so many planes the rest of us shared time in the remaining planes. I flew most of my missions in Corsair number 530, so I had the name "Fancy Nancy" written in white letters on the left side of the aircraft. The guy I shared the plane with was from Texas, and on the opposite side he had written "Dung Ho!"

Each plane was assigned a ground captain who was responsible for maintenance of the aircraft. Our planes were maintained and kept ready for combat around the clock by a fantastic group of ground personnel. Us pilots, like some sort of romanticized knights, received all the glory in the war when so much credit is owed to the men who made our planes function to the top of their ability. The ground crews treated our planes as if they were their own children, and they often worked through the night, if necessary, to make sure the plane was ready the next day. When my ground captain handed me a yellow piece of paper each morning stating that all was satisfactory with the plane, I was 100 percent confident that the plane was working as close to flawlessly as humanly possible.

Most of our combat activity involved ground attacks on enemy troops and shipping. I believe the Marine Corps really introduced the world to modern close-air ground support. There were fourteen Marine squadrons stationed on Okinawa for the purpose of providing close-air support for the Marines and Army infantry and for defensive interception for the ground and naval forces.

We had little preparation when launching ground support strikes. Although there were times the squadron could anticipate action, most likely we were just sitting around the airfield when the call came in for air support. One or two planes in the squadron were usually flying reconnaissance over the battlefield, so when a request for air support was received, these pilots would have a good idea of exactly where the strike was needed and would immediately make an attack using phosphorous rockets to mark the target for the remainder of the squadron to hit.

A squadron of Corsairs could deliver a preponderance of ordnance, often to within 1,000 to 1,500 feet of our ground positions. In addition to the six forward-firing .50-cal. machine guns, the Corsair could deliver eight 5 ½-inch rockets and two 1,000- or 500-pound bombs.

Our approach to a target was made in formation until the lead division spotted our target. The division leader would roll over with his three wingmen following close behind. Each division would follow their lead until all planes in the squadron were single file, heading in towards the target. The attack dive was very brief, and by extending our landing gear slightly we could create enough resistance to allow us to dive much more aggressively (steeper), similar to the SBD dive bomber.

It was wise to be fully out of the dive and heading back up into the air no less than 500 feet above the target, because the Corsair had a tendency to "mush" when pulling out of the dive. In other words, you could pull the nose up, but it wouldn't respond, and this was more the fault of an eager pilot than the plane. We lost a couple of guys when the plane failed to respond and they couldn't escape the dive before hitting the ground. You had to be conscious of the G-forces working on your body and upon the plane. A pilot could withstand a brief exposure to a G-force of up to 9 (9 times the force of gravity), but it was impossible to endure a sustained G-force greater than 3 without passing out. We wore a rudimentary pneumatic suit that covered our midsection down to our feet, and when we experienced G-forces the suit constricted to help keep the blood from flowing from your head causing you to lose consciousness. Another danger was when pilots developed a fixation on a target and lost all measure of everything else, and this was when accidents were most likely to occur.

The attack dive was very exciting because on one hand you're hoping you're not going to get hit, and you're excited about laying it onto the enemy. After a bombing run it was nice to look back on the target to see that your efforts had been a success, but it was nothing like the Hollywood movies when a guy would celebrate or say something vengeful about the enemy after hitting the target. I seldom saw enemy soldiers on the ground because we usually hit tanks, artillery, and supply positions, and I never really looked closely enough to see people. I do remember a time we discovered a large column of Japanese soldiers marching along the road led by an officer who was mounted on a horse. I believe we inflicted many casualties before they even knew what hit them. I seldom saw anyone firing at me, but on some missions against heavily defended airfields I thought of Christmas because the antiaircraft fire flying past me looked like thousands of little red ornamental balls. During my fifty-three missions I was lucky to have never been hit by fire from an enemy plane or an antiaircraft gun.

The Corsair was a very durable aircraft compared to the Japanese Zero we faced in the air over the Pacific. The Corsair could take several hits whereas the Zeros seemed to catch on fire and come apart when we hit them. The Corsair had decent maneuverability that could be enhanced by dropping our flaps at any speed, but it just didn't have the maneuverability to dogfight a Japanese Zero. We engaged all other types of Japanese aircraft without hesitation, but we had to develop tactics against the Zero that involved making a sudden striking pass at high speed allowing us to keep pushing maximum power into a dive or climb to distance yourself from the Zero. If a Zero was on your tail, we had another important advantage that helped us escape. When the Zero went into a dive, it could not turn in one direction and then back in the other as easy as we could, so the way to shake it off your tail was to make a dive, turn sharply right and then back left, and the Zero could never follow and you were free.

Our squadron shot down seventy Japanese planes, but I only saw three Japanese planes in the air when on missions. Some guys in the squadron were so desperate to shoot down a plane they refused to return home until they had shot down an enemy plane. We were told the Japanese were decent pilots, but we had a huge advantage in numbers by the later stages of the war. If there is a single instance to best illustrate our confidence in our skills, and the Corsair, it would be when four guys in our squadron came up against a force of twenty-four Japanese airplanes including eighteen fighters and six bombers. They shot down ten of the enemy planes without a loss of our own.

The Japanese kamikaze pilots inflicted a horrible toll on the American warships surrounding Okinawa, so we began to fly cover over the fleet. When the ships picked up incoming planes on radar, we would try to intercept them before they could attack. The kamikaze attacks occurred most frequently in the late afternoon when it was starting to get dark. The planes used in the attacks were of such a variety that it appeared the Japanese were using any aircraft they had left. It was strictly a one-way mission for the kamikaze pilots, but they were often accompanied by another plane that turned tail once it made sure the kamikaze was on target. The Navy destroyers running the picket around Okinawa really took the brunt of the kamikaze attacks, and I believe the Navy lost over forty destroyers in the waters surrounding Okinawa. I watched one kamikaze strike the battleship *New York,* and although it made a big explosion, it hardly dented her armored decks. The smaller ships were much more susceptible to the attacks because they had less armor and less antiaircraft protection.

One of our squadron pilots, Vic Armstrong, had spent time in China and Japan before the war with his parents, who performed missionary work. Some of his friends were in naval intelligence, and he invited me to go with him to visit some of his friends who were interrogating some Japanese kamikaze pilots. They had been shot down before they could attack any ships, and they were young kids with just a few hours of flight training. I was surprised to learn they were not as dedicated to their divine mission as I had been led to believe. I think many showed a deep sense of regret for failing to complete their mission, but none were too upset over still being alive.

I viewed my combat missions as a job I had to do. We all tried to do the best job we could to help our troops on the ground. I was never really scared flying in combat, and I don't believe any member of my squadron showed even the slightest hint of apprehension flying in combat. We were young, and like kids who drive fast, we all got a thrill from flying. We learned from our mistakes and took a lot of deep breaths when we felt lucky to have survived a tricky situation. I experienced only two moments when I felt lucky to have survived. One was while on a bombing run, when I moved the stick too fast and I inverted my aircraft at 2,500 feet. As with most fighter aircraft, by moving the stick too fast I caused the aileron to stall, which flipped my plane. I was lucky I was not in a very steep dive, or else I might have hit the ground. The other moment occurred while I was in advanced flight training. On takeoffs, the division leader would signal when to switch fuel tanks, and on one occasion instead of switching tanks I turned off the fuel supply, and my plane cut out. Every other day when we performed the switch we were at 250 feet, but for some reason on this day we were at 600 feet, and I had just enough altitude and time to restart my engine and recover.

It was always a difficult experience when members of our squadron were killed. As a fighter pilot, my exposure to death was much more aesthetic than the death experienced by the men who fought on the ground. When I think about the men I knew who were killed, I think about the memorial services I attended, because 95 percent of the guys in the squadron were Catholic. I can still recall not understanding anything during the memorial service except the moments when his English name was mentioned. I was very close to a couple of the guys who were killed. One was a guy named George Hartig, who was killed when he failed to raise his flap during a spin. It was tough, but I don't remember any instances of sitting down and crying. When a pilot was killed, his clothing and bedding were divided among the living, and there was always a moment of reflection that on any given day it could have been your stuff being divided among your friends. We all accepted the risks, and it was just something we never dwelled on.

In June of 1945 the remaining twenty-eight members of the original squadron were reassigned to positions in the States. I was very glad to leave Okinawa, and I married Nancy shortly after returning home. I was assigned to the naval air station in Corpus Christi, Texas, as an advanced fighter instructor. Nancy and I were having lunch when the news broke that the war had ended. We were both relieved, because I was sure I was heading back to the Pacific to prepare for the invasion of Japan.

Flying the Corsair was a fun job. In my experiences as a pilot I was not exposed to the suffering and pain many others may have

Chance receives the Distinguished Flying Cross in recognition of his twenty combat missions on Okinawa between April 9 and May 7, 1945: "For bold and persistent strikes helping to lower the morale and resistance of the enemy forces."

experienced at the hands of the enemy. It would be hard to describe after fifty years if I ever felt any outright hatred towards the Japanese. We never dwelled on how many people we killed, but the Japanese were the enemy, and if killing them meant a quicker end to the war, then I was in favor of doing whatever it took to achieve that end.

After all these years I am still communicating with the men in my squadron, and we call each other periodically and have reunions every few years. The camaraderie formed by men in combat is a brotherhood that is hard to break.

I am amazed today how little young people know about what happened during the war. I hope it's not a matter of not caring, but rather a matter of our education system failing to instill a sense of our history in our young people. A lot of our veterans have never spoken about their experiences, and I hope more men will step forward and tell their families about what happened during the war.

The real heroes of any war are the men who fought on the ground. They were men who crunched the gravel and lived in horrible conditions and had to endure watching their buddies die in front of their eyes. Those poor guys who fought and died in the dirt and mud, and the men in the Navy who went down with their comrades in their ships, are my heroes.

DOROTHY E. STEINBIS DAVIS, R.N.

Rockville, Maryland

57th Field Hospital, U.S. Army Medical Corps

Dorothy Emma Steinbis Davis was born in Tulare, South Dakota, on September 11, 1922. She entered the University of Minnesota School of Nursing in 1940 and upon her graduation in 1944 was recruited by the American Red Cross to volunteer for service in the U.S. Army. After receiving her commission, she served with the 57th Field Hospital in Europe. The hospital's contributions were highlighted when it received a Meritorious Unit Citation for its support of combat wounded during the Battle of the Bulge. She returned home after the war and married the late Col. William V. Davis in 1946. In 2001 the American Red Cross honored her by instituting the Dorothy Davis Spirit of Nursing Award, to be presented to an outstanding Red Cross nurse each year. Davis and her husband moved to Maryland in 1963, and she has three daughters and two granddaughters.

The following profile was based on an interview with Dorothy Davis, and on portions of her personal memoirs, which are reprinted here with permission.

I really didn't know what I wanted to do when I was in high school until I saw an article in *Life* magazine about the life of an airline stewardess. The lifestyle seemed really adventurous, but one of the requirements was that all applicants had to be nurses in case passengers needed medical assistance while in flight. So I decided I would become a nurse in order to qualify for a career as a stewardess.

When the Japanese bombed Pearl Harbor on December 7, 1941, I was a student nurse at the University of Minnesota training in the operating room, and I was returning from lunch at the hospital when I noticed the student nurses were gathered around a small radio in the lobby. Soon we were glued to the reports as to what had happened at Pearl Harbor. Most of us had no idea where Pearl Harbor was, so in a sense it was a surreal piece of news. When I went to work the next morning I walked into the operating room, and there were the nurses and doctors dressed in military uniforms. The university hospital had been assigned as a general hospital in case of emergencies and was already prepared to operate as a military hospital in case it was needed. Once I saw their uniforms, I was immediately attracted to the excitement of the staff preparations for war and knew I wanted to eventually join the service. Perhaps a more compelling reason to become an Army nurse was the reports of the huge number of wounded who needed care, and I felt, as many other nurses, that it was my duty to volunteer to contribute my part in the war effort.

From the moment I was exposed to the other nurses and doctors in the Army, I could hardly wait to join the Army Nurse Corps. In 1943 the American Red Cross began recruiting nurses from our school, and I was the first in line to say I wanted to sign up. The one proud thing about the Army Nurse Corps was that all fifty-nine thousand American nurses who served in the Army Nurse Corps during the Second World War were volunteers.

As a senior student nurse I matured quickly as a person and as a nurse. Because so many of the registered nurses had gone off to the military services, the senior student nurses were responsible for the administration of the hospital wards. Upon graduation, it was a most exciting moment when I received a letter from the War Department addressed to 2nd Lt. Dorothy Emma Steinbis assigning me to the Army Nurse Corps. I reported to Fort Snelling, Minnesota, and was sworn into the Army at twenty-one years of age. I was very anxious to do something finally after three years of training as a nurse and waiting for my orders to report to duty. I felt the same way as the men who trained for so long and who actually wanted to go into battle to put their training to the test.

My first assignment was at Fort Carson, Colorado, which was the basic training center for Army nurses from the Midwest. There were four of us who had come from the University of Minnesota, and we were great buddies experiencing all the trials of boot camp together. The course lasted three weeks, and it taught us how to adjust to the Army way of life. We learned Army protocol including how to salute, ran the obstacle course, and learned how to pull on our gas masks if there was a gas attack. The time we spent at Fort Carson was very interesting and fast-paced, and to my knowledge there was no discrimination against the nurses from the men.

At last I was getting to do something I had wanted to do for a long time. We all felt that joining the Army was a fulfillment of our general patriotic duty to serve our country. As time went by and the war progressed, we all had brothers, cousins, and friends and acquaintances who had gone into the service, and our efforts became very personal. We knew our skills would help save lives—perhaps not the lives of our loved ones directly, but the lives of many others who were someone's loved ones.

After basic training and a month's assignment at Topeka General Hospital (working on a ward for the German POWs who had been sent to the Midwest to help the farmers), I was assigned to the 57th Field Hospital. The 57th was activated in February 1944 at Camp Crowder, Missouri, and by the end of May it was fully staffed, including eighteen nurses, of whom I was one. Many of the members of the 57th were from the Midwest, giving us some common roots such as having lived through the Great Depression and the dust storms of the 1930s. We were also fortunate to have experienced people heading our hospital.

The field hospitals were small mobile units that included 13 physicians, 3 dental officers, 5 medical administrative officers, 18 nurses, 183 enlisted men, a chaplain, and 2 Red Cross workers. This number was then divided into a headquarters unit and three smaller platoon units. Each platoon was equipped to serve as a separate and complete hospital. Small teams of specialized surgeons, nurses, and enlisted technicians, known as surgical teams, would be assigned to each platoon to provide the surgical skills needed.

My introduction into the war was somewhat gradual. On July 24, 1944, we left the States for Scotland. Our first assignment was to staff a holding hospital at the airport in Prestwick, Scotland. Many of the patients had been wounded during the invasion of France (D-Day) and were finally being air-evacuated back to the States for further treatment. Our task was to provide the needed medical and surgical care to the patients waiting to be evacuated. Patients were brought to us, and within five to six hours, barring any bad weather, they were loaded onto transports to be taken to hospitals in England or the States.

While in the university hospital I had been exposed to many wounds caused by gunshots, farm machinery, and accidents, so I had seen some of these types of devastating wounds. During this time the nurses and the Red Cross workers were in much demand to send messages and write letters to the soldiers' families. Another duty of the hospital at that time was to operate a blood bank for the European theater. We received the blood coming from the States, and it was then sent to the military hospitals in Europe. This was my first wartime experience, but what they could not prepare us for was the bombing and how close we were going to be to the front lines later in the war.

With the completion of our assignment in Prestwick, we were sent to a staging area in England where we received equipment and supplies for service on the Continent. On October 5, 1944, we began the trip across the English Channel in an LCI (landing craft, infantry) in what the Frenchmen around us said was the worst storm they had experienced in a century. Three days later we arrived at a broken-down dock in Isigny, France, and we were all horribly seasick. We all decided nothing could possibly be worse during the war than that trip across the English Channel. We were wrong.

Our first assignment was in support of the U.S. Seventh Army armored and infantry divisions in the vicinity of Baccarat, France. We were in a badly shelled building and within sight and sound of gunfire and fighting aircraft overhead. From that time until we departed French soil on April 1, 1945, for Darmstadt, Germany, we were frequently within close proximity of enemy fire as we moved every five to six days, usually during the night and in blackout conditions so we would not tie up the roads being used by our advancing infantry and tanks. Patients had to be prepared for the arduous travel conditions to a hospital in the rear, equipment packed and loaded, and then preparations made for the journey to a new location.

If possible, a schoolhouse or large building would be selected for the hospital by Army headquarters. These sites had served for either German or American troop billets and were often in deplorable condition, so energy had to be spent just cleaning the area so patients could be cared for. Trying to heat the patient care areas with potbelly stoves or oil heaters during the bitter cold was always a major challenge. Frequently, patients on litters would be waiting for us when we arrived at a new site, so the nurses and doctors were busy preparing patients for surgery while enlisted men were setting up the generator for electricity and assembling an x-ray unit, operating room, and post-op ward area.

On several occasions we moved into a building that was still being used as a German hospital. The German medical staff was allowed to care for their wounded and evacuate their patients as quickly as possible. I came from a German family, and my grandfather was a German immigrant, as were most of the people in my community in South Dakota. As medical people, we treated German prisoners of war when needed, and I often thought, "What would I do if I came across a German POW with the name of Steinbis?"

Caring for the sick and wounded during the war proved to be a very demanding and exhausting task and frequently placed the hospitals and staff in close proximity to enemy fire. The closer to the battle lines the hospital could be located, the more lives could be saved because the ice and snow made it difficult for ambulances to evacuate the wounded from the battlefields to the hospitals (this was before helicopters). There were not only the wounded from the ongoing battle situations, but there were also many serious casualties such as severe frostbite and other cold-related injuries from the intense cold and snow. During only forty days of the Battle of the Bulge, the American Army suffered eighty-one thousand casualties, including nineteen thousand killed.

Our field hospital received only the patients who were severely wounded and who might have died if we had tried to transport them further to the rear. All of our casualties were men with head, chest, and belly wounds, and most really were dying when they came to us. It was our job to take these critically wounded patients and provide extensive surgery and nursing care. Many patients were unconscious when they arrived at the hospital, but for the many who were conscious it was a surprise to see women so close to the front lines. I think the fact that the patients saw women in the hospital made them feel that things couldn't be that bad if the Army had women there.

If the patients were conscious, many would ask for their mothers and would want us to send a letter to someone back home. Many asked, "How bad is it?" But the number one question usually was, "How's my buddy?" Often a group of men from the same unit would be wounded and arrive at the same time. The semiconscious patients often called us by the names of their mothers and wives or girlfriends back home.

Upon the patients' arrival in the hospital, we would cut away their filthy clothing so as to see all of the wounds and do a basic evaluation of the patient's condition. The physicians prioritized what patients required immediate treatment versus those who could wait a little longer. Sometimes we nurses would lighten the situation by asking for their shoulder patches and encouraging them to talk about their unit. I have an Army hospital blanket hanging in my office on which I stitched the patches I collected. I think there is an insignia from all the divisions that fought in Europe. Many of the wounded had pictures of their families in their pockets, and they wanted to make sure those were saved from their uniform to be sent back home. We told them someone would write home for them, and we would give this information and any personal belongings to the Red Cross, who performed this service in the hospitals. The nurses just did not have the time to do these things, and it was another way the Red Cross helped comfort our servicemen.

We were told that if a wounded soldier reached the hospital, there was a 97 percent chance that he would survive. It seemed that the mortality rate in our hospital was often higher than that because of the severity of their wounds. This was emotionally difficult for the hospital staff. A patient whom you had tended to over the past twelve to fifteen hours, and who was believed to be in good condition, may have died while you were off duty catching a few hours of sleep. We did see horrible situations, so it was necessary that we stay focused on caring for these severely wounded men. After all these years I cannot recall any faces or a particular patient who stands out in my mind. However, I did try to treat every soldier like I would want someone to treat my little brother if he was lying in a field hospital somewhere.

When a patient was struggling to hang on and death seemed close, we did try to just be there and hold their hand during their last moments. A lot of times we had done everything we could and had to accept the situation. We had to keep moving from one patient to another.

As we crossed France with the advancing American troops, we were often within a few hundred yards of the front lines, and our hospital was bombed once. I was lined up for lunch, mess kit in hand, when I heard this terrible noise and felt the building tremble. I dropped my mess kit and ran back to my patients. None had been further injured from the bombing, but we soon had them loaded on trucks and in ambulances to transport them to hospitals in the rear.

Nurses, of course, had concerns about being captured, but we were too busy to dwell on that for very long. (Some half-heartedly discussed the laws of the Geneva Convention regarding the treatment of female prisoners.) On several occasions, because of the advancing German troops during the Battle of the Bulge, we had to make a hasty retreat from the area. Procuring sufficient transportation to evacuate the patients, hospital equipment, supplies, and personnel was sometimes extremely difficult. We often suffered from the mass confusion of the time, the continuous need for blood, and not knowing the state of the combat situation.

Although we were not assigned to the specific Battle of the Bulge area, we were on the rim of the Germans' furthest advance, and many of the wounded from the battle were cared for in the 57th Field Hospital. During these winter months we were assigned to the 3rd, 45th, 75th, 100th, and 103rd Infantry Divisions, the 12th and 14th Armored Divisions, and the 2nd French Armored Division, but cared for many from any number of divisions. In early January of 1945, Detachment B (the detachment to which I was assigned) of the 57th moved to Sarrebourg, France, into a building also occupied by two clearing companies and a collection station. We were immediately overwhelmed with critically wounded. We later learned that we had been supporting twenty-five battalions of troops.

I remember after one exhausting day during the battle I wearily crawled into my bedroll wondering, "What if we should lose the war?" We had just learned of the massacre of about sixty-nine American prisoners of war at Malmédy, and that seven thousand others had been taken prisoner and the Germans were breaking through our lines. We were overwhelmed with wounded soldiers, and things were going very badly. This was the Battle of the Bulge, December 16, 1944, to January 25, 1945, in Belgium and Luxembourg. It was the coldest and snowiest winter that part of Europe had experienced in fifty years. I think the thing that saw me through the rough times was a constant effort to stay focused on providing the care these men needed so desperately.

After the Battle of the Bulge we were assigned to the 75th Infantry Division during its battle in the Colmar pocket. The frigid cold and the stream of wounded continued. In mid-March the entire 57th Field Hospital was assigned to Toul, France, to care for 355 Allied soldiers. They were mostly Russian, with a few Yugoslavian, Serbian, and Polish nationals who had been liberated from the Germans six weeks earlier. We learned that these few men were what remained of twenty thousand prison laborers who had been forced by the Germans to work in the lime mines near Metz, France. Their living conditions had been reduced to those of animals. They suffered from tuberculosis, a bone deterioration disease called osteomyelitis, and all sorts of physical injuries and nutritional diseases. Our task was to improve their health sufficiently so they could make their trip back to their homes. When we were finally reassigned, a Russian warrant officer and a few enlisted men decided to throw a little going-away party to show their appreciation for our efforts. They went into the nearby town of Toul and found enough eggs, chickens, and other fresh foods to make us a feast. They also entertained us with their traditional dances.

On March 27, 1945, we began the move from Metz through Saarbrüken and into Germany. The devastation and destruction, particularly of German vehicles and other implements of war, were so widespread and total it is almost beyond description. The roads and mountainsides in many places were littered continuously for miles with the evidence of the destruction and desperate retreat of the German Army. The crumbled ruins of the cities of Ludwigshafen and Mannheim were brought particularly to our attention, since it was at this point that we made all our crossings over the Rhine River on the bridges built by General Patton's Third Army Corps of Engineers.

At one point later in the war we were stationed only a few miles from the Dachau concentration camp when it was liberated. Even from our positions a few miles away the stench was overwhelming. One of our doctors, who was Jewish, and several others went to the camp, and they brought back tales of the horrors they had witnessed. They also returned with a woman who was in labor, and her giving birth in our field hospital was one of the more unique experiences of the war. This was the first time any of us had known about concentration camps. It was a dreadful shock to realize something like this could happen in our world. I think it made us all believe more in our mission and why we were fighting. Despite your best efforts, you couldn't help but let such things bother you. If you were in it long enough, the whole war bothered you.

We nurses were not very glamorous during the war. We wore the same uniforms as the combat soldiers. We washed our clothes in our helmets, and during the Battle of the Bulge we went a month without shower facilities and used our all-purpose helmet for sponge baths. We usually wore some lipstick, mostly for our own morale. It wasn't a very comfortable living situation, but we had it so much better than the men who were living in cold and wet foxholes. If we were living in tents, one of the true luxuries was a wooden floor that would be built for us by any Engineer unit in the area. (The cost for that floor was often for the nurses to go to the Engineer headquarters for a night of dancing.) The Engineers will always be near and dear to my heart for those wonderful wooden floors.

When there was a lull in the fighting and we had only a few patients, we would get caught up on letter writing or have a party to share food from home and liquor rations, and on occasion we would get movies. Romance was officially off-limits between the nurses and enlisted men, but officers were allowed to date. I met my future husband during the war, and even though he was in the headquarters of the hospital and I was in Detachment B, we did manage to meet often and develop a deep friendship.

When the nurses had time alone, we perhaps talked about a patient we had treated during the day, but we tried to forget our work and perhaps talk about our human-relation difficulties here and there. We had one nurse in the hospital whose fiancé was killed while in the Air Force, and we were all there to help her through her grief and pain. One of our favorite activities was taking a pressed chocolate bar called a "D-bar." It was so hard we had to scrape shavings just so we could eat it. We would shave some D-bars down, then get some sugar from the mess sergeant and some canned milk and make fudge. It was a little thing that helped make our lives a little more fun. The biggest problem was the sleep deprivation. We would work all day and then move at night. We were given a location to establish our hospital, and on several occasions the front-line troops had been delayed and we were actually in front of the infantry. It always brought a look of disbelief on the faces of the GIs when they saw nurses in ambulances as they marched to the front lines. When we passed by the men in the field we were always treated with respect. I never heard of rude comments directed towards the nurses. We worked very hard to earn a place of respect in the Army, and the soldiers responded accordingly. They always seemed most appreciative of our presence.

Once inside Germany, we were stationed at a number of airstrips to again serve as holding hospitals for the wounded being air-evacuated back to the States. On Easter Sunday of 1945, we received news that some of the first Americans to be freed from the POW camps were coming to our hospital. The commanding general who greeted them told them they would have clean sheets, all the food they could eat, and nurses to care for them. I don't know from where the sheets were obtained, since we had been using only GI blankets for so long, but we stayed up part of the night getting sheets on the cots. The cook was up early making pancakes, and by the time the former POWs arrived we were ready to give them a great welcome. They were all very thin and malnourished. Upon the sight of food they gorged themselves on the pancakes, went outside to throw up, and then lined up in the chow line again for more pancakes. Many of them commented that the American Red Cross food packages had helped them survive their imprisonment. During the war twenty-seven million food packages were assembled by volunteers and shipped by the American Red Cross to the International Red Cross storage centers in Geneva, Switzerland, for disbursement to U.S. and Allied prisoners of war.

When the war ended we were doing air evacuations again from an airbase in Fürstenfeldbruck, Germany. The war was over on the 8th of May, but we were still very busy caring for the sick and wounded coming from the prisoner-of-war camps and taking care of the patients wounded in accidents. We also cared for many others from the general population who needed assistance. We continued with the air evacuation assignment until early June, then we moved to an old sanitarium on the banks of the beautiful Neckar River in Gundelsheim, Germany, where the hospital operated as a station hospital for the remainder of 1945.

By December of 1945 we nurses had enough points to come home. It was a wonderful feeling. It was a bit strange, though, as we thought of leaving our very good friends who had gone through these incredible experiences with us. We were very lax about keeping in touch, mostly because we had gotten married and were soon busy raising our families. For many of the soldiers coming back from the war, they no longer had their best buddies around. Many joined the American Legion and other organizations so they could be around people who could empathize with what they were going through. But there were no places for the nurses to go. The veterans organizations didn't accept women, and the women had to deal with their issues on their own. We didn't help our situation by failing to keep in touch with each other.

I have gotten so many letters over the years from men who think they came through the 57th Field Hospital. Many acknowledge that they considered us their mothers, wives, and girlfriends during their time in the hospital. So many men have tried to identify the nurse or nurses who cared for them during the war. I have had three men send me their charts from when they were patients in our field hospital, and the initials confirmed that I had cared for them. It allowed them to write to me to express their gratitude and hopefully put some closure to a time in their lives they would like to finally put behind them. It makes me feel very good to hear from these men, some perhaps I once thought would not survive, and to know they came home to start families and lead productive and healthy lives. To me the biggest thanks I could get for helping them during the war is to know I have helped provide them with a better life.

Wherever I go to speak about my experiences, people always go out of their way to express their thanks for what the nurses did during the war. The people in Belgium and Luxembourg show a tremendous amount of appreciation for what we did to save them from the Germans and treat us so well whenever we go back to visit. However, I think there is a problem with the way we write history about the war, and many sources do not realize that nurses and the American Red Cross women were right up there on the front lines with the men. Part of the reason I am speaking about my experiences is so young girls can pick up this book and learn that they are capable of doing anything they set their hearts on.

I certainly don't want to convey that I was a hero. I was proud to have volunteered to help care for the wounded men who were called upon to do truly heroic things in combat. I believe every Allied soldier who came through our hospital was a hero of the Second World War.

ARTHUR J. DONOVAN JR.

Baltimore, Maryland
6th and 3rd Marine Divisions

Arthur James Donovan Jr. was born in the Bronx, New York, on June 5, 1924. He attended Mount Saint Michael High School in the Bronx and after a semester at Notre Dame University enlisted in the Marine Corps in 1943. He served as an antiaircraft gunner on the carrier USS *San Jacinto* before being transferred to a machine-gun crew on Okinawa. After the war Donovan attended Boston College, graduating in 1950, and began a career in the National Football League that earned him an induction into the NFL Hall of Fame as a Baltimore Colt on August 3, 1968. He owns and manages the Valley Country Club with his wife, Dottie, and they have five children and five grandchildren.

I guess everyone can remember the day Pearl Harbor was bombed or President Kennedy was assassinated. On December 7, 1941, I was playing touch football around the corner from my home, and we had a radio tuned to the Giants game. Suddenly the game went off the air, and an announcement was made that all military personnel were to report back to their bases. It was a shock, but I was still in high school at the time and too young to do anything about it. I graduated from high school the following year, and I accepted a scholarship to play football at Notre Dame. I really wanted to go to Fordham, but I was afraid my mother would die of a broken heart if I didn't go to Notre Dame. I had a feeling I wasn't going to last long at Notre Dame, and sure enough, after the end of the first semester I said goodbye to South Bend and headed home.

I was so sure I wasn't going to make it at South Bend, I enlisted in the Marine Corps before I even left. Most of my old buddies from the neighborhood had enlisted, and it was only a matter of time before the rest of us went in, too. We were hanging out on the corner one day when someone suggested we go down to Grand Central Station and enlist in something. We went down to where all the different services had their recruiting stands, and as soon as we walked in a guy shouts for us to come over to where he was. We walked over to his booth and he says, "You boys looking to join the service? Then join the Army, we'll give you good jobs as cooks and bakers." I said, "Get the hell outta here. I don't want to be no baker." I think a few of the guys I was with went for it, but the thought of cooking through the entire war didn't appeal to me too much. I kept walking until I saw the Marine Corps booth, and the rest is history. I told the guy I was still in school at Notre Dame, and he said the Marines would contact me at the end of my first semester. That night I told my parents I had joined the Marines, and my old man went nuts. He went through the roof and kept saying to my mother, "Say goodbye to Art, he's going to get his fat ass shot off!" But what the hell; I was excited to go.

In less than a month after returning from South Bend I was in Grand Central Station reporting for duty. I was herded with a bunch of guys onto a bus, then a ferry to Hoboken, New Jersey, and then onto a train. We traveled through Washington, D.C., and finally to Yemassee, South Carolina. All I could think was, "I am in Yemassee, South Carolina; where the heck is Yemassee, South Carolina?" We were let off the train and driven to Port Royal, South Carolina, near Parris Island, the home of the United States Marine Corps. We were herded like cattle into barracks and told to strip off all our clothes. They gave us a shaved-head haircut, and I really began to wonder what the heck I had gotten myself into. We were issued everything but shoes. I remember walking what must have been miles in my dress loafers through the mud to our training barracks.

I was assigned to Platoon 525 and had a drill instructor by the name of Hal Feinstein. Hal was a great guy from Lehigh University, and he really whipped us into shape. I grew to really enjoy boot camp. I was in great shape and everything came naturally to me, and eventually I didn't want to be anywhere else. The Marines needed gunners for the aircraft carriers, so I was taught how to operate the 20- and 40-mm. antiaircraft guns. These were some really great guns that could shoot like hell.

Every Friday night before the movies we had boxing fights, and usually the biggest guys from each platoon were picked to fight. They picked me. I had to fight this big kid in Platoon 524 from Minnesota who was a real loudmouth. He would never shut up about how great of a football player and boxer he was. Where the hell was Minnesota? I hadn't even heard of Minnesota, so I figured he couldn't be all that great. Everyone knew my father was a famous fight referee, and they were real confident I was going to beat this guy, but I was so scared and nervous I think I wet my pants before the fight. I got up in the middle of the ring, and when the bell rang this big kid just put up his gloves to protect his face. I got so mad at myself for having been scared of this guy, I hit him as hard as I could until he fell down. Then I kicked him. He must have been the first guy to get knocked out and win a fight, because after I kicked him I was disqualified.

I was assigned to an aircraft carrier named *San Jacinto* in Norfolk, Virginia, and we left there and traveled through the Panama Canal and arrived in Honolulu, Hawaii. We were given liberty when we arrived, and we had a great time. We were walking back to the carrier, and somehow we ended up on a runway. We heard this noise and all these planes started flying over us, and we scrambled to keep from getting killed. The MPs came and rounded us up and put us in the brig. We got scared, because we thought we were going to miss our departure and spend the rest of the war in jail, but someone from the ship came and bailed us out. In a few short weeks we had sailed to the Marianas, and soon I wished I were still locked up in Hawaii.

I was the second loader on a twin-mount 40-mm. gun, and after we arrived in the Marianas we were at general quarters almost all the time. We were always being attacked, or we were expecting attacks, by Japanese planes. My job was to drop clips that held four shells into the gun, and we didn't know what the heck was going on except that the gun was firing. Those guns were loud, could shoot like hell, and it was exciting.

Those Japs, they were coming down and blowing up our ships left and right. We nearly lost the whole Navy to those crazy kamikaze bastards. These kamikaze guys actually tried to fly into our ships. I guess these guys flunked flight school or something and were told to just act natural and hit something. And boy, did they. The Japs really beat the heck out of us, and a few times there were so many Jap planes in and around us, we fired on our own ships by accident. I would see these Jap planes coming at our ship, and if we hit one sometimes it would explode in midair, or they fell in the water and small pieces of the plane would sail over our heads and land on the flight deck. Seeing that I just thought, "What the hell am I doing here? I'm going to get killed!"

Marines made up only a small portion of the gunners on the *San Jacinto*, and I think they kept us there for tradition's sake, but we held our own. I was never worried about the Japs; I was more fearful of being in the water with the damn sharks. I figured if the ship started to sink I would take my chances anywhere it was still dry.

I remember watching our planes return from missions, and I always had a place to run and hide because some planes would be shot up or the pilot would be injured, and there was a chance the plane would crash into your area. Some planes would hit the deck so hard their machine guns would go off or a bomb they didn't drop would go sliding down the deck of the carrier, and you had to keep low just in case. It was nuts: you survived the Japs just to be killed by your own planes.

When they passed the word that volunteers were needed for a land assignment, I stepped forward. The Japs were sending more and more kamikazes at our ships, and I was happy to say goodbye to the open ocean. I was one of about fifty Marines sent to Okinawa to join a machine-gun squad. I never fired a gun while on Okinawa; I just made sure the people who did never ran out of ammunition. I was on Okinawa for only a month, but it was just long enough to discover there were Japs all over the place. I rarely saw a live one, but I often heard their bullets whistling past my ear when we got into a firefight. It still beat facing those kamikazes. At night I remember watching our Navy anchored offshore during the kamikaze attacks, and I really felt lucky to be on dry land. We could see all the ships blowing up. It was really terrible.

After Okinawa I was reassigned from the 6th to the 3rd Marine Division and sent to Guam. Guam was just like Okinawa: it was supposed to be secured, but there were Japs all over the place. The Japs stole the tent over our latrine, and our lieutenant wanted to go looking for it, at night. Who the hell wanted to get killed looking for a tent? When we didn't find anything after a few minutes, we gave up the search.

I ran into my father while on Guam. He had been a commander in the Merchant Marine, but he was transferred to an overseas USO tour to referee fights. I got the best seats in the house for the fights my father refereed. But my most memorable experience wasn't for fighting. It was for stealing. Or, should I say, my being caught stealing.

I had "found" a case of Spam in the hold of a ship we had unloaded, and I stashed it under our tent. We got hit with a real bad typhoon, and it just so happened a lieutenant, a real greenhorn, ordered an inspection on the same day. The rain was so heavy it had washed the dirt away I had placed on top of the case of Spam to hide it. The lieutenant found it, and he busted me. The next day I was ordered to report to the regimental adjutant. The adjutant was a good guy named Joe McFadden, a quarterback from Georgetown's football team. He got me to 'fess up and said, "What were you going to do with that Spam, Donovan? Sell it to the gooks?" I said, "No, sir, I was going to eat it." He then said, "I told you not to lie to me. Nobody eats that crap." I said, "*I* do. I like it." My price to keep my freedom was to eat the whole case of Spam, and if I didn't, McFadden promised, "my ass would belong to him." I ate the whole case of Spam in nine days. Thirty pounds of Spam. I was eating Spam twenty-four hours a day. I was let off the hook and became the company hero. To this day I have a soft spot in my heart for Spam.

We continued our training for what we all thought was the certain invasion of Japan. Then they dropped the atomic bombs. We were watching the comedian Charlie Ruggles on a rainy night when some general got up on stage and said the war was going to be over, that we dropped the bomb and the Japs would sue for peace. We thought the guy was drunk, but he was right. "What the hell is an atomic bomb?" we said. We had no idea, but who cared? All I cared about was that the war was over and I was going home. If Truman had not dropped the bomb, everything about me might have never happened. Forget the Baltimore Colts, and forget everything. Those Japs were digging in deep on the beaches of Japan, and I probably would have been killed or wounded in Japan. But as it was, four months later I was back in the States.

After twenty-four months of fighting for my country, I came back to the States. I entered a private and left a private; I guess they didn't realize my leadership potential. I was stationed at Fort Mathews, California, and one evening I was with a bunch of guys and we went out to get a beer. The first place we went wouldn't serve us because we looked too young. I had just spent two years overseas fighting for my country, and some rat wouldn't serve us a beer! I got real hot and upset. We talked a sergeant into letting us into the noncommissioned officers' club, and in return we bought all his beer that night. To add insult to injury, I spent Thanksgiving of 1945 in some lousy kitchen peeling potatoes.

I was discharged from a base in Bainbridge, Maryland, and before they would let us out the door they made us watch a movie called *So Long Joe*. It was a film that tried to get us to reenlist. I told the guy to kiss my fat ass. I got on the next train headed for the Bronx.

I walked out of Grand Central and started walking up Broadway when I ran into a neighborhood buddy of mine named Tommy Lionelli. Tommy was a little retarded, and his job was to deliver false teeth all around the city. I had my uniform on with all my service ribbons and was carrying my sea bag over my shoulder. The first thing Tommy says to me was, "Hey, Arty, where you been!" Where have I been?! Are you kidding me?! Jeez, it was good to be home.

After the war was over we all came back and hung out on the same corners, and we really didn't talk much about what we did in the war. There was this other guy from our neighborhood, Jerome "Lefty" Wiseberg. The last time I heard from Lefty was while he was in radio school in the Air Force. He was shot down and wound up in a prisoner-of-war camp, but his parents had gotten the black-outlined letter stating their son was missing in action, and they naturally thought of the possibility he had been killed. Lefty survived the war, but his mother didn't know he was alive until one day she was out shopping, and she sees Lefty walking down the street whistling and carrying his duffel bag over his shoulder. The poor woman fainted right there in the middle of the street. It's a wonder she didn't have a heart attack. A year later Lefty married an Italian girl, so I think his Jewish family considered him dead again. Go figure.

Life returned to normal for me. I enrolled at Boston College and played four years of football. My roommate had flown thirty-nine missions in a bomber over Germany during the war, and he never talked about it. Our war experiences were just another part of our lives, nothing to dwell on, and for the most part I think we wanted to get it all behind us.

I moved to Baltimore in 1950 to play football, and people just loved us. I think Baltimore is the greatest place in the world. Ordell Braase, Jim Mutscheller, and I get together almost every day to drink beer and eat kosher hot dogs. We talk about what a great place Baltimore is to play football. People still recognize us and remember who we are, and they treat us like we were their own kids. It's great being recognized around town. Anyone who tells you otherwise is a liar.

War memorials don't mean much to me. My grandfather fought in the Civil War, my father fought in the Mexican War and the First World War, and I fought in the Second. If they want to build one, fine, but I am not going to march in any parades or put on any uniforms, because the only and last uniform I will wear is the Baltimore Colts uniform. When I took that uniform off me, they had to drag my ass off the field, because I didn't want to retire.

If you want to talk about guys who are my heroes, they are the guys who stormed the beaches in France and all those islands in the Pacific. I went over to Normandy a few years ago, and I can't figure out how the heck they crossed that beach with the Germans shooting down on them. I think they must have been lucky to not get killed. My hat really goes off to those guys. Then there are the guys who won the Medal of Honor. Jeez, to win the Medal of Honor I think you just have to be plain nuts. You must go out your mind after seeing those sons of bitches shoot your friends, and they must go crazy. Me, I was just a big fat guy doing what I was told. But those guys, they are my heroes.

LEWIS B. ELLIS

Baltimore, Maryland

91st Bombardment Group, U.S. Army Air Corps

Lewis Bernard Ellis was born in Baltimore, Maryland, on April 3, 1922. After graduating from the Polytechnic Institute in 1942, he enlisted in the Army Air Corps and piloted thirty-five missions in a B-17 bomber over Europe, eventually receiving an Air Medal with five oak-leaf clusters. After the war Ellis returned to Baltimore and began a career with C&P Telephone, retiring in 1962 after twenty years and beginning work in the insurance industry. He remained in the reserves and the Maryland Air Guard until his resignation in 1964 with the rank of captain. He and his wife, Dorothy, were married in 1945 and have five children, seven grandchildren, and one great-grandson.

My name is Lewis Ellis, and I flew a Boeing B-17 bomber during the war. When I was born my family lived on Goodwood Road in the Lauraville section of Baltimore, about a mile from where I live now, so this nut didn't fall far from the tree. When I was one year old my family moved just a short distance to Iona Terrace on Harford Road. We moved again to Christopher Avenue in 1924, which by then was called Hamilton. Hamilton was mostly farmland back then, and people today wouldn't believe Harford Road was once a mud road with a jerkwater streetcar. If we went out to Carney, we were really out in the country and almost in another world. Today Carney is a five-minute drive by car. Apple orchards surrounded Hamilton when I was a kid, and we never got hungry because we could always steal some apples. Nearby was Kratz Farm, and Mr. Kratz grew strawberries in the springtime. I wonder just how many strawberries Mr. Kratz got, because we sure got our share. When I was old enough I went to Elementary School Number 236, then Saint Dominic's for six years and then went to Polytechnic Institute.

During my senior year in 1942 the war was coming full tilt, and the majority of the guys I knew were joining the service. I knew one fellow I ran track and cross-country with named Jack Shantry. Jack ended up enlisting in the Army and was sent to Europe and made second lieutenant. He was killed early in the invasion of France. There were so many others I knew like Jack, but he is the only one I can think of at the moment. I realized Uncle Sam wanted me too, and I kept thinking I was going to be drafted if I didn't enlist. I didn't relish carrying a gun in the infantry, so in September of 1942 I went down to the central post office in Baltimore City to enlist in the Army Air Corps. On the way to the recruiting station I ran into a classmate of mine named Clifford Bewig. Cliff decided to go down there with me, and we enlisted together. The recruiter informed us that they couldn't take us because we didn't have two years of college, but we were given a two-year college equivalency test, and the recruiter accepted our applications. Our Poly education really came through, I guess. Clifford survived the war and eventually retired from the Air Force in the late 1960s with the rank of lieutenant colonel.

I was ordered to report for service on January 29, 1943. I went back down to the central post office, and things there were just a mess. Groups of men were scattered everywhere, and men were going in every direction. I was placed with a group and stood around for a long time before boarding a train we hoped was headed to Miami Beach. Once we arrived at Miami we began our basic training. Basic training was kind of rough, but it wasn't long before I was sent to the University of Tampa for a college refresher course. I was also given ten hours of flight training to see if I had any flying ability at all. I must have made the necessary impression, because I was then sent to a classification center and preflight training in San Antonio, Texas. Once that was completed I was sent to a civilian flight school supervised by the Army in Ballinger, Texas. I was given my primary

Lewis Ellis and the crew of *Little Patches* on January 15, 1945, upon their return from a mission to bomb the railroad marshaling yards in Ingolstadt, Germany. *Front row, from left:* Joseph Krammer, radio operator; Walter Boenig, waist gunner; Arthur Joseph Jabara, tail gunner; Ellis. *Back row, from left:* unknown substitute waist gunner; William Grimmit, "toggleier"; Will T. Carter, pilot; unknown substitute engineer filling in for John Pitts Rumph, who had been wounded over Cologne; unknown substitute flight training in a Fairchild PT-19, built in Hagerstown, Maryland. I was then sent to Brady, Texas, to another civilian flight school, where I flew the PT-13 and PT-15. While in Brady I was given a choice of whether I wanted go into single-engine fighter training or multiengine bomber training. I asked for single-engine training; I got multiengine training. I requested single-engine because I am a small person, and I thought I would be a better fit in a smaller fighter plane, and it seemed exciting to fly a fighter. So I guess I wasn't too thrilled when I was informed I had been selected for multi-engine bomber duty. But after doing a tour with the four-engine B-17 bomber, I think if we had had a ten-engine bomber I would have taken it. I eventually got to fly the P-52 Mustang during my service in the Maryland Air Guard after the war.

I was then sent to Altus, Oklahoma, where I flew the AT-9. The AT-9 was a twin-engine plane built as a fighter for the Dutch, but when they capitulated we got them as trainers. By the time I completed my training at Altus and received my commission, I had been going for seventeen months straight without a breather. I was once again given a questionnaire asking me to select my preferences for the type of aircraft I would like to fly. I chose the B-26, the B-25, or the Dauntless A-20 attack bomber; I was assigned to B-17s. I knew nothing about the B-17 at that time.

Soon after, I arrived in Rapid City, South Dakota. This was the place where new pilots and other men trained to work in the B-17. We were assembled for placement into crews and overseas duty. We were all gathered in the ready room, and as names were read off the list we were told where to go. My name was read, and I was instructed to report to a commander named Will Carter. Will was a big man from Yorktown, Texas, and one great guy. He had already been trained to fly the B-17 overseas, and he was now responsible for training me to fly it. A lot of the other experienced pilots had an attitude when it came to breaking in newer pilots, but not Will. One of the first things Will ever said to me was, "Within forty-eight hours I'll have you flying this plane." The first day we drew a night flight, and we flew all that night and shot landings (touch and go) for practice. Will was just fantastic and told me he realized the importance of teaching me all he knew because I might have to get him home some day in combat. We eventually split the flying time 50-50 on our missions. I enjoyed serving with Will so much that when my time came to receive my own crew, I passed on receiving my own command. We had a good crew, and we stuck together. Everyone had a good crew, because our lives depended on each other.

As far as performance is concerned, the B-17 was fantastic. The fact that the B-17 was such a fine airplane is the only reason I am sitting here talking about it today. It just performed beyond all expectations. Anyone who flew it loved it. We all knew it was going to get you there and get you back. It would fly with a great deal of damage and get its crew home safely, even on only one engine, which we did. In those days the B-17 was considered a large bomber. It had a 106-foot wingspan and was about 75 feet long and carried various types of bomb loads up to about 20,000 pounds. We didn't always drop bombs. We dropped propaganda leaflets to inform the Germans of their losses in battle, and sometimes just for laughs we dropped newspapers showing baseball and football scores back home in the States. We also dropped German marks and ration stamps. We were strictly forbidden to tamper with the bundles that held the money, and I think this stuff was dropped over Germany to screw up their economy. So what we delivered was not always exploding.

The B-17 was heavily armored with eleven .50-cal. machine guns. She could protect herself pretty well, and more than a few German fighters went down because of B-17 gunners. We flew with a crew of ten men. We didn't have a bombardier like most people think; instead we had a "toggleier." The toggleier dropped on the direction of a bombardier at the front of the formation who was highly skilled and marked the drop point with smoke bombs. All the other bombers in the formation simply dropped their bombs on his lead. Our toggleier sat forward in the glass nose where the bombsight was located. The navigator sat next to him at a little table where he worked his maps. The bombardier and navigator operated a forward nose turret with twin .50-cal. machine guns and another .50-cal. gun. Behind and above the navigator was the pilot's deck compartment where the pilot and co-pilot sat, just behind the plane's props. Directly behind the pilot's compartment was the flight engineer, who stood to fire a twin .50-cal. machine-gun turret. Beyond the bomb bay was the radio operator, and behind him was the ball turret gunner. The ball turret gunner had to sit in a really cramped compartment under the plane for the whole mission and wasn't brought out of the turret until we were nearly back to base. The remaining crew members were the left and right waist gunners, who each operated a single .50-cal. machine gun, and all the way in the back was the tail gunner, who operated a twin .50-cal. turret.

After a couple weeks of flying we boarded a brand-new B-17 and flew overseas. We arrived in England at the end of September 1944. We landed in Wales and arrived at our base by train. Our base was called "Station 121," located near the town of Bassingbourn about 45 miles north of London. Station 121 was strictly a B-17 bomber base and home to the 91st Bombardment Group (Heavy). The 91st Bomb Group consisted of the 322nd, 323rd, 324th, and 401st Squadrons. At the onset of the war each group was assigned three squadrons, but fatigue set in and a fourth squadron was added so one squadron could rest while the other three flew. We arrived as a replacement crew for a crew that was either lost in combat or sent home at the end of their tour. We were assigned to the 401st Squadron, 91st Bomb Group, 1st Bomber Wing, which was part of the Eighth Air Force.

Two views from the navigator's window during one of Ellis's missions over Europe with the 91st Bombardment Group. In the *top photo,* the contrails of the bombers positioned in the high squadron 1,000 feet above the lead squadron can be seen. A bomb group in formation numbered thirty-six bombers, separated into the lead, high, and low squadrons. This tactic dispersed the bomb group at different altitudes, which made it more difficult for antiaircraft gunners to concentrate their fire. The other photo shows a B-17 that has moved into a tight formation close to *Little Patches,* which indicates that the bombers were now nearing their target, closing formation to concentrate their bombing.

We were assigned a B-17G bomber nicknamed *Little Patches*. The previous crew had come up with the name, and we could have renamed it, but it was so full of little repair patches we felt no other name was better, so we stuck with it. We added a lot of our own little patches during our missions. *Little Patches* became our mother. It got us to the job, allowed us to do the job, and got us back. Sometimes we brought the plane back and it would be in such a sorry condition I expected to see it put in the junkyard. But most of the time she would be sitting there with her engines idling, ready to go again the very next day. Things finally caught up with *Little Patches*, and she was put into repairs. When *Little Patches* was taken out of service we had to fly another bomber. We were given, to our eventual dismay, the *General Ike*.

The *General Ike* was a B-17G and was reportedly the ten thousandth or something B-17 built for the war. It received a lot of fanfare upon its shipment overseas and was given to our 401st just about the time we arrived. There was a big press conference when it arrived, and even the queen of England christened it by breaking a champagne bottle filled with water from the Chesapeake Bay and the Mississippi and Missouri Rivers. Unfortunately, the *General Ike* had very poor flying characteristics. No one liked flying it. It was slow and handled poorly because, as our ground crew chief later discovered, its elevators, instead of working together, worked against each other. It seemed the stringers controlling the elevators were reversed when she was built. Even at full power it just couldn't cruise with the other planes. We flew the *General Ike* three times, and we were always above or below and far behind the formation. It was always an adventure flying the *General Ike*. It was so slow it couldn't keep up with the formation. Although we started out in the lead division, we dropped further and further back until eventually even the third division had passed us by. We called to the flight leader to plead for him to let us drop some bombs just to keep up. On one mission to Merseburg the flight leader didn't like the idea of us dropping any of the 4,000 to 6,000 pounds of bombs we were carrying. We kept falling further and further back behind the formation. It got so bad we were eventually given permission to drop some bombs. But we still couldn't keep up with the formation. The entire formation bombed Merseburg and turned to return home, but Will was so pissed he was determined to drop our bombs on the target.

By the time we reached Merseburg we were completely alone. The Germans must have looked up and thought we were the craziest sons of bitches in the world, flying over Merseburg alone. They opened up on us with everything they had. Needless to say, it was hairy. Shells were exploding around us every which way. There wasn't a whole lot of talk—there never was while over the target, so damage could be called out—but I am sure we all had a few prayers flowing through our minds. We somehow made it home and immediately went to inform the squadron commander that we refused to fly the *General Ike* anymore. We would have taken a court martial before we flew the *General Ike* again because it was just a matter of time before we got killed. Flying alone over Germany was a sure death sentence. Sure enough, we were threatened with a court martial for cowardice in the face of the enemy. We had to argue that we just wanted another plane, not to miss any missions. Our only option was to fly a broken-down war-weary wreck. We gladly accepted. The next crew who took the *General Ike* up had the same problems, and they also flatly refused to fly the plane again. Finally our ground crew chief performed a complete overhaul of the plane and discovered the problem with the elevator controls and fixed the problem. The *General Ike* was tested and flew perfectly. It took off on a mission the next day good as new, and it was shot down.

Our evenings were usually spent in the officers' club, and before we went to bed we checked the alert sheet to see what crews were on alert the next day. Being on alert meant making sure you were around in case they called you. We were on alert most of the time. On days we had missions someone would come around to get us up around two in the morning with a rap on the door yelling, "Breakfast now, briefing at three." Breakfast was usually powdered eggs and maybe some Spam. Black-market eggs were a booming business for the local farmers. After breakfast we gathered in the briefing hut where a gigantic map of Europe was hung on the wall. A large curtain covered the map before the briefing began, and we talked about where and how far we had to go that day. We had a little trick to find out before the briefing began by looking on the left-hand side of the curtain where a spindle held a big ball of red cotton string. The string was drawn out onto the map to illustrate the flight plan of our mission, and if there was a lot of string left on that spindle, we had a short mission. If there was a little string left, it meant we had a long one. The briefing officer gave us information on our target and how to drop our bomb load, either in train or salvo (train meant one bomb at a time, and salvo meant all at once). We were given other details on any potential problems surrounding the target like antiaircraft gun emplacements and enemy fighter expectations.

The two most difficult targets we hit were Merseburg and Berlin. The Germans had huge oil refineries in Merseburg where they converted brown coal into oil, and it was an essential plant in their war effort. Berlin was the German capital, so each was heavily protected with antiaircraft guns and fighter cover. I think every time we saw Merseburg come up on the map we all sort of shuddered and took a deep breath. We just knew we were going to catch hell that day.

Antiaircraft was probably our biggest obstacle, and some targets like Merseburg and Berlin had hundreds of guns placed for defense. German fighters were always a concern. The German fighters jumped bombers that flew a little too loose in formation, and if they could get between you and other bombers in formation they would

Ellis flew most of his thirty-five missions in a B-17G called *Little Patches*. Only when *Little Patches* was removed from service for repairs did he fly other bombers. He flew his last mission on March 3, 1945, in a B-17 Model H, which had significant improvements in flight controls relative to the Model G. The B-17H arrived in Europe in small numbers and saw only limited service before the end of the war.

have you for lunch. Keeping formation improved the defensive firepower of the bombers, and the Germans flew right between the bombers in formation to break us up. If they forced you out of formation and you couldn't get back, then you were a sitting duck. Fighters could really be your death once you got separated, and they would hit you from the back and tear your ass off, but they always concentrated their aim on the cockpit area, because once they got the pilot, they got the whole airplane. We had an occasion, I think it was over Cologne, where we were not flying tight, and the Germans flew through us and forced our bomber from formation, but we were able to recover. When a fighter skips within feet of your bomber, the natural tendency is to flinch and move out. Once you got separated a bit they flew in even closer and moved you out even further from the formation.

The majority of the enemy fighters we faced were Focke-Wulf 190s and Messerschmitt Bf-109s. I would say we probably saw more 109s than any other German fighter. There was one German squadron we respected called the "Abbeville Boys." Their planes were easily distinguishable by their front spinners, which they painted black and white. They were named after the base they flew from in France, and they were Hermann Göring's personally selected pilots. The members of this group were the best in the German Air Force, and when those boys were against you, you knew you were in for a fight. They would come right at you with no fear. On our side we had the P-51 Mustang. The P-51s gave us fighter protection, although for a while we did have some P-47s. The P-47s disappeared when everyone got the P-51. The P-51s were a lifesaver. They could escort us all the way into Berlin or further and still have enough fuel to mix it up with the German fighters. They met us on the way over and slowly disappeared when their job was done. We called the

P-51s our "little friends," and they were always there when we needed them. At one point I had a flight of 109s that had decided to take me on personally. I saw this German coming right towards me and I thought, "Oh, no, it's my day." Out of nowhere came this flight of P-51s, and they wiped the whole darn German flight out. They certainly were my "little friends" that day.

Towards the end of the war we began hearing rumors about advanced aircraft being built by the Germans, but I had never seen anything, and it was just hearsay. While attacking the rail crossing in a little German town named Stendal, we dropped down from our normal bombing altitude of 25,000 to 30,000 feet to down about 12,000 feet. I felt like our hip pockets were dragging rocks. As we crossed this target our gunners started calling a bandit at nine o'clock high. We figured we had fooled the Germans who were probably waiting up high for us at our normal bombing altitude. I kind of glanced out, and I never saw anything move so fast as this black dot that was just dropping rapidly at us. The gunners kept calling him and calling him, and finally our tail gunner picked him up, and he was calling him at seven o'clock level. I was waiting to feel the shaking from the vibration of our tail guns when something jumped over us at an incredible speed. I called to our tail gunner, Arthur Joseph Jabara (we called him "Jabo"). I said, "Jabo, did you shoot at that guy?" He said, "No, by the time he got into range he was gone." That was our first sighting of a jet fighter. It was an ME-262 and was the only one I ever saw. Our P-51s took off after the jet, and I heard they got him in his landing pattern at Tempelhof in Berlin and shot him down. This wasn't unusual. The jets had very limited fuel, and by the time they returned to base they had no fuel to make another pass around to land and were easy pickings for our fighters.

Once we were dismissed from the mission briefing, we got our gear together and we were taken to our flight station by truck. It was strictly all work then, and each man had certain things to do to get the plane ready for flight. The gunners loaded their ammunition, and Will and I got the plane ready. There was no joviality, because we all were focused on the job at hand. We had predetermined taxi and takeoff times, and once our time came, we moved out. At the end of the runway Will and I grabbed the yoke (it was a wheel, actually), and we pushed those throttles forward. We were pushing 4,800 horsepower at takeoff. We had a lot of power to move that airplane, and it took all we had with a full bomb load.

We flew our first mission on November 6, 1944. It was a mission to bomb an oil refinery in Harburg, Germany. No one was scared, as such, because you had enough to do to keep your mind off the fear. We had been so well trained that we just did things like it was second nature. Each man functioned properly, and there was never any reason to remind anybody to do this or do that because everybody did their job right. We all knew we were there for a reason, and everybody conducted themselves properly. Sure, there was fear, but there was never any panic. Even over targets when we were just taking a hell of a pounding, we still did the things we were trained to do. Things just fell right into line, no matter what took place and what damage you had. You continued on with your mission, and you continued with your flight. The B-17 was totally reliable, and unless you got split in half, we knew we were going to make it back.

There was one time, I have to admit, that we did panic. Returning from a mission to Kassel, Germany, on the 15th of December in 1944 (the beginning of the Battle of the Bulge), weather conditions were so bad we could not see our wing tips 50 feet away. We were flying the infamous *General Ike* that day. We made a number of landing approaches, eight in all, that day. Not only did the weather prevent us from making the runway, a couple of our approaches were waved off when a B-17 stalled on the runway and then broke out in flames. On our seventh approached to the runway, I saw the road that ran along the 3-foot-high fence that marked the beginning of the number 9 runway. Will had me cut power, only to drop like a rock 30 feet. Our wheels hit hard on the road, and our tail wheel dug into the potato field before the road. We bounced up and over the fence, and our wheels touched down on the runway. It looked like we were going to get the landing I hoped for. But panic set in. Even though we had hit the runway, when we hit the road Will yelled for me to get my hands off the throttles, and he gunned all four engines. Instead of landing, we took off again. We had to come around for our eighth and final attempt.

The story might have ended there but for a chance encounter in a tavern in Bassingbourn fifty-four years later during Will Carter's visit to our old Station 121. When Will entered the tavern he noticed a picture above the bar of a B-17 making a landing. He asked the owner the story behind the painting. The owner explained that as a young man he was employed at the base, and he would watch the bombers take off and land. One day he remembered watching a B-17 hit the road, dig up some potatoes, jump the fence, and hit the runway. The owner had a look of shock when Will was able to complete the story of how that bomber took off again and came around for another landing. The bomber that he had seen that day, the bomber that had been his inspiration to paint his picture, was in fact the *General Ike*. Will told him we had been flying the *General Ike* that day, and they had a good laugh about it. I can assure you, at the time, fifty-four years earlier, we were not laughing.

We did lose ships and men. It was inevitable. Bomber losses during the war were 33 percent. My crew was fortunate. We only had one man wounded, and that was our flight engineer and top target gunner, John Pitts Rumph. He was wounded in the right leg by flak on a mission to Cologne. When we landed he was taken to the hospital, and that night we went to see him. All around were many men that had been injured. Some were in bad shape, but you couldn't let it concern you. It was a horrible feeling to know that some of your comrades went down. We lost ten men every time a ship went down. Bad things happen in combat, but we were so well trained that we just continued to do our jobs. I recall on one mission we were flying deputy lead, and the leader indicated to us he had some damage and we were to take over the lead. He slid out to the side, and just as he passed over and out of view there was a tremendous explosion. His plane and its ten men disappeared in an instant.

I think we all suffered inside when we lost friends. Everybody did, even the fellows in the ground crews. I have seen those fellows in the ground crews sit there and cry when their crews didn't get back. It was upsetting, but you didn't let it get you down. We probably went into town and got a drink. But that's when we were twenty, twenty-one, twenty-two years old; it bothers me more these days. I know one time we went four days without sleeping, and we did do some drinking during those days.

There's always been a question of how we may have felt about bombing civilians. I answer by saying that up that high, everything ran together. There were no civilians, no soldiers, just the enemy. You just didn't think about things like that, and our Air Force did make an effort to avoid collateral damage. One instance was when the Air Force tried to save the Cologne cathedral from damage. Our target was the bridge in the heart of Cologne near the cathedral, and we were instructed to bomb away from the cathedral and down the length of the bridge. This resulted in just a lot of blown-up water and some sand on the banks. We went back the next day to do the job again, and we hit the bridge on a diagonal, which made it a little wider target. The bridge was hit, but we didn't do any appreciable damage. So on the third trip they said the hell with it and told us not to worry about the darn cathedral and just get the bridge. We got the bridge on the next mission. The cathedral was not damaged too severely.

On our last mission to Berlin we were approaching the Zuider Zee in Holland and crossed over a group of islands called the Frisian Islands. The Germans had one antiaircraft battery on one of the islands, and typically they would shoot three or four shells at us and call it a day, I guess to make themselves feel that they were still in the war. Well, they decided to fire at us that day, and unfortunately I was hit in the number 2 engine, the inboard engine on the left, and it damaged the supercharger. The supercharger forced air into the carburetor to increase the burn at high altitudes where the air was thin, and we had to shut it down because we could possibly need the engine again later to get home. We feathered the props, which was to lessen the amount of pitch on the blades, to reduce the vibration caused by the damage to the engine.

We continued to Berlin on three engines, and we dropped our bombs. The flak was extremely heavy, and we took another hit directly on our number 3 engine, the right inboard. From the co-pilot's seat I watched the prop from our number 3 engine take off somewhere. In a moment, another shell took the top off our number 4 engine, the right outboard engine. I looked out, and I could see the pistons going up and down in the number 4 engine. This left only the number 1 engine running at 100 percent. Number 2 was feathered, number 3 had no prop, and number 4 was turning over just somewhat. We kept number 4 running as long as we could until it started burning and shut it down.

We were losing altitude, and the procedure was for us to stay under the flight so our fighters could drop if needed to protect us. By the time we hit friendly territory, we were down around 15,000 feet and considerably below the bomber stream. We dropped below 10,000 feet and brought the number 2 engine back on line in reduced capacity. We began to hunt for friendly territory, because we knew we were going to have to sit this plane down somewhere. We passed over friendly territory at 800 to 1,000 feet, but we decided to continue on because we could see the sun glistening off the English Channel. We thought if we made it to the water, we could ditch and the British air-sea rescue would be waiting to pull us from the water. We got out over the water, and by this time we were holding our altitude at 5,000 feet. We decided again to continue on, hoping that maybe we could make the coast of England. There were several gigantic runways built along the coastline of England just for returning bombers to perform crash landings. We finally reached one of these strips, and by this time we were at 200 feet. Once again we thought we could stretch our trip one last leg to our home base. It was a good thing there were no tall trees, or else we wouldn't have been able to make the base, we were so low.

We finally neared our base, and when we called the base for landing instructions, they couldn't believe we were calling in. Other crews had reported seeing us fall out of formation and thought we had crashed. The control tower seemed confused and wanted us to confirm our identity. I said, "This is *Little Patches!*" There was a moment of silence. Finally, the tower came back and I heard, "*Little Patches,* come on in, you're clear to land." As our wheels hit the runway, the number 2 engine burst into flames and blew up. The fire crew had to come out and extinguish the fire, and we were towed off the runway. We had made it back from Berlin literally flying on one engine most of the way. Things like that created untold faith in the B-17.

That story might have been enough for one day, but it wasn't the only thing that happened on that mission to Berlin. Every crew had its comedian, and ours was our tail gunner, Jabo. Jabo was constantly calling me over the intercom telling me he was hungry and asking if I had a sandwich to eat. I would tell him that even if I had had one it would have been frozen solid. As I said before, we were having our own problems flying that day. We were on one engine and not so sure we were going to get back home ourselves. Another crippled ship called in to the squadron leader. "Red Dog Leader, I have a fire on board and a fire under my number 3 engine, and we may need to bail out." The squadron leader replied, "Try to get the fire out, and stay under the formation, and you'll have fighter protection all the way back." There was a pause. The pilot replied, "No, I can't get the fire out. We have to bail out." There was another pause in the conversation. The squadron leader came back and said, "Well, good luck, son."

With that another voice came on the radio. I knew it was our class clown, Jabo. Jabo said, "Lieutenant, before you bail out I have something to say." The pilot of the crippled plane responded, "What is it?" Jabo said, "I hope you like weenies and sauerkraut!" The pilot immediately told Jabo where he could go. A few seconds passed, and the pilot called the squadron leader again. "Red Dog Leader, we have the fires out, and I am going to be able to stay under the flight. I think we'll be able to make it back." There was a pause. "But I have another problem." The squadron leader said, "What is your problem now?" The pilot said, "Well, my navigator has already bailed out." The squadron leader replied, "It's OK, son. Let him go."

This was too much for Jabo. He comes back on the radio and says, "Oh, Christ, that was smart!" The squadron leader immediately yelled for everyone to get off the air and keep radio silence. Luckily for Jabo the squadron commander didn't know who was doing all the talking. Well, there was a pause, and Jabo comes back on the radio in a minute and says, "Red Dog Leader, can the Germans hear what we say?" The squadron commander was hot. "Yes, dammit, they can. Get off the air!" There were a few seconds of silence. Jabo then said, "But don't you think they know we're here?" The colonel leading the mission then demanded that the funny guy doing the talking identify himself. You have to remember, we had a strict protocol to maintain radio silence during the missions, and Jabo was messing around with getting a certain court martial if he had been caught. There was a short pause, then Jabo said, "Hey, Colonel, I may be dumb, but I ain't that dumb!"

Jabo had many remarkable moments. On our return from our last combat mission, which was a relatively light mission, Jabo called me and asked if we were still over Germany. I said, "Yes, I think we are still over Germany." He then asked, "How long do we have to go to get to unoccupied friendly territory?" I replied, "Well, I don't really know." He then asked, "Well, can't you find out?" I asked the navigator if we were still over Germany. I got the answer and called to Jabo and said, "He says ten to twelve minutes." About ten minutes later Jabo called me again. "Are we over friendly territory yet?" The navigator was listening in on the conversation and came on the radio and said that in fact we were over friendly territory. With that, Jabo said, "I'd laugh if we got shot down now on our last mission." I answered, "Jabo, if we get back I'll kiss your ass!"

Well, we made it back in fine order, and Will Carter and I were the last two out of the plane. I dropped out of the hatch and I hit the ground, and as I looked up there was Jabo, bent over with his behind sticking right in my face. I was so glad my combat missions were over, I kissed his ass.

The Air Force was great for giving you awards. They lined you up in a hangar in Class A's and read off these awards that were being given out. I got the Air Medal. The fellows in the back would heckle, saying we were getting medals not for meritorious services and so forth but for just being lucky enough to be alive another five days. So I got an Air Medal, I believe with five oak-leaf clusters. And that was the only medal I got. I was told that I should have been awarded the Distinguished Flying Cross due to my missions, and I had led two of them. Usually when you were promoted or if you were the lead on just one mission you knew you were getting the DFC. I never got the medal. Like so many things during the war, it was just a minor thing that fell by the wayside, and I forgot about it. I never regretted it. I was just glad we all made it back home.

It had taken me eighteen flying hours to arrive in Europe, and it took me twenty-eight days on a ship to get back. Will Carter had been the last person eligible to fly back home, and I was the first person informed I would have to sail back home. We hit five days of rather rough weather and had some damage to the ship. When things settled down we were allowed out on deck again. I was out leaning on the rail watching bubbles go by with a friend of mine when walking towards us we saw two infantrymen with 29th Division patches on their sleeves. They stopped, and a conversation started when they asked if we were flyers. I said we were, and I asked if they were in the 29th Infantry Division. They said they were. I told them how sorry I felt for the guys in the infantry. They asked me why. I mentioned how during the Battle of the Bulge we flew front-line support and how I would look down at the ground, wondering how the infantry lived in the snow and the slop and how they found anything to eat besides something cold and probably out of box. I mentioned how lucky us flyers were to go back each day, at least those not shot down, to sleep in a room with a dry bed, sheets, and blankets and walk 25 yards to a hot breakfast the next morning. With that the two infantrymen looked at one another and laughed. One of them said, "We used to look up and say how sorry we felt for you poor bastards because up there you couldn't get out and walk home." It was all in how we all looked at things from different perspectives.

After I returned to the States I was trained to fly the B-29 because my fanny was going right over the South Pacific for the invasion of Japan—there was no doubt about that. But as it would happen, Harry Truman, my hero, dropped the two bombs that ended the war. At the time I was stationed in Houston at Ellington Field as an instructor pilot. The day the war ended I was up with some of my

cadets, and I was staying close to the edge of the runway because I knew the news of the war ending was going to arrive at any moment. And boy, when they announced the war was over, I was the first plane on the ground. I told the cadets to go get lost, and I headed into town. I caught the last bus into Houston to meet my wife, Dorothy, who was working at the telephone company downtown. Houston was just bogged down with traffic and people celebrating the end of the war. I got off the bus and walked the rest of the way, which was about twenty minutes. Back then you could walk from the outer Houston suburbs to downtown Houston in just ten minutes. It was a long, skinny town then, not like today.

When I met Dot she was just getting off from work, and I told her the whole thing was finally over. We were naturally in a celebratory mood, as was all of Houston. The whole town was breaking open in celebration. The place was going wild. There was not a lamppost that didn't have at least one serviceman sitting on it looking out over the crowd. I decided to stop into the first church I came to. It happened to be a Catholic church, and I went inside. I broke down. I think a lot of the emotions I had hidden for all that time had come out. I said my thanks together with Dot, and then we rejoined the celebration outside.

We walked home to change clothes and went back downtown and got home quite late that night. It was nothing but dancing and singing in the streets. Everything had closed down but the bars; they were doing a tremendous business. I can't thank Harry Truman enough for dropping those bombs: I was next in line to go to the Pacific. The atomic bomb is a terrible weapon, but it probably killed less Japanese people than we would have killed if we had invaded Japan. Believe me, there are also a lot of Americans living today that would have died had we invaded Japan.

If I got to be twenty again, I'd go and do it all over again. I don't expect to be twenty again, though. We all served and did what we could for our country. Most of the men who fought in the war were so young; one of our gunners was only seventeen years old when he was assigned to our crew. I had one fellow in cadets with me who was twenty-seven years old. We couldn't believe anybody lived that long. I also think kids today would come through if faced with the same challenge. Look at your own kids; they would do it. Sure, they aren't living like we did, but we didn't live like our grandparents, either.

The men in my crew are all still living except for one man. We have had a couple reunions, and on Christmas Day I talk to my good friend Will Carter. On Thanksgiving I stopped to see my tail gunner, Jabo, in Asheville, North Carolina. He was having a little trouble with his kidneys, but hell, I have had a heart bypass and have a bovine heart valve. Our flight engineer has had five strokes, and when I talked to him the other day he had just come in from playing three rounds of golf, so I guess he recovered. We have our pains these days, but we are hanging in there. It is remarkable how we remember things from so long ago but we can't remember what we had for breakfast.

Years ago my daughter and my granddaughter took me over to Washington, D.C., to see the Holocaust Museum. That was very upsetting. I realized then why we fought and sacrificed in the war. We didn't know then what was going on in Europe. Now I understand we were fighting for those people and the millions of others under Nazi rule.

I guess anybody who fought in the war was a hero, but the real heroes are the ones who are still there. They really are. We're here because of them. Sometimes I see and hear things going on in this country, and you wonder if their sacrifices are truly appreciated. I hope they are.

JOSEPH A. FARINHOLT

Finksburg, Maryland
29th Infantry Division, U.S. Army

Joseph Alfred Farinholt was born in Boring, Maryland, on July 17, 1922. He grew up on his father's farm in Catonsville, Maryland, and after graduating from Catonsville High School in 1938 he enlisted in the Maryland National Guard, one day shy of his sixteenth birthday. He was assigned to an antitank battalion in the 175th Infantry Regiment during the war, and his tenacity in thwarting German armored attacks earned him the nickname "Lightning" among his peers. Farinholt was wounded during a shootout with a Tiger tank near Bourheim, Germany, in November 1944, and is a recipient of the Purple Heart. He was awarded the Silver Star for valor an unprecedented four times, and he is under consideration to receive the Medal of Honor. Joe is survived by his wife Agnes "Reds" Marshall and their four children.

I was a platoon leader of an antitank unit, and my primary responsibility was to knock out German tanks. I had a crew of thirty-two men and three 57-mm. antitank guns. The 57-mm. antitank gun weighed about 2,700 pounds and was dependable, accurate, and easy to move. Looking back, I guess I did some pretty dumb things back then.

I landed in France on the evening of June 6, 1944, the day of the Normandy landing. My first experience of war was a memorable one. As we were headed to the shore I heard a "thump . . . thump" sound, so I looked over the side of the landing craft and saw our boat was bumping into the bodies of dead GIs floating in the water. I could only imagine what it was going to be like when we got on land.

I had no feeling on the first day. I was sort of numb to all the destruction I saw. My orders were to expect a counterattack from the Germans, and I was busy setting our guns to defend against an attack from any direction. Our tactics were to deploy our guns in such a way as to prevent the Germans from approaching along roads or breaks in a tree line. Tanks are limited in the type of terrain they can cross, so I could usually predict in which direction they would most likely arrive.

The best way to destroy a tank was to wait until it roamed within the most effective range of our guns, which was about 400 yards. We would sometimes wait until the vehicle passed and throw a bottle of gasoline into the engine, and then finish it off with bazookas or grenades if the crew opened any hatches. On rare occasions it was necessary for one of us to climb on top of a tank and throw a grenade into the turret just before they could close the hatch. We destroyed quite a few vehicles ranging from lightly armored transports to the heavy 50-ton Tiger and 71-ton King Tiger tanks.

The majority of German tanks were superior to the tanks we had and often very difficult to destroy. The smaller German tanks couldn't defeat our tanks, but the Germans built a Panther, Tiger, and King Tiger tank that could knock ours out with ease. The only time I think I felt a hint of apprehension was when I first saw a German King Tiger tank. This German tank was enormous, and it took all three of my guns to knock it out. The Germans used light tanks to support infantry and the heavy tanks to destroy our tanks. The light tanks weighed about 30 tons, and we could knock them out with pretty much anything. We couldn't knock out the heavy tanks unless we caught them from the side or the rear, where the armor was less thick, or placed a shot in a soft spot between the turret and the body of the tank. We never fired on the front of the tanks because the armor was just too thick and our shells just bounced off like peas. If we could immobilize the tank by shooting the tread away, then we had a much better chance of killing it with gasoline bombs thrown into the engine or hand grenades thrown into a hatch when the crew tried to escape.

It took a lot of determination, patience, and strong nerves to attack the big German tanks. They made lots of noise, were very well armed, and could defend themselves by throwing lots of fire in your direction. The thing that concerned me the most was the 88-mm. gun that was fitted on most heavy German tanks. The 88s were particularly accurate weapons and could destroy just about anything they hit. I saw an 88 round take out whole groups of men, concrete bunkers, and several of our tanks with ease.

The first combat encounter I had was sort of comical. I spotted a German mortar position, so I picked up a bazooka and ran forward to knock it out. I fired at the crew, and those not killed ran away. I wanted to search the dead for souvenirs, but as I moved closer to investigate, a German tank suddenly came charging down the road at me. I jumped back into the brush to reload the bazooka, and I was able to knock the tank out as it tried to pass. I ran like hell to get back to our position before more tanks arrived, and as I reached our lines I dove through the bushes and fell flat on my backside. An officer was standing there, and he pulled me to my feet and said,

During a break while on maneuvers in North Carolina in 1941, Joe Farinholt strikes a pose befitting the true fighting man he was. The consummate infantryman, he earned an unprecedented four Silver Star citations for his actions commanding an antitank unit with the 29th Infantry Division. Fifty-five years after returning home, he received the lieutenant's commission he had been promised before being wounded. At the same time, the Army considered awarding him the Medal of Honor that he declined in 1945.

"Son, you are going to get a Silver Star for that." That's how I earned my first Silver Star. The officer eventually wrote the description for my citation completely different than what actually happened, but I imagine that was typical of many citations issued during the war.

Another memorable occasion occurred when I heard the rumbling of a tank for a few seconds, then it stopped, then it started again, and stopped. This was a moment when my heart seemed to stop, and my senses were on high alert trying to anticipate what was going to happen next. I knew there was a 50-ton machine armed to the teeth just a short distance away. I knew what was creating this noise, so I got my men to the guns, and I waited until the tank showed itself. It was a Panther tank, armed with an 88, and when it exited from the tree line it must have been no more than 75 feet from our position. It drove forward with its side exposed to our position so I could relax a bit, knowing if we got the first shot we wouldn't have any trouble destroying it. When it was directly in front of the guns I gave my gunner a squeeze on the shoulder, which was my signal for him to fire. The shot knocked the tread off the tank, and the Panther was stopped cold. We ran towards the tank with bottles of gasoline in our hands, and we burned the tank up before it could return fire.

There was never any thought about the crews inside the tanks we destroyed. Often, killing whoever was still alive in the tank was the best way to relieve their suffering. When an antitank round penetrated a tank, it projected thousands of pieces of shrapnel within the tank and created a hell of a mess. If the crew were not killed instantly, they were most likely in agony from the wounds they had received. I didn't want to kill the men in the tanks, but we never had the opportunity to take prisoners. That is just the way it was: them or us.

I think we knocked out tanks with pure nerve. You get the nerve up because it's a case of do or die. If a tank was coming at you, you knew you had to get it even if it meant climbing on top of it to find a way to stop it. It was natural to be afraid in war, and a tank is a particularly scary thing. But I didn't really think about being scared at the time. I just reacted to the task at hand and made sure I and my men got the job done.

If I had any fears, they stemmed from my concern about losing my men in battle. I soon found that people died so easily in the war, and I had to immunize myself from becoming too attached to my men. When I sent my men out into the field, I just couldn't worry about having my men get hurt. My primary concern was making sure we all did what we were supposed to do so we could get the heck home.

I was sitting with three of my men once, and we had just broken up a chocolate bar to share when a shell burst over our heads in the branches of a tree. I dove for cover, and when I got back on my feet I said, "Everyone all right?" It took a few seconds for me to realize they had all been killed, and I wasn't even scratched. I lost men, and I got a replacement; that's the way it was.

I never had a choice of the men I was sent as replacements, so I had to do the best with what I was given. It took years for my original crew to train to an effective level, and I could only do so much with raw replacements. Most casualties were caused from the inexperience of the replacements, and just dumb luck played a part as well. Although I never worried about it during the war, these days I occasionally wake up in the middle of the night, and I recall the faces of the men I lost. These were often sixteen-, seventeen-, eighteen-year-old kids. I had no men older than their mid-twenties. I had to write home to the parents of the dead boys, and now, forty years later, I still get letters from the wives and children of these boys asking me about what happened to their loved ones. That's when I really feel for them.

I was called on the radio one day by one of my best men, and he said I had better get up to his position because he was thinking about shooting himself. By the time I reached him he was already laying on the floor of his bunker holding his bloody leg. He said he just couldn't take the noise and killing anymore, so he shot himself in the leg and was not ashamed to be going home. I grabbed the soldier and pulled him to his feet and then carried him to the aid station. I told him to never tell anyone what he had done and I would make sure he was sent home. That was the only case in which one of my men cracked up, and I have no shame in doing what I did. The stress of war can weaken the strongest of men, and I think I had a good enough reason to send this soldier home because he was just a sixteen-year-old boy.

The typical German soldier was just like us; there wasn't a damn bit of difference. Most German prisoners were very cooperative and glad the war was over, but most didn't give up until their situation was hopeless or they ran out of ammunition and threw their guns down. The Italians were a funny bunch. They would all be laughing and singing when we came across them asking us why it took so long for us to arrive. We killed the German SS troops and even the Hitler Youth bunch without hesitation, even after they had surrendered.

War is so full of inhuman acts, but below the surface there is an inexplicable bond between you and the enemy despite your best efforts to kill one another. I had abandoned our guns once because our position was overrun, and I had to leave one of my wounded men behind because I didn't think I could escape carrying him. I rolled him into a ditch and covered him with leaves and told him to be quiet. After making it back to safety I started to feel really bad about leaving that boy behind, and I knew I had to go back and get him. I crawled through the first hedgerow and I was not fired upon, so I went to the next hedgerow, the next, and eventually I figured I was in the clear. I found the wounded boy where I had left him and

Opposite page. During a lull in the fighting in northern France in 1944, Farinholt took some photos of his men on the front lines posing with a variety of weapons. *Top:* Corporal Snyder with a 57-mm. antitank gun holding a 57-mm. round; Snyder again, in his foxhole holding a .306-cal. M1 Garand rifle; Sergeant Smith in his foxhole next to a .30-cal. M1 carbine. Replacing experienced men such as these with raw troops was one of Farinholt's most pressing worries while in combat. Both Snyder and Smith survived the war without injury. Farinholt found the undeveloped roll of film containing these pictures thirty-five years after the war and was surprised that they could still be developed.

pulled him from hiding. It was then I saw a German tank at the end of the road with its gun pointed right at me. If the tank crew had seen me I guess it would have been the end of me right there. I pulled the wounded boy through the hedgerow and carried him across a field towards the aid station. Just before I reached our lines, I heard a commotion behind me that sounded like cheering and clapping. I turned to look, and there must have been fifty Germans standing up clapping and cheering me for my little demonstration. I never would have believed it if I had not seen it with my own eyes. The war was funny that way at times.

I earned my second Silver Star when again my position was overrun and I had to leave all of our equipment to escape. After darkness fell I led my men back, and we were able to hook two of our guns to the trucks and get them back to our lines under heavy fire. We went back for the third gun but couldn't get the truck all the way to it, so we had to drag the 2,700-pound gun out by hand. We really baffled the Germans, who thought they really had us cornered, but we managed to pull off a stunt like that. With the use of those retrieved guns we were able to help stop a column of German tanks the next morning.

I was awarded a third Silver Star soon after we entered Germany. While set up in a defensive position around a small town, I watched a company of German infantry enter the far side of the town. Someone called artillery on the Germans, but as our artillery began landing we watched helplessly as some of our troops were caught in the barrage and roughed up bad. I ordered a few of my men to follow me, and we ran into the town to rescue some of our wounded. Without hesitation my men returned time and time again under fire to save as many wounded men as possible. The men I commanded never failed to amaze me. They were all willing to sacrifice everything to help their fellow GIs, and I was proud to serve by their side.

I was awarded my fourth Silver Star for my actions in Bourheim, Germany. I had positioned my guns to stop a German advance, and we were doing a good job of keeping the German tanks at a distance until the gun nearest my command post was hit and the gunner was killed. I ran to the gun to replace the gunner position, and we were able to knock the tread off the right side of an approaching Tiger tank. The Tiger was still in the fight, and while the rest of the crew ducked for cover, I was stupid enough to stay put while the tank sprayed its machine gun over our position. The armor-piercing rounds cut through the protective shield of the gun, and I was hit with shrapnel and knocked to the ground.

It was no fun then, and it's still no fun to recount these events now. I didn't realize how seriously I was wounded until I went to walk away and I fell over because the bottom half of my right leg was just hanging on by the skin. I was able to crawl to my jeep, and I found a way to make it back to the command post and report the events up on the road. As soon as I saw my wounds, I started to get

Joe Farinholt with his new bride, Agnes, nicknamed "Reds," on their wedding day, May 19, 1946. He had to sit this picture out because he was still recovering from wounds that to this day have yet to heal completely. The surgeon in the field hospital who first attended to him wanted to remove his badly wounded leg, but Farinholt told him, "You can't have it. I ain't done usin' it."

scared, but I was reminded that I had just received the "million-dollar wound" and was on my way home. The doctors took one look at my badly wounded leg and wanted to remove it, but I caused such a fuss, General Beachum intervened on my behalf and ordered the battalion surgeon, Captain Tucker, to try and save my leg, and he did.

I spent the next couple of years in the hospital recovering from the numerous wounds I had received. I received my fourth Silver Star from Admiral Nimitz, who had been touring the hospital. The admiral told me that if I wanted to trade in the Silver Star, he would recommend me for the Congressional Medal of Honor. I wish I could take back what I said, but I actually said, "No thanks, I earned it, and I'll keep it."

There were times when we were completely overwhelmed by the enemy, but we found ways to survive because of the training we received in the years leading up to our action in battle. We were fortunate enough to be taught the survival skills we needed when we got into combat. I didn't wash for months at a time. I ate when I had food in front of me and slept in a hole if I made one. We all just used our instincts to make it from day to day, and I think it helped to occupy our minds with thoughts about home, girls, and where we could get beer and food. We never talked about being scared, but we often were, and all we wanted to do was get home.

War doesn't make a whole lot of sense, and I wish it were outlawed forever. If we can get across to people just how much suffering a war causes, I doubt there would ever be another. It's up to us survivors to tell others what the war was like. War is horrifying to everyone involved, on all sides. But people don't think about things like that before they start shooting at each other.

I think I was treated pretty good by the Army, and I still am to this day. They are talking about awarding me the Medal of Honor, but I am not concerned about any medals. The real heroes of the war are still lying where they died. We can best honor them by educating people about the war by retelling our stories. This is more important than erecting memorials, because memorials and statues don't teach a thing about why and how people sacrificed so much for our country.

LORENZO FELDER

Baltimore, Maryland
51st Marine Defense Battalion

Lorenzo Felder was born in Saint Petersburg, Florida, on August 15, 1922. In 1938 he relocated to Baltimore, enrolling in the Booker T. Washington Junior High School, and graduated from Douglass High School in 1942. After graduation he attended Morgan State College until December 1942, when he enlisted in the Marine Corps. He was assigned to the all-black 51st Defense Battalion and promoted to platoon sergeant and chief of fire control for a battery of four 90-mm. antiaircraft guns. After the war Felder graduated from Morgan State and attended law school until his National Guard unit was called back to active duty during the Korean conflict. In 1950 he married his childhood sweetheart, Norma, and began a career at the Aberdeen Proving Ground as an instructor, where he remained until his retirement in 1983 with the rank of lieutenant colonel.

I moved to Baltimore in 1938, and I lived in West Baltimore on Lanvale Street near Gilmore. Since then our house has been torn down so Harlem Park Middle School could be built in its place. I was enrolled in the Booker T. Washington Junior High School and eventually graduated from Douglass High School in the spring of 1942. I then attended Morgan State College in the fall of 1942.

During my freshman year at Morgan State I began working at the U.S. Post Office to help pay for my schooling. It was just before Christmas, and I was hanging out with some of the guys talking about girls, school, the war, and what people we knew who had joined the service and the probability of our getting drafted, too. We starting playing around with the idea of me going down to the Marine Corps recruiting station just to see the look on their faces when I walked in the door and said I wanted to be a United States Marine. As far as we knew, no black had ever been accepted into the Marine Corps, so I thought it was a safe bet to accept my friends' challenge for me to go down to the recruitment office and apply. The worst thing I thought could happen was the recruiting officer would say, "Thanks, but no thanks." If anything, it would give me, my friends, and even the recruitment officer a good laugh.

The next morning I walked into the Marine Corps recruiting office and told the man behind the desk I wanted to be a Marine. I was a little stunned when he told me to grab a seat, and he handed me a piece of paper and a pencil so I could write a paragraph explaining why I wanted to be a Marine. I thought the recruiting officer was just playing a game with me, so I sat down and wrote my little story about why I thought I wanted to be a Marine. Whatever I wrote I have long since forgotten, but it must have been a pretty good work of fiction. When I was finished I handed the paper to the officer and waited to be shown the door. The next thing I knew, I was in a line stripped down to my underwear waiting to be examined by a doctor. I thought the officer was really making me suffer for trying to be funny and that this was still all a charade to put me in my place.

It took some time before the doctor examined all the guys in front of me, and I recall many of the white applicants were rejected right there on the spot by the doctor, so I felt very confident I would be rejected too, for having the wrong-colored skin. The doctor looked me over for a few minutes, and when he finished he told me to hold out my hand. I did, and he grabbed my arm and stamped a big "OK" on my hand. I said, "What does this mean?" He looked up at me and said, "You passed all of our physical examinations. Welcome to the Marine Corps. We will notify your draft board that you are no longer available." I tried to tell the doctor the whole thing was a big misunderstanding and that I couldn't believe this was happening to me.

Just my luck, the Marine Corps had begun accepting applications from blacks in August for the first time in its long history. I did not know that on June 25th of 1941, President Franklin Delano Roosevelt signed Executive Order 8802, which established the Fair Employment Practice Commission to prohibit racial discrimination by any government agency. With one stroke of his pen, FDR opened the United States Marine Corps to all men, black, white, and me. However, blacks' entry into the Marines was so ridden with racism that at times it was difficult to say whether the Corps was more at war with us blacks and itself or with the Japanese.

I was allowed to go back to school and continue my studies, and absolutely nobody believed my story when I told them what happened. The guys at the post office thought I had a great imagination and played along. Eventually I sort of put the whole day behind me. I had forgotten about it until a couple of weeks later I was having supper when I received a call from a Marine sergeant telling me to report to the main post office in Baltimore with a toothbrush, washcloth, and shaving gear. I said, "For what?" He said, "You are to report to the United States Marine Corps for boot camp."

Sgt. Lorenzo Felder in 1943 standing next to a 155-mm. artillery shell during training at Montford Point, North Carolina. Montford Point was the Marines' segregated training camp for black recruits located just a few miles from the Marine training facility at Camp Lejeune.

I immediately hung up the phone and ran over to my Norma's house to tell her what I had gotten myself into. She didn't believe me. My friends didn't believe me. My family didn't believe me. The next morning I called the Administration Office at Morgan to tell them I had to be dismissed from my classes and to make sure they understood it was not my choice to leave, but I had to report to the Marines. The receptionist on the phone reprimanded me for making a prank call on a school phone and hung up on me. I even received next semester's invoice while I was away. I don't think I convinced a single person I had joined the Marines. The next day I packed my belongings and reported to the post office. I bet a lot of people were walking around Baltimore for the next few days asking, "Where's Lorenzo?"

I boarded a train at the old B&O rail yard at Camden Yards, and off I went. The train was not segregated, but I would best describe the mood among the black recruits as "apprehensive." We discussed the fact that we were going to be among the first black men to ever be inducted into the Marines, and there was no telling what we were getting ourselves into.

When the train arrived in Richmond, the men were separated by race; the white guys went one way and us black guys went another. My group from Baltimore was joined by groups of other black men from Philadelphia, New York, Chicago, and points all over the Northeast. We all boarded another train, which took us down into North Carolina and Montford Point.

Montford Point was part of the Marine training base at Camp Lejeune but had the distinction of being reserved for just us black men. We were thus always referred to as the "Montford Point Marines," which made it easier for everyone in the Corps to distinguish us as blacks in comparison to the "regular Marines." The first black recruit to arrive at the camp was Howard P. Perry of Charlotte, North Carolina. He arrived in August of 1942, and was followed by nearly twenty thousand black men who were trained at Montford Point and inducted into the Marine Corps during the war. Of these men, about twelve thousand went overseas in exclusively all-black defense battalions or in combat support companies or as stewards, and were never deployed in combat during the war.

The first five hundred men in our group were all volunteers, and were divided into platoons ranging in number from one to seventeen. I was in the seventeenth platoon, and subsequent platoons were made up of men who had been drafted. Since we were the first black men ever to be inducted into the Marine Corps, an echelon of all-white officers and noncommissioned officers conducted our basic training. There were no black noncommissioned officers in the Corps; all were white, and they all were Southern men who I would describe as "married" to the Marine Corps. The Corps was their God and the sole purpose for their existence. You might think they were harsh on us black recruits, and they were as they would be to any raw recruit, but one thing I will give them credit for is they never asked any of us to do anything without first doing it themselves.

I would assume we performed many of the same basic training rituals as the white Marines, but we were never given equal consideration for anything. Like in civilian life, we never mixed with the whites for any reason, and our Marine uniforms did little to transcend our appearance in the eyes of most of the white officers. We were never permitted to step foot in Camp Lejeune without being escorted by a white Marine. Efficiency reports typically read, "You are one of the best *colored* men I have ever had the opportunity to serve with." When the camp attended the movies, the whites and blacks sat on opposite sides of the theater. When we went on leave, the black Marines stood aside until all the white Marines were loaded on the bus, and we were allowed on only if there was standing room left. On one occasion the camp gathered at an outdoor boxing event, and a Marine colonel stood up in front of the colored seating section and said, "I heard about women in the Marine Corps, and I heard of dogs in the Marine Corps, but when I found out *you* people were wearing *our* globe and anchor, I knew we were in a hell of a mess." The colonel stood there after making his remarks and nobody said a word. I think the colonel was waiting to be cheered by the white Marines. But when nothing happened, I imagined and hoped he began to feel like the real ass he had proven himself to be.

The premise of the Marine Corps is to produce highly trained and hardened men for infantry combat. But black Marines were never trained as combat infantrymen. At the onset, I didn't have the privilege of knowing how our training was different from that of the whites, and it was a long time before we became aware that ours was a lot different, and unequal. I don't think the Marines knew exactly what to do with us. In one phase of the training we were given tanks, and we just played with them on Saturday and Sunday afternoons. Then they tried giving us 75-mm. howitzers. Finally they decided we were going to form a new unit named the 51st Defense Battalion. The white Marines were trained to fight an offensive war in combat, while us black Marines were being trained to fight a defensive war. This was something intrinsically opposite of the Marine doctrine of being an offensive force, but when it came to us black guys the Corps immediately felt the need to firm up their defenses. We were given 90-mm. antiaircraft and 155-mm. artillery guns, and by combining the two the Marines produced a bastard insignia for our unit showing a 90-mm. tube on a 155-mm. carriage, although no such weapon ever existed. The battalion was also given 20-mm. and 40-mm. guns to provide antiaircraft support for the bigger guns.

In December of 1943 the 51st Battalion was loaded onto a train, and we began heading west for deployment in the Pacific. The trip was memorable, to say the least. When the train pulled into New Orleans, the officers ordered us to pull down the shades on the train so no one could see in, and so we couldn't see out. When we arrived in Los Angeles, the stationmaster refused to let the battalion eat at the station. Our white officers didn't take kindly to his refusal, and they defiantly ushered us right into the canteen. The fact that we all carried our rifles with us I think helped convince the stationmaster of our appreciation for his kind hospitality. This was possibly my last impression of a country I had grown up in and for which I and many others were going to risk our lives. The irony, and hurt, was too much for me to put in words.

The battalion boarded a Liberty ship in San Diego, and like all the ships that men had to take to the fronts, it was rough quarters to live in. The belowdecks had no portholes, and the air was stale and had an odor of sweat and dirt from the lack of washing facilities for the men. The bunks we slept in were stacked twelve high, and things were tight. We were given two meals a day, and I had to wait in line for a long time while everyone was served. I remained in good health, but being on the ocean made many men sick. On one

Felder *(kneeling, front row, right)* and members of the 51st Marine Defense Battalion in 1944 while stationed on desolate Funafuti Island near the Marshall Islands. The 51st was one of two all-black defensive battalions formed by the Marine Corps. It was deployed in the isolated reaches of the Marshalls for the duration of the war. Despite deep resentment over their exclusion from combat, the men of the 51st performed their duties with an unblemished record.

occasion while waiting in line for a meal up on the topside deck, the man in front of me became ill, and as he vomited a strong wind blew it back all over me and the other men standing in line. I guess I was so hungry at the time it didn't deter my appetite, but it was little things like this that made me wish to get off that boat as soon as I could.

In early February of 1944 the battalion disembarked on the Funafuti atoll in the Ellice Islands colony (today called Tuvalu), 2,600 miles southwest of Hawaii. We had been assigned to relieve a white antiaircraft unit that had been caught on the island since the war started. When the Marines realized this area was totally out of touch with the war, we were moved to Eniwetok in the Marshall Islands in September. It was a place, we discovered, that was even further removed from the war. In fact, it is so isolated that it was the site chosen by the United States to test the hydrogen bomb. We had occasional alerts of incoming planes and submarines, but nothing ever arrived.

We began to dig our guns in until we received orders to stop and pack up because we had been ordered to join one of the big battles raging in the Pacific. With an excitement we never had before, the battalion dug up our guns from their positions and awaited the next word as to when and where we were going. But word came back down to unpack again and to put the guns back into the pits. It was as if someone had kicked everyone in the battalion squarely in the gut. The battalion was ready for a fight, but instead we all became very demoralized and frustrated not to have the same opportunity to fight against the enemy like the white troops.

We remained on Eniwetok Island through the rest of the war. We guarded an island in the middle of nowhere on an atoll that was completely barren of life except little areas of some grassy vegetation atop the holes that were dug to bury the dead Japanese. The battalion remained there for about a year and a half without ever seeing a Japanese ship, plane, or soldier, and we never fired a single shot in anger. Although we never had any sense of our purpose in the war, we went about our duties without a single instance of exhibiting a rebellious attitude about our predicament.

The personnel in our battalion were rotated back to Montford Point in December of 1945, and we were discharged. There were some guys that stayed in, but the Marine Corps did not go out of their way to express much desire for us to stay around any longer. A group of us gathered that evening, and we pulled off our uniforms and had a big uniform-burning party. We'd had enough. By burning our uniforms I think we were burning away two years of unpleasant memories. You may wonder why, after all the hardships I endured, I would decide to join the reserves shortly after my discharge, but I would just say things were tight back then, and I needed the check.

I came home and got back to the life I had before the war. I did my duty, I served my time, and it was now time to move on. I returned to Morgan and received my degree in political science with a minor in history in 1949. I entered law school, but just about at the end of my first year my reserve unit was called to active duty during the Korean War. Fortunately I was assigned as a casual and sent to Europe for the duration of my time while the rest of my battalion was sent to Korea and served as a transportation unit until the end of the war. I was married in 1950, and when I returned the necessity to make a living meant I couldn't go back to law school. Instead I began working as an instructor at Aberdeen Proving Ground. I was eventually promoted to a supervisor and an evaluation manager until retiring in 1983.

I don't recall any accomplishments that would make me proud to have been in the Marine Corps, but I wouldn't exchange the experience for anything in the world. My time in the Marines taught me I could take hardships in life. I realized I could be treated less well than a person should and still function. The only time I ever felt a sense of pride wearing the Marine uniform was when I came home and walked through my old neighborhood. Baltimore had never seen a black guy in a Marine dress uniform, and I created quite a stir. Children followed me wherever I went, and with all the commotion you would have thought a four-star general was coming around the corner.

Some ask me why I and other blacks fought for a society in which we were segregated and treated as second-class citizens. I answer by saying the black man has fought for this country since the days of our founding fathers, and there was never any question or hesitation in my mind about serving my country. I think I can speak for most of the black soldiers in that I was hopeful our contributions and sacrifices would make a difference in how we were treated when we arrived back home. But this was a false hope. Upon returning home I believe we developed a bitter taste in our mouths when we came to the realization that our condition in society was exactly the same as before the war.

I grew up in a society and culture where I couldn't drink from the same water fountain or eat at the same lunch counter as other members of our society. This was just the way the world worked. When the time came for me to go into the service, I thought we were going to go fight the enemy like everyone else. I didn't have reason or time to stop and reflect about why I was going. I had a job to do, and I spent my time doing that job to the best of my ability. The powers that be made a terrible mistake by not letting black men fight on an equal basis as white men during the Second World War—if for no other reason than that a few more black guys would be under all those graveyard crosses in the place of the white soldiers. In the subsequent wars in Korea and Vietnam our country made sure that mistake didn't happen again.

I think it would be unfair to designate a particular group of people or certain individuals as heroes of the Second World War. I think I would say that any and every person who endured the suffering and difficulties of their time served in war is my hero.

CALVIN S. GEORGE JR.

Frederick, Maryland
USS Peary, *U.S. Navy*

Calvin S. George Jr.

Calvin Shriver George was born in Baltimore, Maryland, on March 12, 1916. While growing up he was a nationally recognized merit badge holder in the Boy Scouts and was rewarded by being invited to participate in President Roosevelt's 1933 inauguration parade. After graduating from City College in 1932, he attended the Naval Academy and received his commission in 1939. He was stationed in the Philippines aboard the destroyer USS *Peary* when the Japanese attacked on December 8, 1941. The *Peary* fled Manila to escape the Japanese, but George was unable to join his crew because of the wounds he had received during the Japanese air raids. His capture by the Japanese began a four-year journey of survival in Japanese prisoner-of-war camps and the infamous "hell ships" used by the Japanese to transport American prisoners of war. He is a recipient of two Purple Hearts. He married his late wife, Margaret, in 1946 and has a son and two daughters.

I wanted to be a Marine when I applied to the Naval Academy in 1934, but I was refused one of the thirteen spots reserved for Marines in each class. Ten of the thirteen Marines who graduated from that class were later captured by the Japanese in the Philippines and China and died while in captivity. If I have learned anything from my experiences in life it is to never ask to be dealt another hand. The second hand you are dealt could be a lot worse than the one you're already holding.

I was eventually accepted to the Naval Academy in 1936 and graduated in 1939 along with 630 other men out of the original 1,200 cadets who had entered in my class. The war in Europe did not seem to concern us much then, and my first assignment was on the battleship USS *Idaho* as assistant navigator and sailing master. I had won the Thompson sailing trophy while at the academy, and the Navy thought it was a good idea for me, and others like me, to

103

teach the new recruits how to sail the old-fashioned way. Every Sunday I would go to one of the three battleships in our group and ask for ten or twelve volunteers to join me to go sailing. The ones who were the first to step forward were always the Marines. I imagine they were most eager to get off their ships because they were the least paid and hardly ever left their ships.

We sailed a beautiful scientifically designed whaleboat that was very tricky to handle because it lacked a keel, and I would have to teach the crew to jump about the boat to maintain its equilibrium. The Marines were wonderful students and were always very quick to obey orders. I remember one occasion we were headed towards the beach and I called out we were "coming around," but the Marines didn't hear me or didn't react fast enough. The boat was never in any danger of sinking, but it began to take on water. I turned to see how the Marines were doing, and they all had been washed overboard. All I saw were their twelve little caps floating in the water. I thought that was the end of my promising career in the Navy, but all the Marines survived, getting just a little wet and embarrassed.

The Navy in 1939 was, pardon the expression, half-assed. A good percentage of the enlisted men were in the Navy simply to escape the privations of the Great Depression, and they did not take their time in the Navy seriously. The Navy itself was beginning to noticeably perk up, in that older ships were being modernized and many began to change their armaments and color schemes to wartime configurations. The USS *Idaho* was assigned to Pearl Harbor with practically the rest of the Navy in the Pacific at the time, and we conducted training exercises more frequently. The exercises were code-named according to colors, with each color representing a nation. In 1939 we primarily ran Exercise Orange, with Orange representing a conflict with Japan. The United States was seriously considering a conflict with Japan, not because there was any outward hostility shown by either side at the time, but perhaps because Japan represented the sole potential threat to the American Navy in the Pacific. The Navy had quietly built Pearl Harbor into the huge naval base it had become, so when the Japanese attacked on December 7, 1941, few American civilians actually knew where Pearl Harbor was located.

When I graduated from the academy they had a rule restricting graduates from marrying until two years after graduation. After serving my two years I fully expected to return to the States so I could marry my Margaret. I met Margaret in grammar school, where I sat behind her in class. One day I put a foot up on the back of her chair, and she turned around and smacked my leg with one of those metal-edged rulers. She drew some blood with that ruler, and it was love from that moment on.

I anxiously awaited my orders, and when I received them I quickly opened the envelope for the good news to return home. To

Calvin and Margaret in a photograph taken after the war. Calvin's thoughts of Margaret helped him survived the trials of captivity.

my dismay, I was instructed to report to the Philippines, home base for our Asiatic Fleet. I was devastated. I knew I had to make the worst phone call in my life to Margaret and tell her the news. When she heard I was ordered "east," she became ecstatic at the thought of me returning home, but when I told her it meant the Far East, it broke both of our hearts.

In July of 1941 I reported to the Philippines and was assigned to the destroyer *Peary* as gunnery officer. In early November we took part in a nighttime training exercise, and another destroyer accidentally collided with ours, causing extensive damage to our ship. Although the bow of our ship was nearly removed, we fortunately had no injuries to the crew. We slowly made our way to the Cavite naval base located across Manila Bay from Manila.

On December 7, 1941, while our ship was being repaired, I was on liberty at the Baguio recreation spot for military personnel, located up in the hills about three hours by car from Manila. A relaxing morning was interrupted with an announcement over the loudspeaker instructing all military personnel to return to their station because Pearl Harbor had been attacked. We all mumbled aloud and wondered what the guy was talking about until at the end of the announcement I heard the words I will always remember: "This is no drill!"

After we learned what the Japanese had done to Pearl Harbor, we all knew we were the next logical target and fully expected the Japanese to show up at any time. The entire area was on alert to the coming Japanese attack, but to my disbelief, the Japanese were able to attack the air bases around Manila with our planes still parked in neat rows, making them especially easy targets to attack. After the air bases were destroyed, Manila was defenseless against air attack, and we all knew we were really going to get hit hard.

When the Japanese attacked Cavite Naval Base in the early-morning hours of Wednesday, December the 10th, the *Peary* was tied up to the repair yard docks with all of her guns removed and dead in the water with no power. All the ship had operating for our defense was our antisubmarine mines and a few Lewis machine guns I had swiped from some old World War I airplanes parked nearby. As gunnery officer, I felt my hands were tied, and we could do little to fight back. There was no place to go, no place to hide, and no cover anywhere. I watched the Japanese bombers arrive overhead, and I was struck with a totally helpless feeling. The Lewis machine guns had a very limited firing range, and shooting at planes thousands of feet in the air was senseless, but it gave the guys some sense of trying to fight back. When the bombs began to fall around the ship, I remember looking over the side and watching a bomb land in the water. I was surprised when I saw the explosion lift a great wooden mast out of the water, sending it high into the air before it crashed back into the water. I imagine the mast had been buried on the bottom of the bay many years before, when Manila belonged to the Spaniards. Moments later a bomb landed in the foremast of our ship, showering the men topside with pieces of shrapnel. We had seen the bomb dropping towards us, so we lay down flat on the deck and held our breaths. The resulting explosion drove pieces of the antennae into my back, making me look like a porcupine, and my head was split open near my left eye. The executive officer next to me was killed instantly, and the man on the other side of me lost one of his legs.

I was carried to a Manila hospital, and during the next three weeks the Japanese continued their attacks on Manila before General MacArthur declared it an open city. Even after the declaration, the Japanese continued the bombing on innocent civilians in Manila. I was immobilized during my recovery, and I remember during one bombing attack a crew mate of mine, who had suffered a broken arm, dove under my cot for protection. It was an odd feeling, listening to the bombs falling around the hospital and having a guy under my cot using my body for protection against falling bombs.

I was still suffering from serious wounds and was not allowed to return to the *Peary* when I learned the *Peary* had been repaired and ready to leave port to join the Allied fleet in Australia. I became very sad. Some of my shipmates came to visit me before they left, and they gave me my last pay and, thankfully, two months of pay in advance. I had no possessions other than a wristwatch, a ring, and a fountain pen, so I was extremely fortunate to have additional money to buy food when our food allowances during our imprisonment became scarce. The Navy was not made aware of my inability to depart with the *Peary*, so I was reported killed when all hands went down when the *Peary* was sunk in Darwin Harbor on February 19, 1942. A plaque was placed in Darwin Harbor honoring those who died on the *Peary*, and my name is on it, making me a walking ghost. As I said before, never ask for second deal in life, because you never know if your new hand is going to be worse than the one you are already holding.

All wounded Navy personnel were moved to a temporary hospital named Santa Scholastica, which was formerly a music school for young ladies. I had experience playing the violin, but it was here I learned how to play the cello when Sister Marie thought I had too much free time on my hands, so she handed me an instrument to play. Living conditions were still pleasant, with clean surroundings and plenty of food brought from other bases in the area. But when the Japanese captured Manila, things started to deteriorate rapidly.

My first experience meeting the Japanese was uneventful, and they seemed rather indifferent to our presence in the hospital. They looked around and asked a few questions about our activities and instructed us to continue our daily routines. I do remember the nurses were terrified of the thought of being captured by the Japanese, but on this occasion the Japanese were on their best behavior. However, there are varying accounts of the treatment of women prisoners at the hands of the Japanese as the war progressed.

After about a month, the Japanese moved us to the old Bilibid prison building in Manila. Living conditions were bad and worsened when the Japanese began to prevent local merchants from standing at the gate to sell us food to supplement our meager daily food allowance. With the extra pay I was holding I was able to purchase food that was essential to my staying in relative good health. The food the Japanese gave us was in very small portions and contained few essential nutrients. Unless a man could supplement his diet with these additional items from the merchants, his health tended to fail rapidly, and he fell ill. The poor sanitary conditions increased the number of cases of disease caused by parasites. I remember watching men shake their bamboo sleeping mats and seeing all the lice and other vermin fall to the floor. Every morning the men were assembled for roll call, and we listened to the count change each day. It told us just how many men were left in the camp and how many had perished the day before.

Because we were all Navy personnel, we had good medical expertise within the camp, but this did not prevent about thirty men from dying each day. I began to suffer from a condition called dengue, or "break-bone fever," which was a very painful ailment and caused a high fever. Those who became infected were usually carried off dead in a short period of time, but luckily I managed to survive. Everyone suffered from some sort of illness, so it was nothing noteworthy for me to claim I was sick, and I was still in relatively good shape compared to many of the men in the camp.

The Japanese generally kept their distance from the prisoners unless one of the prisoners didn't perform in the fashion the Japanese preferred. A man could expect to receive a rifle butt to the gut or in the back if he didn't bow low enough when a guard passed or work fast enough for their pleasure. On some days the guards would just be in a bad mood and issue more severe beatings with sticks and clubs. Men were also forced to stand at attention for hours in the hot sunshine. I don't think it was the Japanese themselves or the punishments given by the Japanese that caused the deaths in the camp as much as the conditions we were forced to live in, but perhaps it is impossible to differentiate between the two.

If the Japanese soldiers saw a watch or piece of jewelry of yours they liked, they took it from you with a smile. As in every army, there are bound to be some men who are just a little meaner than the others, and we quickly learned to recognize which guards were more likely to give you a beating. I think one of the biggest problems I faced as a prisoner were the Japanese soldiers who were very loyal and fanatical about their emperor and wanted to fight. The Japanese lived by a code of honor, shunning surrender, so they didn't think much about us men who had been taken captive. I think it must have been a great embarrassment for these Japanese to be ordered to watch over us prisoners. The best Japanese soldiers were reserved for the fighting, so it was the rejects who were assigned to guard prisoners, and their poor morale, low intelligence, and general resentment towards their task caused much of their resentment to be taken out on the prisoners. There came a point when I began to ignore the Japanese as our captors. I knew who they were and what they could do to me, but as long as I did what I was told, they really didn't make my life any more difficult than what I had learned I could endure.

There was no thought of escape at this point because we were in the middle of Luzon, and any Caucasian would have a very difficult time blending into the countryside. Despair had begun to set into the hearts of many men. I remember watching a group of men climb to the top of a large tower in the center of the camp and jump to their deaths. A couple of the men were ranking officers, and perhaps they had some idea of what was ahead of us and decided to end it sooner than later.

We were moved to an old training camp used by the Philippine Army located in a town called Cabanatuan located in the mountains about five hours by slow truck outside Manila. The camp consisted of large bamboo huts that centered on a command post used by the Japanese. When we arrived at the camp we were assembled on the parade grounds and introduced to the Japanese camp commander. I remember he slowly walked from his office and stood before us without saying a word. He then pulled his sword from its sheath and threw a small melon into the air and sliced it into two pieces before it hit the ground. He stepped forward and in perfect English said, "This is what happens when you do not do what you are asked." We understood very clearly what he meant, and I went along with everything they asked.

We maintained our own command within our ranks, led by a Marine officer named Colonel Beecher. I remember him as a very strong and inspirational leader. The Japanese had control of the camp's exterior, but the Marine colonel had control of what happened in its interior. We adhered to the same discipline expected of an American soldier or sailor, but desperation often revealed a darker side that existed in the camp causing men to steal, act perversely, and even fraternize with the Japanese. In most circumstances these acts were in exchange for extra food, so I am not sure who could be justified in judging these men.

On two occasions we were fortunate enough to have a truck pull into the prison grounds carrying Red Cross packages. It was a great treat to receive these packages containing condensed milk, cheese, candies, and other nice treats. Another amenity was a library that had a large selection of books. Since I was still wounded I was assigned to the library, and this exemption from performing strenuous work in the fields helped me to save my strength.

A bizarre moment occurred one day when apparently a Japanese soldier standing guard in a tower leaned over to urinate and managed to make contact with the electrified fence along the top of the wall surrounding the Bilibid prison. I heard a horrible scream, so I jumped up on something tall so I could see what the commotion was about. At the bottom of the tower I saw this Japanese soldier lying on the ground with his rifle and bayonet sticking straight out of his back, essentially pinning him to the ground. It took us a few minutes in awe to guess he must have dropped his rifle when he was electrocuted, fell from the tower, and his rifle landed on top of him. We had a reason to smile on that day, albeit briefly.

Our daily food allowance remained minimal, but the camp did provide plenty of clean water, fresh air, and, unfortunately, lots of mosquitoes. Mosquitoes posed a grave danger to us because of the diseases they spread, and we had little or nothing to protect ourselves from their ravaging of our ranks. The temperature was always very hot, and even the Japanese refused to work in the afternoon temperatures, so we had respite between eleven in the morning until three in the afternoon. The prisoners worked in the surrounding fields the remainder of the day cultivating crops consisting of a white-colored radish called a *daikon* and *camotes*, which is the Philippine word for sweet potato. The prisoners were given the leaves of the *camote* plants to eat, and the Japanese got the actual potato part of the plant. Our "big" meal of the day was lunch, which consisted of a ball of rice and *camote*-leaf soup that had some sliced *daikon* thrown in, adding little value except for a little peppery taste. Breakfast was a small amount of cereal called *lugaou* that resembled white rice, and in the evening we were given more *lugaou* and perhaps some tea.

I witnessed men deal with our predicament in many ways. I tried to find something positive to escape the reality of my situation, and my thoughts were consumed with my determination to return home to be with my Margaret. Survival was often a matter of luck in maintaining health, but it also required learning how to conserve energy and to avoid beatings from the guards. Some men let the despair of their condition wear them down, and I think they died from a lack of hope. The despair of living in such horrible conditions forced men to give up. When an individual lost all hope, it usually meant his death, but men who had plans for the future were more likely to survive. We spent most of our day with thoughts about what we were going to do after the war. I like to think hundreds of unique inventions were discovered among the men sitting around in the prison camps, and maybe some of those people went home and made a fortune with those ideas. There was no purpose in getting mad at the Japanese. It was a waste of energy. Any extra energy I had was spent playing cards and talking to others about getting home. When I woke in the morning, I said my thanks for still being alive and whispered the words, "I am coming home to you, Margaret." My thoughts about Margaret kept me alive during those years in captivity. She was there with me every minute of the day, whether awake or asleep. My thoughts of Margaret every minute of the day saved my life.

Things became steadily worse as all of our extra food supplements were disappearing, and we had to rely only on the food we were receiving from the Japanese. The Japanese disliked brown rice, and they gave it to us without realizing brown rice was more nutritious than the white rice they preferred to eat. Occasionally we were given a small portion of fish or meat with our rice, and this was big news when it happened. Each prisoner received a small ration of cigarettes, and since I smoked a pipe I sometimes used the tobacco in my pipe. Some men swapped their food rations for additional cigarettes, and since I did not smoke regularly I was able to eat a little better once in a while through a trade.

There was a very slight wire fence surrounding the camp, but the Japanese made the thought of escape impossible. Each man in the camp was assigned to a "shooting squad." Each squad consisted of ten men, and if the Japanese discovered one member of a squad missing, they threatened to shoot the other nine men. Rumors circulated that the Japanese had enforced their threats, but it didn't keep a few Army Engineers from trying to tunnel out of the camp while building a latrine system. When the time came to try an escape, their idea was scrapped because of the thought of condemning nine others to death in exchange for every man freed.

We were losing men to disease at a steady rate, and the best way to deal with the horror was to keep busy. The heat was harsh, and to escape it during the day we dug a cellar under our barracks. We gathered there to play poker, and I did quite well, accumulating a purse of around fifty thousand dollars. I never collected a penny, because the guy who kept the books didn't do a good enough job for us to figure out who owed what after he died. One day I remember sitting in the cellar playing cards when a cobra slithered into the cellar with us. We all dove for higher ground to escape the pit and the snake. There was this cat that hung around the hut, and while we ran in one direction, the cat, curious as always, cautiously peered over the edge of the pit to examine the intruder. I remember a buddy of mine tapped the cat on the hind leg with a stick, and the cat was so spooked it jumped 6 feet into the air. It was little moments like these that made life a bit more interesting for me, and the snake made for a great treat in our rice bowls that night. And no, the cat was spared the same fate.

Another very memorable moment happened while I was watching the Japanese guards perform drills and line up for inspection. A very tough-looking captain was addressing the troops and proceeded down the line of soldiers until he paused in front of a very young-looking soldier. The soldier presented his rifle to the captain and in the process accidentally fired a round that shot the captain's cap off his head, and it tumbled backwards several feet before coming to a rest. I don't think I ever saw such a beating delivered to any man as what the captain gave that poor Japanese soldier—just a little moment that brought a smile to my face because for once it was not one of us being beaten.

Then came the day we heard the rumbling of bombs in the distance in the direction of Clark Airfield. I vividly remember the excitement the sound caused within the camp with our forces being so close. Moments later a single twin-engine bomber flew low over the camp, and we all waved and cheered at the sight of a friendly plane. I hardly recognized the plane as one of ours because since we had been captive the design of American bombers had changed so much, but we saw its insignia telling us it was American. It is hard to recount the joy that pilot gave us when he dipped his wings a few times in salute just to tell us we were not forgotten, and I think he was saying to us, "We'll be back soon." Hope is a wonderful thing.

The sight of the American bomber really cheered us up, but for the Japanese it signaled the time to move us further along. On December 22, 1944, the prisoners were trucked back to Manila, and a few days later we were loaded onto the passenger and freight ship *Oryoku Maru*, to be transported to Japan. The *Oryoku Maru* was a German passenger ship and freighter commandeered by the Japanese. It had no facilities for the prisoners in the hold, which was dark and hot. The Japanese crammed about twenty-two hundred of us into the hold, and within a short period of time numerous men began to pass out and die from the suffocating air and heat. Some went mad and walked back and forth in the darkness screaming at the others. The following morning we were informed that we were passing Mariveles at the tip of Bataan and that gunnery practice was to take place aboard the ship. When the guns began firing I figured it was the practice, but to our surprise it was not a drill but an attack by American fighter planes. The American pilots were attacking an enemy ship and, understandably, had no idea American prisoners of war were on board.

A bomb hit the ship and tore through the cabins above us holding Japanese passengers. There were horrific screams, and blood from the mangled bodies trickled down through the cargo hold covers. Another bomb invaded the hold of the ship, and a hole was torn in the side, forcing the ship to run aground. We endured another two days of occasional aerial attacks until the survivors were ordered out and forced to swim to shore. I jumped through the hole in the side of the ship along with about a thousand other men, and I managed to swim to shore. Men around me were punching and kicking at the water to keep the sharks away. Those who made it ashore were lined up on a tennis court near the beach, where we were held for a day and a half in the burning sun with no water, food, or toilets.

I was in poor shape. I was reaching a point where the events happening around me no longer registered a reaction. When the bombs were falling around me I began to accept the fact that I had no control over whether I lived another minute or not. I closed my eyes, tried to fall asleep, and hoped I would wake up again.

The next day those men who could walk were herded onto trucks, and on Christmas Day we arrived at the Lingayen Gulf of the South China Sea. (Those too weak to continue were left behind on the tennis courts and were executed by the Japanese guards.) We were permitted a swim in the gulf to wash, and my Christmas dinner in 1944 consisted of a ball of rice and a spoonful of vegetables.

We boarded yet another ship, which was apparently a cattle ship, because of the odor and the bits of grain scattered on the floor. We huddled in the dark and suffocating hold of the ship, and shortly after departing we were again attacked by American bombers. The concussion of the bombs landing nearby was terrifying. This period was perhaps the most horrible moment of all my time in captivity. A bomb hit the ship, and the 20-inch beams above us were torn loose and fell among the prisoners. It was a horrible sight to see so many men crushed under the weight of these huge pieces of steel. The ship was again ripped open, and a sailor and I crawled through an opening and began swimming away. We both stopped at the same moment when we realized the futility of our attempted escape. The water was too cold, so we decided to return to the ship. While trying to crawl back into the hold we were both cut and scratched from the jagged metal around the opening. Bleeding, cold, and wet, I sat down and closed my eyes and tried to ignore the horrific carnage around me. Sitting near so many wounded and crushed men was just horrific.

Eventually we were towed into a harbor, presumably Taiwan, and transferred to yet another ship. We were crowded onto shelves alongside the hull in two rows. One row was next to the hull and another toward the center of the ship. Those nearest the hull were worse off because it was coldest there, and many men died from exposure.

In February of 1945 I arrived on the Japanese home island of Kyūshū, and we stayed there briefly until being loaded onto another ship to take us to Korea. I remember during this trip the Japanese lowered a cargo net into the hold of the ship every morning and men would lay the bodies of the dead in the net, and the Japanese would raise the net and the bodies disappeared into the light.

We landed in Korea, and we had our first decent meal in a very long time. The Japanese had ordered the local Korean people to prepare box lunches for the prisoners, and they really outdid themselves with generous portions of rice, fish, and vegetables, much to the chagrin of the Japanese guards. We settled in a camp in Jinsen, a port city near Seoul. The Japanese colonel in charge of the camp was a real gentleman. When he presented himself to the prisoners he admitted how much he disliked his role as commandant and swore he would treat us fairly as long as we maintained his order, and he did. On the day President Roosevelt died the colonel announced to the camp, "Your dear president Roosevelt has died, and in honor of his death all work will be suspended for the day."

The prisoners pooled our resources together from around the camp and managed to assemble a little radio to listen to the progress of the war. At night we huddled around the radio listening intently to how much closer the Americans had gotten to Japan and hopefully to the conclusion of the war. When the news was broadcast of Japan's surrender, we had quite a little celebration, but it wasn't until a few days later that the Japanese colonel officially announced that the war had ended and we were free men. The Japanese guards opened the gates, and we began to flee down the road until our Marine colonel ordered us to stay put while a search party was sent out to scout the nearest town. Hours later the scouting patrol returned leading oxen through the gates, and I had beef for the first time in years.

The following morning we slowly began to walk towards the town, and when we arrived I found a place in a hotel that overlooked the water. From my room window I watched our forces land nearby on the mainland. As far as I could see there were hundreds of ships and landing craft. It was quite a sight to see how much the Navy had grown during the war. I imagine it was like any other invasion during the war, except there was no shooting involved.

Days later I boarded a large landing craft, and I began my trip home. As the boat was leaving the dock the Japanese colonel ran up to the ship waving and wishing us luck, shouting, "Goodbye! Goodbye!" I actually smiled and waved back.

I received VIP treatment from the Navy after my return to Manila, and I flew wherever we went. I was put on a flying boat, and its condition was less than comforting. In midflight we had to make an emergency landing on Johnson Island. As the old crate lumbered up the ramp from the water, the right wing fell off. I was glad to get on solid ground after a close encounter with a plane with such questionable structural integrity. I finally reached San Francisco, and at the first chance I found a phone and I called Margaret. What we said to one another will forever remain between just her and me.

I had survived four years in Japanese prison camps, during which time I had been reduced from 155 pounds to 80 pounds. But I was alive. The single most important thing that kept me alive was hope. Hope is the most powerful thing in the world. During my entire imprisonment, all I could think of was returning home to see Margaret. Although thousands of miles away, she saved my life every day.

Recalling the dark days of my captivity is most painful, but I have put that aside long enough to speak about them. This is just a brief outline of the events that happened to the brave men, not only me, who endured these horrors.

I am no hero, just one who was fortunate enough to survive horrendous difficulties, as were many others. I would reserve the title of heroes of the Second World War for those who sat at home not knowing what was happening to their loved ones so far away. They must have endured an equal or greater pain than those who fought the war.

"For Conspicuous Gallantry"

On March 10, 1943, while patrolling some 650 miles off the coast of Brazil, the U.S. Navy ships *Eberle* (DD-430), *Santee* (CVE-29), *Savannah* (CL-42), and *Livermore* (DD-429) intercepted the German block-ade-runner *Karin,* flying a Dutch flag. Not fooled by the false colors, the *Eberle* and *Savannah* closed on the enemy ship at flank speed and fired warning shots across her bow. The *Karin's* crew promptly set her afire and began to abandon ship. A fourteen-man party from the *Eberle* boarded the blazing ship and attempted to save the prize.

One of the members of that party was Carl Welby Tinsman, seaman second class. Tinsman had been born in Anne Arundel County on March 29, 1924, and had en-listed in the U.S. Naval Reserve on August 19, 1942. Displaying exceptional courage, he worked at putting out the fire until a sudden explosion of a demolition charge killed him. For his heroic action, Tinsman was posthumously awarded the Silver Star with the following citation.

CARL WELBY TINSMAN
(Photo courtesy of Anne Arundel Historical Society)

For conspicuous gallantry and intrepidity while attached to a United States Warship in action against enemy forces. When a hostile vessel was intercepted and attacked, Tinsman, as a member of a boarding party attempted to salvage the vessel, displayed exceptional courage in the face of grave danger from threatening flames and the powerful explosions of demolition charges. While preparing to ascend the ladder of the vessel in order to assist the hazardous salvage operations, Tinsman lost his life as the result of a sudden violent explosion. His exemplary conduct and heroic devotion to duty were in keeping with the highest traditions of the United States Naval Service. He gallantly gave his life for his country.

Source: Anne Arundel Historical Society.

PHILIP A. HANNON

Ellicott City, Maryland

81st Combat Engineer Battalion, U.S. Army

Philip Austin Hannon was born in Fonda, Iowa, on October 14, 1923. After relocating with his family to Northern Virginia in 1942, he enrolled in the University of Maryland for his sophomore year. After fulfilling a requirement to enroll in the campus ROTC course, he enlisted in the Army reserves and was called up in February 1943. He opted to join the 81st Combat Engineer Battalion and was assigned to the 106th Infantry Division. At the outset of the Battle of the Bulge, he was taken prisoner by the Germans and held until liberated in April 1945. After the war Hannon returned home and married his wife, Jean, in 1947 and graduated from the University of Maryland. He worked as a salesman and then partner of a family-owned commercial kitchen supply company until retiring in 1986. He and Jean have two children and three grandchildren.

The following profile was based on an interview with Philip Hannon, and on portions of his unpublished autobiography, "One Man's Story" (© 1990), which are reprinted here with permission.

When the war started on December 7, 1941, I was a freshman at Cincinnati University, and my father was driving me back to school from our home in Fort Wayne, Indiana, when the news came over the radio. I finished my freshman year and then joined my parents, who had moved to Alexandria, Virginia, so my father could take a new sales manager post with his company, which manufactured automatic washing machines. I worked that summer with a company that made oil filters for submarines, and in the fall I enrolled in the University of Maryland for my sophomore year. At the time, the university required I join the campus ROTC program, and in November of 1942 the colonel in charge of the ROTC program told us that if we enlisted in the reserves the likelihood of our being drafted would be diminished. I signed up for the reserves, as we all did, and I often wonder if this was a ploy by the military, because in February of 1943 our entire ROTC group was called up for service into the Army. The University of Maryland ROTC program was assigned to the Army infantry, and my being in the reserves provided me the small advantage of being able to choose which branch within the Army I wanted to join. I had heard the Engineers had trucks to ride around in, so I chose the Engineers, because I was lazy.

All the boys from the Maryland ROTC program were shipped to Camp Lee, Virginia. It was a good month and a half before those of us who had chosen the combat Engineers were shipped out to Fort Belvoir, Virginia. As combat Engineers, we were trained to fight as infantrymen, but we were also taught special skills in handling explosives, laying and taking up mines, and road and bridge construction. Basically the Army Engineers are programmed to get the Army moving through any obstacle it encounters. Our training was all hard work, and they ran us night and day.

After basic training I was assigned to the Army Special Training Corps and stationed on the campus of the University of Maryland. The program was shut down in February of 1944, and I was shipped to the 3rd Platoon, Company A, 81st Engineers, 106th Infantry Division, at Fort Jackson, South Carolina. We proceeded to Tennessee for maneuvers soon after my arrival. It was cold, wet, and dreary along the banks of the Chattanooga River, but despite all the foul conditions I enjoyed my first experience camping in the outdoors. From there we went to Camp Atterbury in Indiana, and then in November of 1944 the division was shipped to Camp Miles Standish in Massachusetts. On November 7 we boarded the *Queen Mary* and sailed for Europe. Five days later we landed in England and spent five days in camp before boarding LSTs (landing ships, tank) that took us across the English Channel, up the Seine River, and we disembarked around Saint-Vith in Belgium.

We arrived at the front lines on December 10, 1944, just six days before the start of the Battle of the Bulge. When we arrived, none of us in the 81st Engineers knew where we were. We moved into an old school building a few days after we arrived and found a map on a wall, and we were able to locate our town of Auw, Germany, and then presume our general location in the war.

The deployment of the 106th along the front was a calculated risk. It was routine for the Army to place a green division in a "quiet" sector where our infantry could get combat training for the big push the Allies had coming. But we were spread too thin along a 28-mile sector, and when the heinies made a last-chance drive, we were caught in the middle.

On Saturday morning, December 16, 1944, we were just getting out of bed when the Germans started sending their greetings with their 88s. They blew one of our jeeps to pieces, but we were green, so we shrugged our shoulders and said, "What the hell, this must happen every so often," and off to chow we went.

Chow was good, as chow always is to guys who are in good shape, and the gang was full of laughs about the close calls that dropped in on us. The heavy firing to the east didn't register, so the talk was about Christmas and the mail that was just starting to come in. The 3rd Platoon had a couple of jobs to finish up front, so we loaded up and off we went. The same old horseplay went on, the KPs got the everyday razzing as we rode by the kitchen, and everyone was in fine spirit as we went up the road to finish a corduroy road we had started the day before.

The front was quiet, the shells were going over and beyond, and we felt safer out on the roads than in the little village we had left earlier. We were throwing snowballs at each other and having a great time when a big major came out of the woods and started yelling at us. He said, "What the hell are you guys doing out here? We don't know what's going on. Get the hell outta here!" We loaded into our trucks and started back to our village. We would never make it back.

We were stopped at our Regiment Headquarters Company, in the little village of Schonberg, and were told we were cut off. From Schonberg we could see our village and the Germans in between. The men of Headquarters Company had been taking a pounding from German artillery, and some of their nervousness got to us. A German "buzz bomb" flew over our truck so low I thought I could have reached up and touched it. We jumped from our trucks and deployed by instinct on the outskirts of the village. No one had to tell us what to do and where to go. We did the right thing automatically and manned a rock pile here, a depression, a ditch, or a manure pile there. Our little village was still ripe for the Germans to pick if they wanted. We were no more than a couple platoons of men from assorted platoons with rifles and a jeep with a mounted .50-cal. machine gun. We remained in our positions for the next four hours and watched our little village of Auw down the road get pasted by German artillery.

On Monday the 18th at two o'clock in the afternoon, we got orders to abandon the village and try for a break back to our lines. Two battalions of infantry were fighting to break us out, and we left the village expecting to meet them and get out. We loaded into the trucks and pulled out under a protecting barrage of smoke and timed fire laid down by our artillery. We moved slowly and in short jumps because no one knew what was ahead of us. At one stop we found a pile of bedrolls, duffel bags, overcoats, and the like left by our retreating infantry. Those of us who didn't have coats and rolls picked them up. Five cartons of smokes were found, so everyone had cigarettes to last for a while. We each had been issued a chocolate "D-bar," so I ate all three portions of mine, which were labeled "Breakfast," "Lunch," and "Supper."

Our convoy got moving again, and it was headed into the middle of a terrific firefight, or so it seemed. We turned parallel to the fighting about half a mile before we got to where the tracers were coming from. I happened to be up front in the truck facing the fighting and could see more than the rest of the gang, so between prayers I reported what was going on in whispers. We were all disappointed, as it looked like we were not going to escape out of the pocket, and I was plenty scared when we were ordered to pull the vehicles off the road into a patch of woods and then de-truck.

We stayed there for the night, and my group of Engineers pulled guard that night. It was pitch black that night, and muttered curses could be heard all over the place: "Get the hell out in the open, a tree burst would kill you as sure as Christ!" and "Dig in, you fool!" I pulled my watch from twelve to two and then decided to dig in. I found an open spot in the field and went to work. While doing that, one guy in my platoon asked to borrow my rifle because someone had stolen his. I let him have it and rolled out my roll and flopped down. I didn't get into it because it would have caused trouble if I had needed to get out in a hurry. I fell asleep with little trouble and slept soundly. My hip boots were like iceboxes, and the next day my feet gave me plenty of trouble.

At about four o'clock on the morning of the 19th, a German patrol found us and started shooting the place up. Tracers were flying up and down the field I was stretched out in. The firing jarred me awake and scared the sin out of me. I glanced into my prone shelter and cussed myself for a damn fool: it was half full of water. I was scared but couldn't see myself in mud and water up to my neck, so I picked a mound of dirt and scrambled for it. Things quieted down, and I went looking for my rifle. I used to cuss that rifle up and down during training, but I sure wanted it then. I finally found the guy with my rifle, and with some argument he gave it back to me. He promptly swiped our lieutenant's rifle, and when the lieutenant missed it he raved and threatened whoever had it. Later in the day the kid gave the rifle back when the lieutenant wasn't looking.

After the excitement died down everyone was up and around, so we talked about home, our situation, and cussed the cold weather while we waited until it was light enough to smoke a cigarette. When daylight did come, we took a look at our position and didn't like it. Our trucks were bumper to bumper on the edge of a small wooded area, which covered a little hill. We drove the trucks into the woods, camouflaged them, and started to dig in to fight it out.

The men dug beautiful two-man foxholes, but everyone seemed to crave companionship, and the holes were too close together. If the Germans had started throwing heavy stuff in, it would have been a bloody mess. One officer started to raise hell (he was the only officer worth anything, as far as I could see), and although we were dead tired we could see he was right and started to spread out and dig in again.

The call went down the line that five Engineers were needed to fill in a crater hole in the road. They wanted men with hip boots because of the mud, so I ended up as one of those five. We found a pile of gravel and loaded a jeep trailer with it and left the woods. We found the road and two kitchen trailers that were stuck hub-deep in the mud. None of us had eaten much for some time, so the first thing we did was raid the kitchen trailers. D-bars and fruit juice were about all we could find that we could eat without cooking, but who could complain when it was better than nothing? Finally we settled down to fill in the hole in front of the trucks.

Suddenly trucks and men came bursting from the woods ahead of us. Men were all over the trucks, hanging anyplace they could, and were yelling, "We're getting out! Pile on!" Sure sounded like a good idea, but first we raided the kitchen trailers again for more D-bars. I got a carton and started hailing a truck. A grenade I had hooked on the buttonhole of my jacket fell off, and when it hit the ground the pin fell out. The boys around me broke and ran, all but one. He reached down, picked up the darn thing, walked about 5 yards with it, and threw it into the field. Surprising thing about that was it was a kid who everyone thought would be the first to crack in a tough spot.

When the grenade went off, the convoy stopped and men sprawled all over the place thinking we were under attack. That gave me a chance to pile into the truck closest to me, which happened to have a 37-mm. cannon trailing behind it. As we started out, it became apparent that we couldn't keep up with the race with the gun trailing behind. The driver stopped, and one of the guys in the truck jumped out and unhooked the thing. Usually it takes two men to heave it off, but this kid practically threw it off. We lost our place in the convoy, but since there were no umpires around like there are on maneuvers, we crowded our way back into line.

We were moving at a good pace until the lead jeep started out of a little village ahead of us and ran headlong into a German King Tiger tank blocking the road. The talk in the truck turned sour: "Sure doesn't look like we are getting out. Throw me that peanut butter." "I wish I had a spoon, it's kind of messy this way." "Chrissake, don't be particular, give me the damn stuff." It was a screwed-up mess; no one knew what was going on and which way to go.

We had one more chance to escape back down the road we had come, and then the lead jeep hit a land mine. We were stopped cold and trapped, beaten without a fight. The order came down to line up and throw up our hands. The sergeant said, "We gotta surrender, fellas." We destroyed our weapons, cussed, and some cried, and I felt empty and lonely inside. Our fight was over. We were beat, tired, hungry, and cold, but we were still soldiers and Americans and expected treatment as such.

When we started for Europe and the war, we talked and thought about being killed or wounded, but we never thought about being captured. We were a sad and silent group when the Germans rounded us together. I had bitter thoughts of having been sold out, and it hurt to have to throw up my hands in defeat. It hurt inside. I pulled out my wallet and looked at the pictures of home and family I had inside one last time. I didn't want the Germans leering at the pictures, so I tore them up and threw my wallet into the mud. The men around me were doing the same as I, and when each man had paid his respects to home, we shook ourselves back to reality and began looking for our buddies.

Our officers told us to throw everything away: "Get rid of your helmets, throw away your knives, and leave your canteens here." We stood around doing nothing for about two hours after surrendering, waiting for orders. Finally Germans began popping up around us from all sides, and it was evident that surrendering had been the right thing to do. We would have been decimated had we not surrendered. Nobody panicked, I think because we were all too tired and confused, but we couldn't believe what was happening. The Germans looked as frightened, tired, dirty, and beat up as we did. Some of the Germans appeared nervous, and that made us a little nervous, too.

They motioned for us to start walking double-time down the road, and we were taken into the square of a small town nearby. The Germans in the town were too busy learning how to drive our trucks and eating our chow to bother with us. When it started to get dark we were herded into a courtyard. In the yard were a few apple trees and on the ground some frozen apples, and I was lucky enough to get one of the apples. A German came into the yard and said, "You will spend the night here. Your latrine is over there. If anyone tries to escape, all will be shot."

For a time we sang. Christmas was just a few days off, so the carols filled our minds with thoughts of home. We sang until the Germans complained that it kept them awake and we must stop or be shot. We lay next to and on top of each other to keep warm. It drizzled all night, and we were soaked to the skin by morning. None of us slept much that night even though we were all dead tired.

In the early-morning hours of December 20 we were lined up four abreast in groups of one hundred and told to start walking and that we would get a break at the end of 18 kilometers. The walking in the morning didn't bother us, and by noon we stopped in a village full of a Panzer Grenadier outfit. These were young, tough-looking troops, and they came up to us, pointed at our overshoes, and jabbed us with their rifle, which was our cue to hand them over. We got stripped of our overshoes and anything else they felt they wanted. About six spuds were thrown out of a window to better than one thousand men. The men fought for the spuds, and the Germans laughed at us.

We resumed our march, and as time went by we grew more and more thirsty, so every time we got a break in the hike we looked for water in the ditches. It was dirty and frozen over, but we were thirsty so we broke the ice and took our fill. As we walked along we ate the ice. By nightfall the march was beginning to take effect on us. Boys were stumbling, and then the column began getting strung out on the road. We passed through a village, and the Germans allowed those who couldn't make it further to spend the night. Our general attitude was that we had to help each other along, and most could still walk but were so tired they needed someone to lean on for direction. We were determined that if the German guards could make it, then we could, too. It didn't work so well as it got later into the night, however, because they kept changing guards and relaying us along. We kept asking how much further, and the guards said, "Six more kilometers." When we walked the six we asked again, and they replied, "Six more kilometers." It was a stall because the guards didn't know any more about it than we did. We passed German troops heading in the opposite direction in tanks, trucks, armored vehicles, and many horse-drawn wagons. I was thinking, "How the hell could a horse-drawn army be beating us?" But at the time they were, and it felt awful.

At about one-thirty in the morning of December 21 we got to a railhead. There was no place to sleep, but we were dead on our feet, so we curled up in little patches of men and slept fitfully. At about four in the morning I untangled myself from the ball of men I had been sleeping with and started looking for water. I couldn't find any, so I bumped my way back to my former sleeping place and worked my way into the pile.

When daylight came we discovered we were a few yards from a stream. The guards were touchy and didn't want us getting to it, and our officers warned us to stay away from it because it was beyond doubt polluted. One of the guys in our gang gave me his canteen, and I made about six trips to the stream. We had halazone tablets, so we threw them in the canteen. The directions said to shake well and let settle for one half-hour, but we shook well and drank the stuff. We were thirsty, and we wanted and needed water then, not one half-hour later.

Around noon we received our first food in three days. Each man was given two packages of hardtack biscuits, and a can of cheese was issued for every seven men. After we ate, we were put back into line and marched to the railway yards. We passed by a group of homes, and the civilians were watching us from the windows. Some small boys dressed in military uniforms were making disdainful gestures at us, and on the other side an elderly couple was allowing some of our men to enter their home to get some water and worked like horses hauling water out for us until the guards stopped them. Those poor people were helping us as best they could, and it made me realize that while Germany as a nation was rotten, its people were human beings with hearts and minds open to good things.

About an hour after we passed the elderly couple we reached the train platforms. An engine came into the yard pulling a load of boxcars. We soon discovered they were full of straw and had just been emptied of horses, but not of what the horses had left in the car. Sixty men were herded into each car, and with some jockeying the Engineers all managed to stick together, and we all got into the same car. I managed to get in one corner that had some straw the horses had left behind, and I settled down. There were no vents in the car that I could see, and soon the air became too hot and sticky for comfort. Some of the men became panic-stricken because of the stories they had read about the death trains and such. We reasoned that if horses had been kept in the cars, there must have been some means of ventilation. After stumbling around and feeling the walls, we discovered two windows about 2 feet long and 8 inches high, and opened them. One of the windows was in my corner, so I got plenty of air and a good look at Germany as we rolled out of the town.

The fact that I was near the window had its drawbacks, however, as I had to serve as the "helmet man." The little bit of (and kind of) food we had eaten, the water we had had to drink, and the fact that we were dead on our feet brought on dysentery, or the "GIs," as we called them. I'd be dozing and suddenly a voice would yell for the helmet. "Chrissake, hurry!" Then after a short time the helmet would come back to me out of the darkness, and I'd throw the contents out the window. The same process was carried out when we had to urinate, only instead of the helmet we used one of the cheese cans, and the cry for it wasn't as pressing as the cry for the helmet usually was.

The hours passed by somehow. There were times we just sat in some yard and others we'd moved at a good clip for a couple hours and then stop and back up half the distance we had traveled. Water became our main want. There wasn't any talk about lack of water because everyone knew that everyone else was in need of it, and talking about it wouldn't help. When we stopped, we would holler "Wasser" or "Essen" at the guards, but they'd shrug their shoulders and walk up and down the side of the train. We slept on and off and tried to work out some way where each man would have room to sit in, but it couldn't be done; there just wasn't room. Quite often during the ride a voice would wake us up yelling, "Get that damn foot off my face!" Sometimes it was my voice.

We talked about the way German prisoners of war in the States were treated, and it didn't seem fair. We had heard stories of Germans going to the States to relax on farms and how some German officers were actually paid monthly allowance. We talked about us working on a farm for some Germans after resting up in a prisoner-of-war camp. All the way we were disillusioned.

On the 23rd we went through Koblenz and got our first look at the Rhine River on our way to Limburg, Germany. When we arrived in Limburg we were stopped in the rail yard for about an hour when another trainload of prisoners pulled alongside us a few tracks over. We could see their patches, and they were from the 28th Division, and we assumed they had been hit as hard as we had.

That night as we lay in the rail yard in Limburg the air raid siren started to sound. An engine that was pulling alongside us stopped abruptly, and the engineer and fireman jumped out and ran. I heard the heavy drone of a flight of planes, and we sat there and sweated. I watched out the window and saw my Christmas tree: the lead plane dropped a flare that burst about 200 feet in the air above, and I exclaimed to the others how the burning red, purple, orange, and yellow lights actually looked like a Christmas tree. Then things started happening.

The first bomb landed with a WHOMP! I watched out of the window, and each time a bomb hit I dropped to the floor. Guys were yelling, and everyone was feeling pretty scared. Voices began shouting, "Crawl out the window if the train gets hit and starts burning!" I couldn't see myself half in and half out when one of those babies hit nearby. A man at the other end of the car was talked into climbing out of the window. As he crawled out, the guard, who was lying in a ditch scared to death, spotted him and said in a pleading voice, "Good soldier, don't run." The man paid no attention to the guard and crawled under the car and unwired the door. We opened the cars nearest to us and then we started looking for water. The bombs scared us plenty, but right then we needed water, and that was our chance.

We found a ditch frozen over and managed to get our fill from it. By then the bombing had stopped, and the guards were getting worked up and started shooting in the air now and then, so we worked our way back to the train. The air raid siren sounded several times during the night, but none of the planes that caused the alarm gave us a visit. We spent that night waiting for another attack and cussing each other up and down for getting panicky. We learned months later that eight men were killed and thirty-six wounded in the bombing that night.

The next day was the 24th and Christmas Eve, and we were still in the yards. Two of our chaplains came up and told us that the bombers had wrecked the tracks up ahead, and it had to be fixed before we could move on. We got some food, which consisted of a loaf of German black bread and a dab of jam. It was more than we could handle in our weakened condition, and the taste and texture of the bread was something new to us. A few of the boys were too sick to even bite. The rest of us ate some and threw the rest away or jammed it in our pockets.

When night came we were still in the yards and worried about being bombed again. We debated if the Air Corps would bomb on Christmas Eve: "They won't bomb on Christmas Eve." "The hell they won't. They're out to win this war, and fast." No bombs came that night, and somewhere along the line of cars a Christmas carol was being sung. Back and forth the carols went, first from our train, then from the other train. That lasted for about an hour or so, then the Catholic boys in our car said their rosary while the rest of us were silent with our own separate kind of prayers, and we settled down to sleep and wait.

Christmas morning found us in the same yard, and as thirsty as ever. Sometime during the morning we started moving again, and our spirits picked up. As we moved through the yards we could see the damage the bombers had caused, and we thanked our lucky stars we were still alive.

By late afternoon the train pulled into a little village just past Frankfurt called Bad Orb. We gathered our belongings, and after a lot of talking among a group of German officers and troops, we were let out. We were lined up in columns of four and waited. Civilians gathered around the ring of guards and just looked. I couldn't see any expressions in any of their faces except pity in a few. We drew ourselves up and tried to look like U.S. soldiers, and we did right well, if you ask me, considering the condition our clothes and bodies were in. It was getting cold fast, and finally we headed out of town and up the mountains. "Three kilometers," the guards told us. I guess it was about that distance, but it was a tough climb.

As we reached the top of the hill, we got a glimpse of our new home through the woods, Stalag IX B. We were marched to the entrance, then around the camp to the rear. There was snow there, so I dropped out of line and grabbed a handful and started back into line, but a guard grabbed me and said, *"Nicht gut"* and motioned to his stomach. He was right, but I was thirsty, so when he wasn't looking I got another handful, and it helped quench my thirst.

The column came to a halt, and the gates opened. As we walked in, faces peered out of the barbed wire. They were Russian troops who came out to greet us, and they were smiling and yelling, *"Russkie! Russkie!"* We smiled and feebly waved as we marched by. It was Christmas Day, and the gates of freedom closed behind us. Wasn't much of a Christmas, but after the battle, the march, and the train ride, this was a place to rest.

We were herded into a quadrangle in the center of the camp and separated. Noncoms, T/5 and up, were moved off first. They emptied their pockets for inspection by the German guards, then lined up and marched to their barracks. After the noncoms the rest of us went through the same process. Again, my group of Engineers managed to stick together, and we were all put in the same building.

The barracks we were led to was a huge barnlike building about 100 feet long and 40 feet wide. Along each side of the room were triple-decker wooden bunks, and two men slept on each layer. The second day in camp some of us were moved to Barracks 24, and each man was issued one half-blanket. My bunkmate and I soon found that one half-blanket under us and one half-blanket and my overcoat on top of us was the warmest way to sleep.

Each layer had a mattress cover stuffed with straw serving as the mattress. The straw was infested with lice and fleas, and every night they would go on maneuvers. Wherever your clothes were tight around your body—the wrists, the ankles, and under the belt—was where they congregated and ate their meals. If there was any humor to this infestation, it was to watch a man sneak up to his bunk, gently take hold of his blanket, fling it back, and flail frantically at the fleas as they leaped about. A major pastime was searching the seams of our clothes, killing lice. As the days warmed up to spring, you could look anywhere around the camp and find groups of men searching their clothes and gossiping like a bunch of old women at a quilting bee.

The windows were about 10 feet apart and laced over with barbed wire. In the middle of the room was an aisle running between the ends of the bunks, and at each end of the barracks there were two cast-iron wood stoves. The stoves were the center of any social gathering in the barracks, and at any time of the day or night you could find at least two or three men standing around the stove talking and holding their hands out to get warm, even when there was no fire in the stove.

After we picked our bunks, we climbed into them and waited for the next move. Our barracks guard came in and introduced himself to us. He was a sergeant and, I should judge, about fifty years old. He explained to us, through one of our men who could speak German, the rules and regulations of the camp. We could not use the inside toilet during the day or when the barracks were unlocked. We were not to lie on the bunks with our shoes on. We were to salute all the German officers, stand count twice a day, and many other minor rules. After he had his say, he left us to ourselves.

A short time later the guard came in and yelled, *"Essen!"* and out we bolted. He lined us up in columns of four and counted us off. We walked across the parade grounds and up ahead around the corner of a building there was a rattling of tin and exclamations. As my turn to round the corner came, a rusty tin can with a wire handle on it was shoved at me, and I had my mess gear. The can was about the size of a coffee can. It was dirty and rusty, but it was all I had to eat from, so I used it. A guard pointed down the street to where the kitchen was. I moved along and stuck my bucket into a steaming window and watched a huge Russian dip his liter-ladle into a barrel of soup and dump it into my outstretched can. Then I headed for the barracks.

Very few if any of us had ever eaten anything quite like the soup we were given. It was made of something green, and for lack of anything better to call it we labeled it "greens," with a few decorative phrases usually tacked on. The stuff wasn't that good, and some of the fellas couldn't eat the stuff. Of those that couldn't, there were two types: those too sick to eat it and those too squeamish to eat it. I was neither, so I gladly helped one of the squeamish guys finish his. There were two kinds of sick men: those truly sick and those mother's boys who just wanted sympathy. The sick ones we did our best for, and the others we let alone. You could pick the men from the boys.

We received three "meals" a day. Breakfast was one can (the one handed out to us the first day in camp) of something that two Russian prisoners served to us in our barracks at about nine o'clock in the morning. We were never sure what it was, coffee or tea. We found all sorts of odd things in this part of our daily menu; the most common were pine needles and small twigs. Before long the "coffee" or "tea" was used mainly to wash and shave, because it was warm when delivered.

The second meal of each day was the green soup. By barracks, the men would form a mess line and proceed past the window in the kitchen building. Each man would thrust his can in the window with some plea: "Dig deep" or "Find the meat and get some solids." On most days the weather was cold, so everyone headed for the barracks. Each man would immediately eat his soup, hunched over his can. We looked like hungry dogs wary that someone would come along and kick us away from our food.

Our last meal of the day was served about four o'clock in the afternoon and was German black bread, and about every other day a dab of jam, a slice of blood sausage, or something similar to cheese, cottage or otherwise, was added.

Food was always in our thoughts. I started craving breakfast foods, and this was my body dictating what it needed, because I have never been a fan of breakfast foods. I remember dreaming of roast beef dinner with mashed potatoes and gravy. I actually could smell the gravy, but I couldn't eat it, and I woke myself up crying. Each of us would make up elaborate meals we would have when we got home, and we would try to outdo each other with our menus.

In early January we were issued a form that when folded properly became a letter envelope and was delivered to the German Red Cross and was then sent to the address in the States. I sent this first letter to my folks, knowing that as soon as they heard from me they would call Jean, who I had become engaged with before I had shipped overseas. As I remember, my letter explained where I was, how I was (well, but not happy where I was), and from there I listed the things to send in their Red Cross package. Everything I listed was something to eat, and I filled all the space in the letter with names of foodstuffs. I learned after the war my folks first heard I was OK on March 9, which was my father's birthday present that year.

The days moped along in a slow and dreary procession. "Dreary" is the word I think best describes the air of being in the camp. Winter was the worst time of year to be in a prisoner-of-war camp enduring the short, cold, and foodless days. All of us were losing weight by the pound. I started out at about 145 good solid pounds; when I was liberated I weighed about 100 pounds, and I was in better shape than a great many of the men.

Fortunately we were issued Red Cross packages at the end of January. Each package was designed to feed one man for seven days, or seven men for one day. Each box had five packages of cigarettes, a box of prunes, raisins, a can of powdered milk, liver paté, sugar, canned meat, crackers, and the like. Anything that could be counted piece by piece was divided among the sixteen men who had to share each package. The powdered milk and sugar, etc., was divided into sixteen piles. We then drew lots to see who got the first choice and so on until it was all distributed evenly.

The Red Cross packages also contained vitamin pills, and everyone was asked to, and did, turn them in to the camp hospital. This was about the only medicine the doctors had to work with, and all kinds of illnesses were showing up. Malnutrition speeds up flaws in the body, and about a man a day was dying. When the first man died, the body was wheeled through the camp with the chaplain and a six-man burial detail following behind. The camp ignored the whole thing. When the next burial detail went from the hospital through the camp to the gate, the entire camp fell out and saluted the body. Each body after that was paid this respect.

The camp cemetery was about a mile outside the camp and in the woods on the slope of a hill. There were about six men already buried there when I was assigned to burial detail. Someone else had already dug the grave, and I am sure we would not have had the strength to do it. The chaplain read the burial service, and we covered the body and returned to camp. The walk and shoveling wore me out for the rest of the day, and I suppose the emotional experience drained me, too.

Trading was a way of life in the camp, and cigarettes were the medium of exchange. One cigarette was worth two dollars cash money. A carton could buy the finest watch in camp. With the sudden riches of the Red Cross boxes, the gamblers went into business. Lotteries were set up. A man would sell ten chances, one cigarette per chance, on a prize of seven or eight cigarettes. I was lucky and won in two of the lotteries I bought into; I don't recall how many I bought into, but it was probably only five or six. This action and carnival-like atmosphere roused one of the men who had given up back into living again. Some of the men simply gave up, turned to the wall, and died. This always puzzled me. I always thought things couldn't get worse, so they had to get better.

On most nights we could hear flights of bombers in the sky. Some nights we could hear bombing and see a glow in the distant sky. We were south and east of Frankfurt and not too far from Hanau. It was probably Frankfurt getting hit. One night a lone plane went over and ditched a bomb. It hit not too far from camp and made us rather nervous about the whole idea. The Germans were rather upset the next day and removed the light bulbs from all the barracks. They thought someone had figured out a way to bypass the master light switch and had signaled the plane. We all figured it was a straggler just dumping his load to lighten up his ship for the run home.

One night shortly after that some nut in the barracks couldn't sleep and whistled like a falling bomb. Every man in the building hit the floor. Some of the men didn't even wake up until they were on the floor, scrambling for cover. If we had found out what jackass whistled, we would have ended up in the "outcast barracks."

The outcast barracks was just that. Any man caught stealing was automatically put in that barracks. First he was thrown in the open latrine pit, and the men of the barracks where he was found stealing stood around the pit and urinated on him. Thieves that stole from their buddies were treated harshly. Stealing from the Germans was accepted practice as long as it didn't endanger anyone else. Others that ended up in the outcast barracks were those who were constantly fighting or had such disgusting habits that the men in their barracks voted them out. The men in this barracks pulled the "honey-dipping detail": their job was to dip out the latrine and haul the mess away. This punishment deterred a lot of thieves, I'm sure. The outcast barracks had nothing in it at all. The men slept on the floor. I'm sure it was hell on earth.

In early February we heard some fighters not too far off engaged in a dogfight. We didn't think anything of it until our planes chasing a German unknowingly shot up a few of our barracks. A couple guys in my barrack were wounded, and one or two in another that was in the line of fire were killed. Everyone was plane-shy after that incident, and many an anxious eye was cast skyward whenever the fighters came within earshot. That day we carried lime from the pile that was used for the latrine and spelled out in huge letters, "p-o-w." The next day one of our fighters flew over and circled the camp wagging his wings and waving. This cheered us because we felt someone now knew where we were.

As March arrived, the weather was improving and we were spending more time outside. The war was moving closer to us daily. Attack bombers were in sight and sound often, which cheered us greatly. The axiom was, "Where there are attack bombers, the foot soldiers follow." These bombers and fighters caused us problems, however, because they would attack anything on the roads that moved, including supply trucks. For a while there was no salt in the camp. The soup was bad enough, but without salt it was deadly. We also had shortages of bread, and we deduced the Germans were telling us the truth—that it was caused by Allied strafing—when one guy in my barrack found a .50-cal. slug in a loaf of bread.

Each night after our nightly count one of the Germans would give us the German version of the war news. We would eliminate what we felt was German propaganda and couple that with the bombings we could hear, the planes we could see, and things kept looking better and better. One night one of the older guards remarked to me, "Pretty soon" and raised his hands in the air, indicating that he would soon be the prisoner.

From about the 20th of March on, our morale went up and down like a yo-yo. Rumors were flying around camp that some of the men had been let out of camp to make contact with the GIs. The Germans were less strict in taking the correct count and were not insisting on our saluting them.

April 1, Easter Sunday, was a waiting day. We could hear the small-arms fire and smell the smells of war, but we couldn't see the fighting. To be quite frank, none of us were in a hurry to go looking for the war. We had lived this long and didn't want a stray bullet to get us now. That day most of the German guards melted away, and by evening there were no Germans around.

On the morning of April 2, three American tanks rode over the gates of the camp, and we were liberated. The troops that followed were front-line infantry, but what little they had they gave to us. It was pure joy to see those big smelly American tanks and trucks roll into our camp. I cannot describe all the emotions we shared. The very next day the Red Cross arrived, and women handed out coffee and donuts. All I could think was what a great Army we had.

Looking back I can close my eyes and picture Stalag IX B, but I have trouble realizing this all happened to me. I do know that I have had my testing in life. A man doesn't know what he can endure until he is tested to his limits, and then far beyond limits he never imagined. Better than two-thirds of the 106th Division was captured in the Battle of the Bulge. The knock against the 106th all these years was that we weren't well trained, but I frankly thought as Engineers we were very well trained, and our predicament during the Bulge was not any fault of our training.

I don't know anything about heroes, but if there were any heroes among the prisoners of war, they would have most likely been the prisoners from the Pacific war. They would also have been the airmen who were captured in the earliest days of the war when they started bombing targets in Europe. I was a prisoner of war for only three months, while those brave men were prisoners of war for years.

E. MASON HENDRICKSON

Hagerstown, Maryland

355th Fighter Group, U.S. Army Air Corps

E. Mason Hendrickson

Edwin Mason Hendrickson was born in Frederick, Maryland, on February 11, 1922. After graduating from Frederick High School in 1939, he attended Washington and Lee University and enlisted in the Army Air Corps at the completion of his sophomore year. Selected as a fighter pilot, he flew sixty-six combat missions in the North American P-51 fighter. In addition to scoring two aerial victories, he is a recipient of the Distinguished Flying Cross and four Air Medals. After the war Hendrickson graduated from the University of Maryland and worked in industry and banking until his retirement in 1987. He and his wife, Virginia, were married in 1943 and have three children and eight grandchildren.

I was a sophomore in college when the Japanese bombed Pearl Harbor on December 7, 1941. During the following two weeks I think every man on campus was exploring what branch of the military he wanted to join. All conversations were about how each of us could get into the military as soon as possible to help support the war effort. My two brothers served in the Navy during the war, but I was still undecided when some friends who were already in the Marine Corps reserves suggested that I join the Marines. I went down to the Marine recruiting office, but it was closed. I knew I had an equal interest in the Army Air Corps and their office was open, so I walked in and enlisted in the Air Corps. Looking back, I am very glad their office was open that day. So many men had enlisted in the Air Corps that I was informed I would have to complete my sophomore year before I was called to duty. I worked through the following summer in a defense plant in Frederick making electronics components until eventually being called to duty in September of 1942.

I was anxious to enter the Air Corps and spent the summer wishing I had been called to active duty sooner. When my time eventually came I was sent to a classification center in Nashville, Tennessee, where I joined other recruits for physical, psychological, and intelligence screening to determine our most appropriate placement in the Air Corps. Most examinations were academic and geared towards measuring our ability to construct commonsense solutions to complex problems. I was classified to train as a pilot, navigator, or bombardier. Inasmuch as the Air Corps was in desperate need of navigators to fill their depleted ranks from losses in bombers over Europe, I was fortunate not to have been assigned to that function.

After qualifying for pilot training I entered preflight training at Maxwell Field in Alabama. I was given academic training in mathematics and physics related to aviation. Two months later I progressed to primary flight school in Americus, Georgia, where I flew a training aircraft called the Stearman PT-17. Each step in my pilot training was a screening process to weed out men who were not suited to be pilots, and primary schooling was the first opportunity for the Air Corps to determine who lacked the coordination to correctly handle a plane in flight, and many men in my class were dismissed. After eight hours of instructed flying I flew solo for the first time and began to perform aerobatics for no reason other than it showed I had a good command of controlling the aircraft. After graduating from primary, I was sent to basic training, where I flew another more advanced trainer aircraft called the Vultee PT-13, or "Vultee Vibrator," as it was affectionately known by the instructors and students. The Vultee was a much more powerful plane, and I continued to advance my flying and navigation skills, flying cross-country and at night for the first time.

At the conclusion of our training each cadet was assigned to either a single-engine or multiengine bomber aircraft at a field for advanced training. The Air Corps conducted the selection process to place men in aircraft they thought they were best suited to fly based on the abilities and skills each cadet had demonstrated during his training. I think my size, coordination, and ability to make quick decisions were among the factors enabling me to become a fighter pilot. Fighter pilots as a group were not tall in stature, averaging 5 feet 9 inches in height, so perhaps my stature at 5 feet 10 inches was a factor in my selection. I imagine I could have flown a B-17, but perhaps not as well as the men who eventually flew it. I did not consider myself a superior pilot to anyone else, but I was elated to have the opportunity to become a fighter pilot, because I felt I had endured and prevailed through the extensive screening process. My selection to fly a fighter gave me a tremendous feeling of confidence in my flying ability.

My training had been hurried so the Air Corps could field the men necessary for the war effort, but I believe I was well prepared, and I was generally optimistic about my abilities to survive in combat. I was not ignorant of the losses occurring in combat over France and Germany in planes and pilots, and I had no illusions about the great dangers each mission would pose to my life.

No contest, the greatest propeller-driven fighter of the Second World War was the P-51D Mustang. In 1943 the P-51D Mustang was equipped with the Rolls Royce Merlin engine, which added 300 more horsepower and included a supercharger that gave it a 50-mph speed advantage over the German FW-190 and ME-109. The Mustang used half the fuel of other American fighters, and its 425-gallon fuel tank gave it a 1,080-mile range that could be extended to 2,600 miles with the use of two 110-gallon drop tanks. When the long-range Merlin-powered P-51D appeared to escort the B-17s and B-29s deep into Germany, the advantage in the air battle over Europe passed to the Allies. Over fifteen thousand P-51s were built during the war.

I received my wings and commission as a second lieutenant in August of 1943 and was sent to operational training in Bartow, Florida, as part of a group of pilots who were some of the first assigned to fly the North American P-51 Mustang. I loved the Mustang from the first moment I saw it. It was sleek, and it just looked so attractive sitting on the ground. We all knew right away we had been provided with the best propeller-driven fighter in the world. When Hermann Göring, the head of the German Luftwaffe, first saw the P-51 he was recorded as saying Germany's battle for the skies of Europe was lost.

The P-51 replaced the early-model Republic P-47, which had a comparatively limited flight range of three to four hours before eventually improving later in the war. The P-51's seven-hour flight range dramatically extended the protection that could be provided to the bombers all the way to the target and back. The P-51A was a fine aircraft, but its Allison engine did not provide enough power to bring the Mustang up to the standard necessary to win the war in the air. The P-51B models were fitted with the Rolls Royce Merlin engine, giving the Mustang the speed and maneuverability for which it would become famous.

Mason Hendrickson *(standing, right)* and members of his 357th "Licking Dragons" Fighter Squadron pose for a publicity photo before a mission. The pilot on the left is the squadron's commander, Capt. Fred Ramsdell, who is demonstrating how he shot down a German FW-190 over Belgium. Over ninety pilots in the 355th Fighter Group were killed in action during Hendrickson's tour of duty. He survived sixty-six combat missions and was credited with two aerial victories.

Hendrickson flew four different versions of his "Gin Rummy" P-51 Mustang, which he named for his wife, Virginia. His first plane was a P-51B that had to be scrapped after he was jumped by an FW-190 over Luxembourg. The second was a P-51C that disappeared over Belgium while being flown by RCAF pilot Miles King on one of Mason's rest days. The third was the P-51D shown here lying on its belly after Hendrickson was forced to perform an emergency landing when the engine malfunctioned on takeoff. He walked away from the crash unharmed and flew a P-51D, "Gin Rummy IV," without incident until the end of his tour of duty.

Flying the Mustang was like flying the Cadillac of all fighters because it was very easy to handle and maneuvered wonderfully. The Mustang was relatively comfortable except for the fact that the pilot had to sit on an inflatable raft and paddles provided in case the plane was forced to ditch in the North Sea, as was a common occurrence during the war. Sitting on these for hours at a time was very uncomfortable. Another inherent discomfort of being a fighter pilot was the long flights (the longest mission I flew in combat was seven hours and ten minutes), during which I had no access to a toilet, and pilots needed as much bladder control as flying skill.

The Mustang was armed with six .50-cal. machine guns, three on each wing, and could carry two 500-pound bombs on short flights. The Mustang had five fuel tanks, three interior and two exterior 110-gallon wing tanks that could be carried in place of the bombs. Towards the end of the war we thought we could be pretty clever by strapping incendiary devices around the fuel tanks so that when we jettisoned the tanks they might make some dent on a target below us.

Men from various operational schools from all over the southeastern portion of the United States were assembled in Tallahassee, Florida, before traveling to Fort Hamilton, New York, and put on the *Ile de France* for our journey to England. There were about ten thousand men on the ship, and I bunked with twenty-four other men in a stateroom built for two people. The trip lasted ten days, and we landed in Greenock, Scotland. I joined a group of six men assigned as replacements for the 355th Fighter Group based at Steeple-Morden Airfield, and of these six men I was the only one to survive the tour of duty.

After my arrival I first flew orientation missions to familiarize myself with landmarks and the coastline so I could find my way home when coming back from missions. Life on the base was relatively comfortable compared to what the men fighting in the infantry had to endure. Our living quarters were huts with a coal stove, and at first I had one sheet and blanket, but as guys left for one reason or another I managed to obtain a good supply of sheets for a weekly change. We had an officers' club we frequently visited for drinks before supper. On occasion, dances or other entertainments were provided on Saturday nights. I never felt like I could get too relaxed, because we were given little notice before missions, and I couldn't afford to excessively indulge in our social activities or risk losing focus on the job at hand.

I had not been in England more than a few days when I developed appendicitis and had surgery the day before I was to fly my first mission in a daylight bomber raid on Berlin. I was in the hospital for three weeks before returning to duty.

After I rejoined my squadron, the 357th Fighter Squadron, I flew my first mission on April 19, 1944. I flew as wingman for my flight leader escorting bombers to a target in central Germany. Each flight consisted of four planes, and the squadron was made up of four flights, equaling sixteen fighters per squadron. Most missions my squadron flew with the other two squadrons in our 355th Fighter Group, which gave us a combined strength of forty-eight fighter planes. There was friendly competition between the three squadrons of our group, but I think we were the best because we were more disciplined than the others. Men advanced within the squadron as others completed their three-hundred-hour combat requirement and were sent home, and through attrition in combat. By the end of my tour I had worked my way up to flight leader, and I led the 357th Squadron on four missions.

I remember the first time I crossed the coastline of France and the Germans sent up a barrage of flak. It made me realize someone was shooting at me and trying to kill me. In combat I exercised caution but was never scared. Any pilot worthy of being in combat was not averse to taking the necessary risks to get the job done. It's a hardening experience when you realize that some other guy you never met wants to do everything he can to kill you and those around you. Ninety men from my group were killed or listed as missing in action during my tour of duty, and while I was saddened at their loss, my feelings of sadness never took on a sense of mourning. Pilots might have talked about what happened and wonder why the guy "didn't do this or that" to save himself. Sometimes a plane got hit squarely with flak and exploded in midair, and no matter how excellent the pilot or the crew, these unfortunate happenings caused many casualties and were considered accidents of fate. We all knew the possibility it could be you next, but if you thought about it too much you were in the wrong business to be flying in combat.

The squadron's primary mission was to escort B-17 and B-24 bombers into enemy territory and protect them from enemy planes coming to shoot them down. A typical mission involved waking at five-thirty to have breakfast followed by a briefing on what the mission was to be that day. We spent time studying our flight plan, which usually involved zigzagging in all directions in order to confuse the enemy as to what was going to be our target. The bombers took off long before us because they were much slower, so we were given the rendezvous point where we would begin our escort and information on what the secondary targets would be if the primary target were not accessible. The stream of bombers sometimes numbered two thousand and stretched for 100 miles. The fighter escort could number up to five hundred aircraft intermingled between the bomber segments to guard against the German Messerschmitt 109s and Focke-Wulf 190s that often attacked the bombers in groups of 200 or 250 aircraft.

When flying escort, we were hunters on the lookout for enemy fighters and ready to engage them before they could get to the bombers. When an enemy fighter was spotted, their location was

357th
LICKING DRAGONS"

communicated, and we reacted to how the enemy fighters moved. If they dove for the bombers, we cut them off; if they stayed in the distance, we kept an eye on them but never left the bombers. The Germans employed many tactics in an attempt to draw us from the bombers, but we never neglected our responsibility to protect the bombers. The escort was performed in shifts because our fighters had a limited fuel capacity relative to the bombers. The length of time we could cruise with the bombers was five to six hours unless additional fuel was expended warding off enemy aircraft, which further reduced our escort range. If we had enough fuel, after being relieved by another fighter squadron we would go down to a lower altitude and search for secondary targets. After the Normandy invasion we were told to hit anything that moved, and we hit our share of trains, trucks, barges, and any other things we thought had military value. We were always very mindful of our fuel levels and had to be very aware of how long it would take to make it back home.

The men in the bombers performed an essential role in our victory and paid a high price in lives because the Germans were determined to do everything they could to bring down as many bombers as possible. I remember watching fully loaded B-17s just blow up after getting hit by flak. Over the Baltic I watched a B-17 go out of control and nosedive towards the ground. Before it hit the ground, its excessive airspeed forced the plane into a loop, and as it neared the top of the loop it lost all momentum, flipping over, and then flopped onto the ground with an explosion. Each bomber contained ten men, and you couldn't help but think about the men who were in those lost bombers. I may have felt some remorse for those men, but I didn't have any guilt about losing a bomber, because every man who suited up and went into the air had to accept the fact that these things happened and to get on with our jobs.

Communication between the bombers and our fighters was kept to a bare minimum. Pilots using unnecessary chatter were dealt with very strictly by the commanding officers when the offender returned to base. Once when returning from a mission I had become separated from my squadron, and I came upon a lone B-17 headed in a southerly direction rather than a westerly direction towards England. I could see the bomber had been damaged, and it was flying on three of its four engines. I radioed the B-17 and asked if they knew where they were headed, and the pilot said their navigator was unconscious and they were losing fuel. I was also low on fuel, but I decided to lower my flaps to reduce my airspeed so I could fly alongside the bomber, and I guided the bomber to Manston Base coded as "Bluefrock." I followed the bomber into the base, and after it landed the pilot called and asked if I would land so they could say thanks, but I wanted to get home as much as they did, so I just wished them luck and headed back to base.

While returning from a mission in the area of Munich, my flight spotted two B-17s who were straggling behind the others, and they had a swarm of ME-109s on their tail. We dove down on the fighters, and I was able to tack on the tail of a 109 without him seeing me approach, making it relatively easy for me to shoot him down and earn my first kill of an enemy fighter. Coming out of the dive, I slid into a position to fire at another 109, and I hit it with a deflection shot by firing ahead of the 109 by estimating its direction and speed. I am not sure where I hit the 109, but the pilot bailed out, and I was credited with destroying my second enemy aircraft.

It was personally rewarding to register those two kills, but I didn't celebrate in any way because my accomplishment was trivial in comparison to those of the fighter group as a whole. On April 24, 1944, the 355th Fighter Group destroyed twenty German fighters, which at the time was the greatest single daily tally during the war of any group. In addition, individual pilots, on both sides, accumulated large numbers of enemy kills, and these men had an unusual natural talent in handling their aircraft that deserves admiration. These men perfected the art of aerial dogfighting and were extraordinary pilots. I don't think the two pilots I shot down were very experienced, and in general we found the pilots like the two I shot down in southern Germany were not nearly as good as those defending key military installations and cities in northern Germany.

I was hit three times in combat, twice from flak and once by an enemy aircraft while over Luxembourg. Immediately after the order was given to drop our external fuel tanks, I heard this thud, and I just thought somebody's fuel tank had hit my plane. When I looked back to see if anything was damaged I was shocked to find a Focke-Wulf 190 on my tail firing its 20-mm. guns at me. I had been flying at 17,000 feet just under an overcast cloud layer, and the 190 pilot was clever enough to jump me from the clouds. My Mustang went into a spin, and I remember thinking if I dropped below 10,000 feet I would bail out, but I was able to regain control. Had the 190 pilot followed my descent he surely would have finished me off, but he probably felt confident chalking me up as a kill and took off for home. He'll never know I was lucky enough to regain control and limp back to base with very limited speed and control.

I flew three hundred hours in combat and was glad to get back to the States with all my skin intact. I would be hesitant to pick one person or group of people as the real heroes of the Second World War. My whole philosophy during the war was based on teamwork, and it was the teamwork between everyone who put on a uniform that won the war.

JAMES A. KANE

Baltimore, Maryland

92nd Infantry Division, U.S. Army Medical Corps

James Albert Kane was born in Baltimore, Maryland, on July 31, 1921. He was one of twelve children, and all six Kane brothers served their country in the armed forces, four during the Second World War. He graduated from Dunbar High School in 1942 and then worked for Bethlehem Steel, becoming the first black welder in the company's history. He was drafted into the Army in 1943 and served as a medic until losing his right leg when he stepped on a mine while attempting to reach a wounded soldier in Italy. He is a recipient of the Purple Heart and the Bronze Star for valor in recognition of his actions in Italy. After the war Kane returned to Baltimore and continued his career with Bethlehem Steel until retiring in 1971. He married his late wife, Kathleen, in 1951 and has one son.

I was born and bred in Baltimore, having been born on Carlisle Street, since renamed Ellsworth Street. In 1942 I was very proud to have graduated in the second class in the history of Dunbar High School. One of my fondest memories at Dunbar was from the football program we started in my junior year. We had to scrape together uniforms discarded by other high schools, and we played with mismatched tops, bottoms, shoes, and our uniforms covered every shade in the rainbow. In October of 1940 we traveled to Manassas, Virginia, to play Parker Gray High School. The first touchdown in school history was a 45-yard pass to me thrown by Melvin Hurt, who became Colonel Hurt, as he was known in the United States Army. Classmate Paul Straver, a future captain in the Army, threw a block for me, opening the way for our first touchdown. I had no idea what to do after I scored. I may have invented the first touchdown dance when I rolled around on the ground for a few seconds in celebration.

After graduation I became an employee of the Bethlehem Steel Corporation. I worked for Bethlehem Steel until December 1942, when I received my greetings from Uncle Sam informing me that my services were required in the United States Army. I worked loading coke into the blast furnaces. It was a hard and dirty job, and I wasn't enjoying it very much and aspired to better my position. I applied for admission to one of the welding schools established by the Defense Department as soon as I acquired the necessary 320 working hours making me eligible. I passed the entry exam and was accepted and eventually became the first black welder to work at Bethlehem Steel. I was issued the necessary equipment and assigned to the ERS (Electrical Repair Shop) and worked in the number 2 yard. I remember the first day on the job very well. As you might expect to see in those days, not too many of the white workers were happy to see my black face as a welder, and I was greeted with a barrage of names and other taunts. The white boys went on strike rather than work alongside me until the government gave them an ultimatum to go back to work or face being drafted. I endured months of name-calling and harassment until I was drafted myself.

I didn't hesitate once about fulfilling my duty to my country. My older brother was already in the Army and enrolled in officer candidate school, and I was actually excited about the opportunity to enter officer candidate school, too. Some people today ask why I would think of fighting for a country in which my color segregated me from the general society. I answer by saying I love my country, as much as any other man, perhaps more so than many. Uncle Sam needed me, and I was proud to have the opportunity to serve. Besides, if I had learned anything in my life at this point, it was when the government called you, you better show up.

I reported to duty at Fort Meade, Maryland, and was placed in a segregated unit, since no part of the service was integrated in 1943. I was assigned to the 3rd Service Command, which was made up of boys from Maryland, Virginia, Washington, D.C., Pennsylvania, and Delaware. I was sent to Fort Clark, Texas, for basic training and joined the 10th Cavalry Regiment. The 10th Calvary Regiment was an all-black outfit except for the commanding officers that were all white. The first few weeks were a little rough for the black draftees. Our drill sergeants were tough white boys from the South, and I think they had a lower opinion of our purpose in the Army than we would have wished. When they said "Jump," we said "How high"? and we all worked hard to earn their respect. I saw punishments inflicted on soldiers that probably didn't warrant the infraction. Soldiers were often singled out for arbitrary punishment and taken to a field where they dragged heavy chains back and forth until allowed to stop. There was a unit from Michigan, and being Northern boys they objected more to this treatment than boys from the Southern states. These Northern boys were subjected to even harsher treatment, including beatings. I know this sounds unbelievable to some today, but it happened just the way I am describing it. I think every one of us had to fight our resentment for this treatment to justify our existence in the Army. I naturally had thoughts of fighting back and getting even, but it was wiser to keep cool and concentrate on moving on. Other soldiers who thought like me were able to stay out of trouble, and we saw beyond the treatment, and within six months I saw an opportunity to move on.

I am not sure exactly how I became assigned to the Medical Corps. Perhaps I showed my dislike for carrying a gun and killing, and perhaps someone in the Army saw I had some education. Either way, it was a ticket to move on. I was shipped to Fitzsimmons Army Hospital near Denver, Colorado. I began a course to study basic medicine making me a Medical Corpsman. I studied physiology, chemistry, and other related sciences. After seven weeks I learned I was qualified for Army specialized training (AST). All AST candidates had to be twenty-two years of age or younger, a high school graduate, and have an IQ of 115 or better.

The AST school was located at Fort Collins, Colorado, on the campus of Colorado State College. I began courses in English, math, and chemistry, and I did well on my exams. Events conspired against me, and it wasn't long before I was removed from the school. There was a movement by married women to keep their husbands at home, and as a result they discontinued these advanced courses to send us single men back into the regular Army.

In March of 1944 I was assigned to the 371st Infantry Regiment of the all-black 92nd Division, which was on maneuvers in the vicinity of Merryville and DeRidder, Louisiana. The 92nd took on the name "Buffalo Soldiers," which is a name given to black soldiers that dates back to the wars with Plains Indians in the West. The Indians nicknamed the black soldiers "buffalos" in honor of their ferocious fighting ability and because of the way the soldiers wore their long, curly black hair that resembled the mane of a buffalo.

The most memorable part of our stay in Louisiana was the swarms of hungry mosquitoes. Someone must have told the mosquitoes we were coming, and they could bite through anything to get to us. We conducted maneuvers, and the rough treatment by the white officers persisted. When maneuvers were complete, the division was stationed at Fort Huachuca in Arizona, and I remember it being a very tumultuous time. The 92nd Division was comprised of all black enlisted men, quite a few black second lieutenants, but the upper corps of officers was still all white. The few black captains or first lieutenants were doctors or other highly qualified specialists. The black officers were treated very poorly, especially by the young white ninety-day-wonder first lieutenants, who made life very difficult for us. Many of my fellow soldiers became extremely agitated or depressed over the harsh treatment, and this led to many cases of men pretending to be sick or mentally ill to escape. I also had thoughts about finding a way out, but there was no way. I just stuck it out and waited for our orders.

I was given a thirty-day furlough before being shipped overseas, and it was a very nice time for me, traveling across the country back to Baltimore. The fact that I was wearing a uniform did not keep a very few people who passed me on the train from calling me "nigger soldier." I had learned to ignore such people because if I reacted I could get in worse trouble, especially so far from home.

In September of 1944 the 371st Infantry Regiment was sent to Camp Patrick Henry, Virginia, and we shipped out from Newport News. This was the first time most of the men were on a ship in the ocean, and many became seasick. I was fortunate not to be among their ranks. The convoy was an unimaginable sight to behold, and there were ships as far as the eye could see. No matter in what direction I looked I saw ships of all sizes and shapes as far as I could see into the horizon. Things became really exciting when we passed through the Strait of Gibraltar, and it was the first time I heard big guns firing from the shore positions, and at what I was not sure. We passed between Sicily and Italy through the Strait of Messina, and after twenty-six days the regiment made land at Bari, Italy, located on the heel portion of Italy's boot.

My first sight in Italy was the appalling conditions of the civilians. They had gathered by the landing area half-starved and begging for whatever food we could spare. Some guys threw candy bars into the crowds, and the people fought over such a small thing. We loaded onto trains and started our journey north. We passed the ruins of Monte Cassino, and the devastation I saw was fascinating although at the same time shocking. I saw destroyed vehicles of all types everywhere. We traveled for three days, passing through Rome, until we reached our final destination of Viareggio, a staging area for the front lines.

Our regiment was to relieve portions of the all-black 366th Infantry Regiment. Black officers commanded the 366th, and despite its good combat performance, its presence was not accepted favorably with the Fifth Army leadership. We marched to the front at night, and I will never forget the terrified feeling I had sitting in the dark during an artillery barrage during that first night at the front.

As a Medical Corpsman, my job was to help GIs who were wounded in action. I carried just the basic tools for treating wounds, including bandages, sulfa powder to fight infection, and morphine to help relieve pain. I did the best I could to help the wounded, but in reality I knew as much about saving lives as a cat knows about Sunday. I had not been given much training for which to perform my duties, but I was ready to do whatever was asked.

I don't think I had too much fear in combat, except maybe for those German 88 guns we all kept an eye out for. The Germans were good soldiers, but we heard rumors about their poor treatment and even execution of black prisoners, and it made me think about it once in a while. The Germans had excellent mortar crews, and all soldiers feared getting caught in the open during a mortar attack.

When it happened, all you could do was to get your head and butt as low to the ground as possible and hope for the best.

Despite having so many people around me at all times, I think being in combat was a very personal and singular experience. Men dealt with situations during the war in very different ways. General Sherman once said, "War is hell," and I agree. War is a matter of personal survival, and I found it hard to question some man who chose to bow out by feigning sickness or wounding himself intentionally. I witnessed one soldier who shot himself in the leg with his rifle, and I think I was too shocked at his actions to react in any way but to treat his wound and send him back to an aid station. It was his way of dealing with being in combat, and I knew he would have to live with the consequences the rest of his life.

When I first arrived in Italy I was attached to Company L, 371st Infantry Regiment of the 92nd Division. We received orders to advance into the Serchio Valley in the Apennine Mountains, and we were on a daylight patrol attempting to capture a small village when our platoon was caught in a mortar barrage. Several others and I took cover under a small rock outcrop, but our Sgt. Willis Allen was hit by a mortar fragment and killed. I ran over to him and administered first aid as best I could before he lost consciousness and died. The platoon began to advance, and I had to leave Sergeant Allen behind, but not before I covered his body with some leaves to hide his body in case the Germans counterattacked. My religious nature tempted me to quickly baptize Sergeant Allen so I would feel comfortable his soul would be accepted in Heaven. Sergeant Allen was a young, tough, and fearless leader, and his death was a great loss to our outfit and me.

As we continued forward I almost immediately saw our Sergeant Thompson laying face down in the road about 30 yards ahead. I ran forward. I rolled him over and saw that he had been shot in the head, and he was dead. I remember the wound in his head looked clean and neat, like cut with a scalpel. The helmets we wore were made of steel, but they were too thin to stop anything coming at your head at high speed, especially a bullet. I thought about moving Sergeant Thompson's body back to where I had left Sergeant Allen, but he was too heavy for me to move. As I let go of his body a bullet snapped over my head and landed in the dirt behind me. I flinched and fell backwards, and then got to my feet and ran as fast as I could back to the platoon. To this day I think about if that sniper had aimed just a little bit lower I wouldn't be here talking today. I had a red cross painted on my helmet that indicated I was an unarmed medic, but that German SOB didn't pay any attention to it and tried to kill me anyway. I think I ran maybe 50 yards, but I felt like I had just run a marathon, my heart was beating so hard.

The platoon retreated, but I made a mental note of where I left Sergeants Allen and Thompson, and I pledged to return to collect their bodies. We advanced back the next day, and inexplicably, both men were gone. I hope they were picked up and properly buried by our troops.

I was very saddened in February of 1945 to come across the remains of our Lt. Col. A. H. Walker. I was bringing up the rear, and I stumbled across him sitting on the ground in a foxhole, half-buried by earth with a carbine across his lap. He was staring straight ahead, and when I tried to assist him I realized he had been hit by a shell and fatally wounded. It should be remembered that Colonel Walker was a very good man and was very kind to the black soldiers in the 371st.

During the next few months the 370th Infantry Regiment was badly mauled, and elements of my 371st and the 365th Infantry Regiment were chosen to reinforce the depleted 370th Infantry Regiment. The 92nd Division was now comprised of my 370th, the all Japanese-American 442nd Infantry Regiment, and the white 473rd Infantry Regiment. The tremendous combat record of these other regiments might have been forgotten if it wasn't for 442nd veteran Daniel Inouye and 473rd veteran Bob Dole being elected to the United States Senate. The 92nd Division was positioned near Strettoia on the west coast of Italy with an objective of advancing north along the coast. I was assigned to the Company A commander, Captain Doiranoff, who was glad to have me around because he thought it a good idea to have a medic around him at all times. If he only knew; but I figured it was safe to hang around the company commander. But the events the following day would prove me wrong.

On April 5 the division renewed its attack north, and our company received tremendous artillery and small-arms fire. It wasn't long before I heard the call, "Medic, medic." Hearing a call for a medic was always pitiful and exciting because it was a call for me into action. The artillery fire was intense, and I have to admit I had some second thoughts about running out into the incoming artillery barrage. I left Captain Doiranoff in his foxhole and ran forward in the direction of the wounded soldier. I had not moved more than 20 yards when I was thrown to the ground by an explosion. I was still conscious, so I sat up and saw the gloves I was wearing were shredded and my hands were bloody. I thought for an instant that my left leg was wounded, but when I looked down I saw most of my right leg was missing; it had been blown off when I stepped on a mine. I was numb, and I didn't feel anything. I think I remember saying, "Well, darn, look at that." I quickly placed a bandage on my leg and crawled into a nearby hole that was big enough to have been a perfect grave if I was to die. I stayed in that hole for almost a day waiting for evacuation because the medics were hesitant to move me because of the possibility of going into shock and because the fighting raged around me all day and that night. I planned my deception of feigning death in case the Germans broke through. Reinforcements arrived during the night to secure the area, and it was a very long, very noisy night. I later was told the soldier I had attempted to help before stepping on the mine had survived. I also learned the shocking news of how Captain Doiranoff and several of his men were cut down by a machine gun soon after I left his position. Doiranoff was literally cut in half.

The next morning I was placed on a stretcher and began my journey down from the hills to the field hospital. On the way down the sergeant stopped to rest, and when he ordered the march to resume one of the guys carrying my litter refused to continue carrying me. The sergeant and the soldier argued until, sitting there in amazement, I watched the sergeant remove his pistol from his holster and point it at the soldier's black face, ordering him to pick me up. The soldier grudgingly complied, and all the way down the hill I was wondering if he was going to tilt my litter sideways, sending me rolling down a hill. I remained in a field hospital for several days and received treatment for my wounds, losing the remnants of my right leg. One nice surprise was seeing my cousin, Herman Briscoe, a Corpsman in the 92nd Division, who helped me through my difficult recovery.

I was shipped back to the States on the USS *West Point* and arrived back at Newport News in May of 1945. I left the States walking and came back on a stretcher. I spent ten months in McGuire General Hospital in Richmond, Virginia, but was able to return home occasionally during the time. It took some time before I became accustomed to having only one leg. One time on returning home to Baltimore I decided to go for a bike ride down to the corner store. As I went to stop the bike I naturally leaned to my right side to use my leg to slow my speed, and it was then I realized there was no longer a right leg to use. Before I could react, I fell over and onto the end of my leg, breaking the fibula. So it was quickly back to the hospital to get fixed again.

Returning home after having lost my leg in combat for my country and having to experience the same racial prejudice and segregation was a very emotional and difficult time for me. I guess I had resentments over the thought of giving a part of my body for my country and still being subjected to the laws of segregation. I never demonstrated any outward resentment, but I sometimes felt depressed thinking that the sacrifice I endured was made in vain. I slowly learned to let go of those feelings, and I began to concentrate on the positives in my life and hope improvements would come along.

There were some people who really went out of their way to make me feel at home. The white driver of the first bus I boarded when I returned to Baltimore saw my wounded leg and insisted I sit next to him in the front of the bus, but I didn't want to make a scene and took my seat in the back of the bus. Others showed a lot of heart and feeling towards me and gave me very kind recognition for my actions. Generally, though, blacks still had to deal with the same old situations of living the life of second-class citizens, and it was a long time before we saw any real change.

As time goes on, the truth about the actions of blacks in World War II has come to light. There are some things that we can't go back and resolve, but at least the general public has some idea that blacks fought and died during the war like everyone else. I think our contributions in the war greatly changed America's impression of blacks, and I am proud to have been a part of our victory.

If I had to pick one group of people who were the real heroes of the Second World War, I would choose the Japanese soldiers who fought for America. My regiment fought next to those Japanese soldiers in Italy, and they were fantastic soldiers.

Training Tips

The following is an excerpt from a handbook on Japanese military forces published by the U.S. War Department in September 1944. The handbook was one of many published by the department during the war to provide American soldiers with insights into the fighting ability and tactics of the Japanese and German soldiers they would face in combat.

Section VI. MORALE, DISCIPLINE, AND EFFICIENCY

1. MORALE. a. The individual Japanese soldier's whole outlook and attitude to life are naturally influenced by his home life, his schooling, his particular social environment with its innumerable repressing conventions, and military training.

b. In the Japanese social system, individualism has no place. Children are taught that, as members of the family, they must obey their parents implicitly and, forgetting their own selfish desires, help each and every one of the family at all times. This system of obedience and loyalty is extended to the community and Japanese life as a whole; it permeates upward from the family unit through neighborhood associations, schools, factories, and other larger organizations, till finally the whole Japanese nation is imbued with the spirit of self-sacrifice, obedience, and loyalty to the Emperor himself.

c. Superimposed on this community structure is the indoctrination of ancestor worship and of the divine origin of the Emperor and the Japanese race. Since the restoration of the Imperial rule in 1868, the Japanese Government has laid much stress on the divine origin of the race and its titular head, and has amplified this teaching by describing Japan's warlike ventures as "divine missions." Famous examples of heroism and military feats in Japan's history are extolled on stage and screen, in literature, and on the radio; hero worship is encouraged. Regimentation of the Japanese national life by government authorities, with their numerous and all-embracing regulations, has been a feature for many centuries.

d. Throughout his military training the Japanese soldier is not allowed to forget all he has been taught in the home, school, or factory. It is drummed into him again and again while his military training proceeds by repeated lectures from unit commanders, given under the guise of "spiritual training" (Seishin Kyoiku). The object of all this concentrated spiritual training is to imbue the Japanese soldier with a spirit which can endure and even be spurred on by further endeavors when the hardships of warfare are encountered. But even though his officers appear to have an ardor which might be called fanaticism, the private soldier is characterized more by blind and unquestioning subservience to authority. The determination of the Japanese soldier to fight to the last or commit suicide rather than be taken prisoner, displayed in the early stages of the war, may be prompted partly by fear of treatment he may receive at the hands of his captors. More likely it is motivated by the disgrace which he realizes would be brought on his family should he fall into enemy hands.

2. DISCIPLINE. a. Because of his training and background the Japanese soldier is generally well-disciplined and very amenable to law and order. With firm leadership, the discipline to which he has been accustomed in Japan can be, and usually is, maintained in the field and in territories under Japanese Occupation.

b. Elated with success in war and imbued with the idea of Japanese racial superiority, the Japanese soldier is apt to adopt a superior attitude towards conquered people and to forget the strict instructions given him during military training. Nu-

JUNGLE WARFARE

SOME JAP TRICKS EXPERIENCED ON GUADALCANAL

JAPS SOMETIMES WEAR U.S. HELMETS

BEWARE OF BIRD CALLS

JAPS PICK UP OUR PASSWORDS

YOU CAN SMELL THE VARMINTS

DO NOT LET PARTY GET WITHIN KNIFING DISTANCE

HOLD YOUR GROUND AND MOW 'EM DOWN

JAP TREACHERY— THE "DEAD" COME TO LIFE

EARLY IN THE PACIFIC WAR the Army Service Forces scrambled to supply U.S. soldiers with basic information about the enemy, in one bulletin picturing the typical Japanese infantry officer's and enlisted man's uniforms and equipment, *above*. *Right:* After the Marines' bloody struggle for Guadalcanal in the late summer and fall of 1942, textbook portrayals gave way to lessons learned the hard way. "Jungle Warfare: Some Jap Tricks Experienced on Guadalcanal" warned against the cunning of the enemy, his unconventional methods, and the peculiar dangers of night fighting. The Army encouraged personnel to clip and post such training tips in common areas. Racial differences and the American view of Japanese treachery helped to account for the extraordinary viciousness of the fighting in the Pacific.

merous instances of breaches of military laws have occurred, and evidence shows that crimes of rape, plundering, drunkenness, and robbery have been committed. Cases of soldiers deserting their posts, or mutilating themselves in order to avoid taking part in combat, are not unknown, and a few cases of insubordination and desertion have been reported.

3. EFFICIENCY. It has already been shown (par. 1) that the Japanese soldier in civilian life is a subservient unit in the Japanese family system, and that individualism is discouraged. In the Army his position is similar. Army training and the Japanese social system place emphasis on teamwork rather than on individual enterprise. As a member of a squad (section), platoon, or company, the Japanese soldier meticulously performs duties allotted to him; he is an efficient cog in the machine and will carry out instructions to the letter.

WILLIAM R. KEYSER

Baltimore, Maryland
4th Marine Division, U.S. Navy Medical Corps

William Robert Keyser was born in Baltimore, Maryland, on November 30, 1924. After graduating from City College in 1942, he attended the University of Baltimore while working for the B&O Railroad as an auditor. He enlisted in the Navy in 1943 and was selected for service as a Navy Corpsman, participating in three amphibious assaults on Saipan, Tinian, and Iwo Jima with the 4th Marine Division. After the war Keyser resumed his job with the B&O Railroad and continued working until his retirement in 1985. He married his late wife, Betty, in 1947.

I grew up in northeast Baltimore on Canyon Avenue off Belair Road. I graduated from City College in 1942, and I was just a teenager when America entered the war, so I didn't think too much about the repercussions of the events going on around me. I went through the motions and registered for the draft when I turned eighteen, but I still didn't think about the war too much. I knew it was likely I would be drafted, but it seemed a long way off at the time. After graduating from City College I began working for the Baltimore and Ohio Railroad in Baltimore in their accounting division while attending the University of Baltimore at night. During the early parts of the war I was assigned to the fire watch at night on top of the B&O building. Baltimore was never bombed, so you can imagine my nights became especially dull after a while.

I received my notice to report for duty in April of 1943, and it came as no surprise to me. My uncle was in the Navy at the time, and after speaking to him I knew I wanted to be in the Navy, too. I disliked the idea of enduring all the marching and walking in the Army, and I figured I couldn't be asked to march too far on a battleship. As it turned out, I found myself at times assigned to a Marine infantry company, so the marching caught up with me regardless of my intentions. I discussed my preferences for the Navy with my father, and he called a friend stationed at the 5th Regiment Armory who was partly responsible for selecting who was being assigned to the various services. My father had a visit with the man, and I was selected for service in the Navy.

When the time came, there was nothing special to mark my entry into the Navy. So many friends had already gone off to the war, and we all knew some would never come back. It just didn't seem appropriate to celebrate or make an issue of my departure. I did say goodbye to people, but I was doing just what so many others were doing, and I was not in the least worried about what was happening to me.

I was sent to the naval training center in Bainbridge, Maryland, and put through a basic training course that tested my physical fitness and swimming skills. We were taught the basics of becoming a seaman, which included learning how to jump from a ship into the water and move away from oil in the water and other survival skills. This was all a little disconcerting for me, because it was not my intention to want to abandon ship somewhere in the middle of an ocean. After basic training I was given a choice of what I would prefer to do in the Navy, and the only activity I was denied entry to was the submarine service because I had an uneven bite that would not enable me to use a Munson lung to breathe underwater. I selected hospital corps school in Bainbridge, because it was close to home.

I remember riding the train at night between Baltimore and Bainbridge, and once we got outside Baltimore it was pitch black, and I couldn't see a thing passing by outside. The train would be packed beyond capacity with men from the various services who were on their way to Aberdeen and points beyond like Philadelphia and New York. As soon as we were moving almost everyone on the train would fall asleep, and without fail someone would walk through the train and shout, "Aberdeen, Aberdeen, next stop Aberdeen!" It was all a ruse to get some men to leave their seats, and the second the men headed for Aberdeen got up for the door, the other men standing around or sitting on the floor would wrestle for control of the vacated seats.

A period of about eight months passed since I first enlisted in the Navy and completed basic training and hospital corps school. Hospital corps school was a six-month training course that condensed nursing care into basic first aid and the application of bandages and medicines. I had scored relatively well in the school, so I was given a choice to be stationed at one of three East Coast naval hospitals, and I think I chose the one in Norfolk, Virginia. When my orders arrived I was a little shocked to see I was assigned to the hospital at the naval air station on the campus of the University of Oklahoma. Up to that moment I had no idea the Navy would have any interest in operating a base so far from the water.

I enjoyed my time at the hospital in Norman, and my most memorable experience was working in what we called the "clap shack." This is where guys who had contracted a venereal disease would be sent for treatment, and the Navy was very aggressive in finding out where the men had been so they could treat the people spreading the diseases. Almost every man who came through the doors insisted he must have gotten his particular ailment while on the toilet seat. The doctor I was working with would always say, "Well, that's a hell of a place to take a girl!"

Men came and left the hospital at Norman so fast the doors were always spinning, but it was four months before I was informed I had been assigned to the Marine Corps. I was devastated. Every Corpsman knew if you went into the Marines you were in trouble because we suffered heavy casualties along with the Marines. This was the worst assignment a Navy Corpsman could receive.

As a division of the Navy, the Marine Corps has no medical personnel of its own, so all the doctors and Corpsmen assigned to the Marines are Navy personnel. During the war a Navy medical battalion was assigned to each Marine division, and a medical company was assigned to each Marine regiment within the division. A regimental aid station was very similar in appearance to those you see on the TV show *M.A.S.H.*, without all the humor and games, I can assure you. The Marines readily accepted and respected us Navy guys because we were there to help them, and after serving with the Marines in combat I attained the highest level of respect and admiration for the Marines.

I was transferred to Camp Elliott, which was the Marine base outside of San Diego, for my indoctrination into the Marines. I arrived with fifteen other Corpsmen, and we traded our white Navy uniforms for khaki green. A drill instructor greeted our bus as soon as we entered the camp, and he immediately ran us onto the parade grounds to march us back and forth. At first the group marched in perfect unison, but then our drill instructor began barking orders faster than our untrained ears could process, and within seconds there were not two of us who moved in the same direction. From this moment on I rarely understood more than a few words those barking Marines ever said.

Our new training was all infantry tactics, similar to what every other Marine received, and it had its challenges for us Corpsmen. I think they made things particularly rough on us to get us ready. One challenge was adapting to the outdoor elements after living in the comfortable surroundings of the hospital. We shared quarters in huts, and despite my preconceived notion that San Diego was a warm place to live, I remember freezing in my bed on most nights. We kept a stove working in the middle of our hut to help keep us warm, but if we let the fire go out during the night, the pan of water we placed on its surface to provide humidity would freeze solid.

In fall of 1943 I received word our group of Corpsmen were shipping out to join a replacement battalion stationed in Honolulu on the island of Oahu, Hawaii. When I arrived I reported to the 24th Infantry Regiment of the 4th Marine Division headquarters near Hickam Field. I learned I was a replacement for a Corpsman who had been killed in the Marshall Islands. When I met my new platoon, I felt green as grass. All the Marines were young kids ages eighteen through twenty-five, except for one guy in the company who was thirty-four, and they called him "Grandpa." Despite all the countless stories I heard retold a hundred times of their fighting in the Marshall Islands, I really had no idea what these men had experienced in combat until I experienced it for myself.

We were loaded onto transports, and only after we left Oahu did we learn we were headed for combat somewhere. Two or three days into our trip they called us on deck, and the officers laid out maps and scale models of the island of Saipan in the northern Mariana Islands, located about three-quarters of the way from Hawaii to the Philippines. This was the first time we learned we were going to join the assault on the island. I don't think our arrival at Saipan came as much of a surprise to the Japanese, because Tokyo Rose had begun welcoming the 4th Marine Division to Saipan on her radio show.

The mood on the ship before our landing on Saipan was solemn. We were instructed to write a letter home, and I imagine during this time the guys who had been in combat were reflecting on past battles and began to focus on what they knew lay ahead. Those of us who had never experienced combat just waited it out with a quiet sort of jittery anxiety. Most of my time before the landing was spent checking my equipment, making sure all was in order. This included a small shoulder bag that held first aid supplies, morphine, bandages, and even some small bottles of brandy to give Marines who had been wounded or to those who needed something to help calm their nerves. I also cleaned my M1 carbine, making sure it was in good operating condition.

The first thing I was issued when I joined the Marines was a carbine and a machete. The issuing of weapons to medical "noncombatants" was technically a violation of the Geneva Convention, but the Japanese had a proven habit of shooting Corpsmen, so we armed ourselves. I never wore the red-cross armband I was given, because wearing it would have increased the odds the Japanese would have shot at me. So I used it to polish my shoes occasionally.

On the morning of June 15, 1944, I was woken by the big guns of the battleships shelling the landing beaches on Saipan. Those who could stomach some food began to eat some of the three days of rations we had been given the day before, and I had some of a "D-bar," which was a Hershey's chocolate bar fixed so it wouldn't melt in the heat, and it was like eating the hardest piece of rubber imaginable. The first waves of Marines landed at seven o'clock in the morning. I landed around two in the afternoon with my medical battalion.

The embarking into our landing craft was a tricky process. The little LCVP (landing craft, vehicle, personnel; also known as a Higgins boat) that was to take us ashore bobbed up and down in the water so much that at one moment it would be 20 feet below your feet, and the next it was near your knees. Timing your drop into the craft was essential to keep from being hurt or, worse, missing it and falling into the water. After loading the LCVP we circled in the water behind the USS *Indianapolis* waiting for the beachmaster to call us to the beach. An amphibious landing craft slowly drifted past our boat, and I could see it had taken a direct hit. I couldn't even make out any individual bodies of the men who had been killed. They were all just lumped together. This was my first image of war, and I knew then I was in the real thing.

When we landed, the beach was under heavy mortar fire, and I took cover in a huge shell hole with several other men. I had crawled to the farthest edge of the hole to look forward when I discovered to my right was a black man dressed in a Navy uniform. I had no idea how or why he had gotten on that beach, and I could tell from the look on his face he was just as scared as I was. We sort of stared at one another for a few seconds, then he smiled and said, "It sure is exciting, ain't it?" With that we both broke up laughing. I spent the night in that hole, and the next morning I was woken when something began tapping on my helmet. I propped myself up on a shoulder and found a big ugly crab had been trying to dig under my head. It scared the heck out of me, and I began throwing sand at it until it decided to retreat back to wherever it had come from.

After the landing area was secured I began working in the regimental aid station. The aid station consisted of a triage area and a large operating room manned by a number of surgeons whose primary mission was to stabilize the wounded so they could be evacuated off the island. The wounded had all types of injuries ranging from superficial bullet wounds to the more severe wounds caused by mines, mortars, and artillery or bullet wounds to the head and chest. There were so many things going on at one time I really didn't stop to notice the blood, the cries of the wounded, or the chaplains who were always giving a Herculean effort in comforting the wounded and dying men.

On more than one occasion I held the hand of a dying Marine and promised to contact his family with a message, but for the most part we all had to be noncommittal with our emotions because there were so many in desperate need of help. We had to move fast around the aid station to help them all. I wasn't being intentionally callous by remaining aloof. It was just a natural self-defense mechanism that prevented us from going insane amidst all the carnage.

Soon after our landing I was assigned to Easy Company, 2nd Infantry Battalion. Easy Company was trying to push around Mount Tapotchau located in the center of the island. During an advance I heard the call for a Corpsman, so I ran ahead to answer the call. The Marines rarely used the word "Corpsman" when in need of medical help because the Japanese recognized the word, so we normally had a code name for me, but mostly it was just "Sailor!" When I arrived I discovered a native woman and her baby lying face down on the ground without a stitch of clothing. She had been shot in the buttocks, so I patched her up and called for a stretcher to carry her away, but not before I found some cloth to cover her and placed her baby in her arms. Although we didn't speak the same language, I could tell her eyes were saying, "Thank you." I remember so many images and places from the war, but my helping this woman was one of my more cheerful experiences of the war.

My primary duty as a Corpsman was to tend to wounded Marines. I was not a doctor, and I could not repair any of the wounds, but by stopping the bleeding, bandaging their wounds, and applying morphine to alleviate the pain I at least gave them a chance to make it back to the aid station where they could be helped more. I even agreed to treat one or two injured Japanese soldiers, although I knew they would have never done the same for me or any other Marine.

Tending to wounded men in combat is hard to describe. There were so many things going on around me it is hard to remember little details of what men said or what I may have said. I do remember some images like having to cut off a Marine's leg that was hanging on by just a piece of flesh below the knee. There was nothing I could have done to save his leg, and the more pressing issue was to get him out of the battle and back to an aid station to save his life. Often, the wounded men would be hollering or crying from the pain or fear while I tended to their wounds, but you would be amazed at how often the wounded men would become at ease when their fellow Marines held their hand and told them everything would be all right. Wounded men reacted in many different ways. I witnessed men who were shot and knocked down but who got up and ran for 50 yards for cover, only to be completely paralyzed by the time I reached their position. Some just fell to the ground hollering, and others just dropped dead to the ground. Death was all around in combat, and those men who we lost were simply left behind where they fell. I had to move on, but not before I took the dead Marine's rifle, attached the bayonet if not already on, and placed it upright in the ground by the body so it could be found later.

I also had to comfort men suffering from psychological wounds. The strain on men in combat was immense, and some men could deal with it better than others. The will to survive in combat is truly amazing, and part of this involves coming to terms with the fact that we had little control over the events happening around us. Prayer was a comforting companion for many men, but some just couldn't accept their situation and were most likely to break down. I once led a man across an open field who was crying hysterically like he had just lost his best friend, and he may have. He would do anything I asked, but he just had no direction of his own. I didn't see too many men in this condition, and I never saw a Marine criticize another Marine who was in this condition because but for the grace of God, we all weren't very far from it ourselves.

It is natural to be scared in combat, but the Marines were so well trained and dedicated to the tasks at hand that I witnessed them do things in the face of almost certain death that defy explanation. I often ran across open fields under heavy fire or jumped from a completely safe place to tend to a wounded Marine, and only after it was over did I think about how stupid of a thing it was to have done. My mission was to save lives, and every time I risked my life, the reward of saving another life made all the risks I took acceptable.

Daily life in combat was just uncomfortable. We didn't have a bath for days and even weeks on end. We were encouraged to change our socks as often as we could, and every so often we were issued new clothing, but it was usually a matter of using what I had for as long as I could. The food we ate was unsavory boxed K and C rations. Later in the war the C rations included hot dogs and beans, and these became hard to find. The maddest Marine I think I ever saw was one who had just killed a Japanese soldier, and while stripping him of weapons he found multiple cans of our favored hot dogs and beans. We hadn't been able to get any for ourselves for a long time, and this Marine just went nuts thinking the Japanese were eating our best food.

When we had advanced to the far side of Saipan, our advance stalled. The Japanese defenses were an incredible maze of fortifications that had obviously been improved for a long time before we had gotten there. We bogged down at the base of some high cliffs that had deep caves in which the Japanese had positioned snipers that picked off Marines trying to approach the caves. A group of Marines eventually made it to the entrance of the biggest cave and threw a satchel charge into its opening. The charge was immediately thrown back out and exploded harmlessly at the bottom of the cliff. The Marines shortened the fuse on the second charge, and again it was thrown back out and exploded at the base of the cliff. A third charge with an even shorter fuse was prepared and thrown into the cave, but the Japanese must have been expecting it because the charge went in and then out in almost one motion. The Marine who threw it in was still trying to find cover when the charge exploded and he was killed. The Marine was disintegrated, and I watched his helmet go flying through the air and roll on the ground until coming to rest beside a tree some distance away.

I respected the Japanese as soldiers because they were fierce and disciplined, but we gave no quarter and didn't expect it in return. They were motivated by their indoctrination in the belief they had to kill ten Marines before fulfilling their sacred honor of dying for the emperor. They were masters of camouflage, and I would bet one could have come across a wide-open field and smacked me right in the face before I noticed his presence. They were skilled at deception and could lie motionless for days pretending to be dead, only to rise up and shoot a Marine in the back after he passed. We never walked past a dead Japanese without someone shooting a couple rounds into the corpse even if it appeared to have been dead for a week. On the other hand, the Japanese were so unbelievably dumb it negated anything they performed well. At night we erected barbwire defenses to funnel the Japanese into our machine-gun positions, and we mowed them down by the hundreds. They just proved again and again that they lacked the will or tactical intelligence to breach our defenses elsewhere. At night I heard the Japanese march shouting a cadence, and although we couldn't see them, it gave us a pretty good idea from what direction they would attack.

At the onset of my time in combat I didn't hate the Japanese. They fired on us, we got mad, and we fired back. But after witnessing so many horrible things happening to the men around me, and losing so many friends, it became impossible for me not to develop a hatred for the Japanese. Our officers were always instructing the Marines to take prisoners for intelligence-gathering purposes, but even the few Japanese who allowed themselves to be captured had little chance of ever making it back to where they were needed. It was not uncommon for a group of prisoners to be led off to the rear, and within seconds of being out of sight I would hear several shots. The Marines escorting them would claim the prisoners had made a break for it and they'd had to shoot them to prevent their escape, but it was clear they'd had no intention of letting them live. It is unfair to judge what men do in battle until those doing the judging walk in their shoes for a while.

I therefore rarely saw a living Japanese soldier on any of the islands I fought on, but I saw plenty who were dead. The very first dead Japanese I saw was lying next to a destroyed 75-mm. cannon. There were about eight to ten dead men, and I was surprised to find a dead Japanese woman among them. I presume she might have been a native Japanese woman who had been dating one of the Japanese soldiers and was killed along with the soldiers.

We spent a couple more days at the base of the cliffs before tanks arrived to destroy the caves and the snipers inside. After all the shooting was over someone discovered a car hidden in the brush. We concluded it was probably a 1936 Plymouth, and it was a curiosity because it was equipped with a steering wheel on the right side. We began to sift through the car when a voice came from behind us: "Uh, I think I would like to surrender, fellas." I turned and saw this Japanese soldier with his hands up in the air. He scared the living daylights out of us, and I must have jumped 5 feet into the air. He spoke perfect English, and while we checked him over for weapons he explained that he was a graduate of the Ohio University and had returned to Japan to visit his parents before starting a job in the United States, but the start of the war had prevented him from returning to the States. He claimed he had been drafted into the Japanese Army against his will and that he did not approve of the Japanese attack upon America. The intelligence guys found out we had a Japanese who spoke English, so they took him away for interrogation. He was one of the few Japanese to surrender on Saipan, and after he was hauled away we began to think he was probably one of the snipers who had killed so many of our Marines but was clever enough to surrender when escape seemed hopeless.

By the first week in July the Navy declared Saipan "secured." As we cleared the last Japanese defenses in the northern part of the island, thousands of native Japanese gathered above the cliffs that overlooked the water. We had guys with loudspeakers who managed to talk most of the civilians down from the cliffs, but thousands jumped to their deaths rather than face capture. I read somewhere the place those people jumped is now called "Suicide Cliffs," and they are one of the more popular tourist attractions on the island.

We spent the next few weeks on Saipan collecting our gear, packing up, and just resting. Someone found a large bottle of sake, so we decided it was time for a drink. We placed some crates in a circle and passed the bottle around. Each man took huge gulps of the sake like it was water before passing the bottle to the next man. The rest of the day was a blur, and the next morning I woke to see only pairs of boots sticking up over the crates from where the men had fallen over and passed out. It was a good sleep, but it didn't last long because we were loaded onto troopships once more to go just a short distance to the island of Tinian. Tinian was so close to Saipan our Marine artillery on Saipan could shell Tinian before we departed.

On July 23 the 4th Marine Division was divided into two forces to assault the island of Tinian. The smaller force feigned a landing on one side of the island to divert the Japanese attention from where the heaviest blow was to fall. Before the Tinian landing I felt I was now an experienced amphibious-landing veteran, so I felt better prepared for what lay ahead. The first waves went ashore in the morning, and our medical battalion landed on Tinian later the same morning, around eleven. One of the things the Marines stressed during my training was to get as far away from whatever brought you to the beach as soon as you could, because that's what the Japanese would be aiming for. The ramp in the rear of the amtrac that brought us on shore could not be lowered because the rear was still mostly submerged in the water, so we were forced to climb out over the sides. The rest of the men jumped out, and it was just myself and another guy left in the amtrac. I was waiting for him to go first, and I think he was waiting for me. We both hesitated, and for good reason, because the sound of bullets hitting the side of the amtrac and flying overhead was enough to make anyone nervous about sticking their head up. I decided I had better get out before something bigger came along and blew us up. I jumped out and landed on the sand, and the other Marine followed behind me, but as he was climbing out he was shot in the head, and he fell to the beach next to me, dead. I didn't hesitate to get off the beach, and I ran forward as fast as I could to find better cover. At the time I had no feelings about what had happened on the beach at Tinian, but today I realize what could have happened to me if I had been the last to leave the amtrac instead of the next to last.

The fighting for Tinian was difficult, but relatively less difficult compared to our experiences on Saipan. It wasn't too long before we were back in Maui gaining some needed rest. We received replacements to bring the division back to full strength and continued training to assimilate the new men into our ranks. A few months passed, and we packed up again and boarded troopships for our next mission. We all had a bad feeling our next mission was going to be a lot closer to the Japanese mainland, and Tokyo Rose was briefing us daily on where we were headed.

When we were shown maps and small-scale replicas of Iwo Jima, we were told the invasion was going to be a breeze. We were told the island would be taken in just a couple days and not to worry because every ship and plane within 1,000 miles had been shelling or bombing Iwo Jima for forty-five consecutive days and that nothing was left but sand and dead Japs. I don't think they killed a single Japanese soldier during all that shelling.

I landed on Iwo Jima on February 19, 1945, at about two o'clock in the afternoon. I had watched the initial invasion from the deck of my troopship, and I could see things were not going well for the Marines who had landed in the morning. The incoming mortar and artillery fire hitting the beaches and the landing craft was horrific, and the stream of dead and wounded being brought back to the ships was a troubling sight. We were told things were not going well before we loaded into the landing craft, and the mood was somber as we headed towards the beach. The water was rough, and some guys became seasick and turned shades of green and gray waiting to vomit. I found that by just engaging the sick men in trivial conversation about where they were from and what were the names of their girlfriends I was able to talk a few of them out of getting sick. The person I really felt sorry for was the coxswain who was steering our boat to the beach. He had to stand above everyone else to guide the boat and was exposed to all the fire coming at us from the island. The coxswain did a wonderful job getting us ashore, and as soon as we hit the beach he dropped the ramp, and everyone got out as fast as we could run.

The beach was littered with men, abandoned equipment, and destroyed tank, jeeps, trucks, planes, and landing craft. We had to negotiate a large hill to make it off the beach, and the island's soft black sand made it very difficult to get a footing to make the climb. I made it 50 or 100 feet past the hill before I was knocked down by a shell blast. I wasn't hurt, and I immediately took out my trenching shovel and scooped out a hole the best I could, and this is where I remained for the remainder of the day and that night.

To say things weren't going well would be to put it mildly. The Japanese shelled us all night, and it was devastating. That night I lay in my foxhole looking up at the sky, and I watched our 16-inch shells from the battleships sail overhead. They glowed a cherry red, and it was nice to see them fly overhead and land on Japanese, and I wished every one would land far, far away. I prayed a lot that night. I promised to give up wine, women, and song in return for being allowed to live through the night. I am sure the good Lord understands if I haven't been able to hold up my end of the bargain all these years.

I spent most of the next few days picking up wounded men and taking them back to the beach to be evacuated by anything still left floating. The beach was still no man's land, and it was a dangerous passage to get off the island because it was under a constant barrage of Japanese artillery and mortar fire. The Japanese still were firing at us from huge concrete bunkers to the right of the landing area high up on a hill. I watched numerous 16-inch shells ricochet off the top of the bunker, and finally the Navy wised up and began to blow the earth away from under the bunker until it tipped over and rolled down the hill.

I was working in the aid station when the first flag went up on Mount Suribachi. I heard someone yell, "Hey! They got the flag up!" I ran outside to look, and we all celebrated, briefly thinking it meant we had won and the battle was over. The battle was to last another thirty grueling days.

Ten days into the campaign I was again attached to Easy Company, 2nd Infantry Battalion. We moved inland and fought our way across Iwo Jima with Mount Suribachi at our backs. The terrain was like a moonscape made up of rocky hills and deep valleys, and the Japanese used every inch of it to their advantage. I rarely saw any Japanese despite being under constant mortar, rifle, and machine-gun fire. The Marines had rocket launchers, and it was always a mixed emotion when they came up to our position to fire, because they were effective weapons but their presence brought every Japanese gun down on our position. The guys driving the trucks knew this, and they kept the motor running so they could run like hell after firing their rockets, leaving us behind to face the music.

Iwo was defended with a fanatical determination we had not experienced up to this time. The company lost eleven second lieutenants who were either killed or wounded. The second lieutenants were the platoon leaders who got us up in the morning and said what time we were moving forward, and when that time came the second lieutenant was the first to jump out of his foxhole, and every last man under his command followed his lead. We might not move more than a few feet at a time, but the first and second lieutenants were the men who were most responsible for leading our assault forward and winning the battles on every front of the war.

Two hundred and eighty men of Easy Company were put ashore

on the first day, and the last time we were all together near the end of the battle, there were only eighteen of them left. The eighteen included me and another Corpsman, so they decided to eliminate one Corpsman and send him back to the aid station. We decided to draw straws to see who would be the one to go back to the aid station, and I won. Winning the draw was the best thing that had ever happened to me, and all I could think about was getting back to my safe little foxhole I had waiting for me back at the aid station. When I returned I was shocked to find my foxhole had been blown to smithereens and all that remained was a crater the size of a bus. I sat down for a while and reflected on how my time spent with Easy Company might have saved me from being in the foxhole when it was blown up.

Word spread quickly when the Navy announced the island had been secured. Two weeks later I was still on the beach waiting for transportation back to Hawaii, and the Japanese were still firing mortars at the beach, and many guys were killed or wounded long after the fighting was declared over. I had one thought when I finally left the island, which was to get as far away from Iwo Jima as possible and get washed. I slept well on the way back to Hawaii, and I was so glad to have survived my time on Iwo. Nothing was ever said about what happened on Iwo during our trip back to Hawaii. I think we all just tried to put it out of our minds.

There was not much time for reflection when we arrived back at our barracks, as we were soon busily packing our gear once more for yet another mission. This time we knew it was going to be the Japanese mainland, and we all were dreading it. When the announcement came the war was over, I let out a sigh and thanked God I didn't have to go back into combat. There was not much celebrating at first. It was the biggest relief of our lives, and I slept the rest of the day in total relaxation and peace.

A couple months later I was on the cruiser USS *Baltimore*, headed for home. Three days into the trip I felt the ship come to a stop, so I went up on deck to see what was happening. We were in a fog so thick I couldn't even see the water. The captain came over the loudspeaker and assured us he knew we were anxious to get home, and that his navigator reported we were sitting just off San Francisco Bay pointed directly at the Golden Gate Bridge. He then said, "My navigator hasn't gotten me lost during the entire war, so I assume that is exactly where we are. That is all." An hour later the fog began to burn away, and through the haze the Golden Gate Bridge appeared looming over our heads, and the ship was as perfectly aligned to the center of the bridge as possible. The ship slowly moved forward again, and all of us landlubbers on the deck thought the tower of the ship was going to hit the bottom of the bridge. The captain must have noticed us staring at the tower and then the bridge, wondering if we were going to clear the bridge. Once again the captain picked up the intercom and said, "I know you fellas must think I am going to hit the bridge, but don't worry. I know the height of my ship, the height of the bridge, the depth of the water, and the current tide. We'll clear it by at least 60 feet. That is all." We were the first Navy vessel to arrive in San Francisco Harbor following the war, and the people of San Francisco gave us a really warm and moving reception. After a short stop at Treasure Island, I was on a train heading back to Baltimore.

I don't know if I could describe combat to someone who has never been in it before. I don't know if anyone ever wins in war, but it was important that we managed to stop some truly evil people who were committing indescribable horrors against humanity in Asia and Europe. The Japanese treated their prisoners with unspeakable brutality, and even to this day I cannot get it out of my mind how horrible they were. I refuse to buy Japanese products because I cannot bring myself to reward the grandchildren of the men who owned the companies during the war who used the slave labor of our troops for profit. I fully supported the dropping of the atomic bombs because it saved countless American and Japanese lives. Years later I saw the *Enola Gay* at the Smithsonian, and I patted it a few times to say, "Thanks."

I imagine my experiences in combat changed me, but in ways I could not be fully aware of. I think about how and why I survived but don't dwell on it too much. I was lucky to have survived numerous close calls. I shed only a few drops of blood, when a 536 walkie-talkie was shot out of my hands and the shattered speaker split my lip. I fired back at the people who fired at me and my friends, and although it's possible I may have killed, I prefer to focus on the lives I saved rather than the lives I took.

The war remains with me in my thoughts, and it took me a long time to return to a normal state of mind. I moved into a house near Patterson Park when I returned home, and on the Fourth of July I was on the kitchen floor polishing my shoes when some fireworks went off in the park. I instinctively dove under the kitchen table and felt a little silly afterwards. Even today I am a little twitchy when people sneak up on me, but I don't dive under furniture anymore.

The real heroes of the Second World War are the men who didn't come back and sacrificed everything for what we have in America today. They are my heroes, and we should never forget their names.

A Baltimorean and the D-Day Invasion

The following article, written by Tom Treanor under the heading "Front Lines," was published in the *Los Angeles Times* and the *Baltimore Jewish Times* in the summer of 1945. The article details the actions of Lt. Raymond M. Rosenbloom of Baltimore and the crew of the Coast Guard cutter *Balsam* in the early-morning hours before the D-Day invasion on June 6, 1944.

RAYMOND H. ROSENBLOOM

Aboard Coast Guard Cutter 62—The night before the invasion the skipper, Lt. Raymond Rosenbloom of Baltimore, called all hands into the galley. "Well, girls," he said, "sometime tomorrow more ships than the world has ever seen will sail from England and put our troops in France." Nobody said anything. "We probably won't reach the beach ourselves and you probably ought to thank God for that." The men stirred a bit but remained silent. They were a weird looking crew, half of them shaved bald except for scalp locks, a pre-invasion stunt on this boat.

"We will be with the first convoy," said Rosenbloom. "As you know, our job will be to pick up survivors from the torpedoed ships. We may have a lot to do, but we hope we won't." He gave them the skeleton of the plan, reminding them that the Navy's job is to put the Army on the beach and that the particular task of Coast Guard Cutter 62 will be to pick up Army men from the Channel and put them on the nearest large craft going to France.

"When you pull these men out of the water," he said, "they will have rifles strapped to their backs. Their first instinct, past experience has shown, will be to get rid of the rifle since even after they are aboard the horror will remain that the rifle is pulling them down. You will not let them throw overboard either rifles or ammunition. The first thing you will let these men know is that the war is not over for them but that they are going to be put aboard another invasion craft."

The men maintained absolute silence throughout as if they were hypnotized. Rosenbloom, who claims to be 24 (although crew members say he has added two years to keep from being the youngest man aboard), spoke slowly in a matter-of-fact voice.

"We're going to have to be callous," he said, "that's going to be the hardest part of our job. When we get a load we are going to have to back off no matter how many men are still in the water. Don't feel sorry for a boy, even if he has a broken leg and is screaming to be pulled aboard. Like a department store, our value is in a quick turnover and a quick return. As soon as we unload a batch of boys on a larger ship we'll go back for more. If the boys in the water won't back out of the way we'll have to back right through them and they'll have to take a chance of being hit by the propellers."

"If a man is dead—." He paused, and asked, "The pharmacist's mate told you how to tell if a man is dead, didn't he?" The men nodded.

"All right, if a man is dead, and the ship is loaded and you're rushed for time, you're not to waste any sentimentality on him because it may mean other lives. You'll cut off his dog tags, put your foot under him and hoist him over the rail. And keep hauling in live men as fast as you can. Even with the nets and ropes they'll have trouble getting aboard. If we lose a big ship there will be lots of men in the water and we won't have any time to lose." He gave them a few seconds to absorb each item before proceeding to another.

"The wounded," he said, "will be a problem. The damage and first aid crew under Chief Dickey will handle them as best they can. The worst wounded will be given a quick shot of morphine, the others quick first aid. Chief, as far as possible, if a man is wounded, let his own buddies take care of him. Men who are able to walk you will herd below as fast as you can stuff them in the wardroom and in the closets. If the ship gets too crowded stuff them in the toilets. The first men pulled aboard, if they are healthy, put to work helping you pull in others. You will find them as meek as lambs, our experience has shown. They'll do anything you ask. They'll be so damned glad to be out of the water, especially at night." He gave some miscellaneous instructions.

"Remember this. Anyone who goes below to light a cigarette must put on a pair of red goggles. The only lights below will be covered with a red shield or orange shield to take care of night blindness." Rosenbloom continued: "These shields will not be removed under any circumstances. We will not fire on any aircraft unless directly attacked. The flashes will give away our position. In case, through confusion, one of our ships fires upon us, we will not give away our position by firing the recognition flares unless a real salvo lands in our neighborhood. Every time we pass a ship Signalman Fernanade will keep his blinker gun trained on the bridge, ready to give the signal. If we are sunk ourselves and washed ashore on the German side, don't touch anything. It may be booby-trapped. Just find yourself a safe place and lie there until you see some of our troops. We will be on the port side of the convoy and will be vulnerable to E-boat attack. You know the E-boats. We will not fire unless we are directly attacked. If we are attacked, do the best we can with the peashooter. Remember, we're specialists, and our specialty is not shooting but rescuing men. Now, have you all read your gas instructions?" Everyone nodded.

"All right. I don't need to tell you that if you use your gas equipment correctly you will be safe. If you don't use your equipment properly—well, you've all seen gas victims of the last war walking about."

WILLIAM S. KIRBY

Annapolis, Maryland

29th Infantry Division, U.S. Army

William Sylvester Kirby was born in Pittsburgh, Pennsylvania, on June 29, 1924. He enlisted in the Army soon after graduating from high school in 1942 and after a brief assignment to the 106th Infantry Division was assigned as a replacement to H Company, 115th Infantry Regiment, 29th Infantry Division. He is a recipient of the Purple Heart. After the war Kirby graduated from the University of Pittsburgh and began a career as a personnel manager, relocating to Annapolis, Maryland, in 1950. He and his wife, Shirley, have three children.

The following profile was based on an interview with William Kirby, and on portions of his personal memoirs, which are reprinted here with permission.

By the time I was transferred to Fort Meade, Maryland, I was a far different young man from when I was inducted into the Army and completed basic training a year earlier. I had been originally assigned to the 106th Infantry Division, and perhaps I was fortunate, because the 106th was severely mauled during the Battle of the Bulge. In late July 1944 I was assigned to H Company (heavy weapons), 115th Infantry Regiment, 29th Infantry Division, as one of the thousands of replacements being assembled to replace the men who would be killed or wounded during the invasion of Europe. During my time in H Company I performed various roles, including squad leader, and was also briefly attached to the platoon leader as a scout.

When my group of replacements was shipped overseas I clearly remember looking at the very small English ship we boarded and wondering how it could get all the way across that big ocean. A few days into our voyage the seas built to heights unbelievable to us landlubbers, and a lot of the convoy was out of sight much of the time in the troughs between the waves. The roll and pitch of that little ship was severe, and the crash of seas hitting the hull forward was deafening and frightening. Many of the men had never been on a ship at sea, and I couldn't imagine how much more weather our little ship could survive. It was terrifying to stand on the deck of that little ship and look fore and aft at the tops of the waves towering over us. Many were so seasick they thought they were going to die, and I think later many of us were afraid we wouldn't. Although I didn't get seasick, I did not feel well and would have given anything for the ship to be completely still, even for a short time. On the other hand, standing on that deck with a cold fresh wind pulling at my hair and clothes, the smell of salt air, and the rhythmic motion of the ship under my feet was a new, exciting experience, and I loved it.

We stowed our gear (rifles, packs, duffel bags, helmets, etc.), lived, ate, and slept in the same crowded compartment. We slept in hammocks slung from overhead beams. The roll of the ship made the hammocks swing in unison, slowly tilting over to the right, pause, then slowly coming back through dead center way over to the left, pause, etc. Sanitary facilities were primitive and inadequate for so many men, and they were difficult and chancy to use in such heavy seas. Two meals a day were brought to our compartment from the galley in open buckets. Too often it was greasy mutton and boiled potatoes. That odor combined with the smell of diesel from the engine room made it difficult to eat. I still find the odor of lamb offensive but manage to eat a little when my wife has it on the menu at home. It was a long ten- or twelve-day zigzag trip across the cold North Atlantic. If nothing else, conditions were just bad enough to make us glad to be off that little boat.

After a short stay in a replacement depot (we called them "repple-depples"), we were loaded aboard a ship and crossed the English Channel on June 29, 1944, on my twentieth birthday. Our ship anchored off the French coast, and we disembarked by climbing down a cargo net slung over the side into an LCI (landing craft, infantry). Both the troopship and landing craft were rolling considerably, and I had to time it so I jumped just as the latter rose up on a wave and slammed into the former. I managed this without injury, all the while loaded with my rifle, pack, belt, canteen, gas mask, rations, etc. The LCI took us into the temporary piers that had been rigged just after D-Day. The beach and nearby coast were littered with the wreckage and stuff of war, and it was very sobering to think of what horrendous conditions the first assault waves must have experienced.

Once on shore we marched past destroyed villages and farms, dead animals, wrecked vehicles, remnants of trees, and litter (pieces of buildings and furniture, farm implements, packs, helmets, empty ration boxes and cans, bullet and shell cases, clothing, and paper) to a replacement depot 5 or 10 miles inland. The depot was close enough to the fighting to hear artillery, a most foreboding sound that told us we had joined the real war and men were dying nearby.

Bill Kirby poses with members of H Company outside their temporary quarters in the German mining town of Aldenhoven, just west of the Roer River, during one of their breaks from the line in the winter of 1944–45. The weather was unusually warm on the day the photo was taken, and from the clean look of their faces and uniforms Kirby believes this picture was taken shortly after they had bathed at one of the nearby mine heads. *From left:* Pasqual "Steve" Marino, Steve Budish, Kirby, Morris Romerstein. All survived the war.

According to the 29th Division history, the 115th Infantry Regiment was relieved on July 20, two days after the fall of Saint-Lô, and went into reserve. Replacements, including me, were assigned to the regiment two days later, on the 22nd. I was assigned to a machine-gun crew in 1st Platoon, H Company, 115th Infantry Regiment. We spent four or five days reluctantly going through elementary training exercises, giving the combat veterans time to recover from a month and a half of heavy hedgerow fighting, and allowing us replacements time to fit into our units. Understandably, the veterans did a lot of griping about that seemingly useless activity.

On the 28th we were taken to our assigned positions in the hills near Percy, first by truck and then by foot along beat-up roads, sunken country lanes, and footpaths. I was nervous and apprehensive from the time we left the reserve area, and I worried how I would handle combat, or if I would be able to. Others must have also been nervous, because they were quiet and introspective, and I remember being very impressed by the calm, perhaps resignation, of the combat veterans.

I had seen the collateral destruction of war, but nothing could have prepared me for my first personal encounter with war. It was indescribably horrible. Words cannot adequately describe the sight of shattered bodies, the sound of incoming shells, the noise of exploding mortar and artillery shells, the rattle of small arms, the "pop" of bullets that came too close, the whine and zip of shrapnel, the roar, clank, and squeak of tanks, the hiss of high-velocity flat-trajectory shells, the cries for medics, the smell of powder smoke and torn-up foliage, earth, and bodies. And the fear, the overwhelming, belly-wrenching, almost paralyzing fear.

You get accustomed to the sounds of war. You quickly learn the sounds of artillery, theirs and ours, incoming or outgoing, close or far away, tank or howitzer, big or small. Mortars, on the other hand, come in from a high trajectory and are almost silent until they explode. The Germans used gunpowder that gave off little or no smoke, and that made it difficult to find snipers and even machine guns. Ours was very smoky, and the amount of smoke around our machine guns made them easy targets. There were times when we would fire a lot and then instinctively dive for cover, knowing the krauts would start firing towards the smoke we created. Another problem with machine guns was that every fifth or sixth bullet fired was a tracer round. Although it was intended to help our aim, it was actually an incredibly stupid idea when used in combat, as it surely showed the Germans exactly where we were. We eventually cannibalized other belts to replace the tracer rounds in the belts we fired. The riflemen liked the extra firepower of our machine guns but didn't want to be too close.

You also become acquainted with the sound of German guns. Their machine guns and submachine guns fired at a much faster rate, and you couldn't hear individual rounds being fired as you could with our guns. At a distance the German automatic weapons sounded like a strong fabric being torn, only louder. It was also very obvious to the infantry that the typical German infantry unit had more automatic weapons than ours.

During our attack in the hills around Percy we were strung up along a hedgerow with a rifle platoon. We came under heavy fire and took some casualties. A GI from the rifle platoon was hit by a bullet that entered his forehead and exited through the back of his head. The bullet must have been an armor-piercing round, because it didn't blow a big hole where it exited. Until then I thought significant brain damage was always fatal, but that GI turned to where I was with a surprised look on his face and said something to the effect of, "Son of a bitch," and wandered off towards the rear. I've often wondered what happened to that GI. I like to think that he was able to return to near normal and live a long and productive life. At one of the hospitals I was in later, probably the one at Braintree, a GI in our ward had a bullet go through his head above his ears. It must have been a hardened bullet, because the exit wound was not very large. Although it was obvious he was going to survive, he mostly sat on his bed quietly staring into his own private world, and rarely talked.

I was far back of the combat area on R&R only when I was wounded or when our division was placed in reserve. I saw a very large number of GIs wandering around who didn't appear to belong to any outfit and, from my casual observations, did little. Our rifle and machine-gun companies could have used these underutilized men. I wondered why we needed so many noncombatants, and I would have liked to be a member of this comfortable part of the war. It is inaccurate for people to suggest that every man who put on a uniform during the war was placed in a situation of grave danger, when in reality only a very small percentage of the men who went overseas did the fighting, the bleeding, and, of course, the dying. But one job I did not envy was the graves registration unit. They were the guys who picked up the bloody and broken bodies, removed one dog tag and personal effects, put the bodies in thin cotton bags, and buried them. How these men continued with a normal life after the war is beyond me. Every GI they put in the ground was someone's son, brother, husband, father, or friend. Every one of them meant immeasurable grief and sorrow and perhaps loneliness to people back home.

Army cooks had a thankless job. Griping about Army chow was a constant activity among the men, and the cooks often had to work under difficult conditions. In the field, cooking was done in tents, abandoned buildings, or maybe in the open. Our kitchens had to move often and had to find whatever quartermaster unit from which they were authorized to draw supplies. That being said, I must add that I have eaten some unnecessarily bad food during my travels in the Army. That was especially true about kitchens feeding transients, as in replacement depots. Greenish reconstituted powdered eggs were not appetizing regardless of whose cooks prepared them. And I think the standard recipe for stew required the use of the whole cow except hooves and horns and some mushy overcooked vegetables.

One day during the fall of 1944 a buddy named Ralph Finke told me he thought his time had come and that he would be killed in the next few days. He gave me a letter addressed to his parents and asked me to mail it after he got hit. As it turned out, he didn't get hit, and I returned the letter to him a week or so later. I was concerned that I'd get killed and someone would find and mail the letter, which undoubtedly would cause his family a lot of pain and grief until they heard from him later.

There is a fatalism regarding survival that was common among the men in my company fighting on the front. There were two schools of thought. Some believed that you were destined to get hit or not get hit. If a bullet or shell had your name on it, you were done, regardless of what you did to protect yourself or reduce the odds. The other school of thought was that the longer you survived, the lower your chances of survival. Combat experience actually improved the chances of survival, as replacements had a much higher casualty rate, but this still did not outweigh the dumb-luck, or lack-of-luck, factor. Experience had no influence over where a shell exploded or the marksmanship of a kraut who was aiming at a ma-chine-gun position or at a specific GI. We knew what was going to happen sooner or later. It was just a question of when and how bad it would be. I think I was more afraid of losing half my face or my arms than being killed. Considering the amount of exposure, it is incredible that some made it all the way from the beach on D-Day without a significant wound. But others lasted less than a day. I lasted only three or four days.

One afternoon near the end of July we paused our advance and were deployed along a hedgerow that ran parallel to a hedgerow the Germans occupied 50 or 100 yards away across a field. We could hear them talk and yell, and presumably they could hear us. For some reason (maybe because he was told to find out exactly where we were), a German soldier climbed over their hedgerow and started across the field with his rifle at ready. Maybe as many as twenty American GIs shot him, as if on cue, and he was knocked backwards some distance, probably without ever hearing the shots that killed him. No others followed him.

During the following days, we experienced heavy fighting against German counterattacks, including heavy armor forces. On August 1, as I paused before running across a gap in a stone wall that was covered by German automatic weapons, I have been told that a German 88-mm. shell hit a tree 3 or 4 feet above my head. I should have been killed instantly but was hit by only one piece of shrapnel that went through my right calf. I did not hear it or know what happened, except that it felt like I had been hit on my leg by a heavy club. There was no pain at first; it came later. I sprinkled sulfa powder on the holes in my leg and bandaged it as best I could. By the time I finished, I looked around and I was alone. I began think-ing about what to do next and finally decided to go back in the di-rection from which we came and to go unarmed to reduce the chances of getting shot by a sniper. I began a slow and difficult jour-ney to an aid station that was made more complicated by German snipers who shot at the wounded. I became as angry as any man could as I watched snipers shoot unarmed and wounded men. I wished I had kept my rifle, because I think I saw one of the German bastards. Someone shot the snipers, and I found a stick to use as a crutch, which I really needed by then, and limped my way to the battalion aid station.

I arrived at the aid station, and by that time my leg was quite swollen. I was placed on a litter and waited three or four days while the more seriously wounded GIs were treated. Some of the wounds were just terrible; shrapnel can do enormous damage. While wait-ing for surgery, a wounded kraut several litters away began talking very urgently in German, but no one understood German, so he was ignored. I told one of the attending medics that I thought he had to urinate (we used more common words than that) and to get him a duck (urinal). I think he came close to filling it. He looked more like a sixteen-year-old than a soldier, and I might have felt sorry for him, but he had just been shooting at us. Might have been one of those snipers.

By the time the surgeon was over me, my leg was a real mess, and I remember it smelled rotten. My wound was cleaned and sewed up, and I was flown to a hospital in Braintree, just north of London. My most vivid memories of my stay in Braintree were the breathless moments from the time the motor of the German "buzz bombs" quit until they hit the ground with a hell of an explosion. Fortunately there were not too many of them.

While in England recuperating I learned of strong German counterattacks in Normandy and how we had defeated and outflanked several German divisions during the battle. The Germans held a single route of escape known as the Falaise gap, and the retreating Germans clogged the roads through the Falaise gap with tens of thousands of troops, trucks, tanks, and horse-drawn carriages in an attempt to escape. This provided the Allied air force and artillery a made-to-order opportunity to slaughter thousands of German troops. The destruction of so many German lives seemed just retribution, and it probably helped hasten the end of the war.

German dead made little impression on me, probably because I felt they had brought it on themselves and death was a small price to pay for bringing so much misery to so many. Seeing dead American GIs and the seriously wounded, however, was profoundly disturbing and instilled a deep sadness and depression in me. All those young men killed or permanently disabled just as their adult lives began. They had had little time to do much of anything, and now their life was over or drastically altered. Many years passed before this sadness left me, and I suspect it will never entirely dissipate.

For some reason that I do not recall, we were in the second floor of a house in one of those small German towns. I was on the second floor of the house, which was not the preferred place to be, because it offered little protection from artillery and mortar fire, and below me an American sniper in a group of trees beside a beet field was hunting German snipers. He had what looked like a World War I Enfield bolt-action rifle fitted with a scope. I thought about how his job must have taken nerves of steel. I wondered who was hunting whom. A sniper's war must be very personal. He gets a man in his sight, pulls the trigger, and sees the man go down. I'd guess many GIs didn't know for sure that they killed a kraut because there was so much mortar, artillery, machine-gun, BAR (Browning automatic rifle), and rifle fire going on all around. You could never know for sure if it was someone else's bullet or a chunk of shrapnel that got the one you shot at, and it made it easier to pull the trigger with things that way.

The Germans were very good at booby-trapping everything, including their own dead, with explosives to kill unsuspecting GIs looking for souvenirs. Bodies with German Lugers or P-38s were irresistible treasures for some GIs, and some went through the whole war recklessly scavenging without the slightest encounter with booby traps. I had a problem with looting German homes unless it was for something I needed such as a stove and coal. I figure being subjected to looting was another worthwhile lesson for the German population about the unpleasantness and destructiveness of the war they let happen.

I recovered from my wounds and rejoined H Company soon after it had arrived in Holland in the latter part of September 1944. On my second day back we were hit by German artillery, and there were casualties as shells exploded up in the trees and showered shrapnel and pieces of trees down on us. As soon as the shelling ended, we all dug our foxholes a little deeper and covered them with logs and dirt. We were soon fully engaged in the battles into Germany. The fighting to the Roer River was over in a matter of two months or so, but it seemed to go on forever. On more than one occasion I was so tired and cold and wet and stressed and hungry (I didn't eat for two or three days at a time) that I sat on the edge of a foxhole inches from relative safety, not caring if I was killed or not. I saw others do the same and often watched as some men took unnecessary risks.

One day at about dusk we started to head back to the cellars we were occupying in Baesweiler, Germany, when we walked past a church, totally exposing ourselves to a German position we had not seen across a big open field. We heard the hiss of a flat-trajectory 88 round, and it exploded against the church before we could hit the ground. It felt like a heavy club hit me in the buttock, and as I lay there waiting for further activity I realized my leg was numb. I was certain one half of my backside was torn off, and I thought, "Oh, no, not again." I was helped back to our cellar, and by the light of a flashlight we discovered no gory wound, just a large red area that was probably caused by a piece of brick knocked off the church by the 88.

Moving around in large groups during the day was risky because we were obviously under observation all the time, and movement usually provoked artillery and mortar fire. Unless attacking enemy positions, units larger than a squad moved at night most of the time, with 8- or 10-foot intervals between men strung out in a long line on each side of the road. Moving at night had risks when there were so many guns in the hands of nervous GIs. When a flare went up it was difficult to overcome the natural reflex to hit the ground, but any movement could prove fatal, so we learned to freeze, duck our heads, and blend into the shattered trees that lined the roads. It was also hard to keep from looking up, but doing so would allow any light to reflect off our faces, giving whoever had fired the flare a bright target in an otherwise black landscape. Most flares burned out within a minute or two, but that was a long period of time when you felt so naked and exposed.

Guard duty at night was stressful. It was often so cold it was painful and so dark you couldn't see much among the jumble of ruins whose shapes made your imagination run rampant. You would find a deep shadow to hide in and strain to see what was or wasn't out there. Then you would hear the squeak of footsteps in the snow, and you wouldn't be able to tell from what direction they were coming. Then maybe you would think you heard a metallic click, perhaps from a rifle safety being released, and again you would wonder how far away it was. After a long time the footsteps would resume, slowly and cautiously, and you would try to stop breathing so some trigger-happy GI or kraut wouldn't see the steam from your breath, and you hoped no one could hear the pounding of your heart. Two hours on watch could seem like an eternity.

After long periods of heavy fighting and shelling, many men were fatigued beyond description. The strenuous effort, insufficient sleep, and the particularly fatiguing effect of great stress and fear caused men to sag, to move mechanically and often very slowly. I don't really know how to describe the look in their eyes. They were blank, staring, glazed, shocked, haunted, and expressionless. The combat infantryman is stripped of everything but the most basic essentials of life. All we wanted was the absence of enemy fire, to be warm and dry, enough to eat, enough sleep and rest, minimum annoyance by stupid orders, and an end to the war. Life was primitive and uncomplicated. Our desire for survival and obtaining any sort of comfort were the driving forces in our daily lives.

Most guys could deal with our predicament, while others couldn't. I think I should mention that in war you know the guys immediately around you, and that's your war. I met guys after the war that were in H Company who I had never known during the war. We had one guy named Larson who was a sort of slap-happy, inappropriately jovial, loquacious guy from North Dakota. I don't think Larson ever experienced fear. He was the platoon messenger and the platoon's contact with the company HQ, and was running back and forth in the worst stuff and probably should have been killed a thousand times. He finally got hit but was sent back to our company too soon. He had lost a lot of one buttock, and there wasn't much left for him to sit on. He wasn't healed enough, and our Captain Leary sent him back to the hospital, and I don't remember him returning after that.

A guy named Eddie was on the other end of the spectrum. I guess Eddie, like the rest of us, was frightened by bullets, shells, grenades, mines, and such. Although nervous and afraid, we went where we had to go and did what we had to do. But not Eddie, who often disappeared when it got rough and showed up days later when the risk level had returned to normal. He was reported MIA several times, and he would say he got lost fighting with another company. I don't remember the other GIs talking about Eddie getting lost, but I was somewhat annoyed. I figured that if others had to take big risks, so should Eddie. Eddie came close to receiving a court martial on a few occasions. Eddie didn't have many friends. I think most of us avoided him during the war and after.

There were a few jovial memories from the war that I can remember. One was while on a break from the line in Aldenhoven, Germany, just west of the Roer River. Aldenhoven was a mining town and had been mostly destroyed when the American Army rolled through a few days before. We found a dry basement for sleeping quarters, and we spent the days relaxing and made it our priority to find a place to clean ourselves, since it had been months since any of us had had a bath. The coal mines around Aldenhoven had showering facilities used by the miners when they emerged from the filth of the mineshaft, and we utilized these facilities at our first opportunity. While showering, a couple attractive German women happened to enter, and they disrobed and began showering. I remember they seemed to be interested in one guy in our midst, and the talk was soon about his chances of scoring with the two Germans. After a quick conversation with the Germans, he discovered they were more interested in the soap he was carrying than his physique. He left without sex, and without his soap.

We had fought our way into one of those small towns in western Germany, and the krauts were retreating into a field just a short distance away. A large armored outfit was following us, moving down the only street, when they came under sporadic mortar fire. The tanks and vehicles had nowhere to go for cover, so they accelerated to get to the other side of the town and out into open fields as soon as possible. I watched as an old man and a little girl, probably his granddaughter, tried to run across the street between tanks and other vehicles. They didn't make it. There was nothing the tank drivers could do. It was very messy and very disturbing.

When the war finally ended, I had a couple experiences that made me realize I was not out of danger. One of my concerns involved the presence of German soldiers, especially the SS, after they had been home long enough to build up anger at our presence, organize, and seek revenge. These were proud, tough men who had conquered a large part of the civilized world and had been pumped full of Aryan superiority for years. Some of them had not actually surrendered; an officer had surrendered them against their wishes. Think of these men coming home tired, dirty, unshaven, hungry, possessing little more than the clothes they wore, picking their way down a street of ruins and stopping in front of a pile of rubble that had been their home. Family dead or scattered, friends gone, no place to live, nothing to eat or drink, no job, and a bleak future. Not that I didn't think they deserved their fate; I certainly think some had made others suffer far more. But I wasn't about to get shot by some of these vengeful German veterans. A GI shot by a bitter veteran after the war is just as dead as a GI shot in battle during the war. I had picked up a Walther P38 somewhere and never went anywhere without it tucked in my belt. The weight of that pistol under my belt was reassuring when I was out alone at night. At times I carried it in my hand with a bullet in the chamber as I picked my way through the rubble on the way back to our quarters.

Not long after arriving in Bremen, another sergeant and I decided to pick up a couple of girls for some common, uncomplicated sex. He had some experience in that sort of thing, while I had none. His first stop was at the mess hall, to scrounge some food. We found a couple of nice-looking girls with little effort (probably at the plaza, where the Dom and Rathskeller are located), drank some beer at a local bar, and went to their house. There was no electricity, so we sat at a little table by candlelight and talked. Then my friend and his girl went into the next room, and he was soon huffing and puffing away, but mine was not at all cooperative. She kept saying, *"Ich bin krank"* (I am sick), which was one of the euphemisms for having VD (now known as STD). I wisely decided not to be insistent. Some time later someone pointed her out with the comment that she had given VD to some friends of his. Thus ended my first and only fling at the promiscuous sex of wartime Europe and occupied Germany, and from that moment I lived a very deliberately celibate life.

The war left me with some residual problems. I permanently lost some hearing, and my wounded leg bothered me for years. For the first few years after I returned home I would get violent shakes at unpredictable times, places, and frequencies. Nightmares were a major problem for more than a decade, and I have an occasional bad dream after I see a war movie, but they rarely disturb me. It took a very long time to return to emotional normalcy even though I didn't experience the worst of the war.

The real heroes of the Second World War are the average men who were ordered into the most dangerous situations, rose to the occasion, and performed their duty despite the real possibility of death or serious injury. They included bomber crews who flew in the early months of the war through flak and swarms of enemy fighters, tankers who fought against superior German tanks, the paratroopers and members of the OSS who were dropped into enemy territory, and the submarine crews who took their boats into dangerous waters. And, of course, the infantry, towards which I may be a little biased because of my personal experience. I prefer to reserve the label of hero for the infantrymen who went ashore on strongly defended beaches all over the world, fought through mine fields and heavy enemy fire, endured terrifying artillery and mortar barrages, and lived with death and physical discomfort day after day after day with little respite or hope of survival.

John Reckord Dies in Action In Normandy

'41 Graduate Noted As SGA President, ROTC Commander

Capt. John Reckord, '41, an important campus leader while an undergraduate, was killed in action on June 23, in Normandy.

Reckord, a member of Kappa Alpha fraternity, was Cadet Colonel of the ROTC and President of the Student Government Association in 1941, during his senior year.

Although he was first enrolled in the College of Engineering, he later changed his curriculum to economics, in the College of Arts and Sciences.

Reckord became a member of the Swim Club while a freshman, received the National Society of Pershing Rifles Silver Medal in his sophomore year, and was appointed a lieutenant in Pershing Rifles.

The next year he spent at West Point, but returned to Maryland to finish his undergraduate work.

In addition to his other activities, he was elected Secretary and Treasurer of Men's League, Captain of Pershing Rifles and a member of Scabbard and Blade. Later in his senior year, the Citizenship Prize was awarded to him.

Immediately upon graduation, Reckord entered the Army, working his way up to the rank of captain. He had been overseas for sometime.

Capt. Reckord, nephew of Major General Milton Reckord, noted Maryland alumnus and former commander of the 3rd Service Command, leaves a widow, former Kappa Betty Catling.

Campus Leader Killed

JOHN RECKORD

RAYMOND V. KURSCH

Glen Burnie, Maryland
64th Antiaircraft Battalion, U.S. Army

Raymond Vernon Kursch was born in Baltimore, Maryland, on October 10, 1921. He enlisted in the Army in May 1941 after graduating from vocational school and was assigned to the 64th Antiaircraft Battalion. On December 7, 1941, his battalion was garrisoned at Fort Shafter on the Hawaiian island of Oahu just a few miles from Pearl Harbor. After the war Kursch worked at the Maryland Shipyard and Drydock Corporation as an electrician until his retirement in 1985. He survived his late wife, Ella, and has four children and eight grandchildren.

On the morning of December 7, 1941, I was a member of Battery G of the 64th Army Antiaircraft Battalion assigned to the 25th Infantry Division. We were stationed on the island of Oahu, Hawaii, after having arrived in May of that year. We were garrisoned at Fort Shafter, and we stored our guns and equipment in buildings that were more like stables. Fort Shafter was located on a bluff that overlooked Pearl Harbor a few miles away.

Our battery consisted of eight 3-inch antiaircraft guns. Each gun had a crew of about six men. I was a gunner, which meant I would set a new round into the breech with my left hand, pull the firing lanyard with my right, and then eject the spent casing, again with my left. Two men seated in front of where I stood aimed the gun with wheels that when turned would raise, lower, and traverse the gun. A crew of men behind me would calculate range, set the shell fuses, and load the shells into the breech. Most of our days on Hawaii before December 7 were spent perfecting our gun skills, and we got to a point where we could fire thirty rounds a minute. We also spent a considerable amount of time practicing our loading and transportation procedures.

In the weeks before December 7 my battalion received a "non-drill" alert on three occasions. The first was about two weeks before the attack, the second a week later, and the final alert occurred on Saturday, December 6. The December 6 alert was memorable because we were issued live ammunition for the first time. We had heard so many rumors that our radar was picking up enemy planes and ships offshore that we really thought that something might finally be happening.

When we were alerted, we retrieved our guns from the stables, hooked them to the rear of our trucks, and drove to our gun positions at Ahua Point about thirty minutes down Kamehameha Highway. Ahua Point is located between Pearl Harbor and Hickam Field, and it was intended that my battalion would provide Hickam Field with antiaircraft protection from an enemy air attack.

On the December 6 alert, we manned our guns and stood ready for anything that might come our way. We stayed on alert for the remainder of the day, and at just about sundown we were given the all clear. We packed up our guns, drove back to our base, and stored everything away. That night half of the battalion was issued a forty-eight-hour pass, and there was lots of talk about parties in Honolulu giving out free booze. I was not fortunate enough to receive a pass, so I went about my normal duties around the base. It was the evening of Saturday, December 6, and no one had given us any reason as to why we stood down from alert, but the Army never gave us a reason for anything they told us to do.

On the morning of December 7 I was assigned to guard duty, and I remember it was a beautiful morning. I walked the perimeter of the base with a Marine stationed at Tripler Army Medical Center who was also on guard duty that morning. We walked and talked about just how pretty the view was.

In the distance we noticed some airplanes that looked like they were just hovering over Pearl. At first we didn't give it a second thought because the Navy had sent a notice to our base that they were conducting exercises and that we could expect flights of planes overhead on Sunday morning.

We couldn't hear anything, but there was a lot of smoke starting to come up from Pearl Harbor. More and more planes began arriving, and when we saw the first explosions I think we knew that something was terribly wrong. I am not sure what we would have done had we had the time to think about it, but just about the same time we saw the explosions, someone spotted what seemed like a hundred planes coming right towards us. All we could do was stand there with our rifles and watch the planes get closer and closer. Just as they passed over, a few planes dropped out of formation and turned around to strafe our position. I could see clumps of the ground explode into the air as the planes machine-gunned our base. The Marine on guard with me started yelling, "Holy shit, that's live ammunition! And I think those are fucking Japs!" We made a run for the barracks, and as soon as I entered we literally bumped into a lieutenant whose name I don't recall. He was one of those of-

Raymond Kursch in front of his bunker in the latter part of 1943 on Guam, where his 64th Antiaircraft Battalion had been stationed to protect one of the island's airfields. The heat was so intense on the island that the uniform of the day was typically a pair of cut-off shorts and a cap. Kursch remained on Guam until September 1945, when his battalion was sent back to the States.

ficers we called "shave-tailed ninety-day wonders." Guys like him were hurried through the promotion process real quick because the Army must have known the war was coming. They had more attitude than brains.

The lieutenant stopped us and said for us to follow him. I think I said something to the effect that I was still assigned to guard duty. He hollered back, "Not anymore, you're not! You're one of our truck drivers, and I need you right now!" We walked outside and were headed to the stables when the Japs made another strafing pass overhead. We had to dive back under the barracks to avoid being hit. The lieutenant yelled out, "Oh, I think I'm hurt!" And then he said, "I think I just got the first Purple Heart of the war!" He rolled over and asked me if I was hurt. I said, "I'm cut, but I'm not going in for any Purple Heart!"

We crawled out from under the barracks and headed back to the trucks. This time the lieutenant was grabbing as many men as he could to help get the guns hooked up to the trucks and the trucks loaded with ammunition. There were only about eighteen guys left on the base from our battery; all the rest of our outfit was still in town on leave. It took about twenty minutes to hook up our guns to the trucks and get ready to move out.

The lieutenant and I drove off the base first with a column of trucks behind us headed down Kamehameha Highway to the Army air base at Hickam Field. There were abandoned cars all over the road. At first I tried to drive around the abandoned vehicles, but the lieutenant hollered for me to push through the wrecks.

When we neared Hickam Field we ran into more trucks that had been shot up. There were bodies on the road, so I stopped the truck and started to get out to move the bodies out of the way. The lieutenant grabbed my arm and said, "No, keep driving!" There was nothing I could do, and a Japanese plane was making a strafing run along the road. I got back behind the wheel and just looked ahead as I hit the gas and drove through the wreckage. I could feel the bodies under the wheels as we passed over them. It was a horrible feeling.

When we arrived at Hickam we saw more dead and wounded off to our right by the barracks. It looked as if a group of men had been assembled for roll call and were sprayed with machine-gun fire. We sped past the gate to the airfield, and as we drove through Hickam Field I witnessed one of the strangest things. A meat delivery truck sped past the guards at the gate and us and then proceeded to drive down the runway purposely knocking the rudders off all the fighter planes that were neatly lined up on the field for inspection. We just drove on, and I don't know if they ever caught the man driving that meat wagon. In all the years since, I have never seen a record of the incident, either.

The lieutenant pointed out some bomb craters along the runway and ordered me to drive close so we could set up our guns in the craters. We set our guns and began firing back at the Jap planes in about half an hour. The sky was thick with black smoke that hindered our visibility, but we fired our guns as best we could for the next few hours until we were given the all clear. We brought down several Jap planes, and some of our guys drove a jeep over to the wreckage of one downed plane to check it out. When they returned I think we were all completely shocked to see they had found maps of the island as detailed as any I ever saw. They had the locations of our bases and military positions all over the island marked with red ink. After seeing those maps, it was no wonder how the Japs managed to do such a good job that day.

After the attack, Hickam Field was a mess. Pearl was on fire, and you could hardly make out anything recognizable. Our commander, Capt. John Walker, assembled the men of my battery and began to inform us that this was probably the start of a major invasion. I remember he said we would fight to the last man and would never surrender. A chaplain stepped forward and gave us our last rites and handed out communion. Everyone who attended the meeting took communion, no matter what religion they were. Some of the guys were pretty broke up. We stayed by our guns all night thinking the Japs would land at any minute. I was nineteen years old, and I was pretty scared. I had never seen dead people before, and I couldn't forget our drive to Hickam Field and having to run over those bodies.

During Sunday night and into the following morning the Army began landing troops near Pearl brought from outposts around the island. There was poor communication between outfits, and when elements of the 24th and 25th Infantry Divisions garrisoned at the Schofield barracks landed near Hickam, everyone on land thought they were Japanese invaders. A battle ensued in the confusion between our own forces for about forty-five minutes. We finally learned that they were our own guys, but not before our battalion lost one man during the shooting. Ironically, this was the only casualty the battalion had during the Japanese attack.

When December 7 comes around every year, I can't help but remember how poorly prepared we were for the attack. We were definitely asleep somewhere to have let it happen. I think someone knew what was going to happen at Pearl, and they just let it happen. I am not afraid to say it. If we had been ready, the Japs wouldn't have stood a chance. Maybe history would have changed if we had been, but as it was, we suffered a great defeat, and the nation rallied behind the war effort.

I really hated the Japanese during the war, but over time I realized it was just a few who were to blame. I feel very sorry for the Japanese-Americans who had their whole lives torn away and were placed in detention camps. I am glad it's all over now, and I hope we don't have to go through anything like that again. But as long as there are two people alive, I guess there will be disagreements, and there will be more wars. It's just the way it is.

ALFRED J. LIPIN

Glen Burnie, Maryland
629th Tank Destroyer Battalion, U.S. Army

Alfred Jerome Lipin was born in Pasadena, Maryland, on March 16, 1920. He attended Pasadena Elementary School and graduated from Glen Burnie High School in 1938. He enrolled in the University of Baltimore before being drafted into the Army in 1942 and assigned to the 629th Tank Destroyer Battalion. He is a recipient of the Silver Star for valor in recognition for his actions in helping to stop a German advance in Belgium. After the war Lipin joined his father in the hardware business and then entered politics. He was elected to the Maryland House of Delegates (serving from 1966 to 1970) and then the Maryland Senate (serving from 1970 until his retirement in 1977). He and his wife of fifty-eight years, Irene, have four children and eight grandchildren.

I grew up on Lipin's Corner in Glen Burnie, Maryland, which was a store and garage my father established in 1918. He had seven gas pumps in front of the business establishment, and he later built the Sherwood Gas Station. He eventually converted it to a general-merchandise store and then as time went on into a restaurant. I was in the restaurant when I heard the news on the radio that Pearl Harbor had been attacked. Pearl Harbor was a wake-up call for America. The Japanese did it behind our backs and declared war on us after it happened. I spent the next few months after the attack going to school at the University of Baltimore studying business administration, and I waited tables at the family's restaurant. I talked to people and listened to the radio, so I knew a little bit about what was going on with the war, but in those days the news did not tell you much except that we had some vessels at sea preparing to fight the Japanese.

After my junior year I received my draft notice. I expected my notice sooner or later, but at least it did not arrive until I had finished my third year. I think they did that purposely with us college kids because they could draft other people sooner who were not in school. I felt going into the service was something that I had to do. I was not necessarily enthusiastic about going off to fight, but it was my duty to go.

I was instructed to report on a certain day to the local draft board, which was located in the old Sanitary Commission Building in Glen Burnie. From there I and the other guys who had to report that day were taken to the Glen Burnie railroad station, and we got on a train and went to Baltimore, arriving at Camden Station. We then got on a military truck, which drove us to the 5th Regiment Armory downtown, and we had our physical examinations. We were also given a written exam, and I was surprised to discover that while I was trying to answer all the questions honestly, a lot of the other guys were trying to figure out how to answer the questions so they could get out of the service. In talking to them about it, they were surprised at me for trying to answer the questions accurately. I was then interviewed by a psychiatrist who asked me a lot of questions about sex and so forth. I happened to know the guy who interviewed me because I served him lunch while working at my dad's place, and I think he was shocked when I told him I had never had sex. I overhead all these guys around me talking about what they had done with girls the night before and how they had used some kind of excuse that they were going off to war and might never come back, just to have sex. I began to think maybe that was why they wanted to get out of the service, because they wanted to go back and do it again.

After all the tests and examinations, a group of us were shipped to Camp Lee, Virginia. We were once again asked a series of questions, and the group I arrived with was dispatched to various rooms. I immediately got a fifteen-day pass, which they said was normal so I could go home and close out whatever personal issues I had. I spent the time with my girlfriend, Irene. At that age I didn't have too many points of business to conclude, so the time passed quickly, and before I knew it my father was driving me back to the Glen Burnie train station to return to the Army. I don't think my father and I knew exactly what to say to each other. What is a father supposed to say to a son when he goes off to war? Anyway, it was just something like "goodbye," but I don't really remember. I do know it was a sad time, but I had no reluctance about leaving. It may sound strange, but I was actually excited about experiencing whatever adventures were ahead.

I went back to Fort Lee and then to Fort Bragg, North Carolina, for basic training. I spent thirteen weeks there learning artillery. The artillery piece was a 105 howitzer, and we studied how it was put together, tactics, and things like that. At the end of thirteen weeks a small group of us from Bragg were shipped to the armor training center at Camp Hood, called Fort Hood today. We trained to operate self-propelled artillery carriers that were actually pickup trucks with a two-by-four attached to the hood of the cab that acted as the gun. We were then informed our group was being formed into the 629th Tank Destroyer Battalion. We did not have any real tank destroyers, but we practiced the basic skills of moving a mechanized unit in combat.

The first time I ever saw a tank destroyer was when we moved from Camp Hood to Camp Young in the Mojave Desert in California. Our company commander and all the drivers had gone to California before we left Camp Hood, and on our first or second day at Camp Young they arrived with our new tank destroyers. Camp Young was just a spot in the desert and consisted of numerous five-man tents and no buildings. For the most part the men assigned to each tent became the crews that would work together from then on. The crew of each tank included the sergeant who commanded the tank, a corporal who was the gunner, and three enlisted men who were the driver, radio operator, and assistant gunner. The first crew I was assigned to included a thirteen-year-old boy; somehow he had deceived enough people to get into the Army.

We spent about eight months in the Mojave Desert getting accustomed to our new tank destroyers and learning the tactics of maneuvering to destroy other tanks. We learned how to perform reconnaissance, how to establish defensive positions, and how to move forward into enemy positions and gain the high ground to fire down on the enemy. Perhaps the most memorable feature of our training was the incredible heat of the desert. This only made the extreme temperature inside the tank escalate even higher. It was hot. We were given a fifteen-day pass while training in the desert, and I returned home by way of Pennsylvania Station in Baltimore with three other guys who lived in the Baltimore area. When we walked through the station, the people stared at our faces because the sun had baked our skin almost black, and we really stood out in the crowd. We thought having all the people staring at us was really funny at the time.

After eight months more of desert training, the unit moved to Camp Maxey, which is near Paris, Texas. I received a three-day pass and returned to Baltimore to get married. Irene and I were engaged before I left for the Army, and we had just one day to spend together after our wedding. My father arranged for us to honeymoon at the Carvel Hall Hotel in Annapolis. He paid for all the expenses. It wasn't too hard to leave again because that was the schedule Irene and I had set for us, and lots of other couples were doing it. After our wedding I returned to Texas, where we began preparing to go overseas. We were given physical examinations and any necessary dental treatments, and we updated all of our records and insurance policies. We were then transferred to Fort Dix, New Jersey.

We were at Fort Dix for just a short period before departing for Fort Kilmer and then on to Europe in December 1943. We went over in an English boat, and the food was terrible. The boat rocked quite a bit, and many got sick. Our boat stopped for twenty-four hours in the middle of the Atlantic because the engines failed, and if it had not been for the American submarines protecting us during that time, I think we would have been in trouble because the rest of the convoy had kept on going, leaving us all alone.

After some more training in England our battalion landed in France on the Fourth of July. The Allies had not advanced very far by then, and we didn't have to go very far to get to the front lines. We were set up as artillery to support our infantry fighting in Saint-Lô, where the Allies were engaged with tough German defenses. From our positions I saw our airborne troops jump near Saint-Lô, and I unfortunately saw men fall to the ground when their parachutes didn't open, and I could see the Germans who were shooting at those who floated down to the ground. It was amazing how many got down and got their job done. We broke through Saint-Lô within a few days, and the beachhead was finally opened up.

Our battalion consisted of three companies (A, B, and C), and each company was made up of three platoons. I was assigned to Company A, 3rd Platoon. There were four tanks in a platoon, twelve tanks in a company, and thirty-six tanks in a battalion. Each company was also equipped with what was called an M2. The M2 was like a tow truck that could retrieve tanks that were broken down or damaged.

The typical types of tanks used by the Army were designed to fight the infantry, but that does not mean that they didn't fight other tanks, because they did. The basic purpose of a tank destroyer battalion was to destroy enemy tanks. Our tank destroyers normally followed behind the other tanks, and when they encountered a situation against an enemy tank they couldn't handle, or when they needed a little extra firepower, we would then move into position to lend a hand. Each platoon sergeant had a jeep and a driver, and they scouted ahead to locate enemy tanks and then came back to direct the attack.

There were a few types of tank destroyers (TDs) used in the war, but we used the M10. The M10 was based on a variant of the M4 tank chassis. The M10 was relatively lightly armored compared to other tanks, and instead of an enclosed turret the M10 had an open turret. The open turret allowed enough room for three men to stand up at the same time to operate the main gun. In the turret there were two seats, one on each side of the main gun, where the gunner and commander sat while operating the gun. While sitting there their heads would stick out above the armor to see forward. The third man stood behind the gun to load rounds into the gun. The main gun was a 3-inch, or 76-mm., antitank gun. The gun had been developed as an antiaircraft gun before the war and was very powerful. It had an effective range of about two city blocks and could penetrate the armor of all but the heaviest of German tanks. The M10 also had a .50-cal. machine gun mounted on the turret.

The big German tanks, like the Tiger, had twice the armor of our tank destroyers, and our shells just bounced off them like peas. Even more impressive were German tank destroyers, and I was amazed at how heavily armored they were. We knew the Germans had stronger tanks than we did, and they were harder to destroy, and it would take a couple of volleys to take care of one of theirs. Their Tiger tank had a distinctive sound that you could recognize a few seconds before it went by, and that helped alert us so we could get out of their way. The German guns were much more powerful than ours, too. The biggest German tanks had the 8.8-cm. guns that had a long range we had to be wary of. We were constantly maneuvering around trying to get a shot at them first before they could get us, and the M10 was perfect for this role.

The number one question in a tank battle is who can fire first, and the first to shoot usually wins. The M10's speed and maneuverability gave us a tactical advantage to get into a position to fire first. Its tracks were made of rubber, making us quieter than the tanks that used steel tracks, and this allowed us to do a little more sneaking up on the Germans. We lost a bit of our stealth when the Army decided to upgrade the diesel engine with a gasoline engine that was much noisier than we would have preferred. These new tanks, made by the Ford Motor Company, were M36s. They had a 90-mm. gun, which was significantly more powerful. If anything, we beat the Germans because we had more tanks than they did. I don't think that Germany could produce as many tanks as we could. They could destroy ours quickly, but we would have another right around the bend to replace it. It was a matter of quantity over quality. We also had a far superior advantage in the air, and if all else failed we could always rely on our Air Force to back us up.

I would say that under the circumstances the M10 was comfortable. Sometimes in combat we could sleep in a bedroll outside next to the tank, but most of the time we slept in the tank. It was very uncomfortable trying to sleep sitting on a hard stool, but because you were so tired, you fell asleep pretty fast. If we did sleep outside we slept very near our tank, because otherwise you might get run over by a tank or some other type of vehicle. We rarely bathed, and when we had to go to the bathroom we did it in our helmets and then threw it out of the tank. When we hit the Siegfried Line we were stopped for I don't know how many days—more than a week or so. We didn't get out of our tank for a long time, but we got used to the smell from our poor hygiene and didn't notice it much after a while. We mostly ate the rations we had with us in combat, and we didn't enjoy it much, so it was always great when we had chow brought to us from the company headquarters. If we could stop and get out of our tanks for any amount of time, some guy would make an "egg call" over the radio to begin a search for chicken coops to gather some fresh eggs or anything else we could find to eat.

The M10 Wolverine tank destroyer featured a pentagonal welded turret equipped with a 3-inch M7 gun mounted on a Sherman tank chassis powered by a General Motors twin diesel engine that gave the M10 a speed of 25 mph on roads. An estimated seven thousand M10 tank destroyers of various varieties were produced during the war. Their mission was to engage and destroy enemy armor so as to allow Allied tanks to concentrate on the destruction of enemy infantry, fortifications, and rear areas.

All of our clothing and everything else we owned, like our bedrolls and supplies, were strapped to the outside of our tank. Our tank was hit once on the side of the turret. Nobody was hurt, but when we were hit it blew all of our equipment, clothing, and supplies all over the place. We were shaken up at how close a call we'd had, and we stumbled around trying to gather all of our stuff, and the mood was pretty bleak until someone passing by told us to look up, and above us hanging from an electric line was someone's underwear, so we found something in our situation to laugh about.

The first time that we ever encountered a German tank was in the Battle of Mortain. Mortain is a small French village that became the focus of a German counterattack on August 6, 1944. The Germans tried to force their way between the American First and Third Armies, and the roads through Mortain were essential for their objectives of driving towards the French coast. We were ordered into a defensive position around Mortain, and we dug in our tanks and loaded sandbags and logs on the front of the tanks for extra protection. A fierce battle occurred, and our tank scored a hit on a tank, and we knocked it out. We held our positions, but we would not have won the battle if it were not for the Air Force. They sent a forward observer to our platoon, and I had become a sergeant by this time, so I went forward on a reconnaissance mission with the observer. I will never forget the devastation I saw. We walked through a field, and strewn from one end to another were dead Americans and Germans who had fought and died on top of each other. It was something that you did not want to look at, but you had to get through it.

That was my first dose of that kind of stuff. Afterwards we saw lots of dead infantry, mostly American infantry that had been killed along the way. All I did was glance at stuff like that and keep on going. You are so busy doing the things in war that you have to do that you don't have time to worry about the bad things you see around you. You become immune to seeing death and destruction, and it doesn't bother you after a while.

I received a letter from my eldest brother's wife, and it must have arrived in late September of 1944. In the letter she said that my brother had died. My parents had told her not to tell me because they did not want me to know about it for fear it would upset me. I wrote a responding letter to her a few days later, which amounted to telling her that these kinds of things happen and so forth and how sorry I was, but that life goes on. At the time I read her letter I was probably more upset about my brother's death than anything else. But by the end of the day we had to move on, and things started happening, and I forgot about my brother's death. In combat, you start a fight before dawn and the next time you look at your watch it is after lunchtime. Time just passes so fast you don't think about looking at your watch. You don't think about anything except what you see in front of you.

There is fear in combat, and it is going through your mind most of the time. But you forget about your fear because you know that there is something that has to be done. We were trained to automatically do the things that we were supposed to do. We were trained over an eighteen-month period to kill. We were trained to fire at the enemy and fire at whatever was firing at us. I guess I did some praying for comfort, but I do not remember praying very much. I didn't have much time to think about praying, and I am not sure how much prayer can help you in a war. While at the Siegfried Line we were pinned down for days with infantrymen dug in all around us. A new fellow came in one night, fresh from eight weeks of basic training. It was quiet when he arrived, and I overheard him comment that nothing was happening around us and that he had nothing to worry about. The experienced infantrymen laughed and told him to wait a bit and just see what happens. When I woke up the next morning, that boy was dead. A mortar shell had landed on him during the night, and we just forgot about it and went about what we had to do and on to the next day.

The Germans were well disciplined and good soldiers, and they fought hard, there is no doubt about that. When they started on the offensive, they were especially good and gave no quarter. I felt fighting them was just part of our daily activities, and I never developed a hatred for the Germans. We were there to kill the enemy, and I didn't take anything they did in the war personally. On one particular occasion during the month of November in 1944 our company commander came to me and said we were going for a ride. He told me he had a job for me to do in the morning. We got into his jeep, and he took me to a hill in a wooded area overlooking a scenic valley and a house tucked in the edge of some woods. He told me he wanted me to come to the house before daybreak with two tanks, and whenever I thought the time was right, I was to fire as many rounds into the house as quickly as possible. The next morning we moved up into position in the dark, and when the sun shone over the horizon I did as I was ordered. I informed the company commander our mission was accomplished, and it was then he told me they had discovered the Germans were having parties every night with women in the house I had destroyed. How much damage we did, how many men and women I may have killed, I cannot say. I did what we were supposed to, and it was always a matter of them or us. That's the way it was throughout the whole war.

On the night of December 16, 1944, I was sleeping in the snow when the Battle of the Bulge reached us. I heard lots of tanks coming through our area, and we thought they were American tanks. All night long these things kept moving, roaring like anything. The next morning we found out it was a German attack, and we were ordered to move out of that position and travel as fast as we could all the way around the German thrust to meet it head on and try to stop the Germans from getting further through our lines.

At the height of the Battle of the Bulge the Germans surrounded our position. We had one long night where we didn't sleep and didn't know what was going to happen, waiting for the Germans to overrun our positions. Then in the morning we began to receive radio messages from someone who was telling us to get out of our vehicles and relax because the Germans had retreated. There was a guy in our platoon who was a German immigrant, and we always made fun of him because he liked to speak in broken German and English together, but never all of one or the other. He radioed everyone not to get out of our tanks because he could tell the person calling us to get out was not an American but a German pretending to be. He probably saved all of our lives that night. We spent another restless night alone thinking we were surrounded, and the following morning we woke to discover that the 82nd Airborne had landed on top of us during the night, breaking the German attack in our area. I think that would have been the end of us if the weather had not cleared to allow the paratroops to come.

On January 15, 1945, we were attached to the 83rd Division. We were on the forward side of the hill in a small town in Belgium whose name I do not remember. Off in the distance we saw a puff of smoke come from a thickly wooded area, and we knew it had to be a tank or something like it, so we and a few other tanks fired at the smoke. We began to receive greater fire in response, and I ran back and forth between my tank and some buildings to help direct fire on the enemy positions. I needed a better view, so I told my crew I was going upstairs in a nearby house to find two artillery observers who I knew were in the house. I found the artillery observer, a second lieutenant, who was looking from the window at the wooded area off in the distance. I moved to the other window in the room, and I was telling him what I had seen when a shell came right through his window and completely obliterated him. It must have been an armor-piercing shell that hit him. Another shell hit the building, knocking me off my feet, and the dust and falling debris made it hard to see.

I found the door on the right-hand side of the room and headed down the stairs. I bumped into the other observer, who had blood all over his eyes, and when I grabbed his arm he said he couldn't see. I led him down the stairs, and when we reached the door to the house I pointed him towards a safe place behind the house and told him to run like hell for a while and then lie down on the ground. After he ran off I followed him, and I fell on the ground next to him. I overheard my tank crew radio back to headquarters saying they thought I had been killed when the house was hit. I stayed there for another minute or so, laughing to myself, and thought I would wait a little while before I told them I was fine. I hollered out, "Here I am, I'm OK" and indicated I was going back to the company headquarters to report on the situation.

I am not sure why I did the things I did at this point, and I think the explosion might have knocked out some of my senses. I was trying to tell the captain what had happened up in the village when a first sergeant looked at me and grabbed my arm and had me look at my side. I looked down, and I saw pieces of body parts splattered all over me from the artillery observer who had been killed next to me. I was given a new pair of overalls, and I changed right there in the company headquarters before walking back to my tank. When I returned, the wooded area we had been firing on was engulfed in a hail of artillery and tank fire. I'll never forget how the woods were just blown to bits. When the smoke cleared we advanced and found we had destroyed an enemy tank, a half-track, two houses, and had inflicted casualties on nearly 150 German troops.

I was awarded a Silver Star for my actions that day, and I was sent to the 83rd Division headquarters to receive my citation. Their headquarters was near Paris, and the sergeant planning my trip knew I had a brother in Paris, so he recommended to the captain that I be given a three-day pass to visit my brother. To my knowledge, I do not know anybody else from my company who got a three-day pass during the whole time we were in the war. At the time, our battalion was waiting to cross the Remagen Bridge over the Rhine, and I felt awkward waving goodbye, headed to Paris while the other guys had to go forward.

My time with my brother in Paris was fun, but when I returned to my platoon I was told that one tank—not in our company, but in the 629th—did not make it across the bridge. I don't know the details, but I was told the men drowned when it was knocked off the bridge by an artillery shell that had landed nearby. Our battalion suffered heavy casualties fighting in the Remagen bridgehead, and I felt guilty I had been in Paris visiting my brother while all this was happening.

When the war ended on May 5, 1945, we were in view of the Alps somewhere in the southern part of Austria. We were told to stay in place and don't move an inch in any direction. We stayed there for about a day or two before we got orders to move back to a place where we established a border-crossing point between the American and Russian zones of occupations.

The Russian troops were friendly at times and at other times incredibly brutal. I remember one occasion when a German soldier was trying to get home and he had to cross from the Russian sector into ours. The Russians fired on him when he ran towards our sentry post, and we picked him up and brought him into company headquarters. The Russians had already made it clear to us they wanted him back, but we told the Russians he had escaped and we couldn't find him.

The Russians were always looking to buy stuff from us, so I began selling my monthly liquor ration of whiskey. I sold it to a Russian for five hundred dollars, believe it or not. The Russians paid us with five-hundred-dollar bills that no American had ever seen before, but when I took it to a nearby German bank they gave me smaller dominations I knew were legal tender, and I sent most of it back to Irene. One time someone had drank half of my whiskey, so I thought I would just fill it with water and sell it to two Russian majors anyway. A few days later I heard there were two Russian majors looking for a second lieutenant who thought he was pretty clever, so I stayed away from the border for a while after that.

The last encounter I had with the Russians was a pleasant one. Some Russian brass and other soldiers visited our headquarters and there were no interpreters, so the situation was a bit awkward with everyone standing around staring at one another. Finally we opened a couple cases of Coke, and the Russians greeted this gesture of friendship with big laughs and entertained us with their traditional dances.

In July the first group of men who had enough points earned during the war were allowed to go home. I had trained with many of these men and saying goodbye was hard, but I had to stay because as a second lieutenant I didn't qualify. I became an instructor in tactics, training a new crop of tank destroyer crews for the coming invasion of Japan. The war ended in August, and it was December before I was on a boat headed for home. I boarded a boat in Marseilles, France, and as we left I was told the ship next to us was taking on French soldiers heading for Vietnam.

We arrived at New York Harbor fifteen days before Christmas, and I will never forget us all on the deck looking for and finally finding the Statue of Liberty. Fireboats greeted us as we pulled into the harbor, and I remember looking up the busy streets of New York and seeing all the cars moving up and down the avenues. I was discharged from Fort Dix and sent to Fort Meade, where my father-in-law met me to bring me home. The war was over for me, and I was home for Christmas.

If I had to pick one hero of the Second World War, I would say Gen. James M. Gavin of the Airborne was my hero. Perhaps second would have to be Winston Churchill. Both men were very different but equally great leaders during a very difficult period in our history.

Le Carrefour—"The Crossroads"

On the night of June 9–10, 1944, after fighting and marching for twenty-two hours, the 2nd Battalion of the 115th Infantry Regiment began to rest in the fields outside of the French village of Le Carrefour, Normandy. Those not assigned to guard duty or supply detail dropped into the field and fell fast asleep. For thirty minutes nothing happened. While supplies were distributed, the staff met to discuss the next day's plan, and the men began to set up defensive positions as best they could in the very restricted areas typical of the hedgerow country.

Suddenly the noise of approaching vehicles was heard, challenges were exchanged, and shots were fired. A retreating German force consisting of parts of the 352nd Division, members of a workers battalion, and bicycle troops had stumbled upon the weary 2nd Battalion and quickly infiltrated into positions from the west and north sides of the battalion. The Germans unleashed a barrage from two assault guns, machine guns, machine pistols, rifles, and mortars. The 2nd Battalion returned fire, but the Germans cut down many men of the 2nd Battalion before they could react. The Germans gunned down many of the men who resisted, and the wounded who called out for help were killed where they lay. At the far end of the field the 2nd Battalion organized a line of resistance where the wounded were gathered for protection, and fire was returned. Members of the 2nd Battalion charged forward and fired their bazookas, which resulted in the destruction of the two German assault guns.

When the Germans withdrew they collected their wounded and the American prisoners they had taken and began moving again down the road towards Cartigny. While passing the American positions at the end of the field, fighting broke out again until the American POWs, who were in the middle of the column, cried out for their comrades to stop firing.

The wounded were carried on litters to an aid station of the 175th Regiment guided by the antiaircraft tracers that could be seen firing at German planes attacking the shipping off the beach. The following day the survivors assembled and trucked back to the ambush site, where they recovered lost equipment and found the bodies of their battalion commander, Lieutenant Colonel Warfield, and Captains Onder and Scott, who when called upon to surrender had said, "Surrender, hell!" before being machine-gunned as they tried to reach their men. The body of Lieutenant Tucker, the supply officer of 2nd Battalion who had gone forward to investigate the noise created by the advancing German column, was found in Le Carrefour at the base of the wall he had been stood against before being executed by the Germans.

The German records of the events indicate that they thought the idle American troops were actually a strong position intended to prevent their escape west. German commanders ordered an assault led by armored assault guns, or "Stugs." The Stugs could not penetrate the thick hedgerows, and the Germans had to resort to firing through the hedges. Confusion ensued as German elements became intermixed, and many held their fire for fear of hitting their own troops. The attack broke down quickly. It was noted in German action reports that if the Americans had been better prepared, the German assault would have been a failure.

The following are excerpts from an account of the German ambush at the French village of Le Carrefour, written in 1997 for the *29th Infantry Newsletter* by Donald C. Van Roosen. On the night of June 9–10, 1944, Private Van Roosen was the number 5 man in the heavy-machine-gun squad of H Company, 2nd Battalion, 115th Infantry Regiment, 29th Division of the Maryland National Guard. His primary responsibility was to haul ammunition for the squad and to man the bazooka when required. His actions in response to the German attack that night earned him the Bronze Star for valor with an oak-leaf cluster. (He is also a recipient of the Silver Star and the Purple Heart with three oak-leaf clusters.)

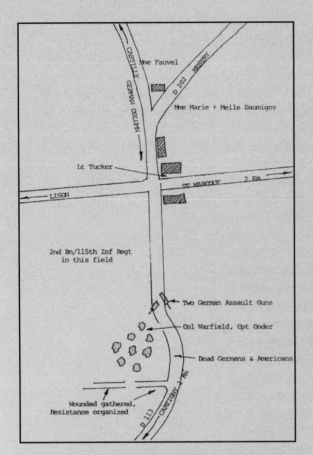

A MAP DEPICTING the movements of American and German forces on the night of June 9-10, 1944, when 2nd Battalion, 115th Infantry Regiment, was overrun by a retreating battalion of German infantry supported by assault guns. Those Americans not killed or wounded retreated to the far side of the field the battalion had bedded down in for the night and returned fire until the German column departed.

DONALD VAN ROOSEN POSES WITH ACTOR MICKEY ROONEY near Durboslar, Germany, during Rooney's visit to the front lines in February 1945. Van Roosen is holding a model M1 Thompson .45-cal. submachine gun. The Thompson was relatively heavy at 11 pounds and had an effective range of under 75 yards, but its .45-cal. round fired in full automatic mode was devastating at close range. Prior to and during World War II the Auto-Ordnance Corporation in Bridgeport, Connecticut, and the Savage Arms Company in Utica, New York, produced approximately 1.25 million Thompson submachine guns. The fully automatic M1s were fed by a 30-round box magazine and had a rate of fire of between 600 and 750 rounds per minute. The Thompson was very popular among specialized troops such as Rangers, Marine Raiders, and armored and parachute units. Possessing one became something of a status symbol, and it was an eagerly sought-after weapon.

The 2nd Battalion suffered thirty-one killed, seventy-seven wounded, fifty-eight taken prisoner, and ten missing—a loss amounting to 22 percent of the battalion's strength.

On the night of June 9–10, Company H, 115th Infantry Regiment, came to the field at Le Carrefour and proceeded to set up a night defense. Sergeant Hanson and I took the machine gun out into the road and set it up. When flares went up and firing started, I opened up and fired about half a box of ammunition down the road. A light machine gun from G Company also fired. The gun jammed, and I was unable to clear it. I saw two Germans coming down the road firing their Schmeissers, so I ran back into the field. The two Germans picked up our abandoned machine gun and disappeared.

I then heard tanks coming down the road so I gathered my bazooka and a round and went back up to the road. Fifty yards down the road a German assault gun was turning into the field. I fired at the side of the vehicle, and it stopped and caught fire.

I returned to the field and began collecting about twenty wounded and placed them behind a hedgerow in the next field for protection. I dressed the wounds of as many as I could while fighting off the Germans who were trying to advance down the road by our position. As more riflemen came through the entryway into the field, I placed them in defensive positions around the wounded. Senior noncoms and a group of officers came through our position, and when I asked for orders they said, "Keep up the good work."

I do not agree with the often-expressed statement that those who died are the real heroes. There are a lot of ways to die in war: through stupidity, bad luck, being at the wrong place at the wrong time. Anyone who did a heroic act during the war is a hero. The rest served honorably and deserved respect, but a blanket award of the title "hero" is not appropriate, in my opinion.

Donald Van Roosen later described his own actions that night in more detail.

CLARENCE A. MOORE

Reisterstown, Maryland

VF-31 Fighter Squadron, U.S. Navy

Clarence Alan "Bill" Moore was born in Peoria, Illinois, on August 5, 1923. After moving to Baltimore in 1929, he attended Garrison Junior High and Forest Park High School. He enlisted in the Navy in 1942, becoming a fighter pilot assigned to Fighter Squadron 31, and is a recipient of three Air Medals with three gold stars. On August 15, 1945, he was credited with downing a lone Japanese kamikaze plane, which eventually earned him the distinction of scoring the final aerial victory of the Second World War. After the war Moore returned to Baltimore to pursue a career with the C&P Telephone Company, retiring in 1988 with forty-seven years of service. He and his wife, Betty, were married in 1946, and they have three children and six grandchildren.

I grew up in the Howard Park section of West Baltimore and attended Garrison Junior High School. Things were a little different then. Unlike today, we had no school buses or anything of that sort. I walked the 3 miles each way to Garrison Junior High, which was way up off of Garrison Avenue. I didn't even think about the walk, because it was just an everyday occurrence. In the summertime my father rented a cottage in Stony Creek near Riviera Beach, and I learned how to swim, fish, and crab, and I developed an appreciation for all the good things about the seafood industry in Maryland. We caught a lot of crabs. My grandfather came up from Brownwood, Texas, one summer, and I took him crabbing. We used chicken necks for bait, and we were catching so many crabs that every line we threw in the water had a crab on the end of it within minutes. My grandfather asked me if we could put more lines in the water, but I told him I didn't have any more anchors to take the bait to the bottom. He then pulled out a beautiful pearl-handled pocketknife and told me to use it as an anchor. I refused, saying it was likely to get lost. He said, "I don't care; this time we have together is more important than any old pocketknife." That kind of stuck with me my entire life. I have lots of great memories from that place.

After graduating from Forest Park High School I took a job with the C&P Telephone Company as an installation and repair technician. On December 7, 1941, I was at a meeting of my high school Gamma Sigma fraternity when the news came over the radio that Pearl Harbor was being attacked. We were all kind of shocked, and we really didn't know the meaning of it. We all ran out in the street yelling and hollering that we were at war. We were kind of happy about going to war, but you have to remember we were eighteen-year old kids with no idea what war was like. I am sure my reaction would have been different if I had known then what I know now.

Things settled down a bit over the next couple of months, and in February 1942 I decided to go down to the main post office in Baltimore and enlist. I went with a high school classmate, Garland Myers, and when we got to the steps of the post office we realized we had not thought about what branch of the service we would join. We decided to each flip a coin to decide if it was going to be the Navy or the Marine Corps. He flipped his coin and it came up Marines. I flipped mine and it came up Navy. So we walked into the post office, and he went one way and I went the other. I saw my buddy just one more time before we were called to duty. I never saw or talked to him again, despite some efforts since to locate him through the years.

When I walked into the recruitment office I had no intention of wanting to become a pilot. I walked up to the desk and told the recruiter I wanted to sign up. He handed me an examination, and I sat down and completed it and gave it back. I answered questions related to math, English, and science. The recruiter took my exam and told me to have a seat, he would be back in a minute. When he came back he told me I had qualified for the V5 program. I said, "V5? What's that?" The recruiter explained to me it was the introductory course to enter the Navy's flight training program to become a pilot. I thought it sounded exciting, and I accepted.

The next few weeks were very exciting, and I was anxiously anticipating my being called to duty. When my notice arrived, the telephone company gave me a good going-away party with a luncheon and so forth. They were very kind to me and gave me assurances they would have my job for me when I got back and I would be granted any raises that would have occurred while I was away. It made me feel very good, and I was naturally very pleased. I was relieved to be going into the Navy because I had been classified 1-A, which meant I was most "qualified" to go into the Army infantry.

I boarded a train with ten other guys from Baltimore at Pennsylvania Station, and we went to Charlottesville, Virginia. We were met by a couple of junior-grade officers who told us to "fall in." We figured out what that meant after a minute, and they marched us through Charlottesville to the University of Virginia. The first thing I discovered was that we were forbidden to ride in cars or use any form of transportation to get around campus; we had to walk wherever we went.

I was pretty green and ignorant of the traditions of the Navy and still maintained a carefree attitude in my first few weeks in the Navy. I worked really hard one day so I could earn a weekend pass so I could visit a young lady I knew in Charlottesville. I arranged to get word to her I was coming to see her, and I got all dressed up in my Navy white uniform with hat and everything. I began walking across campus feeling as happy as I could to have a few days off, whistling as I went. All of a sudden this voice came from behind me saying, "Cadet Moore! Attention!" I stopped in my tracks and froze. The voice then said, "Cadet Moore, front and center!" I swirled around, and standing there was our commandant. He said, "Cadet Moore, do you know who whistles in the Navy?" I said, "No, sir." The commandant said, "Well, only boatswains and damn fools! Are you a boatswain?" I said, "No, sir." "Well, then, you are a damn fool!" The commandant then proceeded to inform me my weekend pass had been withdrawn and instructed me to change into my work clothes and report back to him immediately. I ran back to my room, changed, and ran back to report to the commandant. He handed me a rifle, and I stood guard outside the officers' quarters for the remainder of the weekend. I never whistled in the Navy again.

The V5 program was an introductory course to prepare us to become pilots. We didn't fly while at the university but were taught naval history and Navy regulations and procedures. We also studied meteorology and navigation, which was important when flying from a carrier that moved from the place you took off from. Our courses at UVA lasted three months, and from there we went to the Virginia Polytechnic Institute for basic flight training, where we learned how to fly.

We trained in the Piper Cub, and I was taken on three training flights with an instructor before I was sent up on my first solo flight. I picked it all up very easily, and it was a great experience for me. My first solo flight went as smooth as could be until it was time for me to land. We were flying from a field carved into the mountainside in Blacksburg, Virginia, and the winds always whipped through the mountains, tossing around our little Piper Cubs. The wind was especially harsh during my first solo, and I tried and tried to get the plane on the runway, but the wind kept lifting me back into the air. Finally they radioed me and said I should expect two guys to run out onto the runway during my next attempt and grab the struts of the wings to hold me onto the ground. My first solo flight ended inauspiciously with the help of two greasy mechanics holding on to each wing as my plane finally came to a stop.

Accidents happened in training and during the war, but my class managed to escape without any incidents. I think it was due to a combination of luck and confidence in my skills that I never had an accident. I never so much as blew out a tire on all those carrier landings, although it was a common occurrence. The cause of most accidents was pilot fatigue and anxiety. Missions were emotionally draining and sometimes lengthy, and the anticipation of getting back on the carrier and out of the plane had to be tempered with concentration. We had a landing signal officer (LSO) who helped guide us down onto the deck of the carrier. He spoke to us through the radio and used colored panels in each hand to visually indicate if we were too high, too low, and if our wings were out of line with the deck. If things didn't look right, he would wave us off, and we would have to come back around for another try. If things were looking good, the LSO flipped his panels over to red, and we cut our engines and hit the deck. A hook in the tail of the plane grabbed the restraining chains, and the plane was brought to a stop. The most exciting thing that I ever did was to land a plane on a carrier deck, because it was moving. As long as you paid attention to the LSO, you knew you were going to land on that deck without any problem whatsoever. I had complete trust in his judgment. The guys who were exhausted and anxious wouldn't pay attention to the LSO. That's when they would come down hard and bounce over the side or, worse, hit the end of the deck head-on.

We completed our basic flight training in three months, and we were sent to Memphis, Tennessee, to fly a biplane for advanced flight training before heading to the University of North Carolina. The Navy tested our mettle and tried to toughen us young kids up by having us box and wrestle to see who was the toughest guy. We pounded on each other, and when it was all said and done, we had become closer friends. During these weeks we also had classes in aerology teaching us how to use the stars for navigation across the oceans. We also had to prove we were capable of escaping from a plane dunked into a pool of water while wearing all of our gear, to see who could keep his cool and swim to the surface. Some guys panicked and flunked out. We were then sent to the University of Georgia for similar training and played soccer against an Army squad at Fort Benning.

I arrived at Pensacola, Florida, sometime in the spring of 1944. I flew the SNJ-186 Navy trainer learning how to fly in formation and aerial gunnery. Ted Williams, the great hall-of-famer from Boston, was one of my instructors. He played on the Pensacola baseball team, and I remember he didn't like flying so much with eighteen- and nineteen-year-old kids, who took a lot of chances while learning how to fly. It was at Pensacola I learned the skills I would eventually use in combat. We started by doing a lot of target practice by shooting skeet. The skeet shooting got us familiar with shooting at moving objects, and shooting at another plane in the air was done by leading your aim at a target the same way you shot skeet. We practiced aerial gunnery by shooting at a sleeve trailed by a plane, and we performed practice attack dives with each guy firing a different-colored bullet so they could see who was hitting the target. Hitting the target was an indication of how well you could fly the plane, and if you didn't hit the target, you were going to get in trouble and eventually flunk out.

The art of being a fighter pilot is basically about getting behind your enemy and shooting them down. We learned and practiced these skills by chasing and being chased. The lead guy could go wherever he wanted, just as long as he didn't go into the clouds. If he did, he lost. I didn't think the Japanese were very good fighter pilots because there were a few times they got the jump on us and only managed to do a little damage when they had the opportunity to shoot us from the skies. I was able to get on the tail of one Japanese fighter, but as soon as he saw me he hit the throttle and pulled away from me. I flew the Grumman F6F-5 Hellcat during the war. It was a great plane, but pretty slow. The advantage we had with the F6F-5 was that we had much more maneuverability. It may not have been as fast as most of the Japanese planes, but we could cut inside the Japanese planes every time. The Japanese couldn't follow us when we dove to the deck to escape, and when they tried to follow they often flew into the ground. There was always a moment of terror when you discovered a plane was on your tail, but you would react instinctively and your thoughts changed real quick to getting the hell outta there. You had to react quickly to get moving to maneuver yourself. As soon as I saw a plane on my tail, I flipped over and headed as fast as I could for the trees or water. If it was a Zero on my tail, I knew I could lose it by feinting left and then making a quick and hard turn to the right. The Zero just couldn't copy the move.

I graduated from Pensacola in September of 1944 and received my commission as an ensign. I was sent to Daytona Beach Naval Air Station and learned how to fly at night and land on a short runway with an arresting wire that was similar to what was on the carriers. This is where I flew the F6F for the first time.

The F6F Hellcat was designed to replace the F4F Wildcat and to better compete with the Japanese Zero fighter. I thought flying the Hellcat was the best experience of my life. It was a marvelous and dependable airplane, and the F6F won the air war in the Pacific. To me it was a big airplane, but it was only a single-seat fighter designed with collapsible wings so it could be fitted on the aircraft carriers. It had a performance ceiling of 37,000 feet with a cruising speed of 200 mph and a maximum speed of 400 mph that we reached in our attack dives at full power. It had a large fuel capacity, giving it a range of around 1,100 miles, and a drop tank could be used to increase the range. The F6F could carry up to 2,000 pounds of bombs and three 5-inch rockets under each wing in addition to the six Browning M-3 forward-firing .50-cal. machine guns (three in each wing) with four hundred rounds of ammunition for each gun. The throttle was located on your left, so even the left-handed pilots

Bill's Moore's 2nd Division of VF-31 Fighter Squadron in front of an F6F Hellcat aboard the carrier USS *Belleau Wood* in 1944. *From left:* Lt. K. H. Sommerville, Ens. Bill Moore, Lt. James S. Stewart, Ens. Harold Mokwa.

had to reach over their left arm to adjust the throttle. The Navy was definitely a right-handed Navy, and the F6F-5 was a part of all that.

Perhaps the single most important feature of the Hellcat was the 2- to 3-inch armor plating located behind our pilot's seat. The armor outlined our body, protecting us from getting hit by enemy fire from behind. The Japanese didn't have anything like this, and I think it was a big reason we gained the advantage in the air. My plane was shot up from behind a few times, but I was only grazed once in the left arm when it was hanging out from the protection of the armor plating. The armor-plating design feature was indicative of the difference in theories of how pilots were expendable to the Japanese but they weren't to the Americans. The Japanese had little value for their lives.

On one occasion I had been chasing a bogey up to 30,000 feet and the engine was running rough, and I tried to make an adjustment but only managed to flood it with water. I called an SOS, and the captain of the *Belleau Wood* actually ordered five destroyers to circle the area where I was to splash. All that for me. A big part of the task force was waiting for just one man. When I returned to the carrier the captain called me into his quarters and asked if I was all right. Of course, I never did admit it had been my fault.

We left Daytona for Great Lakes Naval Training Center in Illinois. We were asked what we wanted to do, and I chose to be a fighter pilot. The group I had trained with from the beginning was split up, with some joining me as a fighter pilot and other guys choosing to be torpedo or bomber pilots. I was sent to Hollister, California, near Monterey, and it was there my VF-31 Fighter Squadron was assembled. There were thirty of us from all over the country, and we stayed there for several months perfecting our formation flying. The Navy knew we were headed to the northern part of Japan, and we had to practice flying in similar conditions. We took off in the morning and flew into fog banks to practice flying by instruments, and we had to trust our squadron leaders implicitly that we wouldn't get lost. On one flight we entered a fog bank near the Golden Gate Bridge, and when we cleared the fog bank our commander, Lt. Comdr. Don Wallace, was gone. We never saw him again. It was a quite a shock, and it was worrisome to me that if our most experienced pilot had problems, what might happen to us?

While at Hollister we had gone out for the night in San Jose, and we were late getting back to the base. We missed our curfew, so we decided to cut through a few buildings to sneak back into our barracks. The last building we cut through was a kitchen, and as we ran through someone grabbed a meat ax and threw at the wall. The ax stuck perfectly into the wall, and the next day we had a good laugh about it. When the Navy asked us if we had a preference for a squadron insignia, it didn't take long for someone to suggest the "Flying Meat Ax" as our squadron insignia.

We left Hollister for Oakland Naval Air Station and boarded a transport that took us to Hilo, Hawaii, then Saipan, Guam, and the Philippines, where we boarded the *Belleau Wood*. The *Belleau Wood* was a French cruiser converted into a carrier at the beginning of the war. On October 30, 1944, it was hit by a kamikaze that claimed over one hundred lives. The damage was repaired and the carrier was returned to service by January of 1945. Our squadron boarded the *Belleau Wood* in San Pedro Bay in the Leyte Gulf. We conducted a training cruise in the Leyte Gulf until steaming northward with Task Group 38.1 for Japan in July. We were part of an operation named "Empire Strike" that continued to the end of the war on August 15, 1945. The objective was to bomb and strafe the defenses on the Japanese home islands of Honshū and Hokkaidō.

Life on the *Belleau Wood* couldn't have been better. I was never an organized youth when I was growing up. I didn't make my bed every day, and I didn't have a regular schedule as far as work is concerned or what to do around the house. In the Navy things were much different. I had one roommate, who was also a pilot, and every morning at 6 A.M. a sailor would come by and rap on the door and say, "Ensign Moore, it's 0600 hours, breakfast is being served in the wardroom." We would take a shower, shave and get dressed, and meet in the wardroom. We always had to present ourselves in the "top Navy way" because the ship's officers were always there. During the day a sailor gathered our clothes to wash and then iron them, and they were ready for us when we returned from our mission. Not a bad life for nineteen-year-old guy. When we had free time we played bridge, and I learned how to play poker. I never played in the craps games that were all over the ship because I didn't understand the game or know the odds of rolling an eight or

Moore sits in the cockpit of his F6F Hellcat shortly after the conclusion of the war in August 1945. The squadron's "Flying Meat Ax" logo can be seen below his name. To the right of Moore's name is the Japanese Rising Sun emblem, which represents the Japanese kamikaze he shot down at 2:30 P.M. on the afternoon of August 15, several hours after signing of the armistice that ended the war. His downing of the kamikaze was later determined to be the last official aerial victory scored by an American pilot in the Pacific, and the last of the Second World War.

seven or six or whatever. The most important thing we had developed was our fellowship, and we all became very close friends. When I wasn't playing games, I just loved being around the planes. I spent much of my free time jogging up on deck or just sitting around watching the other planes take off and land. I was much more fortunate than the poor guys in the Army who were out in trenches full of mud who had to worry about where they were getting their next meal or when they could get their next bath. I had it all handed to me aboard our ship.

Every evening instructions were posted as to who was going up the next day and at what time. Two flights were launched each day, and I flew a mission every day. One went up in the morning and the other in the afternoon, and each had a different target. I preferred the morning flights, and so did my flight leader, James Stewart, and we would always volunteer if we could. We would be in the ready room at 0600 hours for our mission briefing, and we were told the objective and location of the targets. Our squadron put up three flights of four fighters on each mission. The primary mission of our squadron was to protect the carrier and provide cover for the dive bombers and torpedo bomber squadrons on missions. When we entered the war the Japanese had far fewer planes in the air, and we were used more for bombing and strafing missions. The objectives of our missions were prioritized to hit airfields, manufacturing, railroads, and shipping, in that order. We were given navigational information and the codes the ship would be broadcasting so we could find our way back home. The chaplain would then say a few words, and we were out the door and to our planes. We were normally over the target by 0800 hours and back before lunch.

I never really thought about the dangers of flying in combat. I thought every mission was exciting and actually fun. I was naive, perhaps, or I must not have been very bright or something, because I never felt an ounce of fear. But that is why we want young and naive people to fight our wars. There were some guys who just seemed hard pressed. They were frightened about going up on missions. One of the members of my flight had a habit of flying halfway to the target and then coming up with some excuse that he felt sick or his plane was acting up and had to return the carrier. He was just a nervous guy, but we didn't respect him very much. I felt like he was letting us down, and his absence left someone without a wingman, and that endangered lives. He eventually did it so often the commander of the squadron took his wings away from him. How he went home and went about his life knowing he had failed himself and his fellow pilots I could never know.

On bombing missions our flight approached a target above the flak, maybe at 20,000 feet or a little bit higher. We were on oxygen at this altitude, and when we were over the target the flight leader would start our attack. He would peel off to the left, and the rest of the flight from left to right would follow. I don't recall ever peeling off to the right, and it was follow-the-leader all the way to the target. You could see what the guy immediately in front of you had done, so you didn't want to hit that target because generally speaking, once you hit a target with hundreds of tracers, rockets, or a bomb, it would catch fire or be destroyed. After the run, we would gain altitude again and the flight leader might say, "Let's hit them one more

The Grumman F6F Hellcat was the Navy's successor to the F4F Wildcat. Although the Hellcat was less agile than the Japanese Zero, it earned a great reputation as a fighter and fighter-bomber. The Hellcats were better armed and far more powerful, durable, and numerous than their Japanese counterparts, which gave the U.S. Navy and Marines the advantages they needed to win air supremacy during the last two years of the war in the Pacific. According to U.S. Navy records, of the 6,477 enemy planes destroyed in air combat, 5,150 were destroyed by Hellcats flown by Navy and Marine pilots. By the end of the war Grumman had manufactured nearly 12,200 Hellcats.

time" or "Good job, let's get outta here." We wouldn't form up, but we would follow one another around in a circle to come back and hit the target again if needed.

On July 13, 1945, we attacked the Japanese naval ships in Tokyo Harbor. It was a treasure trove of Japanese ships, including two aircraft carriers, a heavy cruiser, and a few destroyers. The jewel my flight was after was a massive battleship named *Ise*. We dove at the 35,000-ton battleship almost straight down so our 500-pound bombs would hit the deck of the ship, and I was actually aiming for the ship's smokestacks. We let the throttle all out because the flak and small-arms fire was intense, and we wanted to get in and out as fast as possible. The battleship *Ise* had 16-inch armored decks, and our general-purpose bombs just bounced off the deck. We did some damage to the towers and main guns, but nothing we could tell at the time. When I came out of my dive on the *Ise,* I saw a carrier right in front of me across Tokyo Bay. Well, I'm thinking, "I've got six rockets, and I'm going to get myself a carrier." I flew a few feet above the water across Tokyo Bay, scraping the prop of my plane along the water. The carrier was huge, and I was very close when I let all six rockets go. I watched them explode on the side of the darn thing, and they didn't do anything at all. The rockets were not made for armor piercing, and my efforts were like scratching a match across the side of the carrier.

Getting back from a mission was always a great feeling. You usually let out a deep breath and said a little "Thank you." We were interrogated after each mission we flew over Japan, and we would report what we had seen and what the guy in front of us had done and what we had hit and missed and so forth. Our fighter group had a flight surgeon who looked after us. He was a really nice guy and a unique doctor. He didn't bring any of his own tools, medicines, or other tools of his trade aboard ship but used those belonging to the ship's infirmary; but, we discovered, he had brought a large stash of booze. When we came down after a flight, and sometimes it was after a tough mission and perhaps we had lost a guy or two, there he would be waiting for us with a bottle of Old Crow bourbon in his hand. We often needed the drink. The doctor helped loosen us up, and it helped the interrogators get all the details of our missions they needed for their reports. This was also about the time my plane captain would come looking for me. Each plane was assigned a plane captain who was responsible for the maintenance of the plane. They were revered men, for our lives depended on their attention to the details of our craft. He would come looking for me to give me hell if I had gotten "his" plane shot up. I also had a bad habit of firing my guns too long, and I burned out more than my fair share of barrels. I could still hear him coming down the hallway towards the wardroom, cursing and moaning, looking for me to yell at.

I had four wingmen during my time with the squadron. Three of them were shot down, and two of them were killed. On a mission to

Ens. Edward R. White, the first of three wingmen Moore lost during the war, suddenly and without warning climbed from formation to stop a Japanese fighter that was on a collision course with Moore's F6F Hellcat. White's Hellcat collided head on with the Japanese Zero, and he was killed.

bomb an airstrip in northern Japan I lost my first wingman and best friend, Edward R. White. I was the lead pilot of our flight, and I was watching the sky from 0 to 15 degrees and Ed was watching from 270 to 360 degrees. We were up at about 15,000 feet, and the sun was above and to our left. I didn't see it coming, but Ed saw a Japanese Zero come out of the sun headed right for me. Ed didn't say a word. He left formation and went full throttle up to meet the Zero. They both began firing their guns, and they hit head on; I've got that picture right here in my head like it happened yesterday. There was a massive explosion, and I had a glimmer of hope that Ed had survived when a parachute emerged from the black cloud of smoke. But it had only been blown off Ed's back, opened, and drifted slowly down under its own weight. I was Ed's best man at his wedding in San Francisco before we were shipped overseas, and I remember saying to him, "Don't get married, Ed. By God, man, you're gonna go over there. What are you gonna do if you have to leave a widow back here?" And that's what Ed did. I went to go see his wife when I got back to the States, and it's tough to talk about even now, after all these years.

I wasn't angry; it was sadness. No anger. My friend had saved my life. It had happened so quickly, and if he hadn't of done that, I would have been a goner. I was not angry. I mean, what was I to be angry about? Ed gave his life for me. At the time, during the war, I have to admit I hated the Japanese. I still harbor resentment for the Japanese for what they did to our boys in World War II. But as I have gotten older, and hopefully wiser, I have come to the realization we are at a point in history where we have to learn not to hate anymore. Our enemies these days have hatred for us, and we should defeat them, but I don't want to be part of that hateful consciousness anymore. I don't want to be that kind of a guy who carries a grudge, even though I still carry those kinds of feelings deep inside. I am not proud of it, and I am sorry about it, but it's the way things happened to me. I've had some bad experiences, as I have said.

On the flip side, I was never so blinded by hate during the war that it made me forget the difference between right and wrong. I had a real bad experience when we were sent to Hiroshima to seek out targets to bomb. This was before the atomic bomb was dropped, and from 100 feet up the city was beautiful. We were given strict orders to not do anything except locate possible targets and nothing else—nothing. Our orders stated, "Don't touch Hiroshima, it is a religious community." We completed our mission, and on the way back we decided to pass over Tokyo to find some real targets we could hit. Our bombers had pounded Tokyo, and the place was a mess. We flew over the Tokyo train station, and it was a horrible and sad thing to see these thousands upon thousands of people below us jammed in there trying to get away from the place. One can only imagine the horrors they had already endured. Anyway, my wingman Lt. Bill Hall, God rest his soul, peeled out of formation and turned on four of his .50-cal. guns and opened fire on the crowd of people below. I don't know how many hundreds of people he probably killed or injured. I couldn't believe I saw him do something like that. For no reason at all, he killed those innocent people. They weren't soldiers; they were just innocent people in that station trying to run for their lives. When we landed back on the carrier I ran over to his plane and punched him in the mouth, I was so angry. He killed innocent people. That's not the way Americans fight. Anyway, Lieutenant Hall flew the next day as my wingman, and he was hit after a low-level strafing run by some small-arms fire and killed. It was as if God was punishing him for what he had done. The guy owed me eight hundred bucks, too.

The third wingman I lost was named Herb Laws. We were over an airfield in northern Japan strafing it to keep the Zeros from getting into the air, but some did, and Herb got a Zero on his tail and was shot down. He was able to perform a belly-landing in a field, and he got out of the plane and was standing on the wing and waved to me when I flew past. I flew over a second time, and the last time I saw the Japanese surrounding his plane. He became a prisoner of war and survived the war and today lives in Boston, Massachusetts. When we met after the war, he was not the same person; the Japanese had killed him psychologically. When the war was over one of my most rewarding missions was to drop cigarettes and candy bars into his and many other Allied prisoner-of-war camps in Japan.

Our last mission of the war was on the morning of August 15, 1945. We were headed to bomb the Japanese electric works in Tokyo. The entire city had been leveled by the B-29s except for this one large stone building. And, of course, the Navy just had to level it for good measure. There was nothing else within miles—really, absolutely nothing except for this one building left standing in the middle of what used to be Tokyo. Most cities in Japan were just like Tokyo: we destroyed every urban area in their entire country. We were running a little behind schedule and should have been over the target by 0800 hours, but by this time we were still twenty minutes away over the ocean. Then we heard the message over the radio, "Now hear this. Air Group 31. All pilots. An armistice has been declared. Return to base. Jettison all bombs, ammunition, and rockets. Jettison and return to base." We were given the order to release our belly tanks, and we fired all of our rockets and guns at the same time until we were spent. It was a fun time, and we started doing barrel rolls. I was performing a barrel roll when I released my two bombs, and I watched one roll off the end of my wing. At a reunion fifty years later, a guy in my squadron said he had seen me do that and thought it was the craziest thing he had ever seen. I thought that was the last time I would fire my guns during the war. But it wasn't.

When we got back aboard the carrier I planned on doing a little partying. The war was over, and we had survived; I was elated. Before I could unwind and relax I heard the announcement, "Ensign

Moore, report for duty." What the heck they wanted I had no idea. I went back up to the ready room, and they told me I was to fly cover with my flight at 10,000 feet over the fleet because they were afraid a lot of the Japanese pilots had not gotten the message the war was over, and radar had picked up a few planes heading our way. I was then handed a message that read, "Admiral Halsey has issued an announcement that all Japanese sniper (kamikaze) planes were to be shot down, not in the spirit of vengeance, but in a friendly fashion." I appreciate what the great admiral was trying to say, but I was unsure how I could shoot down a guy in a "friendly" fashion.

I got my flight up into the air again, and nothing happened until about 1400 hours, when over the radio came the message, "Enemy at two o'clock, 12,000 feet." I was at 10,000 feet, and I immediately decided I was going to go get it. I gave it full throttle, and since I was the flight leader I was well ahead of the others and got to the Japanese plane first. I got on his tail, and after a couple of maneuvers I was able to get some fire into his wings, and the plane exploded. I didn't know it at the time, and even for many years after the war, but someone did some research on the subject and discovered I had shot down the last plane of the war. My name made it into the history books.

When the war ended we entered Tokyo Bay with the fleet. We went ashore, and we discovered we could buy anything we wanted with only cigarettes and candy. I bought some little brass pots used to burn incense, and I still have them. The Japanese were very friendly to us, and I was very sympathetic to what we had done to them during the war. I had no bad feeling towards anyone. When I got back to the States a few weeks later I was asked if I wanted to stay in the Navy and become an instructor. I said, "No thanks."

I have always talked about my war experiences in a positive light, and my family understands what I went through. It's important that we talk about our history, or else the younger generations will never know the history of America. My Navy years were a pleasure to me because there was always something exciting going on. It taught me how to be organized, and taught me about the good in life and how precious life is. Looking back on my experiences in the war, the one thing that sticks out in my mind is the organization and fellowship that we all acquired in order to do our jobs. You couldn't do it alone. We did it together by learning how to get close to people and to learn how to protect each other as best you could. We all had our share of good friends we lost, and I always thought that God was on my shoulder to help me get home.

The real heroes of the Second World War are the dead ones. Like my friend Ed White. He was a hero to me. I wasn't a hero. Being a hero in the war meant being at the right place at the right time and being able to handle it with whatever skills you had. But in the end, the guys who were lost were the real heroes.

JOSEPH W. PURNELL SR.

Berlin, Maryland
366th Infantry Regiment, U.S. Army

Joseph William Purnell Sr. was born in Berlin, Maryland, on August 29, 1914. After graduating from Flower Street High School in 1934, he worked for the Worcester Board of Education as a bus driver until being drafted into the Army in December 1942. He was assigned to the all-black 366th Infantry Regiment, which was sent into combat in Italy attached to the 92nd Infantry Division. After the war Purnell returned to his bus-driving career, retiring twenty-eight years later in 1973. Since retirement he has been active in local politics and veterans affairs, serving in the NAACP, the Maryland Service Corps, Project Shore Up!, and the Veterans Commission. He married his late wife, Ruth, in 1946 and has two children and six grandchildren.

I remember the Pearl Harbor attack like it was yesterday. My girlfriend, Ruth, and I were walking out of church when someone started running around saying the Japanese had attacked Hawaii, and I think we all were in shock. Exactly a year to the day later I was inducted into the Army. When I received my draft letter, the first person I told was my mother, and I said I had to go away for a while. I wasn't given much notice before I had to report, and there was hardly any time to have any family gathering to say goodbye. I didn't go out of my way to tell many other people, just those who I happened to run into on the streets, and I began to discover other blacks from the area had been drafted as well. Thirty-three blacks from Worcester County were inducted into the Army on the same day. Two other black guys from Berlin, Olin Washington and Leon Duncan, went into the Army with me that day, and I was the only one of the three who survived the war and came home. I felt I had no choice going into the service; I was told to report, and I did. Blacks were not given the opportunity to enlist, and I am sure we all would have gladly enlisted if the opportunity had been there. By serving my country I sincerely hoped my service would gain respect from both black and white people. I also knew if we didn't fight the war there was a good chance there would be no freedom for anyone in the entire world.

We all assembled in Worcester County in Snow Hill, where we boarded a train to Fort Meade, Maryland, and after a short layover we were sent to Fort Devens in Massachusetts to join over two thousand other black draftees from the Northeast. I was assigned to Company E of the 366th Infantry Regiment. Every single man in the 366th was black, from the commanding officer all the way down the chain. We trained to become soldiers and received our Expert Infantryman's Badge, meaning we were ready for combat. The 366th was assigned to patrol the Eastern Shore for German U-boats, but the whole regiment was moved to A. P. Hill Military Reservation in Virginia for more training. Before we left Massachusetts our colonel, Howard D. Queen, gathered us together and said, "Men, we're moving out. We're going to A. P. Hill in Virginia for special combat training. You're going below the Mason-Dixon Line now. It's going to be different for all of us, but I don't want to hear any talking about it." We were not a transportation or trucking outfit, but we moved ourselves in trucks without incident.

We lived in tents the whole eight weeks we were at A. P. Hill, performing more drills typical of boot camp, and we learned more combat techniques including how to blow stuff up and all that kind of stuff. The black troops were treated harshly by the white officers, and when we went into town on leave we were met with an equal amount of racism and prejudice despite wearing the same uniform as the white soldiers. When the regiment finished training we moved out to Camp Atterbury, Indiana. We received a less than warm welcome when we arrived in Indiana, and on numerous occasions the regular Army guys told us they didn't want us there. The base had a white colonel who didn't like the fact that he was the same rank as our Colonel Queen, and he told Queen he didn't want him telling him or anyone else what to do around the base. Word spread our Colonel Queen told the white colonel they were the same rank and he had in fact been a colonel longer, so he couldn't tell him how to behave. Five days later the white colonel reappeared, but in place of his colonel's eagles, on his shoulders he had a general's star. He had been promoted in five days just so he wouldn't have to be equal to our Colonel Queen. This is the kind of stuff we went through all the time, and it would actually be funny if it weren't the truth.

We finally received our orders to ship out overseas, and Captain Green, a graduate of Dunbar School in Baltimore, told us we were to pack up. We left for Hampton Roads, Virginia, in February of 1943 and remained there for about eight days before we loaded the transport taking us to North Africa. Colonel Queen gathered us together one more time and said, "All right, men, y'all are wondering where you're going and what's going on. Well, I am going to tell you exactly what's happening and where we're going." I remember the whole regiment got excited and began shouting, "Where are we going?" He said, "Men, I'll tell you. We are going overseas." This was an amazing development for us, because up until this time blacks had been primarily used as a labor force in the Army, and our motto was "Labor" (not battle) "conquers all things." I read somewhere only 15 percent of all blacks enlisted in the war saw combat because our generals were unwilling to test our abilities.

On March 28 we got all of our equipment loaded onto trucks and went down to the docks where a brand-new troopship named *Billy Mitchell* had pulled up to the docks. The ship was too new-looking for something the Army would give us, but sure enough, they told us to line up and get on board, and I felt like we were cattle being loaded onto a boxcar. I noticed the radar at the top of the ship that kept going around and around, and when we asked the captain what it was all about he told us to watch it closely, because when it stopped and pointed in one direction, it meant a submarine was nearby in the water. This was not a good way to help many of us who had never been on a ship before relax. The radar stopped a few times during our trip, and when it did the ship whirled around and started to zigzag all over the place. We felt better when we learned the ship was fast enough to outrun any submarine, which explained why we went out on our own without the protection of a convoy.

By the time we landed in North Africa it was about Eastertime, and I thought it was exciting when we arrived at Casablanca, where the movie with Humphrey Bogart was to have taken place. The fighting for Africa had ended a long time before we arrived, but there were some Germans and Italians around working at the big Army prison called Newsit Hill for American servicemen who couldn't deal with Army life or messed up in some way. While in Casablanca we met soldiers, presumably Egyptian, who carried these long decorative swords that were razor sharp. The British troops told us these native soldiers had fought alongside the British and how they slit the throats of the Germans with their swords. They loved us Americans, and despite our attempts they refused to show their swords to us because they had a practice that if they drew their sword, they couldn't place it back in the sheath without spilling the blood of their enemy. I was glad they were on our side.

It wasn't long before we were loaded onto a transport once more and sent to Italy. We landed in Foggia, in the southern part of Italy, and were assigned to the Fifteenth Air Force under General Twining guarding the Air Force base in Foggia. The 92nd Division had not arrived in Italy by this time, so the 366th was on its own. Although the 92nd had an all-white commanding staff, the 366th officers were all black. When the 92nd arrived it was sent directly into combat north in the Po Valley, where it ran into heavy German resistance and suffered heavy casualties. When men were needed to fill the ranks of the 92nd, they came and took our 366th.

We were relieved by military police and sent to the front to join the 92nd Division. The commanding general of the 92nd, General Almond, greeted us and said, "You know, you all want to go into combat, you all wonder why you are going into combat, but remember this, your own people did it to you." He was right. The black newspapers back in the States had caused all kinds of trouble asking why black troops had not been put into combat.

We were immediately sent to the front lines, but instead of entering combat as a cohesive unit our 366th Infantry Regiment was fragmented and sent into the line as replacements. This destroyed our morale and eventual effectiveness in combat. General Almond didn't care for our 366th Infantry Regiment much, and our Colonel Queen resigned his command because of the mistreatment he received at the hands of the general and the grief brought on by the dispersion of his 366th Infantry Regiment. When the 366th was split up, I said goodbye to many of the men I had known from Worcester County, and I never saw many of them ever again.

On December 1 we arrived at the front lines, and our new colonel, Colonel Ferguson, addressed the men. He said, "Men, this is it. We're going up there tonight, and remember, your M1 rifle will be your mama and the bayonet your baby sister. We'll move out tonight, and don't think the Germans don't know we are coming; they do. They are watching every move we make. Combat is rough, men. Some of you are going to go up there and you're not coming back." To my right was my good friend Leon Duncan from Berlin, and when he heard the stuff about not coming back he leaned over to me and said, "Joe, I'm one of them not coming back." But I said to him, "Man, I'm coming back." Then my other friend, Olin Washington, says, "Joe, I don't think I'm coming back, either." I said, "Hey, guys, I'm coming back." Olin then said, "When you get back, tell my mom that I've got ten thousand dollars for her and to buy that little house she wanted." The colonel then said, "All right, men, I want to wish all of you the best of luck." We immediately loaded onto trucks and went right into the battle. I was an aide to our Captain Green, who I sat with on the way to the front. All the men were quiet during the drive to the front. I was frightened to go into combat, but what I think helped me through these tough times was my total faith and trust in the Lord. I prayed constantly.

The Germans were up in the hills looking right down on our positions, and they could see everything we did. We quickly learned we couldn't move during the daytime, and even at night we had to move quickly or else risk getting shelled. At night we listened to Axis Sally on the radio, and lying there in my foxhole it was troubling to hear her talk about our unit like she knew everything we were doing. She would say, "Oh, look what we have here, it's the 366th Infantry. You're an all-black unit, and we wonder what you are doing here when your own people treat you so poorly back home—look at yourselves." She also talked about the Japanese-American troops fighting alongside us in Italy. When Axis Sally signed off at night she would say, "Sweet dreams, we'll be shelling you."

I first went into battle on December 26, 1944, without any additional equipment or training than what we had arrived with months before. A superior force of German and Austrian troops, which had more tanks and artillery guns, overwhelmed our forces. All we could do was find cover and pray we would have a chance to move without being discovered. I was in combat for six months, but I wasn't in combat the whole time because we would fight for seven days, and then we would be relieved and go back down the hill for a rest, and then we would eventually have to go back, of course. When I was out on a mission, I felt death was facing me at every turn, and I had little control over what might happen to me. I found the best way to deal with the killing and death in combat was to put my total faith in God, and believing his presence was with me was comforting. I quickly learned the best way to survive in combat was to stay ahead of the enemy and try to anticipate what they might do next and act accordingly. Daily life was something other than my own, and I felt I was being dragged along by the circumstances of war with all the other men in my same position. Witnessing the sudden death of so many men I had known for such a long time was a shock, and at times I lost all sense of control over what I was doing.

On the 28th we were given orders to move forward against a German stronghold, and we were instructed we would have artillery support before our attack. The support never came, and we were told our artillery had been "rationed," if you can believe it. The greatest Army in the world, and we couldn't get a hundred shells thrown in our direction. Without artillery, Captain Green assembled a patrol to go forward to scout the German positions, and my friends Olin Washington and Leon Duncan volunteered. A group of Italian Partisans volunteered to lead the patrol through the German positions, but they were actually a group of Fascists who led our patrol straight into a trap. The Germans ambushed the patrol, and the German machine guns cut them to pieces. The Germans killed all but one man, the first-aid man, who they told to go back and tell us how they had laughed when they killed our friends. The Germans really didn't care much about any Americans, let alone us blacks, and we heard rumors they had refused to take blacks prisoner, so many of us agreed not to surrender and to fight to the death. We never recovered the bodies of the men who were killed, and we never found their dog tags or anything else to process their deaths. I guess they were all buried together in an unmarked hole somewhere in those hills. The deaths of my two friends from Berlin were a great emotional shock to me, and I felt traumatized at how they had been tricked into their deaths.

We fought our way through Rome-Arno, the North Apepnine Mountains, and the Po Valley. In January we had resumed the attack, and fighting was difficult, and we lost a lot of guys. We had just a handful of tanks with our company, and I was walking with Captain Green just to the side of a tank when a shell, probably an 88, hit the tank and killed Captain Green. I wasn't wearing my helmet at the moment the shell hit, and I was knocked senseless. I crawled around in the dust until I found the captain's body. I was yelling, "Cap! Cap!" When I realized Captain Green was dead, I started running blindly through the dust and smoke. I ran until a sergeant named Mickey yelled out to me and then ran after me until he grabbed me and pulled me to the ground. We laugh about it now when we get together, and he says I was a little crazy for a bit, just repeating his name: "Mick, Mick, Mick, Mick." I was taken down the hill and put into an ambulance that dropped me off at a general hospital. It was one of the big hospitals they had near the front lines, and I was there for about four weeks. I had not received physical injuries but had suffered a physical and mental breakdown. I remember two fine nurses, Miss Goetz and Miss Carol, who took fine care of me. I also became friends with a guy from Macon, Georgia, named Roy who was wounded on Hill 606 in Salerno, where his division lost eighteen hundred men. When I found out I was being let go, Roy grabbed me and said, "I was taught by my parents a Negro was no good, but they taught me wrong. When I get home I am going to change my ways." I said, "Roy, you know what? Those Germans don't care if you're white or black. Those 88 shells kill no matter what color you are."

After I was released from the hospital I began my trip back to my outfit, and a colonel in a jeep pulled up to me and asked if I wanted a ride. I told him I was fine and was just trying to do the best I could to get back to my unit. He asked my name, and when I arrived back at the front I was ordered to report to an all-black quartermaster outfit in Milan, Italy. I thought I was going home, but it turned out the unit was to be transferred to the Pacific to help prepare for the invasion of Japan. This was about when Italy was just quitting the war, and before I left Italy I had the distinct pleasure of being in the streets when they dragged Mussolini's body through the streets of Milan. I was helping to guard a group of German soldiers at the time, and one of them turned to me and said, "You got a cigarette?" I said, "Man, if this was you holding this carbine, do you think you would let me smoke? Keep moving." We boarded the *Billy Mitchell* I had taken from the States to North Africa, and after a long trip we made it to Manila, where we learned about our coming invasion of Japan. Truman dropped the bomb just a few weeks later, and it was all over. If Truman had not dropped the bomb, a lot more boys would have died in the war.

When things settled down each man was called into an office to receive our discharge papers. I had accumulated enough points to return home and was excited to get back to the States. A lieutenant sat me down, opened up some sort of file, and said, "Now, Private Purnell, looks like you have done a wonderful job. Wouldn't you like to stay in the Army?" I said, "Lieutenant, sir, I want to get out of this place so bad, I don't know what I am doing!" I arrived home a week before Christmas 1945. I married Ruth and tried to put the war behind me.

The 366th was the first and last all-black outfit in the Army, and today people just wouldn't believe how we were treated. The 366th trained together, crossed the ocean together, but was completely pulled apart before we could prove our merit in combat. Thirty-three black men from Worcester County went into the Army with me, three of us from Berlin. We all went into combat with the 92nd, and only nine of us came back home, and just a few are still alive today. During the war we often wondered if things would be better for us when we got back to the States. I can't speak for the other men, but since I was the only one to have made it back to Berlin, I can say things didn't change much for a long time. Leon Duncan, one of my friends killed in the ambush in Italy, once asked me if I thought we would be allowed to sit on the bench on Main Street when we got back to Berlin. He'll never know the answer was still no for many years after the war. I sit on that bench these days, and I think of Leon, Olin, and all the other friends I lost in the war. They gave their lives despite the bigotry we encountered so Hitler wouldn't win. If Hitler had won there would be no Eastern Shore or Berlin, Maryland. Our homes today would be just another small percent of his world under Nazi rule.

The real heroes of the Second World War are the black soldiers who fought and died in the midst of bigotry and prejudice and never gave up. I hope someone recognizes the contributions of the 366th while there are a few of us around. If I had to pick just one person, it would be Lt. John Fox. Fox was a member of the 366th who sacrificed his life in the small Italian village of Sommocolonia to stop an attack by calling our artillery on his position. He was killed along with seventy enemy soldiers, and his actions went unnoticed until his widow received the Medal of Honor on his behalf fifty-three years later in 1997.

CHARLES A. SERIO

Perry Hall, Maryland
5th Marine Division

Sgt. Charles A. Serio

Charles Andrew "Chick" Serio was born in Baltimore, Maryland, on July 20, 1922. He attended Saint Edward's Grade School and is a 1941 graduate of Mount Saint Joseph High School. He enlisted in the Marines in 1942 and was assigned to the 5th Pioneer Battalion, 5th Marine Division. He is a recipient of the Silver Star for valor in recognition of his resourcefulness in the closing battle for Iwo Jima, which helped halt a Japanese attack. After the war Serio attended the University of Baltimore, graduating in 1951, and worked for the USF&G Company for ten years before forming his own insurance agency, which he operated until his retirement in 1988. He married his wife, Marguerite, in 1951, and they have three children and one granddaughter.

My grandfather, Joseph Serio, immigrated to the United States from Sicily in 1906 and started a small business delivering cases of limes and lemons to local bars. I was told my grandfather was especially proud to have had Babe Ruth's father, who owned a bar in Baltimore, as a customer. His small business eventually grew large enough for him to establish a stand in Lexington Market, and he and his five sons, including my father, John J., built the business into the largest produce business in the area. The business lasted in Lexington Market for nearly fifty years and provided the five Serio sons and their families with homes and private educations.

I worked at the market for my dad when I was only eight years old. Dad would purchase a hundred shopping bags at one and a half cents per hundred, and I went around the market and sold them to shoppers for three cents each. At the end of the day I had to reimburse my father for his investment, and I would go home with a few bucks. Doesn't seem like much these days, but back then it paid for a lot of fifteen-cent banana splits and five-cent movies at the Dixie Theater on Baltimore Street. After I purchased a ticket I would sneak into the back of the theater and open the door so my buddies who didn't have any money could watch the movie, too.

My father married Sara Marsiglia, my mother, and her parents and their twelve children grew up around the corner from our house in Walbrook. I was fortunate enough to grow up with my uncle Joe, the youngest son in my mother's family. Joe was an excellent athlete, and we were friendly competitors. Joe was a great leader for me and the other kids in the neighborhood, and he was someone I tried hard to emulate. We played baseball and football together in Gwynns Falls Parkway or Bloomingdale Oval, or go to Leakin Park for baseball and hiking. The natural dams created little ponds on the Gwynns Falls, and we would spend our afternoons swimming and fishing for tadpoles. We had several nicknames for each pond, including the "Seven-Footer," the "Ball Freezer" (for reasons I hope are self-explanatory), and "Granite Quarry." We had some good times back then.

In the summer of 1942, after graduating from Mount Saint Joe High School, I took a job at Bethlehem Steel working as a clerk in warehouse number 2. That summer my uncle Joe received his draft notice, and I decided I wanted to join up with him. We went downtown to the Marine recruiting office together and told the recruiter we wanted to sign up. We figured we should join the Marines because they seemed the smallest outfit and might need more guys. They handed us and five other guys a test, and after a short while they informed us that only my uncle and I had passed, and that we were going to be Marines. I was so excited to tell my father that I ran all the way back to my father's produce stand in Lexington Market to spread the good news. However, my father was not pleased when he heard the news. He actually flew into a rage and began yelling, "You did *what?* Are you crazy?" My father was a Navy man, having served on the USS *Ohio* during the First World War before he was legally a citizen of the United States. He sat there and lectured me about how Marines slept in holes while Navy men had clean bunks to sleep in every night and ate good food. Never could I have imagined at that moment just how right he was.

My basic training was at Parris Island, South Carolina, and it was tough. When all was said and done, we were made into Marines, and we were trained to the nth degree. The drill instructors kept on telling us, "A United States Marine can do anything." After you go through boot camp, you feel like you *can* do anything. They told us to take on three or four Japs at once because we could handle it. At the same time, they warned us not to do stupid stuff because a dead Marine was of no use to them. I always wondered how the heck I was going to do both. We were all just kids seventeen, eighteen, nineteen, and twenty years of age, and I guess we were capable of believing we were ready for what lay ahead. In the weeks following boot camp we really learned how to fight. We practiced advancing on an entrenched enemy and learned how to stay alive. This train-

Serio *(front row, far left)* with other marines and sailors in front of the NBC offices in Hollywood, California, before shipping out to Hawaii in 1943.

ing saved lives, but there were always some foolish guys who thought they could do anything their own way, and these fellows almost always paid the ultimate price later on.

We left Parris Island in August of 1942 and went to Camp Lejeune in North Carolina for more training and schooling. In December of 1943 we were taken to Camp Pendleton, California, by train. We spent the majority of the next year receiving advanced training and conducting mountain-climbing exercises that began at five in the morning and included 30-mile hikes with full packs and rifles. We were lucky if we got more than five hours of sleep a night during our training.

In mid-January of 1944 I was promoted to sergeant, and we were loaded onto transport ships and sailed out to Hilo, Hawaii. When we arrived we practiced assault landings on the quiet beaches, which at the time had only two hotels. I recently returned to the spot where we made those practice landings, and those pristine beaches are now packed with tourists and countless hotels. While on Hilo, I played for the battalion baseball team. We had some good players, and several went on to play professional baseball after the war. We had no baseball diamond on the base, so we loaded into an old Marine dump truck and traveled around the island to play against teams comprised of Japanese, Chinese, and Filipinos. I was the only one with a driver's license, so I drove us around the island. When the ignition was turned off, the truck backfired, and I was chewed out on a couple occasions for purposely frightening the local natives during our jaunts across the island.

We were loaded onto the ships again and spent the next forty-two days in what seemed like hell. We slept and ate in the dark hold of the ship. It always smelled of body odor and vomit. Things finally got interesting when we were called together on the deck of our ship. We gathered in a large semicircle around an officer who had placed a three-dimensional map of an island in front of the group. This was the first time any of us had ever heard of a place called Iwo Jima. I remember a few guys had trouble trying to pronounce the name. The officer told us it was a 5- by 2-mile-wide island, and that strategically we had to take it for the invasion of Japan. He also said we had to capture Iwo Jima because the Japanese had spotters on the island that alerted their homeland of a pending bombing raid, and that our bombers needed a safe place to land if they were damaged or low on fuel returning from bombing Japan. (After the war I read that landing on Iwo saved the lives of thirty thousand or more airmen.) As he pointed at places on the island, he would tell us of all the potential dangers we would encounter. After we got back on the ship forty-five days later, I could have added a few nasty particulars to his list.

That was the beginning of our Iwo Jima experience. The education we received on the deck of that ship was very important for our success. A few of us had been in combat before, but for the most part we had no idea of what we were getting into. All we knew was that we had a job to do. I think I had some fears, but I tried to keep that fear in the background, and I didn't think or talk about it much.

The next morning I remember walking onto the deck of our ship to stretch my legs. The night before the seas had been empty, but that morning there had arrived what seemed like thousands of ships of all shapes and sizes. You could see ships as far as the horizon. We just stared at the aircraft carriers, not really fully believing the immense size of these ships. During the next day all these ships and planes bombed the hell out of the island, and it disappeared into one huge cloud of dust.

On February 19, 1945, the first waves of Marines made their landings on Iwo Jima. My battalion was to land later that same day, but we did not get onto the island until the next day because we were told there was just no room for us to land. On the deck of our ship, we watched the first wave go in. I really wish I had been a photographer, because I had the opportunity to see the whole battle right in front of me. I could see all the Marines on the beach trying to move forward and getting shot and thrown around by the exploding mortars. It was like a movie. It was a sight to behold, and I have never forgotten watching all those boys fall over in the sand. That same night, I was standing on the bow of our ship when a huge spotlight from one of our ships was turned on and located a crew of Japanese soldiers trying to move a cannon from one cave to another on top of Mount Suribachi. In a moment, the guns from a nearby battleship boomed, and it took that one blast and the whole

Japanese crew was blown to who knows where. Just as suddenly, the spotlight went off, and the sounds of the explosion faded into the darkness and all was absolutely quiet again. Now that's a scene I have never forgotten and that can never be duplicated.

The following morning we had a breakfast of steak and eggs, and we couldn't get over it; we never ate so good. Our battalion was ordered to pack up our equipment and report on deck. It was our turn to land on Iwo. The seas were pretty rough, and coming down the rope ladder into the landing boats you had to be careful. Many guys broke legs or fell between the ship and the landing craft, and we had no chance to rescue them before they were drowned. It was hard to accept the fact that they didn't even get a chance to fight. We were heavily loaded with ammunition, grenades, packs, rifles, and food, and those moments during loading time were quite an experience. We were each given two bottles of brandy before going over the side. I thought it was foolish to liquor guys up before going into combat, and I gave my bottles away to a guy who I think collected most of the bottles given out to the men in my boat.

We finally filled our landing craft, a Higgins boat, and set out to rendezvous with the other landing craft circling offshore before we headed to the beach in formation. The choking black exhaust from the diesel motor of our boat blew right over my head, and I had to crouch down to get some fresh air. To this day when I see a bus and all that exhaust come out, I run in the other direction to keep away from all those awful fumes.

We rolled slowly over the waves, and that's when I said, "Lord, I am getting sick!" We all were so sick from the motion of this tiny boat, we just wanted to get on that island as soon as possible—forget the Japanese. The Japs were very good with their mortars, and they were dropping in all over. Some other boats were hit, and you could see Marines thrown up in the air when their boat exploded. We just wanted to get the hell out of that boat. I was thinking at the time that if we got hit, I was going to dive deep into the water under everyone else. I would cut off all my equipment and make my way to the surface. I had learned how to hold my breath for a while under water, so I just thought about that during the trip to the beaches. We were all scared; after having seen what was going on in front of us for a couple days, you had to be.

As soon as we felt the bottom of the boat hit the sand and heard the front flap of the boat come down, we just flew down the ramp and charged the beach. It took just a few steps to realize there was no way to run in that black volcanic sand. The first thing I saw was a hill in front of us, so we crawled our way to the base of the hill and used this for our only protection. There was debris everywhere: ruined boats, planes, crates, and stuff just blown to hell. There were Marines, alive and dead, scattered all over the place. We sat there until the beachmaster told us we could all move forward. The Japanese were shelling the heck out of us, and we couldn't really dig

Chick Serio and fellow 5th Marine Division buddies during a rest period in Hawaii following their combat tour on Iwo Jima. *Front row, from left:* Jack McLaughlin, Serio. *Back row, from left:* Jack Gavin, Bill Carpenter, Lloyd MacCreary. The 5th Marine Division suffered eighty-seven hundred casualties in thirty-six days of fighting on Iwo Jima.

down for protection. The soft sand was more like ash, and it just kept falling in on any scratch you made in the ground. We learned to use pieces of destroyed airplanes and pieces of debris to make walls for our foxholes. The Japanese were still so deeply hidden we didn't actually see the enemy when we landed. By the amount of incoming bombs, I figured they sure could see us.

On Iwo, the 5th Pioneer Battalion was responsible for unloading equipment from landing craft and managing the ammunition and supply dumps, and we also worked in the division cemetery. I was assigned to the Headquarters and Service Company, and we spent most of our days during the first couple weeks guarding our supply areas.

We quickly learned that the Japs would try to infiltrate into our foxholes at night and try to stab at us, so we always had to have a top over our foxhole to make it hard for them to slip in on us. Sitting in my foxhole on the third day after we had landed, I realized it had been a long time since I last ate, slept, or used the facilities. They had told us in basic training to use our helmets while two guys watched out for the enemy, but I just couldn't do it that way. I saw a tank come rolling by, and I hollered at the guy sticking his head out of the turret to park in front of our position so I could jump out and do my business. He nodded and pulled up in front of our foxhole. Just as I dropped my pants, a Jap mortar crew started dropping shells around the tank. The tank took off in one direction, and I, with my pants around my ankles, dove back to my foxhole in the other direction. I spent the rest of my time on Iwo looking for that damn Jap mortar crew.

It rained all day when the second flag was raised on Iwo atop Mount Suribachi. I was tired, and I hadn't taken my boots off since we landed, so I sat down and had started to remove my boots when I was startled to hear a whole lot of commotion going on behind me. I looked over my shoulder and saw some guys standing around a flagpole with our flag there. All the guys started clapping and cheering, and the whole time I was soaking my sore feet in my helmet.

In the Marines, it doesn't matter if you are a cook, baker, or whatever; if there is fighting to do and you are nearby, you fight. On Iwo there was plenty of fighting, and we found ourselves assigned to the 26th Marine Infantry Regiment to support their offensives.

The Japanese were damn good soldiers, and they rarely surrendered. We never really saw the Japanese. We would shoot at movement, but I never knew if I hit anything. They had built 26 miles of caves on that 5-mile by 2-mile island. I can't imagine what must have been under us all that time.

I had a buddy, a Corporal Barr, who we nicknamed "Candy." As we approached the entrance to a cave I boldly decided to go inside and check for Japs. Before I stepped a foot into the cave, Candy came running over and grabbed me by the collar and then harangued me for my stupidity. Candy had been in on the invasion of Tarawa, and he had seen what happened to Marines who wandered into caves. There could have been a hundred Japs in that cave, and I wouldn't have known it until it was too late. We threw explosives into the cave to seal it, and moved on. My life had probably been saved by Candy that day. All of us who walked off that island had our lives saved probably at least once by another Marine at one time or another.

The only way to take that island was to clear every hole and every cave and drive the Japanese out with knives, bayonets, rifles, grenades, and explosives. The flamethrower was the most effective way to flush them out, and those guys did a magnificent job. The Japanese came out of their caves and bunkers only when we burned them out, and the men who carried the flamethrowers on their backs were the favorite targets of the Japanese snipers. We would wait for the flamethrowers to shoot their flame into the cave, and when the Japanese came running out we easily picked them off. There were so many Marines firing, I couldn't tell who actually hit what.

Towards the end of the fighting things finally started to quiet down. We were ordered to return most of our unspent ammunition when it was determined that the island was "secured." We spent a lot of time in our foxholes, and we had to continuously move around because the sand got too hot if you stayed in one spot too long; that's how hot that volcanic sand got during the day. It was still a dangerous time, as we found out. I remember watching this Marine stand up in his hole and try to be funny shouting, "Where did all the Japs go?" An instant later that boy was shot dead by a sniper.

To my amazement, bomber crews were landing on Iwo long before the fighting was over. Their presence set the stage for one of the most brutal episodes of the battle on the very last day of the fighting.

In the very early morning hours of March 26, 1945, I was in my foxhole guarding a field hospital when two figures approached me. We kept our guard up at sunrise and sunset because in our experience the Japs would attack during these times, when it's the most difficult to see. These two figures ran to within 150 feet, so I raised my rifle and said, "Halt. Who goes there?" I had hardly finished challenging them when I saw they were Japs, and they started running faster towards me, screaming. I tried to fire, but my rifle jammed. Lucky for me, my friend Cpl. Jim Cannon jumped up and got both of them with just two shots, and the two Japs fell dead in front of me. In the heat of the moment Jim was so excited that he then pointed that rifle at me. I started yelling, "Cannon! Wait! Wait! It's me! It's me!" Moments like that can make your heart stop.

This was the start of a well-organized attack by a group of Japs who had been hiding in some caves. We gathered on top of a ridge and watched in horror as a group of about two hundred Japs ran like madmen through the startled bomber crews, killing and cutting off the heads of numerous airmen. We figured the Japs were officers because the majority carried swords. The horror then dawned on us that we had just a few rounds in our rifles and in our shirt pockets with which to fight back. I was one of a few that had a Marine Corps driving license, so Col. Robert Riddell threw me the keys to a jeep, and I drove down to the dump on the beach to get more ammunition. I got to the dump and began loading ammunition, but a noncommissioned sergeant refused to allow me to continue. I grabbed my rifle and leveled it at his head. The major in charge of the depot came running up to me, demanding to know what was happening. I just snapped, I guess. I pointed the rifle at the major and told him I desperately needed the ammunition to stop the Jap attack. The sergeant said something to me, and I yelled back, "You son of a bitch, you're just another one of them to me. Get out of my way!" The major ordered the sergeant to step aside, and I loaded the jeep. They gave me a Silver Star for my actions that day. I don't think the major would have approved.

With the jeep loaded with ammunition, I drove back to my unit. Our lieutenant, Harry S. Martin, had assembled an assault team to counter the Jap attack. Lieutenant Martin had almost single-handedly destroyed several enemy positions before he was killed before my eyes. I saw the Jap who killed Lieutenant Martin come over a ridge about 10 or 15 feet in front of us. I yelled out to the lieutenant, but I was a split second too late. I saw the puffs of dust come out through his shirt, and he fell down dead. We were able to rescue several Marines and airmen who had been surrounded during the fighting, and Lieutenant Martin was posthumously awarded the Medal of Honor for his actions that day.

One image that I remember from that day was when a Jap came running over the crest of a little dune waving his sword at us. Nothing had ever looked so big as that sword heading right for us, but I shot him in the chest. We just couldn't believe that the Japs really tried these banzai attacks with those swords. He wasn't yelling "Banzai" but something that sounded more like "Yah! Yah! Yah!" Well, as I told a reporter all those years ago, "Yah, I got him, too." Another Marine tried to pick up the sword, and I made it very clear to him he had better remove his hands, or else. I still have the sword tucked away somewhere, and when I come across it occasionally it brings back memories of those days I spent on Iwo.

We mopped up the remaining Japs on the island, and that marked the end of the fighting for my outfit. A jeep came by with a plow on the front of it and piled all the dead Japs into a crater and then buried them. We all got on top of the pile and pissed on it. Afterwards I had the biggest headache of my life. My buddy Ed Burns told me lie down in his foxhole, and I got some needed rest until I felt better.

The Army landed, and we were finally relieved. My buddy Mac-Creary, who was a real scrounger, went down to the beaches to find us some beer, compliments of the U.S. Army. He came back carrying a case of what he thought was beer, and we got real excited. When we opened the case we discovered it wasn't beer but cans of grapefruit juice. It was not exactly what we had in mind, but it was a nice treat for some thirsty Marines.

Some Navy guys came ashore, and I overheard one of them asking if anyone was from Baltimore. I said I was from Baltimore, and he took me back to his ship, where he introduced me to a Navy officer named Vernon Schlutter who was also from Baltimore. We talked about home, and I remember it was so nice to have a shower and a hot meal despite it being stewed tomatoes, my least favorite item on the menu. We parted after dinner, and I returned to the island and never thought I would see the Navy officer ever again. Almost thirty years later, I met Vernon again through my insurance business, and he remembered our meeting off Iwo, and we have been close friends since.

A few days passed before we were loaded onto troopships and headed back to Hawaii. As I departed I remember looking back and telling the guy next to me, "Let's get the hell outta here!" It was nice to shower once more, and I spent the next few days alone on the deck of the ship. All I wanted to do was read, sleep, and not talk to anyone for a while.

After arriving back in Hilo, Hawaii, we were loaded onto trucks for the trip back to our camp. One of our guys was waving a captured Jap flag from the rear of the truck near us, and as we passed some Japanese civilians, supposedly, as I was told later, one man seemed to bow towards the flag. It was senseless, and I am not so sure the Japanese man *was* bowing to the flag, but a Marine lifted his rifle and shot that man dead on the spot. We all were quarantined to the base for two weeks after that, but we had all the beer and food we wanted, and we got fat and lazy. We started training again soon after for the invasion of Japan, but the atomic bombs were dropped and, thankfully, the war ended.

My battalion was shipped out for occupation duty, but I stayed behind in Hilo because I had enough points to be discharged. I took a ship to Oahu and was quartered in the Royal Hawaiian Hotel in Honolulu. I was given good food and drink and entertained by the Glenn Miller Orchestra. It was a thrill I will never forget.

My experience of war was something I feel fortunate to have lived through, but I would never want to do it again. I never really talked about it much, but you never really forget. My experiences are always in the back of my mind somewhere, but I put it aside and concentrated on the new problems of life. I remember images from the war like seeing pieces of arms, legs, and heads torn away. I learned to kill to stay alive and never once hesitated on pulling the trigger. I sometimes think about the Japs that had tried to surrender. They yelled some kind of babble at us, but we wouldn't listen; we shot them down regardless. It's just the way it was. I feel sorry for the wives, fathers, mothers, brothers, and sisters who suddenly lost loved ones or who had to care for the men who had come back severely disabled. This is a lingering suffering put upon so many men who served that perhaps many of us have forgotten about.

I don't want to be made a hero. We Marines fought together and protected each other, and as a Marine I don't use the word "I," it is always "we." We don't enjoy being singled out, and so many Marines did their job above and beyond the call of duty with no recognition. So few of us were seen doing something that earned a medal, and it's unfair not to remember all those "unseen" heroes.

If I had to say who were the real heroes of the Second World War, I would say it was the men who were killed. My 5th Pioneer Battalion lost forty men on Iwo, and each one is a hero to me.

Perhaps just as heroic were the men who were wounded or disfigured in battle. My uncle Joe and I were separated after we enlisted together, and he fought on Guadalcanal and Bouganville, and was severely wounded on Guam on July 24, 1944. Japanese bullets hit him in the shoulder and tore part of his jaw away. Joe came home and married his sweetheart, Doris, and they have seven children and a wonderful life. But it pains me to have seen men like my uncle Joe live with the pain and suffering caused by their wounds for the remainder of their lives. They are the real heroes, and our country should never, ever forget them.

JOHN T. SINDALL

Reisterstown, Maryland

9th Bombardment Group, U.S. Army Air Corps

John Truman Sindall was born in Baltimore, Maryland, on February 19, 1926. He attended Pimlico Elementary School 223 and Garrison Forest Junior High and graduated from Baltimore Polytechnic High School in 1943. He enlisted in the Army Air Corps before graduating from high school and completed twenty-five missions as a blister gunner on a B-29 bomber. He is a recipient of the Distinguished Flying Cross and the Air Medal with three oak-leaf clusters (in lieu of the Air Medal). After the war Sindall began a career with the C&P Telephone Company and retired in 1987 after thirty-nine years of service. He married his wife, Peggy, in 1948, and they have two children and two grandchildren.

In 1943 I was attending Poly and was in my senior year when most of us realized that it was only a matter of time before we were going to be drafted into the service. I knew I didn't want to be in the infantry, so my two friends Marbury Councell and James McDermott and I decided we would join the Army Air Corps. All three of us were called up after our eighteenth birthdays. Marbury and James eventually became gunners on B-17s in Europe, and both survived, although Marbury was wounded and lost an eye. We all shared a very patriotic feeling about what we were doing, and we were excited to serve our country.

In March of 1944 I reported to Fort Meade, Maryland, and I was issued my clothes. I was given winter ODs (olive drabs) because it was still cold at the time, but I stayed in Maryland for just two weeks before being shipped off to Biloxi, Mississippi. Here I was, wearing winter ODs and crammed onto a train riding through the South. It was hot as Hades in Biloxi. Marbury and James were riding with me on the train, which helped pass the time. The train took five days to make it to Mississippi, and I thought we would never get down there, it was so long and uncomfortable. Once we got to

Biloxi and started our basic training, we were all sent to different units and were separated from then on until the end of the war.

We received our basic training, and we were all tested for the air cadet program. At that time, we found out later, the Air Corps had all the pilots, bombardiers, and navigators they needed, so they washed my entire class from the air cadet training program. There was just one guy they let stay in. A week later I was shipped to Fort Myers in Florida and entered aerial gunnery school.

In gunnery school I was shown how to operate a .30-cal. machine gun, and when we felt comfortable with that we were shown how to operate a .50-cal. machine gun. I learned how to completely dismantle the .50-cal. gun, field-strip it, and rebuild it. I was blindfolded and had to put it back together in two minutes, and our instructors tried to foul us up all the time. On occasions the instructors thought it was a good idea to have some sort of tear-gas drill to make our assembly task a bit harder. We did a lot of skeet shooting from the back of a moving pickup truck and had to hit clay targets that were thrown from the side of the road in such a way as to simulate angles of flight. This was important because it showed us how to lead and hit a moving target, something important in aerial combat. We were then taken up in B-17s, and I think some B-25s, and did aerial target shooting. A plane would tow a long sleeve behind the aircraft, and we fired at it. The instructors changed the bullets in the guns so that each student fired a different-color bullet that left their marks on the target so the instructors could tell how well each guy was doing or not doing.

Gunnery school lasted about six to seven weeks, and when we completed our training they didn't seem to know exactly what to do with us, so we were shipped to Naples, Florida. Today Naples is a very exclusive and expensive area, and then it was just as wonderful, if not so busy, as it is today. I spent the next six weeks lounging around, and the only thing that was bothersome were the mosquitoes that attacked at night. After we left Naples I was given a brief leave and was able to return home to visit my parents before reporting to Lincoln, Nebraska. It was in Lincoln that I was assigned to the B-29 bomber program. We spent a week in Nebraska, then shipped out to Alamogordo Air Force Base, New Mexico, and I was introduced to my crew. We were assembled and our names called out and we were formed into crews, and this is how I met the men I was to serve with in combat.

We had eleven members in our B-29 crew, including the airplane commander, co-pilot, navigator, bombardier, flight engineer, radio operator, radar operator, central fire control gunner, left blister gunner, right blister gunner, and tail gunner. We all got along from the first time we met, and we were a fairly close-knit group. We had some trials and tribulations when we began our missions. Our airplane commander evidently did not like the officers and enlisted men being so familiar with one another. Despite all of our natural

John Sindall and his crew at Mather Field, Sacramento, California, in April 1945 before flying overseas. *Front row, from left:* Bill Morgan, central fire control gunner; William McLaughlin, radio operator; George Reinert, tail gunner; Sindall; Norman Lombardo, left blister gunner; Mark Snivley, flight engineer. *Back row, from left:* Chris Prehoda, airplane commander; William Henderson, co-pilot; Warren Warchus, bombardier; John Kraft, navigator; Curtis Everett, radar operator.

instincts to form close bonds within the crew, the commander enforced what became almost a class distinction drawn between the enlisted members and the officers.

We trained at Alamogordo for several months, flying and practicing bombing missions across the country. We then flew to Harrington, Kansas, to pick up our new B-29. The B-29 was a very large aircraft for its day. It was a first-generation aircraft that could be pressurized when flown at an altitude over 8,000 feet. The B-29 was a big plane with a 10-ton (20,000-pound) bomb load capacity and had an operating ceiling of 34,000 feet, which permitted us to perform high-altitude bombing that put us above the common antiaircraft defenses of the time. The plane was defended with eight .50-cal. machine guns with three more (sometimes replaced with a 20-mm. cannon) in the tail.

The B-29 had four large supercharged engines that created the biggest problems for the B-29 because they had a large component

High-explosive and M69 incendiary bombs on racks being prepared to be loaded into Sindall's B-29 before a mission to Osaka, Japan, in May 1945. With their 10-ton bomb load capacity, multiplied by the hundreds of bombers that participated in an average raid, the B-29s of the Twentieth Air Force dealt a catastrophic blow to Japan.

of magnesium, which was prone to catching fire. The plane had a built-in fire-extinguishing system, but if the fire was not controlled quickly the engine could completely burn out of the wing, forcing the crew out, or in some cases the fire spread so quickly the crew had no chance of escaping. At the end of the war we were transporting some infantrymen from the Philippines back to the States in an old war-weary B-29 and an engine caught fire. The extinguishing system failed to put out the fire, so the airplane commander put us into a very steep dive until the flames went out. It was quite a ride, and a little frightening. The infantrymen were beyond consolation for the remainder of the flight. I felt so sorry for those guys.

Boeing lost their entire test crew in the initial test flight of the B-29 when fire consumed the plane and it crashed. When subsequent test missions cost even more lives, Boeing told the Army it didn't want to continue the program. In response, the Army informed Boeing that it would have to return their fifty-million-dollar deposit, or give the Army what they had ordered and the Army would fix the problems. Boeing didn't have the money to give back, and I am not sure if the Army was completely aware of the hurdles they would face trying to fix the problems, but the planes began rolling off the assembly lines. Other than the problematic fire risks, the B-29 was a substantial aircraft and brought many of us airmen through some difficult times.

Flying in the B-29 was comfortable because it could operate at a height of 34,000 feet, which required the plane to be pressurized to protect the crew from the extreme cold and lack of breathable air at this altitude. We were fortunate in that we didn't have to worry about the cold air at high altitudes the crews of other bombers had to endure. We didn't have to wear heavy flight suits to protect us against the cold and wore just a light flight suit. We didn't even wear helmets, although I notice in a lot of the pictures some guys did. We had flak jackets that we sat on more than wore because the little wooden stools we sat on didn't offer much protection from the flak that came at us from below; it became necessary to sit on the jackets to protect the "family jewels," as the saying goes. During night missions we tended to put on more flak gear because we were more concerned about attacks from enemy fighters and bullets flying through our cabin. You couldn't see the Japanese fighters at night. All you would see were the machine guns firing and the tracers being fired back and forth between the fighters and our bomber. Our bombers were spread out in a long line during the night missions to avoid collisions, so we were essentially alone. If something had happened to us, no one would have ever known what or where. This happened with many crews that were lost.

A photo taken from a 9th Bombardment Group B-29 during a mission to drop supplies to POWs following the conclusion of the war. (The words "POW Supplies" are visible under the wing of the nearest plane.) Bombers of the 9th Bomb Group were distinguished by the circled "X" on the vertical stabilizers. The B-29 Superfortress was adopted by the Twentieth Air Force for the planned destruction of the Japanese homeland. With pressurized crew compartments and remote-controlled gun turrets, the B-29 was very advanced for its time. Although it had been designed for high-altitude bombing, Gen. Curtis LeMay discovered that its greatest successes were obtained with low-level nighttime incendiary bombing. The two most famous B-29s of the war were the *Enola Gay* and the *Bockscar*, which dropped the atomic bombs on Hiroshima and Nagasaki, respectively. The cost of a B-29 in 1944 was $639,000.

We took along bottles of juice for the missions, but we never did get any of the sandwiches I had read somewhere would be prepared for us each mission. There were no bathroom facilities on the plane, just a relief tube to use that led to the outside of the plane. The early B-29s even had bunks in the rear, and someone once told me the Japanese thought we used them to bring women along on our missions. As much as we wished it was true, of course, it wasn't.

From Harrington, Kansas, we flew to Mather Field near Sacramento, California, and stayed there overnight. From there we flew to Hickam Field on the island of Oahu in Hawaii. From Hickam Field we flew to a layover strip on Kwajalein Island in the Marshalls. The Marines had been on Kwajalein for a while, and the most remarkable things about the island were how hot it was and how there was not a single tree anywhere on the entire island; it was completely bare and incredibly hot. From Kwajalein we then flew to our home base on the island of Tinian. When we arrived at Tinian we learned that our plane had been assigned to the 1st Squadron, 9th Bomb Group (Extra Heavy), 313th Wing, Twentieth Air Force. The planes of our 9th Bomb Group were distinguished by the large circled "X" on the vertical stabilizer on the tail of each plane.

The airbases on Tinian were specifically built for B-29s, and the bombers in our 9th Bomb Group were based on the island's North Field. The 9th Bomb Group consisted of forty-five B-29 bombers divided into three squadrons, with fifteen bombers in each of 1st, 5th, and 99th Squadrons. The 9th Bomb Group consisted of a little over two thousand personnel, including aircrew and ground crew. Tinian is located about 3,000 miles from the Japanese mainland, so we considered the distance as menacing an enemy as the Japanese. It was a fifteen-hour flight round trip every mission. The Japanese had occupied Tinian after the First World War, and they had maintained a large sugar plantation. Once we occupied the island, it looked more like a desert island, and all vegetation and other facilities were removed and two large airfields were built. The Seabees had transformed a desolate piece of land into a modern airbase with a 10,000-foot runway, the longest in the world at the time.

We lived in Quonset huts, which were oval-shaped buildings covered with galvanized steel. The weather was not too hot, with average temperatures around the eighties. There weren't too many activities on the island, and between missions and training exercises we could use a library on the base or go swimming. The food was not that good, and it consisted of a lot of lamb, and to this day I just can't eat lamb, I got so tired of eating it during the war.

Our mission schedule was posted daily in the orderly room, and someone would check and see if our plane was scheduled to fly. We had no regular schedule; whenever they decided we were needed, they told us. Sometimes our full squadron was sent up, and other times only a few crews were selected to fly. We had briefings before each mission, and if it was a daylight mission we got up very early, but if it was a nighttime mission—and we had a good many of those—we got up at a more normal time, and it made for a long day. Before each mission we went down to the plane to check it over and make sure all the guns were in working order and the turrets were working fine. The ammunition and the 10 tons of explosives or incendiary bombs the B-29 could carry were already loaded by the time we arrived. Even with such a long runway, we were so loaded with bombs that on occasion the props of our plane skimmed the water after takeoff. More than a few heavily laden bombers just couldn't gain enough speed and/or altitude and performed belly flops at the end of the runway or in the ocean.

My role in the B-29 was as a waist blister gunner. The pressurized interior was divided into sections, with the bomb bay being the only nonpressurized section of the plane. A padded tunnel connected the portion of the plane behind the bomb bay, where the radar officer, central fire control gunner, and left and right blister gunners were positioned, with the forward section of the plane, where the remainder of the crew, minus the tail gunner, was located. Once we were in the air and the airplane was pressurized, the tail gunner was totally cut off from the rest of the crew. If anything happened to him, we could not get to him to help. All the gun positions on the plane were in turrets, and we looked through a Plexiglas bubble, or blister, and the gunners remotely fired the guns housed in turrets above and below the plane using an electronic computing sight. The B-29 was unique in that the machine guns were controlled by an electronic fire control system. This system was very advanced for the time, and it gave us a lot of mobility and provided a good amount of firepower. The firing system linked all the guns on the plane together and was controlled by the central fire control gunner (CFC). The CFC sat between the two blister gunners and was elevated on a swiveling chair that allowed him to look out of a blister at the top of the cabin. The CFC could scan the skies for enemy fighters and switch control of the turrets to a single gunner so all guns could then be brought to bear on a single target that the gunner had in his sights. The CFC could also control the tail gun if the gunner was incapacitated.

I think I may have scored a kill during a daylight mission, but it was hard to tell; so many other planes were shooting at the same plane. It should be mentioned what a great help our escorting P-51 pilots were to us bombers. They really looked out for us.

There were certain targets that caused some concern among the crews, and of course we were not happy when we learned we were scheduled to hit them. Most of the missions were long, and you were very tired by the time you got back. Sometimes you had some pretty bad experiences, which you would just as soon forget. One of the worst feelings I ever had was when we lost two engines on a mission and we were trying to make it back to Iwo Jima, wondering if we were going to go down in the ocean. The very first mission we

A B-29 lies at the end of Tinian's North Field after having run out of runway trying to gain speed for takeoff. Tinian's 10,000-foot runway had been specially built for the large B-29s, but many of them were so heavily loaded with ordnance that their props touched the water on takeoff. Other less fortunate bombers belly-flopped at the end of the runway or into the ocean.

flew, we had fuel problems on our return leg, and we had to land on Iwo. Iwo was quite a welcome sight to see for any bomber crew struggling to get back home. I think our crew alone landed on Iwo three times, and on each of those three occasions our survival would have been in doubt if it hadn't been for our base on Iwo. During one of my visits to Iwo we had to stay overnight, and I was able to roam the island for a few hours. I could not get over the number of crosses in the Marine graveyards, each cross, I knew, indicating a piece of the price in American lives it took to capture the island. Thousands of airmen were saved by the sacrifices of those Marines, and every airman who landed on Iwo owes some unknown Marine who died on Iwo a tremendous expression of thanks for sacrificing so much so we could live.

When we were briefed on our missions, we all knew over which cities we would encounter the most amount of flak or Japanese fighters. In the Pacific we encountered Japanese fighters that were more interested in becoming kamikazes to ram your plane than trying to shoot you down. A few planes came close to ramming us, and the only defense was to shoot them from the sky before they got too close. We realized that the Japanese were very fanatical, and I worried because I didn't want to think I was giving up my life in that fashion, and none of us wanted to become a prisoner of the Japanese. If I ever had to bail out, I had a .45-cal. pistol to defend myself and a knife to cut myself free if I should get tangled in my parachute. I figured the .45 would probably be useless because I was only given eight bullets, so I often wondered just exactly what the purpose of the pistol was. The Japanese didn't care much for the crews of B-29s, and captured fliers were given a rough time. I learned sometime after the war that it did not pay to become a captive of the Japanese. Only 40 percent of the B-29 crew members captured ever survived to return home. At a reunion recently I met a fellow who was the only one from his eleven-man crew to survive the prisoner-of-war camps after they were forced to bail out over Japan. When the Japanese surrounded him, he figured he had no chance of running or shooting it out, so he just threw his .45 away.

Soon after our arrival Gen. Curtis LeMay evaluated our bomber effectiveness and decided we were not hitting our targets because we were flying at altitudes that were too high. Until the B-29s began flying, we had no working knowledge of the jet stream and how it affected our airspeed and the accuracy of our bombing. LeMay scrapped high-altitude daylight bombing at 30,000 feet in favor of a new philosophy: to get below the jet stream and begin flying low-level missions at 6,000 feet. The change in flying altitude saved fuel, decreased wear on the planes, and certainly made it easier for us to hit our targets, but it also made it easier for the Japanese antiaircraft guns to hit us. Needless to say, when we were told of this change in plans none of us were at all happy, and we had real concerns. We began to fly nighttime missions dropping incendiaries from about 6,000 feet, and at that altitude we were big fat targets for the Japanese antiaircraft gunners.

In addition to the altitude changes, LeMay also ordered that much of the automated fire control system be removed and the gunners be left behind so we could load more bombs into the plane. My function during these nighttime missions changed from worrying about fighters to going to the back of the plane to drop stuff we called "rope" from a camera hatch; the "rope" was actually aluminum foil that jammed the radar that guided the antiaircraft guns. LeMay also had us run missions to drop leaflets over cities telling them beforehand we would return and level their city. It may have helped save some civilian lives, making us feel better about annihilating their homeland, but it also gave the Japanese an idea where we would strike next, and they could prepare their defenses.

It was estimated that one B-29 fully loaded with incendiary bombs could start a thousand fires. If you multiply this number times the one hundred, five hundred, or one thousand bombers we launched on a single target, you begin to get an idea of the destruction we were capable of causing. Flying at low altitudes I could smell the horrible stench that came up from the burning cities below. The heat was so intense I could feel it on my face when I looked down from the camera hatch. I just cannot begin to explain the odor and the heat we experienced over all those burning cities. Perhaps the only way to describe it is to say it was an inferno that one could expect to see nowhere but in hell. We must have created hell on earth in those Japanese cities.

During one of our early missions we were at 6,000 or 7,000 feet and we had just unloaded our incendiaries. A firestorm developed, and as we flew over the target the massive uplift of superheated air drove our plane violently upwards. I think the pilot said afterward we were jolted 2,000 to 3,000 feet straight up, and then as we passed over the fire below us we dropped just as suddenly at least another 1,500 to 2,000 feet. I was in the back of the plane, and I had no idea what was going on. I naturally thought we had been hit and were out of control. It was terrifying. The floorboards of the plane were all torn completely loose, and the cabin was filled with so much dust and dirt I couldn't see a few feet in front of me. A large container holding our sea rescue equipment was thrown against the top of the cabin and then landed on top of me. I couldn't move. I began calling for help for someone to remove the large container lying on top of me.

The pilot said he had learned his lesson and would never fly us through a firestorm ever again. It is a wonder the wings of the plane were not torn off. It was an example of how well built the B-29 was. Another example was when I saw a B-29 come back with no rudder on it at all. How the pilot managed to get that plane back safely, I'll never know. On another occasion a B-29 in our group was witnessed completing a 360-degree roll when the pilot momentarily lost control of the plane. No one, including the pilot, could explain how he did it, but he was able to regain control. When the plane landed on the base, the ground crew was amazed to see that almost every rivet in the plane had popped, and how the pilot got it back to the base was again amazing. The same pilot was killed on his very next mission.

Flying at low levels through flak could be pretty rough. I am sure we all prayed a little more and hoped someone was looking out for us. I think for the most part none of us thought anything was going to happen to us; it was always going to be some other crew. I guess being young and naive are the best qualities for a good soldier. Our crew was lucky and we didn't suffer any losses, and we often said somebody must have been watching over us. We knew other crews that were not as fortunate, and you just had to realize that death is the unfortunate part of this awful thing we call war. You are not happy about it, but life has to go on, and you know that in the next two to three days you are going to be fine again.

So much of your survival in war depends on your skills and those of the men around you, but often it was just dumb luck. It often amounted to being in the right place at the wrong time, as it often seems in life. When we were still in the States flying training missions our crew had been scheduled to fly on Good Friday during the Easter holiday. Our scheduled flight was canceled, and the next crew who took the plane up was coming in for a landing when a fire broke out. The only three men who escaped alive were gunners, and of those, only one survived because the others didn't have time for their parachutes to open because they were too low when they had to bail out. That was the plane I was supposed to be on. It made us all think. When that one crew member came back to our hut that night and told us what had happened, we were all pretty shaken up.

In March of 1945 our 313th was assigned to the mining of Japanese ports. We dropped nearly thirteen thousand acoustic and magnetic mines in the western approaches of the Shimonoseki Strait and the Inland Sea and in the harbors of Hiroshima, Kure, Tokyo, Nagoya, Tokuyama, Aki, and Noda. We flew these missions usually at low altitudes at night, and we mined these areas so effectively that by the end of the war no Japanese ships could get through the Sea of Japan. In May the Japanese became desperate and tried to make a breakthrough of our mines, and eighty-five of their merchant vessels were sunk.

When the 509th Composite Group flew into Tinian, we were all very curious and surprised because they were in an area that was completely removed from the rest of the base. Their hangars were surrounded by a high fence and closely guarded by a special police force, so we never got the opportunity to meet any of them or talk to any of them. There were some rumors about who they were and what they were doing, but all we thought was that they were a very select crew. We had absolutely no idea they were preparing to drop a new type of bomb. We really had no clue. It was the greatest secret of the war as far as I am concerned because I was so close to where they were. We had never heard of an atomic bomb until they made the announcement that the bomb had been dropped and we could see the results. Looking back, it was amazing that they had prepared for the delivery of the atomic bombs on Tinian because there was usually nothing that went on around the island without someone finding out what was going on. We were all amazed to think that one bomb could do as much damage as usually took us hundreds of bombers to accomplish. The ramifications of the new weapon were startling to me. It meant one plane could do what it had taken us hundreds of bombers and the lives of many men to do before.

One of the last missions we flew was to Yawata on the western coastline of Japan. Yawata was one of Japan's biggest steel-producing centers, and the 313th Bomb Wing had been trying to erase it from the map since the beginning of the war when they were in India. The city had been left relatively unscathed because on all the previous missions there had always been heavy cloud cover and a lot of antiaircraft flak over the city, which made bombing the steel plants difficult. Again on this mission the city was concealed under a blanket of thick clouds, and a bomber in our group was shot down. The crew managed to bail out successfully except for the commander, who hit the tail of his plane after bailing out, and he was killed. The others managed to inflate their life rafts, and a few bombers dropped out of formation to fly cover to keep the Japanese fishing boats from capturing the crew until they could be rescued. Despite our best efforts, the Japanese eventually picked up the crew.

When the war ended we flew missions to drop supplies on prisoner-of-war camps. This gave us a feeling of being able to help those who had been held captive for so long. We flew over Hiroshima once or twice during these missions, and I actually saw the damage that the one atomic bomb had done, and none of us could fathom the amount of damage that single device had caused. It was just unbelievable. I have that picture of the devastated city in my mind, and whenever I see the news footage on TV I remember having been there over that spot, and I know it is the truth.

When the war finally ended we had flown twenty-five missions, ten short of the thirty-five we would have had to fly to return home. Japan was pretty well destroyed by this time, and the continued destruction of the remaining parts was assured with or without atomic weapons. One amazing thing we began to realize after the war was how many planes the Japanese had brought out of hiding. It was estimated that the Japanese had probably four to five thousand aircraft they had hidden to be used in the final battle of Japan. They were flyable and could have been used for kamikaze attacks. You can only imagine the devastation they might have caused, when you look at what they had done to our Pacific Fleet in the closing months of the war.

I don't recall any big celebration when the war ended. The only thing I recall was knowing that the war was over and that I could not wait to get home. I think back and perhaps I have just blanked out all the other details from that moment from my memory. I think my only thought was, when were we going to go home?

Soon after the war ended the Air Force began to send our B-29s on photoreconnaissance missions along the coast of Russia. The Russians responded by harassing our planes, and General LeMay responded by launching two missions that were labeled "Show of Force." We put every single plane into the air we had and flew over Japan and close to the Russian border to prove to the Russians we had the capability, and will, to take care of anything the Russians thought they were capable of doing to us. The striking power we possessed at the end of the war was almost unimaginably awesome. I cannot describe the scene when we returned from these missions and watched hundreds of bombers circle overhead and land one after another for hours on end.

A photo taken by Sindall from his right blister gun position over an unidentified Japanese city following the war. Most of Japan's major cities were in a similar state of devastation, with few buildings remaining standing above the rubble. The heat created by the firestorms from the heavy bombing of the B-29s was so intense that the bomber crews could feel it 6,000 feet above the target. Many bomber crews used the same word to describe the burning Japanese cities: "Hell."

When we were shipped back to the States we were barracked at Fort Meade. After a few days I was one of just four to five others in this huge building, and they did not know what to do with us. They told our small group to go to an empty building and sleep for the night and that they would decide by morning what was going to happen to us. When we woke up the next morning we went back to see the base officers, and they said we had been given a furlough and when we returned they would make a decision. We walked back to our bunks, and as we were packing up our gear we were ordered back to the orderly room. When we arrived, an officer told us to pack up our stuff, go home, and don't come back. I had been discharged. That was one of the happiest moments in my life.

I don't think I really hated the Japanese during the war, but I think we all realized that they were our enemy and we had a war to win, and we were doing our best to win the war. When we flew over the Japanese cities I could not help but think about the people below us, but it was our job, and we all did it to our fullest ability and without hesitation. It was sometimes hard not to hate when we watched our planes shot from the sky and when crews returned all shot up. I looked at the dead and wounded men, and I just thanked God that it wasn't me.

My wartime experiences were an interesting experience. Even though most of us who served never had any doubts about performing our duties and fulfilling our patriotic duty, I think we were all glad when it was over with. I wouldn't want to do it all again and wouldn't want to even think about my children or grandchildren having to experience war as I did. I don't know if people will ever learn that we have to find a way to live in peace with one another, but I have seen the destruction that results from our failure to do so.

I think the real heroes of the Second World War are the men who had to lead the invasion in Normandy. We will probably never know or understand the suffering that they had to go through. Just as heroic were the Marines and Army men who did their fighting in that dirty island warfare. As beautiful as those tropical islands were, they were filthy and deadly. If people don't learn and understand what deprivations those brave men endured, their sacrifices will be lost into history.

CHARLES W. SLAGLE IV

Baltimore, Maryland
10th Mountain Division, U.S. Army

Charles William Slagle IV was born in Baltimore, Maryland, on January 11, 1922. He attended the Gilman School until the completion of his junior year, when he began a career as a professional ice skater. He was drafted into the Army in 1942 and volunteered for the 10th Mountain Division, participating in the 10th's daring breakthrough of the German Gothic Line on Mount Belvedere. After the war Slagle resumed his career on the ice, performing until 1953 when he and his wife, Gloria, retired from the entertainment business. Since 1976 he has operated "Shorty's Shop," a well-known wooden-toy store in Bethany Beach, Delaware. He has one son from a previous marriage, one daughter with Gloria, and six grandchildren.

I grew up on Roland Avenue in Baltimore and learned to ice skate on the fishpond at the Roland Park Apartments. Most people don't remember or know that Gilman had a hockey team back then, and I played on two teams that won consecutive national championships in 1938 and 1939 at Lake Placid, New York. We played all the top hockey schools in the country, including Andover, Choate, and Exeter, and they all knew the name Gilman when we were finished with them.

I began figure skating with the Ice Club of Baltimore over at the Carlins Rink on Park Circle, and for us to keep the club operating we held a carnival and performed a show each year to raise funds. I started doing a comedy routine with a classmate, Tommy Lee, to help with the show, and people loved our routine, so we started doing shows on our own, performing as "Zig-Zag" around the region. While performing in Washington a talent scout happened to see us skate, and a week later I received a telegram from Chicago asking if we would join his show for $125 a week. In those days $125 a week was a lot of money, so my dad didn't hesitate to put me on the next train to Chicago. The show was called "Ice Vanities," and it opened and closed within a week, and I found myself stranded in Chicago without a penny to get home. Fortunately, Sonja Henie had seen one of our performances, and when she learned our show had gone belly up she offered us a three-year contract to appear in her show, "It Happens on Ice." She also covered all of our outstanding expenses from the previous week.

Sonja Henie was from Oslo, Norway, and was an Olympic ice-skating champion who won the gold medal four times. Her Olympic fame carried over into a Hollywood career, and between making movies she produced a traveling ice show that performed in the big metropolitan centers around the country. Sonja died of leukemia on the plane taking her home to Oslo in 1958.

On December 7, 1941, I was having breakfast in Rockefeller Center in New York when the radio announced that Pearl Harbor had been bombed. Upon hearing the news one guy ran over to a Gillette razor advertisement featuring a mannequin dressed as a soldier, and my first impression of being at war was this guy running around Rockefeller Center yelling that we were at war, waving a toy rifle he had taken from the mannequin in the Gillette display.

The start of the war didn't affect my daily life too much, and I continued performing with the Sonja Henie group. Between shows many of us skaters spent our free time skiing at Bear Mountain, and when our being drafted appeared inevitable, fourteen of us decided to join the National Ski Patrol, because membership would certainly help with our entry into the 10th Mountain Division (10th Light Division, at the time). The National Ski Patrol is a civilian organization founded in 1938 by Charles Minot Dole, who created the patrol to provide safety, rescue, and training for our nation's skiers. When the United States entered the war, Dole wrote a letter to President Roosevelt citing the accomplishments of the Finnish ski troops against the Russians and offered to help recruit experienced skiers to help train new American ski troops. Dole's letter was forwarded to the Army, and Dole eventually convinced the War Department that it was more reasonable to try to make soldiers out of skiers than skiers out of soldiers. Dole then established the requirements for acceptance into the 10th Division, which included submitting three letters of reference attesting to a recruit's competence in mountaineering or skiing. This was the only time in the history of the American armed forces a civilian sports organization helped recruit, screen, and approve applicants for military service.

I joined the Ski Patrol so I could become a part of the 10th Division partly because I wanted to avoid the regular infantry, and when my draft notice arrived I immediately applied and was accepted. My father put me on the train once more at Camden Station, but this time I was headed into the Army, and the mood was much less festive. My mother refused to see me off at the train station, she was so upset at my leaving. I said my goodbyes to my father before boarding the train, and he was also visibly distressed, so it was hard to leave them both behind worrying about me. The train arrived at Fort Dix, New Jersey, and I immediately boarded another train heading to Camp Hale in Colorado, home to the 10th Mountain Division. I arrived at Camp Hale on the evening of February 11, 1943. The temperature was about twenty below zero, and I lined up with the other men and began a march through a mile of ice and snow wearing only a light jacket, issue pants, a pair of silk socks, and a thin pair of leather shoes issued to me at Fort Dix. I hoped Army life could only get better.

The fourteen of us from the Sonja Henie show who had joined the Ski Patrol were now members of the 10th Mountain Division. We all arrived on different days and were assigned to various companies, but it was good to know we were together again in the same place. We spent our free time skating together at Colorado Springs and started performing shows to raise money for the war effort. In the two years before I was sent overseas I was given numerous four- and five-day furloughs to travel around the country to participate in ice shows to promote war bonds. I often went to Chicago to perform in the *Chicago Times Show* and New York for the *Ed Sullivan Show*, and although I wasn't paid a penny for the extra work, just getting the time off from training was often reward enough for me.

Charles "Shorty" Slagle thrilled crowds during the passes he was granted from his training with the 10th Mountain Division to participate in shows to promote war bonds. He achieved fame by performing daring jumps in specially modified stilt ice skates. Shown here with his 16-inch stilt skates, Slagle also performed in stilt skates that measured 3 feet tall. His stilt-skating routine has been duplicated by only a few since his retirement, and his skating technique and innovative performances are still recognized as some of the most spectacular to have ever taken place on the ice.

Camp Hale was 12,000 feet high in the Rocky Mountains, and the oxygen at this altitude was thin enough to require a period of acclimation before I felt completely comfortable. Our officer ranks were made up of professional skiers who had been drafted from all parts of the country, and many had been fierce competitors before the war but had put those personal battles aside for the time being. My first sergeant was Harry Wagner. Harry was a marvelous instructor, and I thought it was remarkable that he had been a first lieutenant in the German Army before moving to the United States. He brought with him years of experience in living and training in rugged terrain, and he managed to guide us out of a number of tight spots while in combat.

The 10th was an all-volunteer division, and it was the only division to promote enlisted men to officers from within its ranks. Like me, many of the men in the 10th had known others in the division before joining because we had belonged to the same ski clubs and gone to the same colleges and skied and climbed in the same competitions before the war. A large percentage of the men were successful high-salaried professionals or from wealthy families who lived the lifestyle in which they could learn how to ski and frequent the finest ski ranges in the world. One platoon in our company had a sergeant who was a *cum laude* graduate from Princeton, and in any other Army division he would have been a lieutenant or captain.

The primary function of the 10th Mountain Division was to conduct mountain warfare. Like any division, it was comprised of three regiments, the 87th, 86th, and 85th Infantry Regiments, with an additional artillery regiment attached to the division. I felt we were generally an elite group of physically fit men who were immune to the physical stresses caused by extreme altitude and who had no fear of heights. Our training was difficult and diverse, and it prepared us to fight on flat land or in the mountains while climbing or skiing. We believed in our training, and our manual was a constant work in progress as we incorporated tactics of mountain divisions from other countries or discovered our own approaches to different problems.

When I arrived at Camp Hale I was assigned to the 87th Infantry Regiment and attended armor artificer school. An armor artificer is basically a military mechanic who is skilled in assembling, maintaining, and repairing weapons. I had no idea why I was selected for this role, but I was not complaining when I was elevated from private to corporal upon my graduation and reassigned to Company A of the 85th Infantry Regiment. I began working in the company supply room, and it wasn't long before I was promoted to supply sergeant. My job as supply sergeant was to provide the men of Company A with everything they needed to perform their duty. Before our time in combat this meant making sure all the new guys arriving at Camp Hale received a comb, handkerchief, uniform, helmet, rifle, bayonet, and just about anything else a man could need.

In combat my duties were similar in that I prepared food, distributed ammunition, replaced worn or lost clothing, and repaired broken weapons. One of the most important aspects of my combat responsibilities was to help keep the company's feet warm and dry to prevent foot problems that could cause men to be pulled from the line. I made it a personal mission to scrounge for extra socks every day in places you would not believe, just so I could give every man in the company a pair of clean and dry socks with their daily food ration. The men really appreciated such a little added comfort in their daily life, and I like to think it helped keep the company fighting at full strength.

In training we moved our equipment with amphibious M29 jeeps, or Weasels, which were completely white, down to the leather seats, and had 20-inch treads to traverse the toughest terrain. Unfortunately, the Weasels were nothing but a problem in combat, and we stopped using them because they were constantly breaking down. Supplying the battalion was a difficult task in peacetime but a nightmare when people were shooting at me at the same time. Making things even more difficult was the fact that we often advanced in single-file columns that could stretch along a line 4 miles in length on a narrow mountainous trail with the lead elements 3,000 feet higher up the mountain than the rear just 1,000 yards behind. Sometimes getting transportation to move supplies forward was a daunting task. Our jeeps broke down, were blown up, or just went missing. In the most mountainous terrain we used mules to haul our supplies, but the mules were useless in deep snow, which not only prevented supplies from getting up to the men but also ground our artillery battalion to a halt. It was the worst feeling in the world to be stranded with no transportation when the entire company was waiting for me to deliver ammunition and other supplies. I had to improvise transportation on numerous occasions, and it meant taking horses or oxen or anything with legs from farmers to get our stuff moving forward. When we overran the German positions, I would find little of value to supplement our shortages, and their lack of food stores explained why I thought the German prisoners always looked half-starved.

Surviving the elements was as important as learning how to survive the enemy, and much of our equipment was specialized for portability and use in cold climates. Every move in an intensely cold environment had to be calculated, and precautions to protect myself against the cold were ingrained in my mind. Most of the men in the division had prior experience in cold climates, and this helped prevent casualties in training and combat. It was not necessary for anyone to tell us we should breathe through our noses; we all knew breathing the bitterly cold air through the mouth would freeze the lungs and cause serious injury. We often discovered new ways to combat the cold to keep our bodies and equipment functioning, and for the radio operators this meant having to sleep with

Members of the 10th Mountain Division pause at an overlook in the Rocky Mountains where the division trained (based at Camp Hale). Members of the original 10th Division were hand-selected for experience in skiing or climbing, and the division was unique in that all of its officers were promoted from its ranks of enlisted men. The 10th Division first entered combat in the Italian Apennine Mountains, where they were given the task of breaking through the strong and previously impenetrable German defenses atop Mount Belvedere along the Gothic Line. The 10th Division's daring and successful nighttime assault on Mount Belvedere was immortalized in the 1950s movie *Climb to Glory*.

their bodies wrapped around their sets to keep them warm and ready for operation at any moment. The medics had a very difficult task in treating the wounded because the intense cold prevented the use of blood plasma, so they were limited to bandages and morphine. Any plasma or other liquid they required had to be carried under their clothing to prevent it from freezing solid. The altitude and cold increased the rate at which wounded men lapsed into shock, so evacuating the wounded to a warm place at lower altitude was essential. The medics in the division were selected for their physical strength, which enabled them to carry the wounded through rugged terrain to an aid station. It often took a team of six or seven medics to evacuate one wounded man down the mountain using ropes, sleds, and pure determination.

The equipment and clothing I carried at any time greatly depended on the season and the mission. My weapon was always an M1 Garand with bayonet and a few grenades, but my clothing and the other supplies I packed varied. During the warmer months I wore only a light uniform, but as we entered higher elevations or when the winter set in the amount of clothing I wore naturally increased. In the winter months I wore a ski parka designed to protect against severe cold, and it could be worn reversed between white and olive green, depending on the terrain. I wore ski boots that had an oversized toe to fit into my skis, and the extra toe space also served a more important function of allowing adequate movement of the toes to prevent them from freezing. I often wore a wool hat under my steel helmet and a pair of wool gloves that fit under a pair of camouflage canvas gloves. Both the wool and the canvas gloves had a hole near the right index finger to expose my trigger finger when needed.

We were given the best skis available at the time, but they were still nothing like what is available for use today. They were made from solid oak and were long and heavy, weighing 12 pounds each. After cross-country skiing for hours or hauling them up the side of a mountain, we began to refer to our skis as "torture boards." Our division is often shown in photographs on skis or carrying our skis on our backs, but in reality we never once used our skis in combat because we were always climbing. Skis were also useless in deep snow, so we utilized two different kinds of snowshoes to help us get around. The first type of snowshoe was called a "bear paw" because it was round and was useful in very deep snow when walking forward in open terrain. The other type of shoe was a more typical version of a snowshoe and was used in wooded terrain because its shape provided much more maneuverability in confined spaces. Walking was still difficult in either shoe, and you tended to perform more of a gliding motion than a normal walk.

I carried my sleeping bags, food, extra clothing, medical kit, ammunition, and other essentials I needed to stay alive in a metal-frame rucksack capable of holding up to 90 pounds. It was essential to carry as much as we could in our packs because once we entered the mountains we were completely on our own, with no possible means of receiving additional supplies. Getting supplies in combat was always a problem because we were moving so fast once we got the Germans running, and we kept at them so they couldn't turn and fight. My diet in combat consisted of K and C rations, and the most remarkable item I found in these rations was a concentrated chocolate bar that was so hard I had to gnaw and scrape at it with my teeth to eat it. If our mission was abbreviated we could carry canned food, but it was much heavier than the rations so we were limited as to how much we could carry. The canned food froze solid in the cold, so we used an old trash can or our steel helmets to melt snow for water and to defrost our supplies, to cook, and even for bathing and shaving. The canned food was much more palatable than the rations, and my favorite type was some sort of chicken noodle meal, and it was always nice to see the words "Packed in Cambridge, Maryland" printed on the label.

Each man was issued two down sleeping bags lined with goose feathers. One bag was fitted to tightly conform to the shape of the body, and the other was larger, to fit over this first bag. They were extremely light and could be folded tight into small bundles to be easily carried in our packs. The bags were more than sufficient to protect us from the extreme temperatures at night, which on occasion dropped to thirty-two degrees below zero. Instead of piling on extra clothing at night, I actually stripped off every stitch of clothing before crawling into the sleeping bag. This allowed my perspiration to evaporate inside the sleeping bag instead of entering my clothing and possibly freezing, which in turn would have frozen me. To protect against extremely bitter air temperatures, we buried our sleeping bags in the snow because the constant thirty-two-degree temperature of the snow protected us from the colder air temperatures. Once I was settled down for the night I was quite comfortable, but it was always very difficult to leave a warm sleeping bag the next morning to venture out into the cold again.

In late June 1944 the division left Camp Hale for flatland training at Camp Swift near Austin, Texas. Additional recruits joined the division, and we began 10-mile marches in the Texas heat with full gear. The activity included carrying simulated wounded, but the heat provided real experience in handling numerous heat-exhaustion casualties. In November our new brigadier general, George P. Hays, greeted us. He had been an artillery commander in France after the D-Day landings before assuming command of our division. He addressed the division and concluded his speech with, "We are going to have good times and bad times in our combat overseas, and it will be my policy to make everyone as comfortable and to have as good a time as possible as long as we accomplish our mission. If you are going to risk your life, you might as well do it in good company. Men, you are in good company." A few days before Christmas we were moved by train from Camp Swift to Camp Patrick Henry in Virginia and from there to Hampton Roads, where the division was loaded into transports. Baltimore was just up the road, and it was an awful feeling for me knowing I was so close to home before leaving to go overseas. The 85th was put aboard the USS *West Point,* formerly the USS *America* and the largest and fastest ship in the commercial fleet. We sailed alone across the Atlantic until we reached the Straits of Gibraltar on my birthday, January 11, 1945. I spent most of my time on the deck of the ship because so many of us were so seasick, I had to escape to the fresh air above.

On the 14th the regiment was loaded onto LCIs (landing craft, infantry), and after a night docking in Naples we sailed northward up the west coast of Italy until offloading in Livorno as antiaircraft fire filled the sky over our heads. We boarded trucks and arrived at Pisa the next day and found our staging area, known as the King's Hunting Grounds, a mile west of Pisa. I was able to visit Pisa long enough for me to fully appreciate the pitiful condition of the Italian people. There was little food for the people, and they rummaged through our garbage looking for some scraps to eat. The Italian forces had sided with us by this time, and the Italian mountain troops were very eager to assist by providing detailed information that helped us to plan our advance. For the next three weeks the division conducted reconnaissance and combat patrols in preparation for our assault on Riva Ridge and Mount Belvedere in the Gothic Line.

The Allied offensive against the German defenses along the Gothic Line had stalled because the Germans held the advantage of commanding the high ground along all routes leading north. The Gothic Line was an impressive network of defenses the German general Kesselring had built along the slopes of the Apennine Mountains. The Apennine Mountains are a 50-mile-deep range in northern Italy that runs diagonally from coast to coast, and they afforded the Germans a natural barrier for defense. The Germans considered their positions atop Mount Belvedere impregnable to Allied attacks, and they were successful in mauling two American divisions who had tried to prove them wrong. The German positions atop Mount Belvedere commanded Highway 64 into Bologna, and its capture would mean a tactical victory for the Allies, so the 10th Mountain Division was brought to Italy to circumvent the German defenses on Mount Belvedere and attack from its rear, where the Germans were less prepared to defend.

The division marched out of Pisa on the 16th of February, and it took us two days to navigate our way around the base of Mount Belvedere to where the Germans couldn't see us. On the evening of the 18th, seven hundred men of the 86th Infantry Regiment began their successful assault of Riva Ridge, which rose steeply 2,000 feet above the Panaro River. After the flank was secured, the assault on Mount Belvedere could begin. Just before midnight and without artillery support, five battalions including mine began our attack on Belvedere. Our climb was almost vertical, and we moved slowly in the darkness with heavy packs and rifles strung on our backs. Orders were to use only grenades and bayonets so we could be confident any rifle or machine gun fire would reveal a German position. I affixed about six grenades to the harness of my packs so the safety pin was automatically pulled out when I yanked the grenade and threw it with the use of just one hand. The tactic worked well, and we caught the Germans with their pants down. By the next morning we were on top of Mount Belvedere clearing the last remnants of the defenders from deep caves and bunkers. I saw many dead Germans on that first day, and most had defended their positions with a fierce determination, but many more were completely stunned at our arrival and surrendered.

With the initial object achieved, the division fought towards Monte della Torraccia, our final objective. We encountered fierce counterattacks, and it was not taken until the 24th. The battles for Riva, Belvedere, and Torraccia cost the division 909 casualties, including 203 killed and 706 wounded. One of those wounded on the first day was my good friend Richard Norris. Dick had skated with me in New York and was wounded in the heel and leg by an explosion. I was able to visit him in a Bologna hospital a couple weeks later, and he told me the story of how the doctors had come close to removing his leg when a delivery of penicillin arrived to cure the infection threatening his leg. As skaters we both understood the implications of losing a leg, so we shared a common praise of the penicillin that enabled Dick to continue his skating career after the war.

In early March the division continued its drive north and the 85th captured Monte della Spe, an important victory because it cut the Germans' main line of communication and supply route to the Po Valley where the Fifth Army was driving against heavy resistance. We were pinned down for weeks fending off heavy counterattacks, and we endured intensive artillery. It was the worst shelling I experienced during the war, and it was no fun getting out of my hole every night to collect some cooks and distribute food, ammunition, and clean socks to the men counting on me to arrive each night. I dug a hole as deep as I could for protection against the artillery, and when I hit rock I dug sideways under some rocks for added protection; it was that bad. It was around this time that I learned my friend Torger Tokle had been killed. Tokle was born in Norway, and after coming to the United States he had gained fame by winning the National Ski Jump Championship in 1941. A mortar shell in the village of Iola killed him.

The division finally broke through the Gothic Line and began our fight through the Po Valley, and we led the way out of the Po Valley to reach the Po River on April 22. We had advanced so rapidly that we outran our bridging units, so we crossed the river on a makeshift flotilla of rubber rafts. By midnight on the 23rd the 85th was across the Po River and charging full speed ahead to cut the Germans off from escaping into the Alps, but the Germans had escaped across the Alps and blown up the alpine highway tunnels leading into Austria, so we couldn't follow. This forced us to cross Lake Garda in another amphibious assault on April 30. Elements of the division loaded amphibious trucks (DUKWs) and crossed the lake, suffering heavy losses when several DUKWs capsized with all hands lost but a few. The 10th Division was in Austria at the conclusion of the war a few days later. The 10th Division had suffered 4,888 casualties in just four months of combat, including 978 men who would never return home. Our replacements were men from the general pool of reinforcements, and although they were good men, none had the extensive training similar to the original members of the division. One of these men was a future senator, Bob Dole. Dole was assigned to our 87th Infantry Regiment and was severely wounded by machine-gun fire soon after the division crossed the Po River in April 1945.

I didn't really have time to reflect on what was happening around me while in combat. The division was moving so fast, at times I didn't even have time to feel tired, and I just never knew what was going to happen to me from day to day. It was absolutely a matter of luck as to who survived and who died, and if a bullet or a shell had your name on it, there was nothing you could do. I was standing along the side of the road and a sniper took a pot shot at me, and the bullet missed me by a few inches and hit the hillside over my shoulder. On another day I had just gotten out of my hole to take a leak and a piece of shrapnel passed so close to my head I felt the heat on my neck.

When the war was raging around me I just didn't think about being scared, because we were all asking ourselves what it was we needed to do to stay alive. I had little concern about what was going to happen the next day or the following week or month, as all my thoughts were concentrated on the here and now. We all tried to help one another the best we could, but everyone was pretty much fending for themselves. We all had orders and knew what each man had to do, but there wasn't anyone to hold your hand and show you how to do it. There are really no cowards in combat, just some men who can't handle the stress of war as well as others. On one occasion I was the sergeant of the guard, and when I checked on one particular guy he was never at his post. This was a critical disregard of his duty, because the lives of the men in the company were dependent on our vigilance. The third time he was found missing from his post, his ass was hauled away in shackles, and I never saw him again. The man was panic-stricken at the thought of standing guard at night, but I had no sympathy for the man. Our duty was to protect our sleeping comrades who trusted us by putting their lives in our hands, and this fact alone should have negated any concerns he had for his own safety.

I don't think there is any easy way to describe combat, other than it's something you just don't want to experience for yourself. Combat is frightening, but at the same time there was nothing I could do but try to survive the best I knew how. Sergeant Wagner made it very clear to us, from the very first day, that there was no bargaining with the enemy. I had no prior impression of what the Germans would be like when I encountered them in combat, and I didn't hate the Germans because I think they disliked fighting and the thought of dying as much as I did. When we searched prisoners they were scared to death, and we found they all had pictures similar to ours of their girlfriends, mothers, fathers, sons, and daughters. After the shooting stopped I don't think they were any more interested in killing me than I was in killing them, so it was hard not to share a mutual feeling of respect and understanding. But I had to kill or be killed, and if I wanted to survive, it was that simple. I am not overly religious, but I am sure I prayed while in combat when things were rough. But I am not sure how much prayer can keep you alive, because men who were a lot more spiritual than I were killed just the same as everyone else.

After the fighting in Europe ended, the division was slated for redeployment to the Pacific for the invasion of Japan, but Truman ordered the use of the atomic bombs, ending the war. The 85th left Naples on July 31 aboard the SS *Marine Fox* and arrived at New York Harbor on August 11. The ship had just reached New York Harbor when someone on a tugboat steering us into port yelled out that the Japanese had surrendered and the war was over. Some USO girls were brought aboard and distributed cartons of fresh milk to all the men. It was the first I had tasted milk in a year, and we all toasted the end of the war with our cartons of milk raised over our heads. We offloaded on the Hudson and arrived at Fort Drum later in the day. After a thirty-day furlough the division assembled at Carson in Colorado.

On my first weekend pass I went to a nearby hotel to take advantage of their fine skating rink, and I was out on the ice when two MPs grabbed me and told me to report back to camp immediately. The camp commandant instructed me to report to Fort Sheridan in Illinois to meet Mr. Arthur Wurtz, who at the time owned the Sonja Henie show. Wurtz arranged for me to be discharged the next day, forgoing all the routine discharge procedures. I was out of the Army and within twenty-four hours I was performing with Sonja Henie in Indianapolis. It all happened so fast, I was back to my prewar routine without catching my breath, and while my wartime experiences were not forgotten, I managed to put them far behind me. I stayed with the Sonja Henie show until 1947, when I joined the Ice Capades, and I remained there until my wife and I retired in 1953.

After retiring from show business I needed something to keep me busy, so I began to explore the interests in woodworking I had discovered during my skating career. Between shows I had spent much of my free time fiddling around making wooden ships, and while some of my creations were not so good, others were quite good. With so much more free time on my hands after retirement, I created more elaborate wooden ships and toys, and my basement evolved into a woodshop to support my hobby. When the flow of sawdust from my work began to accumulate in the rest of our house, I was given the ultimatum to build a woodshop elsewhere. I was lucky enough to find a vacant shop along Route 1 in Bethany Beach, Delaware, and this is how my second career running "Shorty's Shop" began.

My time in war was something I would never want to do again, but if I had to do again, I would. I learned a lot and met some fascinating people who I still keep in touch with after all these years. At the conclusion of the war only 5 of the original 175 men in Company A of the 85th Infantry Regiment, including me, had escaped death or injury, so I feel very lucky to be sitting here talking about the war when so many men I knew were not as lucky.

I don't think there is any one individual who can be called the real hero of the Second World War, except maybe my first sergeant, Harry Wagner. There are a lot of men who were in my company who can thank Harry Wagner for their having lived through World War II.

GI Diary—Battle of the Bulge

DECEMBER 2, 1944—We are in Germany. It was a quiet night. It was cold and damp, again. Addressed a few Christmas cards. Slept the rest of the day, had chow, and went back to the firing line at 1600 hours. Sat in a foxhole and listened to the Army vs. Navy football game. Army-23 Navy-7. Played in Baltimore. Sure would have liked to have been home for the game. Made me a little homesick to hear them say Baltimore over and over on the radio.

DECEMBER 5, 1944—Got up at 0730, had chow. It cleared up enough for our planes to come over. The British started to advance on our left flank. Jerry was too busy to bother us today. Didn't get any sleep in the pillbox. A boy played the harmonica all evening. Doesn't play all too well but helps pass the time. Went to chow. Had a swell dinner! Beans, soup, ground beef with chopped macaroni, beets, corn and chocolate pudding for dessert. Best meal yet. We have been lucky and have not missed a meal yet. Those mess guys treat us all right.

DECEMBER 7, 1944—Been three years at war today. Was in Ft. Bragg 3 years ago today. They play Have I been away too long on the radio. You bet your life we have! Be glad when this is over and to get back home. Had hot cakes for breakfast, sure was good. Went to position and it rained all day. Fired 12 rounds. We had Tetanus shots today, I feel a bit sick I think from it. Jerry sent over some planes but the AA was so heavy they ran away like scared rabbits. Have been at the front for a month, sure gets monotonous. That boy keeps playing the harmonica, too much noise to sleep in the pillbox.

DECEMBER 9, 1944—In Waubach, Holland on 48 hours pass. Red Cross has brought us beer. I had just a couple. Don't want to be hung over. Lady invited us in her house to stay. She got on her knees and wiped the mud off our shoes. The Dutch can't do or give us enough. No guns or planes here, just nice and quiet. Went to see a band play.

DECEMBER 17, 1944—Cloudy and cold, finished digging the gun in. Rained off and on all day. Jerry planes diving all day bombed and strafed but did no damage. Fired 11 rounds at 13,000 yards. Some German paratroopers were found and caught in the town. Have a cold. Makes it tough.

DECEMBER 18, 1944—Still in Feilenkichen, Germany. Went to gun at 2400 hours, no fire missions today, all quiet. Jerry sent bombers over again all night bombing rear positions. Noise kept me up all night. Came off at 0800 and did some wash and shaved. Still a lot of Jerry planes over us. Fired all night, hope to get some rest tomorrow.

DECEMBER 19, 1944—Slept well all night and got up at 0800. Jerry started shelling us and we ran to our holes fast. He really was throwing the TNT at us today, lasted about 1 1/2 hours. Three men were killed including McCashin and a new guy I did not

The following are excerpts from the personal diary of Staff Sgt. John Dix, of Baltimore, Maryland, who was a member of Battery C, 327th Field Artillery Battalion, 84th Infantry Division. The excerpts cover the days before, during, and after the Battle of the Bulge.

"I wrote the diary," Dix later explained, "because keeping one was something I have always done, even before the war and to this day. The Army told us not to write a diary because if we were captured it could help the Germans with intelligence information, but a lot a people did, including our officers. I didn't know most of what was going on around us during the war. They may have told us what our objective was in terms of the battle, but my objective was just staying alive, and if it meant killing, that was part of the game I was willing to accept and play along. We had no TV to tell us about what was going on, and it was some time before we figured out the Germans had counterattacked."

know. They died instantly. Incoming fire is a strange thing. It's like a tornado. It sweeps in and does its damage, then passes on leaving behind a path of debris and wreckage all around. Another shell landed close to our hole, put the fire out, the concussion was terrific. They finally stopped the firing and I thank God for that.

DECEMBER 24, 1944—Quite a lot has happened since I last wrote and I'll put it all down here. On the 20th, we were completely shelled from our positions. Jerry had us plotted in perfectly and there were a lot of close calls but everyone is O.K. We had to dig out all of our equipment that was buried during the shelling. I was scared as the shelling began when we returned and we sweated it out. It was a good day to move out, it was foggy and Jerry was grounded like we were. Just as we pulled away another barrage began and we all would have been killed if we had stayed a minute longer. On the 21st, we got orders to join the 1st Army group and reported to the vicinity of Marche, France. We learned that Jerry had broken through in several places and that we were going down to plug a gap. We went the 120 miles and it was extremely cold and we had only K rations to eat. I felt weak after cutting all the logs to dig our guns in. We created a circle of guns because we had no idea in which direction Jerry would attack. A big difference in X-Mas this year. No food and cold as hell. I am thankful I am alive and healthy, which is quite a lot to be thankful [for] over here. Many dogfights overhead as the skies cleared. We counted 2,000 of our bombers, stopped counting after that. Some Jerry planes crashed near us, what a mess, all very young. Went to church, sang some songs, it was beautiful.

DECEMBER 25, 1944—X-Mas day, had K rations again as our cooks are somewhere trying to catch up. Our little tree was pretty. A case of beer showed up and it was pretty good. Very little activity we sat around and talked about what we would be doing if home.

DECEMBER 26, 1944—In Belgium. In reserve waiting for a push forward. Jerry started another attack and the AA guns were busy all night. We didn't fire because we couldn't cover the sector where all the action is.

DECEMBER 27, 1944—Kitchen arrived last night and we had hot food!! Pancakes. We have been ordered to get ready to move out, looks like we are going back onto the attack. Took new positions and surrounded 40 SS Jerry troops. Arrogant bastards. Refused to sleep and stayed up all night in the snow. So much wreckage on the roads, I think Jerry must be on their last leg.

CHARLES H. SMELSER JR.

Westminster, Maryland

490th Bombardment Group, U.S. Army Air Corps

Charles Harold Smelser Jr. was born in Uniontown, Maryland, on July 4, 1920. After graduating from the University of Maryland in 1942, he enlisted in the Army Air Corps and piloted thirty-five missions in a B-17 bomber over Europe. He is a recipient of the Distinguished Flying Cross and Air Medal with five oak-leaf clusters. After the war Smelser returned to Carroll County and married his wife, Betty. He was elected to the Maryland House of Delegates, serving from 1955 to 1963, and held a seat in the Maryland Senate from 1967 until his retirement in 1995. In 1958 he was elected director and later president of the New Windsor State Bank, a position he held until retiring in 1997. The senator and Betty have lived on a dairy farm in the Unionville area of Frederick County since 1947. They have two children, a granddaughter, and a great-grandson.

Having been born on the Fourth of July, I always thought I was a bit more patriotic than the next guy, so I didn't hesitate about going down to the main post office in Baltimore to enlist for military service. I wanted to avoid all the mud that came with the infantry job, so I decided I would take my chances in the air, and after graduating from the University of Maryland in 1942 at age twenty-two, I enlisted in the Army Air Corps.

I was called to duty in March of 1943 and was immediately shipped off to classification school, where I was graded according to how I performed on tests and a number of interviews. It was here that men were selected as radiomen, mechanics, potential pilots, or whatever the Air Corps needed. I was selected for pilot training and sent to preflight school at Maxwell Field, where I learned aviation basics, code, meteorology, and aircraft identification. Next was primary flight school, basic, and then advanced flight school, where I earned my wings. I really wanted to fly the B-17 and was very excited to learn I was being shipped off to Hendricks Field in Sebring, Florida, to be introduced to the B-17 bomber.

Training to fly the B-17 was intensive and exhausting, and my first flight piloting a B-17 was a memorable experience. Training was done in old war-weary B-17s brought back from combat, and they had definitely seen better days. During one preflight inspection I was surprised to see that one of the tires was so worn several belts of the tire had been worn through. The instructor, Captain Selby, was very laid back and did not seem worried and told me to suit up and get aboard, but I hesitated and voiced my concern. The captain just smiled, patted me on the back, and said, "Lieutenant, just make sure you land with the bald spot facing up." I think the captain gave himself a real chuckle, but I didn't think it was too funny at the time. He must have had nerves of steel or else was a complete fool. The fact that I was a raw trainee did not deter him from sleeping right through many of our flights together.

The single most important aspect of my training was to perfect my formation-flying skills. I took pride in my ability to keep the plane in a tight formation, and my crew knew when I was flying because I kept us in a much tighter formation than my co-pilot, Carter, who tended to drift away from the other bombers when he was flying. The Germans tried to break up our formations, and when successful in separating a bomber from the rest of the flight, they would have it for lunch. A good flying formation was a bomber's best defense against enemy planes because it concentrated our guns on attacking fighters. With twelve .50-cal. machine guns on each bomber, the amount of fire we could return made attacking a formation very risky, and I think the B-17 was appropriately named the Flying Fortress.

At the end of transition school I was assigned a crew for the operational phase of our training. The crew of a B-17 consisted of ten men, and our crew ranged in age between the radioman, who was thirty, and the tail gunner, who was just sixteen. I was very lucky to have a crew who took their responsibilities very seriously, and we all got along fine. To me, as the airplane commander, it was important that I maintain the proper level of discipline that combat required. Our crew was very conscientious and well disciplined, and I helped them as much as I could and made sure they received their promotions when due and deserved.

We were assigned to the 848th squadron, 490th Bomb Group (Heavy), 93rd Wing, which was part of the Eighth Air Force based in Eye, England. Eye is located between Norwich and Ipswich and was home to four squadrons, each squadron consisting of twelve to thirteen planes. Our base would normally send out three squadrons with the fourth in reserve, but all four squadrons would sometimes fly together when a maximum effort was needed. We were a replacement crew, and so we were not assigned our own aircraft

Charles Smelser *(back row, far left)* with his crew during operational training at MacDill Field in Tampa, Florida, in June 1944. *From Smelser's left:* Larry Iverson, co-pilot (later wounded flying with another bomb group after being transferred as punishment for returning half an hour late from leave); John Walter, bombardier; Neil Johnson, navigator. *Front row, from left:* Leonard Kail, tail gunner (at seventeen, the youngest member of the crew); Herman Kautz, assistant engineer and waist gunner (killed by flak over Brüx, Czecho-slovakia); Walter Hale Jr., radio operator (at twenty-eight, the oldest member of the crew); John Jackson, ball turret gunner; John Hoyak, waist gunner; Joe Poor, engineer and top turret gunner.

and flew whatever plane was available. I flew the same bomber for my last twenty missions, but I never had any thought about giving it a nickname like many of the crews who flew the same aircraft during their missions. I don't know why I didn't; I just never did.

The cumulative destructive power of the Eighth Air Force in 1944 was tremendous. On one mission in December of 1944 to Berlin our group was the last to leave the coast of England as the leading group was returning over the English Channel. The bombers of the Eighth Air Force were stretched from England to Berlin and back, which indicated to me that the war would soon be over. The punishment we were dishing out was staggering.

Our living quarters on the base consisted of corrugated-steel Quonset huts that had minimal heat, but we didn't complain because we were all in the same boat. I didn't have too many of the luxuries we take for granted today, but at least I had a dry and relatively safe place to rest my head at night, which was a lot more than the infantrymen, who didn't have it half as easy as I did. When we had free time we spent it at the officers' club on the base or in the library, perhaps watching a movie, or just sleeping. We even had a softball league, and my greatest achievement was getting a hit off Cleo Mace, who was a professional softball pitcher from Oklahoma City.

On the day of a mission we were called sometimes at three-thirty in the morning and treated to fresh eggs and sausages obtained from local farmers. Following the meal the officers assembled in the briefing room for the mission briefing, and while we waited there was a lot of anxiety as to where we were headed on our mission. The room was set up theater-style, with a stage and a large map of the European continent at one end. A curtain hid the map so we couldn't tell where we were heading until the officer pulled the curtain back to reveal our flight plan. In the early part of the war the bombing campaign concentrated on ball-bearing and oil-manufacturing plants. Towards the end we hit synthetic oil plants and provided tactical bombing support for the troops after the D-Day invasion.

Smelser's B-17 crew following a tough mission to Merseburg, Germany, in early 1945. The smiles in the photo taken during training in Tampa are noticeably absent and have been replaced by expressionless glares. Three members of the original crew were now missing: engineer Kautz had been killed, ball turret gunner Jackson had asked to be reassigned, and co-pilot Iverson had been transferred before the crew went overseas. *Back row, from left:* Smelser, co-pilot Carter Younts, navigator Neil Johnson, bombardier Walter Johnson. *Front row, from left:* engineer Joe O'Hare, ball turret gunner Harold Pickerill, waist gunner John Hoyak, tail gunner Leonard Kail, radio operator Walter Hale Jr.

Missions to heavily defended targets would cause a long and collective sigh as the group thought back to all the antiaircraft guns we had encountered on a prior mission. The briefing officer would inform us of our primary and secondary targets, probable flak concentrations, enemy fighter strengths, weather, and information regarding other missions flown by other wings. Briefings lasted about thirty minutes, and before the conclusion we were issued the time we were to report to our planes, the time to start our engines, the time to begin the taxi to the runway, and the time to take off. We never questioned a mission, but we knew some targets were just going to be worse than others. When the meeting adjourned, all you could say to the guys next to you was good luck and hope for the best.

You had thoughts about not coming back, but you just hoped it wouldn't be you. The best thing you could do under the circumstances was to stay positive and hope for the best. I was very confident in my skills as a pilot, but being a good pilot was no guarantee that you would return from your mission. Many good pilots were in the wrong place at the wrong time. With a little bit of luck thrown in I was sure we would get through the mission just fine.

Of course I felt fear, but as the commander of other men I couldn't let it show. My men looked up to me for leadership, and if I stayed cool I think they all felt a little less tense. I don't believe anyone who flew in a B-17 was a coward, but I did expect everyone to put forth an effort to make every mission. If one guy had to go do it, that's just the way I approached it. After being airborne on a mission to Merseburg, Germany, my co-pilot said he was just too sick to fly. If you pick up any book about the Eighth Air Force, you'll see lots written about our missions to Merseburg. I flew three missions against Merseburg, and it was the most heavily defended target in Germany. We always took a punishment flying over Merseburg. After listening to him complain about not feeling well, I think I got a little pissed at first, since I felt he was no sicker than I was. I was willing to give him two options. The first was that I would fly over the base and he could bail out for everyone to see. The second was that he could stick it out and I would fly the entire mission. He chose to come along, and I flew the entire eight hours to the target and back. You didn't have to rock me to sleep that night.

On another occasion my ball turret gunner, John Jackson, from Mount Vernon, Texas, came to see me after our sixteenth mission to say he just couldn't take another mission in the ball turret. Our first few missions were real rough, and the fact that he was our ball turret gunner didn't make it any better for him. The ball turret was just about the toughest place to be in a B-17 because there was no place to duck and hide when the German fighters began firing 30-mm. shells and when flak was coming straight up at us. He sat exposed outside and under the body of the B-17 in a glass enclosure and fired the twin .50-cal. machine guns that were critical to the defense of our plane. It was a cold and cramped space compared to the rest of the plane, and I really felt for the kid, so I did everything I could to make sure he could be reassigned to another crew where he no longer had to be a ball turret gunner, and he completed his thirty-five missions with that crew.

Taking off in a loaded B-17 was a delicate process, and the preflight inspection was essential. We checked every gauge and every switch to make sure it was functioning. The B-17 could carry 2,780 gallons of fuel and 5,000 to 6,000 pounds of ordnance, so one careless oversight on your checklist could lead to disaster. A fully loaded bomber that didn't have enough power to lift off most likely ended up performing a belly flop at the end of the runway. Making things worse was the usual short runways and typically foggy weather we had to endure. Fog was so dense at times it obscured my view of the runway, and my co-pilot had to guide us down the runway by watching the runway lights on his side get closer or further away and telling me to correct my direction accordingly. The sky around the base during takeoff and landing was filled with aircraft, and the whole crew was called upon to keep an eye out for other aircraft, but we still had some close calls.

On the way to the target I was naturally tense, but I was so busy concentrating on leading the other three bombers in our element, staying in formation, and monitoring the condition of the plane that I didn't worry about much else. I kept my eyes moving or else I would start developing vertigo from staring in one direction too long. I was not worried about enemy fighters or flak because they were just things I couldn't do much about. Like all pilots, I was constantly observant of the plane's fuel levels, and on the way to the target I would watch the fuel gauge drop lower and lower until by the time we got to the target we would have maybe one-third of our original fuel supply remaining. I would be thinking about how the hell we were going to make it home with so little fuel, but once we dropped our bomb load, the plane felt as light as air and we cruised all the way home. On one occasion we did run out of fuel just as we touched down, even though the fuel gauge read 125 gallons.

Bombing missions were long, and a round trip could last as long as eight hours. My co-pilot would help fly part of the way, but he was uneasy flying in close formation, so I did most of the flying to the target. At high altitude the temperature outside the plane would drop to fifty-five below zero, so to combat the cold we wore heavy flight suits with lighter ones under them containing electric heating coils sewn into the liner to provide extra warmth. We seldom left our pilots' seats, so if we had to relieve ourselves the co-pilot and I each had a funnel with a rubber hose for us to use.

There were moments of suspense waiting for the first call to go out over the intercom when we spotted an enemy fighter. The crew then jumped to life to fire at the German fighters. In the latter months of the war our fighter escorts did a great job of keeping enemy fighters off our backs, and by the end of the war we saw very few enemy planes. A more dreaded threat was the antiaircraft guns. The Germans had very accurate antiaircraft guns, and a lot of them. The targets with the highest concentration of antiaircraft guns were Berlin and Merseburg in Germany and Brüx in Czechoslovakia. Enemy fighters could pick you apart, but flak could completely destroy an entire plane in a flash. Flak made a "thump, thump" sound. If the flak exploded close enough, I would hear it hitting the plane. When we saw the flak explode, it was no threat; it was the flak we never saw that did the most damage. I saw B-17s go up in puffs of smoke leaving little evidence that there had been a bomber, and a crew of ten men, there just moments before. I guess it was just dumb luck if a bomber was hit by flak, and it didn't matter how good of a pilot a man was when flak destroyed a plane in an instant. Two things I distinctly remember from the war are the thick clouds of flak over Berlin that burst in huge red fireballs, and how I would often look ahead at the dense flak clouds over our target and later wonder how we had managed to fly through it all and return to base.

During the bad moments under heavy fire I saw images of my life race through my mind. On one tough mission I made a promise to myself that if I made it home I would never worry or get upset over things like if I ever got stuck on the side of the road while driving. Everything else in life just seemed so insignificant compared to the trouble I was in. Years later I made good on that promise when my car broke down and I got stuck on the side of the road. I could have become upset, but I remembered the promise I had made to myself back in the war. I think being in combat puts everything else in perspective, and I learned not to take things so seriously anymore.

The stories about the B-17's durability are legendary. The B-17 could take a huge amount of punishment and remain in the air. I saw B-17s with so much damage after a mission I couldn't believe they could have still flown back. I was lucky enough to survive thirty-five missions with relatively light damage. We lost two engines on one mission, and except for the loss of our engineer gunner on the sixth mission, I think the worst damage we ever received was when we counted about a hundred holes in the fuselage following a mission. The engine on the B-17 could take a direct hit from flak, sending hot oil flying all over the place, but it would just keep on humming along, and even if one, two, or three engines were lost the B-17 could limp home on just one engine running. The B-17 was a well-designed and well-built airplane, and it brought countless airmen home safely from tough missions. The B-17 was just a beautiful plane. I can't say enough about it and how thankful I am for it helping me and so many other airmen survive the missions we flew. As far as I am concerned, the unsung heroes at the bomber bases were the ground crews who kept our planes in top flying condition in all types of weather, working through the day and night.

Smelser is presented with the Distinguished Flying Cross by an officer of the 93rd Bombardment Wing: "For extraordinary achievement while serving as pilot of a B-17 aircraft on combat missions against the enemy. Despite extremely adverse weather conditions and severe flak damage to his plane, Lt. Smelser, by his determination, flying skill, and courageous devotion to duty, materially contributed to the success of missions on Brüx, Czechoslovakia on 11th September 1944, and over Merseburg, Germany on 28th September 1944, and 21st November 1944. His actions on these occasions reflect the highest credit upon himself and the Army Air Forces."

The bombing of the target was sort of an automatic thing. The lead crew of the formation had a bombardier, who was the real hot-shot of the group and could put the aiming hairs right where they belonged. When he dropped his bombs, he would also release a bomb trailing smoke, and the remainder of the formation dropped its bombs along the same path. If the lead plane was on target, we all were; if he was off, we were all off. It was a crucial job for that lead bombardier to get it right.

We were never told to purposely bomb civilians, but I think we knew any target we hit in the confines of a city could cause the death of civilians. I didn't want to hit civilians, but it was a part of war, but I surely hope some of those bombs landed on the heads of those antiaircraft gun crews. After seeing what we did to Germany I had a real good appreciation of how lucky we were our country was to be spared such devastation.

After we came back from a mission we would have a debriefing to record our observations. The bombardier would assess the damage to our plane and determine who got credit for any enemy planes shot down by our plane. Debriefing gave me some time to unwind from the mission, and I would start to hear about what crews had yet to return home. Anytime I learned of a crew that had been shot down, I just thought about how but for the grace of God it could have been me. Some missing crews would turn up in a day or so with outrageously concocted stories about how they had bailed out over France only to be rescued by beautiful Frenchwomen and how we had really missed out on all the fun. There were times we just never saw certain crew members ever again.

On one mission we were out of gas and were forced to land in France. We sent a message to our base that we were all fine, but by the time I got back to the base the other guys had folded up all of my belongings to be shipped home like I had been killed. We all got a good chuckle out of things like that, although it did make you think a little.

Losing a crew member was traumatic. On our sixth mission to Brüx, we were hit hard by flak. Our engineer, Sgt. Herman Kautz, had his leg nearly sheared off by flak on the bomb run, and he died from loss of blood and oxygen. It was tough to fly all the way back home with a dead crew member on board, but it was just the nature of war. War isn't nice, and we just had to keep going about our business. It was something every man who served in combat had to deal with and put behind him to get on with the war.

After completing my thirty-five missions I stayed on as an operations officer until the end of the war in Europe. Then we flew what we called a "chow hound" mission to parts of Europe desperately in need of food and supplies. On one of these missions we dropped food in a park in Amsterdam, Holland. We would load up our B-17s with food and fly over open areas to drop our cargo on a target marked with a white "X." I think this was the most rewarding experience of the war for me. I never had to worry about if I was going to come back from these missions, and I much preferred doing something constructive for a change after contributing to so much destruction.

So many people think flying the B-17 was a glamorous job. I don't think it was too glamorous, and it was actually an extremely dangerous job. So many planes were lost; I realize how lucky I was to have survived. I attribute much of my good fortune to the training I received, and it taught me to not get too excited about things and to relax when things got tough. I don't think I did anything special, and I saw many men do the same things I did and more. If we honor anyone from the war, we should honor everyone who contributed to the war effort and not just the soldiers who carried the weapons. There are so many people who were home building our weapons, making the uniforms, preparing our food and medicines, and saving and sacrificing so much for the war effort.

Years after the war I was out in Tucson, Arizona, and visited Davis-Monthan Air Force Base. Locals out there call it "the graveyard" because it is the final resting place for most of the planes used by the Air Force. I saw some B-17 bombers that had my bomb group's red tail markings, and for a moment I thought about how I just might have flown one of them during the war. I turned away because I just didn't want to think about the war any more than that.

I have always been a firm believer that something good always comes from something bad, and the Second World War was no different. The supreme sacrifices made by so many left the world in a better condition, and I am just proud to have been part of the whole thing. If our nation ever faced the same perils we did during the war, I would gladly do it all over again.

BORIS R. SPIROFF

Severna Park, Maryland
OSS—Balkan Group, U.S. Army

Boris Robert Spiroff was born in Baltimore, Maryland, on February 14, 1920. He attended Edgar Allan Poe Junior High and in 1937 enlisted in the U.S. Army. He was assigned to Company L, 14th Infantry Regiment, Canal Zone, Panama, and was later selected for service in the Balkan Group of the OSS (Office of Strategic Services). He participated in operations on the Dalmatian Islands off the coast of Yugoslavia and is a recipient of the Bronze Star for valor for his actions during a mission on the island of Hvar on February 24, 1944. After the war Spiroff remained in the Army and was assigned to Company G, 7th Cavalry Regiment, in Korea. He was again a recipient of the Bronze Star for heroism for his actions in leading an assault on a heavily defended position near Paiu-Ri, Korea. He retired from the Army in 1962 after twenty-five years of service and began a career as a security investigator with Westinghouse, retiring in 1991. He married his late wife, Catherine, in 1950, and has one son.

The following profile was based on an interview with Boris Spiroff, and on portions of his autobiography, Korea: Frozen Hell on Earth *(Baltimore: American Literary Press, 1998), which are reprinted here with permission.*

My parents, Anthony and Maria Spiroff, came to America in 1916, and although they didn't know it at the time, they arrived on the same day on the same ship. They were both sponsored by families living in Southwest Baltimore, and they eventually met, fell in love, and were married in 1918. I was born in Baltimore in February 1920. In 1922 my father received a letter stating that his mother was very ill, and that if he wanted to see her again he should return to his hometown of Skopje, Yugoslavia, immediately. My father returned home with my mother and me, promising we would return as soon as possible. But we never did.

Soon after our arrival, my grandmother died. My father then became ill, and after a short illness he also died. This left my mother and me alone in Skopje, but my mother wanted to stay with her family in Kikinda near Belgrade. We moved to Kikinda and lived with my mother's brother, Uncle Alexander, while preparing to return to America. It was another six years, when I was eight years old, before my mother wrote to her sister Milka in Baltimore to ask for the money we needed for passage back to the States. In October 1928 the money arrived, and my mother purchased tickets for a ship to America. However, my mother had caught a cold in the days before our departure and was not allowed to board the ship. Her cold developed into pneumonia and we had to return to Yugoslavia, and after a long illness she also died. A month after her death my aunt Milka in Baltimore provided passage for me to board the liner *Leviathan,* bound for America. My uncle Alexander made arrangements for someone to look after me on the ship until we arrived in New York.

The ship arrived at Ellis Island, New York, on November 22. I had no clue where I was. I didn't speak any English, so I couldn't ask for help. All I had was a tag hanging around my neck that instructed people to put me on the next train headed to Camden Station, Baltimore. I arrived at 9 P.M. and was met by my aunt Milka, and I lived with her and her five children on Woodyear Street in Southwest Baltimore. To learn English, I was enrolled in an Americanization class at Elementary School 75, on the corner of Poppleton Street and Lexington Street. During my first two years in America I got into quite a few fights with boys mocking me because of my accent and lack of knowledge of the English language. By 1932, having learned enough English, I was transferred to Edgar Allan Poe Junior High School at the corner of Greene and Fayette Streets. The school was approximately 2 miles from home, which I had to walk. More often I hitched a ride from the rear end of a streetcar or from a truck. I chose to quit school before graduating to find work to help support my aunt, who worked hard to support six children. At this time we moved to a larger house on Calhoun Street. Work was hard to find after the Great Depression, but after just a few days' search I was fortunate enough to find work on the docks unloading ships of their cargoes of bananas. The work was very hard, and the pay was low. I soon found an opening at the Postal Telegraph Company delivering messages, and I left the docks. This work was also hard. I pumped a bike eight to ten hours a day through the streets of Baltimore earning three to five cents for each telegram I delivered. The job earned me the hefty sum of eighteen dollars a month. The money for my bike was earned delivering shoppers' groceries from the Hollins Street Market to their homes.

A friend of mine, Jack Mills, had been laid off and was unable to find another job. He told me he was thinking about joining the Army because it paid twenty-one dollars a month. The messenger job was becoming difficult. He asked me to quit my job and enlist with him. So I decided to quit my job and join him. It made no difference to me into which branch we enlisted, but Jack preferred the Navy, so we went there first. He was accepted, but I was rejected because I didn't meet their weight requirement, a minimum of 135 pounds. I then went next door to the Army recruiter and was accepted. On February 15, 1937, I enlisted in the Army, one day after my seventeenth birthday, telling them I was eighteen, but they never checked or caught on or I'd have had to have my aunt's signature. Jack Mills never enlisted. When the Navy didn't accept me, he decided that he didn't want to go into the Navy, and he didn't want the Army, either.

The United States was at peace when I enlisted in the Army, and I figured the best way to get the most out of my time was to volunteer for foreign service so I could see a bit more of the world. I was assigned to the 14th Infantry Regiment, Canal Zone, Panama. Our duty in Panama, other than normal Army training, was to guard the locks from being sabotaged. In March of 1939 my two-year enlistment expired, and I returned home with the hope that economic conditions would be better and jobs would be available. Things were still the same, the conditions no better, and Jack Mills was still unemployed. I decided to reenlist, returning to Panama and to my former unit, Company L, 14th Infantry.

In March of 1941 I was promoted to corporal. In November, while on outpost duty at the locks, I received a letter from Jack stating that he had found work in the shipyards in Baltimore, and that he had work lined up for me. My enlistment was due to expire in March of 1942. I was elated that in just four months I would be home with a job. But it was not to be. A week later, on December 7, 1941, Japan bombed Pearl Harbor, forcing us into World War II; hence all discharges were frozen during the war.

I was sent to Camp Livingston, Louisiana, in March of 1943, as part of a two-hundred-man cadre. Prior to that I had been promoted to staff sergeant. Our cadre was composed of a sufficient number of NCOs and officers to form a regimental-size unit once replacements arrived. Camp Livingston was a holding area for troops destined for overseas assignments. We learned we were scheduled for the Pacific theater.

While in the post movie theater watching a training film, I was called out with seventeen other men. All of us knew a foreign language. We had been called out to be interviewed for the Office of Strategic Services, otherwise known as the OSS, for action against the enemy occupying the countries we knew the languages of. Being of Serbian descent I knew Serbo-Croatian, and after an extensive interview and background investigation, I was accepted and assigned to the OSS. I knew nothing about the OSS or their activities prior to the interview. The OSS was a new branch of service organized by Gen. "Wild Bill" Donovan. I didn't choose to be part of the OSS; the OSS chose me to be part of them.

During the war the OSS operated in both the European theater, with headquarters in Bari, Italy, and the China-Burma-India theater, with headquarters in Burma. The primary function of the OSS was to perform intelligence-gathering operations and to support Partisan soldiers engaged in guerilla warfare. As a covert military branch of the U.S. government during World War II, it was imperative that the existence of the OSS, and the various missions conducted against the enemy by the agency, not be made public. Due to the agency's short existence from 1942 to 1945 and the secrecy involved, only a few knew of the missions performed by the OSS and of the consequences we faced if captured. Even to this day much of the public has never heard of the OSS, and those who have do not know what the letters stand for. At the conclusion of the war, President Truman ordered the abolition of the OSS and transferred all of its activities to the War Department. A number of former OSS members were retained and formed the core of what was to become the Central Intelligence Agency.

I was assigned to Company C, 3rd Contingent of the OSS Balkan Operations Group, stationed on the island of Vis, Yugoslavia. I was among those chosen for this group for interpretation purposes. Most men in the Balkan Group were of Slavic, Serb, Croat, or Greek heritage. The group also operated in Italy and Greece. I was especially proud to have returned to my parents' homeland to help liberate it from the Germans, though I never got to visit any relatives there.

The operations groups (OGs) of the OSS were best comparable to today's Special Forces, who perform covert fighting where needed. Those of us in the OG were not the "glamour boys," which was a term the OGs used to describe the men assigned to the special operations (SO) or secret intelligence (SI) groups. The SO and SI groups were like the spies seen in movies and read about in books. They performed secret intelligence operations and didn't get "dirty" in performance of duty unless there was no alternative. The OGs were the combat unit of the OSS, trained for guerilla warfare including parachuting, mountain climbing, hand-to-hand combat, sabotage, and various covert operational techniques needed to infiltrate and operate in enemy territory. The OG personnel operated under the most hazardous, nerve-wracking conditions against a fanatical enemy, in relatively unknown territory far from friendly troops, and with no fanfare.

All members of the OSS received special training. My initial orientation occurred at the Maryland Congressional Country Club near Washington, D.C. It was a surreal experience to be surrounded by the green expanses of the club while learning espionage and guerilla warfare. Our instructors were British Commandos, members of the world's most elite commando organization. Their exploits were something legendary read about in newspapers and seen in movies. They had been fighting the Germans long before we entered the war, and the experience they brought to us was invaluable.

Orientation at the country club lasted only a few days. We were then transferred to a former CCC (Civilian Conservation Corps) camp in Triangle, Virginia, opposite the Marine base at Quantico. Most of us were already experienced in basic infantry tactics. When we arrived in the woods at the old CCC camp, the British Commandos instructed us in advanced commando tactics. We received hand-to-hand combat training and were instructed in how to handle and fire a variety of weapons. Fortunately I never was in a situation where I had to perform hand-to-hand combat. The nearest I came to a German soldier, other than a prisoner, was within 20 feet during a shootout with a German patrol on the island of Hvar. We finished our training in Virginia in mid-September 1943. We were given a weekend pass before our planned departure for Europe. I returned to Baltimore on September 29 during my weekend pass, and that was when I met my future wife, Catherine.

We sailed from Norfolk, Virginia, aboard the Liberty ship *J. W. Brown* on October 2, 1943. The *J. W. Brown* is presently docked at the Inner Harbor in Baltimore. It is one of only two Liberty ships saved from the over two thousand Liberty ships used during World War II. The other is in California. The ship wasn't that big, and it was overcrowded. The water was choppy, and many got sick on the first day, including me. We picked up additional ships at various ports heading north along the Atlantic coast, adding numbers to our convoy. Midway across the Atlantic a torpedo from a German submarine hit the ship behind us, but we kept on going. The loudspeaker informed us that the last ship in the convoy would lend aid and pick up any survivors in the water. We were all scared, not knowing which ship would be hit next. Fortunately there were no more torpedoes. A few days later we sailed through a vicious storm. I didn't think we were going to make it. I was in the hold of the ship with the other men, and it was hell. All the beams were creaking, and the ship rolled back and forth, and men were throwing up everywhere.

It didn't seem possible, but twenty-one days after we left the States, we docked in Oran in North Africa. We had been scheduled to land in Italy but were held in Oran for six weeks while Allied foreign ministers met in Moscow and Cairo and then, in Teheran, Roosevelt, Churchill, and Stalin pondered large war plans. Oran, with the surrounding desert, was an extremely hot place. We did some desert training during our stay in Oran. This took us up as far as Alexandria, Egypt. There was evidence everywhere of the recent desert war. There were destroyed American, British, and German tanks, jeeps, half-tracks, and trucks everywhere.

We were finally given clearance to continue our mission. On January 3, 1944, we were flown from Alexandria to Sicily in Italy, where we spent the night. The next day we were flown to Bari, Italy, which was the location of the OSS headquarters for the European theater. Our unit was designated as the 1st Special Recon Battalion commanded by Maj. John Urban.

After our arrival at our training camp outside of Bari, we received additional training in compass orientation, mountain climbing, and airborne operations. Our airborne training was at Brindisi Airfield not far from our camp in Bari. We learned camouflage techniques and how to live off the land if stranded behind enemy lines; also, how to gauge the amount of equipment and supplies that would be needed for a particular mission. We were instructed in using specialized weapons and were issued new clothing that the Army was testing. There were some little features added to our uniforms—including buttons on our jackets that were actually small compasses and maps of Yugoslavia hidden under the silk lining of our jackets—that would help us if we were lost. It would have been terrible to be lost in the rugged mountains of Yugoslavia.

Parachute jumping back then was dangerous, even in training. We didn't have the quality parachutes of today. Being a British jump school, we jumped with one chute only—no emergency chute. You landed where the wind took you. We had a few members who were seriously hurt during training. One lieutenant was hurt when he crashed through the roof of a barn. He had large wood splinters embedded in various parts of his body. My easiest jump was my first because I was the third in line, and I just moved along following the others in front of me and jumped without thinking. It was a lot different during my second jump when I was the first man in line to jump. I stood in the doorway waiting for the green light and looking at the ground passing far below. I began to have thoughts about my chute not opening, since we had no emergency chute.

I was especially frightened during our night mission into Yugoslavia. We had no idea who or what was going to be waiting for us to land. The Balkan OG operated from the forward OSS base on the island of Vis in the Dalmatian Islands chain off the coast of Yugoslavia. Here I received my initial enemy fire, being bombed by a low-flying German plane as we were moving into our area from the ship. Two bombs were dropped. Much damage occurred, but no casualties. Thank God, the plane made only one swoop, and the two bombs missed the intended target. Was I scared? And how. Everyone was.

The Germans occupied the other eight islands in the Dalmatian chain. It was our mission to liberate them. The island of Vis was under British control, so our OG was under British command. Maj. Randolph Churchill, a nephew of Winston Churchill, Britain's prime minister during the war, commanded some of the missions on the various Dalmatian Islands. The OSS contingency on the island of Vis numbered approximately two hundred OG officers and men. We were part of a larger operational group that included a brigade of British Commandos and a brigade of Yugoslav Partisan soldiers.

Our OG was divided into three patrols designated "X," "Square," and "Circle." The patrols, in whole or part, took turns going on raids with the Partisans and or the British Commandos. I had the Circle Patrol, Sergeant Jimmy Zevitas had the Square, and Pete Panagakos had the X.

Before we could attack any island, we needed to first determine the strength of the occupying force so we could tell what size force we would need for the mission. The first part of any operation was to conduct small intelligence-gathering missions on the occupied island that sometimes lasted for a week or more. We ascertained the location of German garrisons, how they were being supplied, how often and where they conducted patrols, and how many men were in each patrol. Once it was determined that we had enough information, we returned to our base and informed headquarters, who would then initiate a bombing raid, if needed, or lay down plans for a ground assault.

The raids ranged in size from small hit-and-run raids of ten to fifteen men to full-scale combined operations with the support of Partisan, Navy, and Air Force units, if needed. When our operations began in the early part of 1944, the German occupation forces were scattered throughout the islands in small, isolated, and lightly held garrisons that offered ideal targets for our small patrols. Soon after our arrival and initial successes, the Germans concentrated their forces on each island into one or two strongly held positions. It then became essential to expand our operations to include larger forces to eliminate these larger German positions. All of our operations were at night, and it was difficult to avoid the German searchlights sweeping the water.

The Germans were very hard on the civilian population in Yugoslavia, and the civilian population harbored a fierce hatred for the Germans. The Germans responded to attacks upon them by going into a village and executing anyone they thought had some connection with the Partisans. If no men were present in a household, they would demand to know from the women where their husbands were. The women might have known where their husbands were, but perhaps they did not know at that moment. More likely, their husbands were already dead. If they could not convince the Germans that this was the truth, the Germans would torture, rape, and kill the women without mercy. They also took their children, who were also tortured and killed. It was a horrible situation for the civilians.

Fighting the Germans didn't affect me much. I was young and carefree, and I considered what I experienced during the war as simply a matter of "all is fair in love and war." I don't think that I shot at the enemy in anger. It was more of an instinct for self-preservation—either him or me. I didn't enjoy the killing, ever. Whenever I pulled the trigger to shoot at the enemy, my stomach felt sick.

During my ten months' tour of duty in Yugoslavia, I took part in several operations. Every reconnaissance, patrol, or raiding mission I participated in is an endless story of details regarding the area, terrain, time, weather, the enemy, and the risks involved. The occupying forces were regular Wehrmacht soldiers, who fought hard. Not all of our missions were successful, and some required a second or third attempt with additional personnel. Our missions had an inherent added element of risk because unlike regular warfare, our exercises were conducted behind enemy lines and were considered acts of espionage. If captured, we would have been considered spies, and shot. This was also true for the SO and SI groups. To my knowledge, no one in my OG was captured or executed, although I estimate we did have two killed and thirteen wounded.

Of the many missions I participated in, two stand out as the most memorable. The first occurred on the island of Hvar between February 20 and March 1 of 1944. Capt. Andy Rogers and seven OG personnel, including me as patrol sergeant, arrived in Hvar at night by boat accompanied by a Yugoslav guide. Our goals were to destroy shipping, take prisoners, and harass the enemy. The first objective was to locate a suitable CP (command post) area and an OP (observation point) without being detected. After a few days of reconnaissance it became clear that the first two goals could not be performed; thus four members of our patrol returned to Vis. The remaining four members of the patrol set off to the village of Vrbaska, and we were met by six to eight Partisans, who introduced us to pickled squid contained in jars and to some very dark bread. Quite a change from our Army rations.

On the night of February 24, we entered Vrbaska to ambush what we thought would be a four-man German patrol. A curfew on the island was in effect. We had noticed from our OP that at five o'clock each night a four-man patrol left from the school, their headquarters, and strolled the waterfront checking the dark areas for violators. No villagers were to be out after 7 P.M. Captain Rogers thought it was possible, before returning to Vis, to take at least one German prisoner and at best all four. We prepared our ambush, but instead of the four Germans we were expecting, there were eight, along with a dog. Captain Rogers thought we could still by surprise overtake the eight-man patrol, but the dog sensed our presence and started barking at us before we could get into position.

We were in a single file at the end of a narrow alley. Our guide and I were the first in line; Captain Rogers was to my right rear; Sergeant Jimmy Zevitas and Pete Panagakos were in the rear. The Germans ran forward toward us, closing in to approximately 30 feet. We couldn't run away up the narrow street without getting shot in the back, so we opened fire. All hell broke loose as both groups began firing at one another at close range. One of the lead Germans had a round headlamp in front of his chest shining at us. As I fired my carbine I stumbled, tripping on a protruding brick, and fell forward, still firing. I saw the light go out and heard him scream. The Germans returned fire. A burst went over my head and hit Sergeant Zevitas, who was behind me, in the groin area. Had I not fallen, the burst would have hit me. The exchange lasted less than a minute. During the silence I reloaded my carbine. We killed six of the Germans and wounded the other two. Captain Rogers, who was next to me, said, "Let's get the hell outta here!" We left expecting that the Germans would come running out of the school building a block away.

Everyone in the OG understood that if wounded, they might be left behind. A wounded man hindered the chances for the remainder of the group to escape; thus a sacrifice would have to be accepted. But when we were faced with the reality of the situation, we were not able to leave Sergeant Zevitas behind. His wounds were not so severe that he couldn't be transported. We took a mule from a nearby yard to carry Jimmy from the village.

When the German garrison had heard the shooting, they had fired flares into the air and sent search parties with dogs after us. We traveled all night, stumbling along in the dark and cold to the other side of the island. We could hear Germans and their dogs in the distance behind us all night. We were somehow able to evade the Ger-

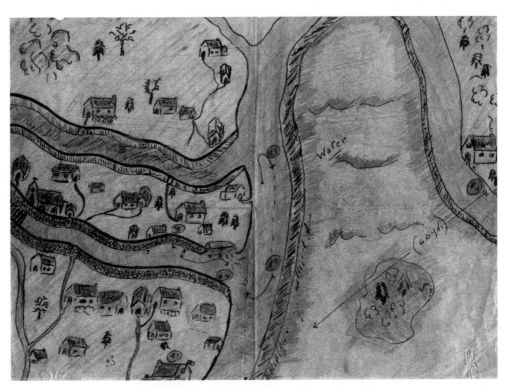

The map produced by Capt. Andy Rogers for British intelligence detailing the movement of the German patrol his OSS party ambushed on the night of February 24, 1944, in Vrbaska on the island of Hvar. *Arrows* indicate the location and movement of the German patrol, and the *numbers* represent the members of the OSS party, which included Boris Spiroff.

mans temporarily and arrived at the town of Verbanic at eight the next morning. We were cold, wet, hungry, and tired. Jimmy was a big problem, not being able to move fast.

A villager from the shootout area arrived in Verbanic a little later with news of the incident. The villager told us he had heard that the Germans knew it was Americans on the island because we had left some clues behind at the scene of the shootout. Sergeant Zevitas had lost his wool cap when shot, I had lost one of my gloves while reloading my carbine, and Sergeant Panagakos had accidentally dropped a pack of Camel cigarettes. I was sad to learn that the German commander in the village was sure we had escaped with Partisan help, and he ordered six teenage boys shot in retaliation. I felt terrible. I couldn't understand why they would take their frustrations out on innocent children.

Soon after speaking to the villager we heard dogs barking and saw the Germans closing in, coming at us from the woods. Captain Rogers told us to scatter and eventually to meet at our prearranged point at the beach. We all scattered in different directions. I ran into a nearby barn and climbed up into the loft. Someone ran behind the house; I thought it was Pete Panagakos. I could see through a small opening that one of the dogs was barking at the barn. The German holding the dog started walking towards the barn, and just as he approached the door, another German spotted Sergeant Panagakos running from the house into the woods. They all gave chase, even the one with the dog. I quickly climbed down. My heart was pounding, and I narrowly escaped a certain shootout or capture and headed for the woods, ready to shoot if confronted.

After a few minutes we somehow worked our way to the prearranged point on the beach and spotted a motorboat with two Commandos who were looking for us to take us off the island. At the last moment we all got in the boat, including Jimmy, and motored away. The Germans came running from the woods onto the beach, yelling and shaking their fists at us. If the Commandos had not rescued us at that moment, we would have been surrounded and captured. The Germans were frustrated. When we arrived back at Vis we informed the British Command of the location of the German garrison. They sent Spitfires to bomb and strafe the school building. I was promoted to tech sergeant, finally.

Following every mission, two men were selected to receive a five-day leave. Those selected traveled together. On July 5, 1944, Corporal Hlodash and I were given leave. We decided to visit Rome. We caught a plane to Rome from the airfield in Brindisi, which was near our base in Bari. We arrived in Rome at five on Thursday afternoon and registered with the Red Cross for overnight lodging. We then went to a nearby park and met two Italian girls. We went out for drinks with the girls that evening. The girls knew where to go. We had already made arrangements at the airfield in Rome to return to Brindisi the next morning, but to prove our sincerity in wanting the girls' company we promised to meet them the same time next evening. However, the next morning Hlodash and I had breakfast and soon began walking to the airport.

Our plane was to take off at 10 A.M. A British soldier in a jeep stopped and asked if we needed a ride, so we climbed into the jeep. I had the two girls from the previous night on my mind, so I asked Hlodash if he would spend another night with me in Rome. He refused, fearing that we would be considered AWOL if we missed our flight. The morning was very foggy. I asked the soldier to stop the jeep at the entrance of the airport. I decided to stay another day, and Hlodash still wanted to get back. I watched him get onto the plane with several other passengers. I went back to the hotel but never found the two girls and spent the night again at the Red Cross. I returned to the airport on Saturday morning but discovered there were no scheduled flights to Brindisi. It dawned on me I would have to hitchhike the 400 miles back to Bari, and I worried I would never make it back in time, but I was fortunate enough to catch a ride to Naples, which was halfway to Bari. Again luck was with me. I caught a ride from Naples to Bari in a 2 1/2-ton truck and arrived in Bari on Sunday morning. A truck from our camp brought me and some others that were on pass back to camp at eleven on Sunday evening. I found my tent and went to bed.

Roll call was conducted the next morning at seven. All the members of my Circle Patrol were present and accounted for. So were the members of X and Square Patrols. Headquarters had one man missing; it was Corporal Hlodash. First Sergeant Stimenos asked me if I knew Hlodash's whereabouts, since we had been on leave together. I told him we parted in Rome because I stayed an extra day, and that I saw Hlodash get on the plane headed to Brindisi. Hlodash was placed on AWOL, which I thought he would be. Right after eating breakfast, the Red Cross called informing our CO that the plane carrying Hlodash had hit a mountain Friday morning shortly after takeoff due to the heavy fog. All seventeen passengers on board were killed, including Hlodash and five Australian nurses. The Red Cross was able to locate our unit from the ID around Hlodash's neck and from the pass in his pocket. I'll never know what kept me from boarding that plane. To this day, I keep thanking the two Italian girls we met, even though they never showed up the following evening.

My other memorable mission took place on the Yugoslavian mainland in an area near the city of Zara from September 2 to October 6, 1944. The operation was code-named "Adairville," and our objective was to destroy German oil and gasoline supplies, harass lines of communication, and attack patrols and outposts. On September 2 I made a night jump with Lt. Jack McConnell and six others in the area just east of the village of Zara. We landed in a cornfield, which was our DZ (drop zone), at 10 P.M. and gathered our equipment. We were met by a group of Marshal Tito's 19th Infantry

Brigade. The Germans, who knew we were coming because they had spotted the burning corn stalks marking our drop zone, gave chase. We followed the Partisans through the field heading for the mountains to get away from the Germans. They did not follow us into the mountains, knowing that the guerilla forces controlled them.

We organized the following day and spent the next few days searching for targets defined in our mission briefing, but we found nothing suitable to strike. The order came for us to redirect our efforts by attacking convoys and other road traffic. We were reinforced on September 16 by only seven of the other twenty OG personnel who were to join us. Bad weather prevented two of the planes from making their drops, and they returned to Italy. We harassed German convoys departing Greece and traveling through Yugoslavia back to Germany. We did this by mining critical roadways, which halted the convoys. The stalled German vehicles were sitting ducks from our firing position on the steep mountainsides above the roads. The mission was abruptly halted. The Partisan command informed us that we were no longer needed in Yugoslavia. We began to make our way to depart, being 40 miles from the coast. Our radioman called Vis informing the base that we were leaving for Kornat and asking for the boat to meet us there.

We were given a Partisan guide to escort us back to the coast so we could return to Vis. We were loaded on two wagons, six men in each, and told to follow the main road south. I was in the lead wagon with Lieutenant McConnell and our guide. We came to an unexpected fork in the road, not knowing which was the main one. The wagons stopped. It was 9 P.M. and exceptionally dark. I volunteered to go forward on foot for a short distance, to see what road was the best to follow. I had walked about a half block when a voice yelled, *"Stoy! Halt!"* I froze, and from the darkness behind two large trees, two figures dressed in long dark coats and black caps armed with machine pistols walked towards me. They looked like Chicago gangsters. They evidently thought I was a German soldier. The one figure yelled, *"Hände hoch!"* (meaning "Hands up!" in German). I raised my arms, and one man yanked my Tommy gun from my shoulder. The other tried to remove my .45 and its holster from the belt, but he couldn't get it out. Without thinking I reached to unbuckle my gun belt. He yelled, "Hands up!" and smacked the back of my hand with his gun, breaking a blood vessel. It hurt like hell, and it started to bleed profusely. Scared, I raised my hands again, realizing he could have shot me in the chest thinking I was reaching for my .45. I considered myself lucky. At that moment, Lieutenant McConnell and our Partisan guide came forward to see where I was and what all the commotion was about. The guide saw me with my hands raised, one hand being bloody. He started yelling at the two guerillas dressed in black, evidently knowing them. The guide presented a letter saying that we were Americans, signed by Marshal

Spiroff *(arrow)* with members of Tito's 19th Infantry Brigade on September 4, 1944, in the mountains near Mostar, Yugoslavia, after returning from a raid against German columns heading back to Germany. OSS personnel cooperated successfully with Yugoslav Partisans to delay the retreating Germans until Tito ordered the OSS out of Yugoslavia.

Tito, which guaranteed our safe passage, and showed it to the two men. The man who had cut my hand handed my Tommy gun back and started kissing me on the cheek. He was very apologetic, and both shared their wine and bread with us before showing us the correct road. After they bandaged my bloody hand, we started back down the road toward Kornat on the coast, where a boat was waiting for us.

We reached Kornat on September 28 at 6 A.M. and crowded onto a small Partisan boat in the middle of a severe storm and returned to Vis. This was the final mission the OSS performed in Yugoslavia. For political reasons, after high-level meetings in the fall of 1943, the relationship between the western Allies and Tito's Partisans had deteriorated sharply. It was an unfortunate reversal from the cooperative spirit of our missions against the Nazis.

On October 6, 1944, the operational group in Vis was disbanded. All the OG personnel were reassigned to various front-line Army units in Italy and France. On January 5th of 1945 I arrived in southern France to join the 13th Airborne Division. The Allies had just broken out of the Battle of the Bulge, forcing the German Army to retreat from France into Germany, and the 13th Airborne was preparing for a jump across the Rhine River into Germany. I, however, was recalled by the OSS for an anticipated jump into Norway, which was still occupied by the German Army. I was flown to London and processed for my trip to Scotland to join other OG members training for the mission. We already had some OSS personnel with the Norway underground. The German Army was on the verge of surrender, but the Army commander in Norway indicated that he was committed to fight to the bitter end. The Germans, however, also surrendered Norway just as we were preparing to depart to the airfield to begin our mission. This was on May 8, 1945, and victory was declared in Europe.

With the war in Europe finished, I returned back to the States. On July 30 I arrived at Fort Meade and was given a thirty-day furlough. At the end of the furlough I was to report back for assignment to Burma for OSS action against Japan. During my furlough, on August 6, 1945, the atomic bomb was dropped on the city of Hiroshima. On August 9 a bomb was dropped on the city of Nagasaki. Japan surrendered unconditionally on August 14, 1945, thus ending World War II. My orders for Burma were canceled.

I was discharged from the Army on October 25, 1945, and assigned to the ready reserves, ending my initial eight years of service. It was the end of my World War II experiences, but not the end of my military career. During the postwar years I served in Germany with the 16th Infantry Regiment and later fought in Korea with the 7th Cavalry from September 1950 to October 1951, retiring in August 1962 with twenty-five years of service. But that is another story, which I describe in my book *Korea: Frozen Hell on Earth*.

My time in the war was exciting, but I was glad when it was all over. Everyone who contributed to any of our wars should receive some special recognition for his or her service. The real heroes of the Second World War, however, were the men who never returned and gave their lives for all of us. We should never forget them. May their souls rest in peace.

DOUGLAS H. STONE, M.D.

Baltimore, Maryland
4th Auxiliary Surgical Group, U.S. Army

Douglas Hoffman Stone was born in Baltimore, Maryland, on March 29, 1911. He attended the Friends School and the Johns Hopkins University and was a member of the 1932 Hopkins Olympic lacrosse team. After graduating from Harvard Medical School in 1937, he was trained in general surgery and completed his residency at the Union Memorial Hospital in Baltimore in 1941. That same year he volunteered for the Army and joined the Johns Hopkins 18th General Hospital, eventually volunteering for a battlefield assignment with the 4th Auxiliary Surgical Group. After the war Stone entered general surgery private practice in Baltimore. He retired as General Surgical Section chief of the VA Medical Center in Asheville, North Carolina, in 1980. He is survived by his wife Essie, four children, and one grandchild.

The following profile draws on an interview conducted by George S. Rich. Portions of it, which are reprinted here with permission, appeared in the Maryland Medical Journal *(March/April 1999).*

I had just graduated from Harvard Medical School, and things in my life had more or less pulled me along once I had made up my mind in high school I wanted to become a surgeon. I took my studies seriously and had been made chief resident during my general surgical training at the Union Memorial Hospital in Baltimore. I wanted to locate my private practice in my hometown of Baltimore, but less than a year after entering private practice, war was declared on the United States. I decided soon after Pearl Harbor was attacked that I wanted to join the service to contribute my part to the war effort.

The Marines appealed to me, and I went down to the Navy recruiting station and said I wanted to be a Marine doctor. The officer smiled and said the Marines didn't have a medical corps, but I could join the Navy and then ask to be assigned to the Marines. I asked if I could be guaranteed of getting an assignment to the Marines, and he responded, "No, sir." So I left feeling sure I did not want to join the Navy for fear of being confined on a ship and having my surgical training underutilized. The next morning in the locker room of the Union Memorial Hospital an older surgeon on the staff at Johns Hopkins Hospital told me Hopkins was organizing a volunteer Army general hospital, and he wondered if I would be interested in joining with a rank of captain. This seemed like a good opportunity. I joined the Johns Hopkins 18th General Hospital, which was activated at Fort Jackson, South Carolina, on April 20, 1942, and received a commission as a captain in the Army.

The 18th General Hospital was dispatched to the South Pacific in April of 1942 and was initially stationed in Auckland, New Zealand, for six weeks. Being the first shipload of Americans to arrive in New Zealand, we were met with bands and crowds of people as we disembarked. It was hard to know what they thought. Our disheveled group from Hopkins was mostly made up of people in their thirties and forties, and we walked down the gangway carrying our own duffel bags and were very unmilitary-looking. After an indoctrination of six weeks here we went to Fiji. I served there with the Hopkins unit for another nine months, during which time we cared for fifty wounded Marines from Guadalcanal. In Fiji I ruptured a tendon in my right shoulder while helping to build huts for personnel. My shoulder was swollen and black and blue. Our hospital commander offered me the choice of having it repaired right there or back in the States. Since the danger of infection in the tropics was much greater and the war had passed us by, I chose to return to the States for an operation, and I was checked into the Letterman General Hospital in San Francisco.

The night I arrived in the surgical ward a young doctor came to my bedside and informed me that he was scheduled the next morning to perform the surgery on my shoulder. I asked him what his specialty was, and he said, "Ear, nose, and throat." He admitted that he had never operated on a shoulder in his life or even seen one done. Later that night I slipped out of the hospital and ran to the Western Union office about a mile away and sent two telegrams explaining my plight. The next morning orders arrived for me to proceed to Walter Reed Hospital in Washington, D.C., where surgery was to be performed. My telegrams had been effective. My shoulder was successfully operated on by a former resident in orthopedic surgery at the Johns Hopkins Hospital.

While convalescing I met with the surgeon general, who discussed new Army surgical assignments that were available. He also told me about the newly established auxiliary surgical group units, which had proven so successful in the North African campaign. Each auxiliary surgical group unit was comprised of forty teams, which consisted of three officers (a chief surgeon, his assistant, and an anesthetist), a nurse, and two GI technicians. He gave me a choice of assignments, and I was appointed as chief surgeon of Surgical Team 20 in the 4th Auxiliary Surgical Group. I was allowed to choose my own assistant from a cadre of other medical officers who had volunteered for surgical service on one of the teams. The auxiliary surgical groups functioned with the field hospitals, with evacuation hospitals, and even at times with the most forward battlefield clearing stations. When the situation demanded, each surgical team might actually have to act independently to provide initial care to the severely wounded on the edge of the battlefield. The surgical teams, being unattached, were utilized on a random basis and were sent wherever they were needed most urgently. Nurses, all young women in those days, were usually detached from the surgical teams to serve with the evacuation units located further from the fighting when their teams entered combat areas. Nevertheless, the nurses were also exposed to the risks of combat, and some were killed in bombing raids. Several of our officers and enlisted men on other teams were also killed in action. Two of them were close friends of mine.

The field hospitals were divided into three platoons, each with a surgical team and about twenty Army technicians, tents, operating tables, and all the additional mobile equipment needed to perform forward battlefield surgery. They were the first definitive surgical units in the field and usually backed up the clearing stations, which were designed to administer first aid and triage on the edge of the battlefield. This enabled serious casualties to reach us promptly in the field hospital. Our primary mission was to provide life-saving surgery to soldiers with nontransportable chest and abdominal wounds who could not survive without immediate attention. The less seriously wounded were transported back to the next surgical unit in line, which was the evacuation hospital. These planned arrangements were frequently disrupted, however. Sometimes the surgical teams were the very first to treat severely wounded soldiers right on the edge of the active battlefields.

After a ten-day voyage as part of a large convoy leaving Taunton, Massachusetts, in late April 1944, we arrived in England. We were billeted in private homes for six weeks, during which time I bought a ten-dollar bike for a hundred dollars (prices were really inflated). I enjoyed roaming the English countryside while getting the needed exercise. We really didn't do much training as there were no casualties to treat, and we were never subjected to the "military" regimen. One night in late May we were ordered to pack up for the coming invasion of France. A tough-looking and battle-hardened Army sergeant sat twenty-four of us down and proceeded to lecture us. The sergeant said something like, "You medics shouldn't be going in with us assault troops. You're all gonna die. You can't do us any good. We'd rather have twenty-four more fightin' men in your place. The only reason you're here is probably because some congressman has a son here, and he demanded that we have a certain number of medics along. If you've got a letter to write, write it; it'll be your last letter."

After being trucked to Wales, we marched about 30 miles in the rain carrying our duffel bags before arriving at Milford Haven about 4 A.M. Twelve surgical teams were packed onto an old British steamer named the *Lady Connaught,* which had been converted into a hospital ship painted white with large green crosses on her sides and decks. We formed a convoy with two other hospital ships, painted as we were, and stayed at anchor for ten days eating British rations. Our ship's captain was an old Scottish fisherman who was never without a bottle of Scotch whiskey, usually opened and in his hand. On the night before the D-Day invasion he managed to get us to the east end of Juno Beach, about 70 miles from our assigned debarkation point at Utah Beach. The Germans had surreptitiously mined the marked-out lanes we were to follow, and the two hospital ships ahead of us hit mines. The first quickly sank with all hands, and the second one was badly damaged. We were the third ship in line, and our old skipper had drifted out of the marked-out lanes, and this actually may have saved our ship from a similar fate. In the panic to escape he kept on going and didn't stop until we reached Le Havre, which was about 80 miles south of our objective, Utah Beach. After the captain was relieved of his command, we spent most of D-Day itself going back the way we had come, creeping back past battleships and cruisers. Their tremendous shells whistled over us before we reached Utah. An LCT (landing craft, tank) full of infantry picked up our group from the *Lady Connaught.* We only had our packs—no medical equipment except my canvas bag, which contained my precious assortment of excellent Army surgical instruments and a pair of surgical gloves.

My Surgical Team 20, 4th Auxiliary Surgical Group, waded onto Utah Beach two hours before midnight on June 6, 1944, D-Day. We were without orders and had no supplies. We followed white tape across the beach, which marked lanes that had been cleared of mines. In the pitch black of night and a cold light rain we were almost run over by blacked-out tanks and trucks roaring up the cleared lanes. We stepped out and over the tapes to avoid being squashed like bugs and with our helmets dug a round depression 8 feet wide and 2 feet deep for the five of us. Even though that part of the beach wasn't cleared of mines, it seemed a better bet than being run over by our own tanks. Shortly before dawn a beachmaster approached us and hollered, "You dumb SOBs, you're in a minefield!" He then took off before I could get any information out of him. I stepped out onto our still visible footprints with one of our technicians and found a clearing station a quarter-mile up the beach, where we started operating using their basic supplies. I sent the tech back to bring the others up.

From then on, around the clock, we operated only on patients with severe chest and abdominal wounds who would die without immediate surgery. On D+1 a German tank pulled into the head of a drainage ditch about 150 yards from our clearing station straight inland from the beach. This gave the tank a good vantage point to fire at our disembarking troops. It began to fire with both 88 cannon and machine guns on the incoming troops along the beach. Although it wasn't aiming at me, it sure felt like it. An enterprising young Navy ensign and a gob (another name for a seaman in the Navy), armed with bazookas, crawled up the ditch and blew the bottom out of the tank. The tank crew did not survive. Everybody who saw their actions cheered themselves hoarse. We heard later that the ensign and his gob both were awarded Silver Star medals for their bravery. Well deserved!

During this early period our "sterile technique" was truly a fruitless gesture. The sterility of the instruments and the gloves ended with the first patient. Thereafter, we soaked everything in a bichloride-of-mercury solution and used it over and over until fresh supplies began to reach us a day later. Living conditions were crude for everyone. For me, as the only surgeon, sleep amounted to a tenminute catnap on a blanket on the ground, wet or dry, near the sawhorses (our operating table) while the next patient was being prepared. Food was K rations whenever the opportunity presented itself, and our water, laced with chlorine, came from a canteen. Later, every two or three days there was a chance for a shave and a bath out of a helmet.

For the first two days, D+1 and D+2, there was an acre around us covered with severely wounded American and German soldiers waiting to be cared for. We were terribly overwhelmed, and many of our patients were dying while awaiting surgery. It was heartbreaking. Our technicians were told to bring back the nearest American soldier who looked as though he could be saved. We operated day and night without rest for three days. Our anesthetist cracked up after the first day and couldn't function. I poured ether, operated, poured ether, operated. Since I had to do my own anesthetizing I would put a gauze mask over the patient's face and drip ether onto it until he went to sleep. If he started to tense up, I would stop and apply more ether and then resume operating. The next day I got a new anesthetist in answer to my emergency radio call plus new operating supplies, plasma and blood, and IV pentothal. The anesthetist technician who had cracked up remained petrified and jumped into a foxhole on D+3 with a carbine he'd picked up. He refused to come out and threatened to shoot anyone who tried to pull him out. Later the fear of battle caused a few other replacements to break out in hives or begin vomiting and have diarrhea uncontrollably. Finally I got a replacement named Mike, a "dead-end kid" from New York City. He was a reject from everything you can think of in the Army. He had a terrible service record, but when we understood each other, he was excellent. He became my best team man and my best friend in Europe. Mike had a heart of gold and was a real doer. If I needed anything, he would just go get it.

On D+3 we moved inland about 400 yards and set up near a crater from a 16-inch naval gun shell explosion. We used this shell hole as a depository for helmets, boots, uniforms, arms, legs, dressings, etc. On the same day word got around that the Allies might not be able to hold the invasion beachheads. I immediately told my team to gather up every "Mae West" life preserver and all the rope and wood they could find to make a raft. The only choices available to us were either to surrender to the Germans or to try to get back to England any way we could, so I decided that we should take a vote on what to do. My team voted unanimously to make a break by sea to avoid capture. We hoped to paddle out far enough to be picked up the next day. Luckily, the next day word came down that we had broken through the German defenses, and the fear of a Dunkirk-like departure disappeared. This unrelenting three-day battlefield experience gave us a fine honing in emergency techniques and in teamwork, which prepared us well for the challenges to follow. Though there were a few replacements, the teamwork remained superb.

Every two or three days we got orders to proceed to a new battle area. All of our equipment was stuffed into a weapons carrier, and off we went. It was my duty to reconnoiter to find new sites to set up our hospital, and incidentally I became the consummate souvenir hunter. After the war I filled a room in my house with all kinds of German artifacts. I was uniquely able to ship almost unlimited quantities of relics home in ration and medical supply boxes. The order was out to retain spent shrapnel and bullets from the patients. Although I was told they were to be used for medical study, they were never collected, and I still retain a fair number in the same original bloody gauze as a grim reminder of the war. When I ran out of gauze and bandages on the beaches of Normandy, I used the silk parachutes of the 82nd Airborne, which were scattered all over from their predawn air drop on June 6, and I still have some of that, as well.

In late June, as we moved through a small French town, we began to receive devastatingly accurate artillery fire. After the steeple was blown off of a small church, our troops grabbed a wounded priest and also a wounded young woman with a German radio. They had been spotting for the German artillery. Regardless, I operated on both, and neither was too badly wounded. Not long afterward we were driving into a village square. There was a clutch of people around a little seven-year-old girl who was badly injured. Her shoulder was mangled, almost completely blown off, and her chest was punctured. I immediately got all my gear from the weapons carrier and right there on the cobblestone street operated on her and tried to save her life, but she died. The story was that she and her little circle of friends had been playing jackstraws on the

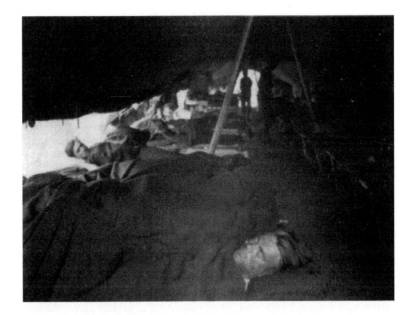

Wounded soldiers, American and German, rest in the ward tents of the 101st Evacuation Hospital in France in August 1944. The hospital did not have enough facilities to separate the German and American troops, but it didn't seem to make any difference to those tending to the wounded.

German prisoners of war are put to work erecting the 101st Evacuation Hospital in France in August 1944. Within hours an empty field was turned into a fully operational hospital. German prisoners willingly worked to help transport and erect the field hospitals and in return were treated very well by the American hospital staffs. The groups of prisoners assigned to the hospitals were exchanged frequently.

sidewalk in the town square when a group of retreating SS German paratroopers in trucks passed them, and one of these Hitlerized brutes dropped a grenade into the group of little girls, killing all but this little one who was still living. I tried my best to save her, but I just couldn't. She was the sweetest little girl. After fifty-seven years, I'll never forget how she looked at me with those beseeching eyes, desperately hoping that I could save her.

We loaded our gear back into our weapons carrier and moved on. The weapons carrier was very much overloaded with my team of three officers and two medical technicians. Also, we had a driver, plus an x-ray technician with a portable battery-operated machine and lights. We were equipped with a Heidebrink anesthesia machine, my Army-issue bag of surgical instruments, and a dozen bottles of type-O universal donor blood. In addition, we had containers of sterile dressings, antiseptic solutions, rubber gloves, adhesive tape, needles, sutures, etc., and, finally, we had two sawhorses (my operating table) tied on. Every day we received a generous number of units of whole blood. A little later in the war, most were drawn in the United States within the previous twenty-four hours, were flown overseas in bombers, then in light planes, then in mail planes, and were finally delivered via jeep to our surgical teams in action. Blood transfusion in itself saved many lives of the severely wounded.

On July 3rd of 1944 my surgical team was sent forward, shortly before daylight, to provide surgical support to the ferocious attack on Saint-Lô, which was part of the all-out effort to break out from the Normandy beachhead. When we arrived, it was raining and the battle was raging. We pulled up as close to the action as we dared, behind a little rise. Just beyond, and on the other side of the rise, we saw a big excavation in the ground, perhaps 10 by 12 by 6 feet. The rise was probably the dirt thrown up from the hole. The opposite side of the pit was sloped and marked by fresh tank tracks. No doubt it was an abandoned German tank pit or gun emplacement. The rise had been thrown up by the enemy toward the English Channel for protection from our expected invasion forces. The Germans had been driven out, so we used the pit to give our weapons carrier some shelter. We jumped into the excavation, unloaded our sawhorses and other equipment, and prepared to go to work immediately. It was raining steadily now, and we were all out in the open getting soaking wet and muddy. Now that the rise was behind us, we were not as well protected from German fire, except for being down in the tank pit. For a while the rain fell on us and into the open wounds as we were operating. Later our resourceful men rigged a makeshift cover for us, taking canvas from the top of the weapons carrier. There was a shell burst nearby, and very shortly afterwards two corpsmen slid a litter with a badly wounded soldier on it over the muddy edge of our hole. He was not breathing and had no detectable pulse. The Corpsmen looked at me, shook their heads dolefully, and scrambled back over the rim of the hole to return to their rescue of the battlefield wounded. These brave battlefield Corpsmen saved many lives, sometimes losing their own in their attempts.

We immediately decided to give this man his chance, as slim as it seemed. The litter was put across the sawhorses, and while I rinsed my hands in bichloride solution and pulled on sterile gloves, our technicians cut way his shirt with their combat knives. This exposed a sucking wound of the upper right chest. The wound had been stuffed with a piece of a GI raincoat to prevent the sucking action. The patient, Pvt. Terry Fitzgerald, said later he remembered the

Corpsman doing this on the spot where he was wounded, "to keep me from suffocating" before he lost consciousness. Terry also remembered that it was raining and even remembered passing the German pit that just minutes later would be the site of his operation.

The patient Terry was unable to breathe on his own. Our new anesthetist immediately applied a mask and pumped in oxygen under manual pressure to the rubber bag attached to the machine. This artificial respiration also helped to inflate the remaining functional lung, the other having collapsed. Simultaneously, one of the technicians swabbed the chest wall with antiseptic solution, and then he soaked his hands and became our instrument man. I quickly threw four sterile towels around the wound site and made an incision around the wound in order to remove the damaged skin and muscle tissue and lead me along the path the shrapnel had taken to disclose the damage it had done.

It was necessary to rapidly remove a section of four ribs in one piece to give myself room in which to operate. The chest cavity was full of blood. I actually had to bale it out by the handful. Our technicians had gotten the suction working, which enabled me to see the damaged area. They were unable to insert needles into the collapsed peripheral veins to give the crucial blood and electrolyte fluids. I told the technicians to remove the blood pressure cuff from the patient's arm and to wrap it around the blood donor bag. The improvisation was in anticipation of the need to steadily force the blood to flow faster through the tube into the heart. By this time I had the heart exposed and moved gently to the patient's right. I had only seen an actual living heart rarely in lung operations during my hospital training, and had never touched one.

The critical wound was an elongated vertical gash into the right ventricle, now barely oozing blood. I plugged the gash by laying my right index finger along the wound and while holding the flaccid heart in the same hand gently and rhythmically massaged it. With my left hand I took the large donor needle from the technician, having to ignore the "sterile technique," and inserted it directly into the right atrial chamber of the heart. Three liters or more of blood were given as rapidly as possible. The effect was magical. Veins grew visibly in the arms, and more blood was started in them. The above actions were crucial, making it possible to proceed with the definitive operation.

With my finger still plugging the deep gash, I took a large curved Bloodgood suture needle in the left hand, passed it deep through the full thickness of the heart muscle on one side of the gash, under and around my finger and into and out through the full thickness of the heart muscle on the other side. This was done quickly four times in a row. Then, as I slid my finger out, Bill, my assistant, pulled up all four sutures gently. I quickly tied square knots in each, snugly but not tightly, and then sutured a flap of pericardium to cover and support the closure. The sac itself was not fully closed for

The pile of torn, cut, bloody uniforms and boots that had accumulated outside the surgical tent of the 32nd Evacuation Hospital in France south of Verdun after a long night and two days of work in September 1944. Doug Stone and his Surgical Team 20 endured long hours repairing the butchery of war amid rain and mud.

Near Verdun, France, in September 1944. Doug Stone's assistant, Mike, is shown holding a rusty American helmet from the First World War. Hidden in the woods, it marked the grave of an unknown American soldier. These woods had been occupied moments before by a group of nine German snipers, but a firefight killed three, and the rest were captured.

fear that a possible accumulation of blood in the empty sac might compress the heart and inhibit its action or cause localized infection. After closure of the heart wound had been completed, I resumed cardiac massage to the flaccid heart muscle and could feel it perceptibly firming up and fibrillating. Soon a little rhythm or beat was detectable. As I continued this action, the patient began to change color from paper white to pale pink. We all gave a heartfelt sigh of relief. We knew we had won the all-important first round and had made a good start.

By now all bleeding had stopped. The patient had received and retained an estimated five liters of whole blood, was showing an even better color, and had a detectable pulse. Finally, we checked around the chest cavity for "bleeders," using the suction apparatus to empty all fluids and to get a "dry" chest. A couple of hemostatic sutures were quickly placed in a shallow laceration of the right lung. We then inserted our drains and suction catheters through stab wounds into the chest cavity, instilled 40,000 units of penicillin into the chest, sprinkled sulfanilamide powder into the chest and tissues, and carefully closed the incision in layers.

The patient did not develop an infection, despite the primitive circumstances of his wounding and operation. We were constantly amazed at how few infections there were in these hardy, healthy young soldiers. It was only towards the end of the beachhead action that penicillin became available to us in the field and seemed to be so effective and precious.

Our battery-operated field x-ray machine films revealed to us that there was a jagged piece of shrapnel about 1 inch long by 1/2 inch wide that appeared to be embedded in Terry's liver below the diaphragm, slightly to the left of center. Experience had taught us that to attempt to remove this now would have required major additional surgery, which was out of the question in this situation. It had also taught us that unless such metal fragments were the cause of major bleeding, which was not the case here, they seldom caused trouble. To this day, the shrapnel is still visible by recent x-ray and has caused Terry no further harm.

It was fifty years later in 1995 when I next saw Terry Fitzgerald. While my wife, Essie, and I were on an automobile trip through the West we made a search for Terry and found him in his comfortable home in Fonda, Iowa, doing well at age seventy-one. I had not seen him since July 7, 1944. We talked, and he informed me that he is sure he was wounded by a fragment from a shell fired from a German tank that had been hiding behind the little village church. He and his patrol had been ordered to knock out that tank with rifles but couldn't, of course. Then they were sent again with bazookas, and the others in his platoon were successful after he was wounded. It was probably the same tank that had previously occupied our pit.

We surmised that Terry had thrown himself forward when the shell exploded and the shrapnel had entered his chest just under the right clavicle, cut a tangential slice through the muscular wall into the chamber of his heart, and passed through the diaphragm and into the liver, slightly to the left of center.

When Terry was brought to us by the medical Corpsmen, our technicians could not find his dog tags and could not fill out his EMT (emergency medical tag). It was deduced from the location of his wound that the shrapnel had cut the chain supporting his identification and that his dog tags were lost on the battlefield. We did not know who he was or what outfit he belonged to. We couldn't identify him from the contents of his pockets. It was only when he regained consciousness, days after the operation, that he established his identity. Terry said that if he hadn't survived, he might now be occupying the Tomb of the Unknown Soldier.

Reporters from the military newspapers came to our hospital and wanted to talk to me about this unusual case. I was simply too busy to take the time, so they put together a version of what had happened from accounts of our platoon personnel who had been on hand during the operation and also from others who were not there when the operation was performed. Their resulting description of the event was the one that was published, and it was pretty accurate. From this came all the subsequent press releases in the United States. The factors that were brought together then to save Terry's life were excellent training in general surgery, fine teamwork, the right instruments, effective anesthesia and oxygen, ample quantities of whole donor O blood, penicillin, sulfanilamide, and the youth and health of the patient.

Our team moved on through France with the Third Army. When I wasn't operating, I would borrow a jeep and driver from whatever unit we were with at the time to select a new site where we were going to set up our operating team next—generally the nearest to the fighting that we could get (and you could tell where the fighting was without any problem). As the weather got colder and we got closer to Germany, we moved our surgical operations into commandeered buildings. I did the reconnaissance and selected our new location most of the time. On the way I would go to the local *Rathaus* (the German word for city hall) and pick up all kinds of guns and equipment that had been turned in. I took orders for shotguns, binoculars, Lugers, dress Nazi daggers, cameras, etc. Most GIs who had been in combat would have Lugers, and I would sometimes buy them. I would never take souvenirs for free from a GI even if offered, but I also found a lot on my own. I carried a tarp in the back of the jeep and would just load up the tarp, tie it up, and when I got back I'd start distributing the stuff. I'd fill boxes with my own selections and send them home. Also, I'd take orders for our other officers and our enlisted men and usually could fill them eventually.

Later we were operating at the town of Metz where there was an incredible system of individual fortresses. They were built with specially hardened concrete and in a dome shape so that shells would not penetrate but carom off. This beehive-like complex was still literally impenetrable. Now it was the holdout of the SS, and the Germans were under strict orders from Hitler himself to defend it to the death if necessary. So our GIs had the desperate task of overcoming each fort, room by room, even having to root Nazis out of the food lockers and closets.

From one unit of these Nazi defenders a young German officer was brought in by our litter bearers. He was SS and had been indoctrinated with that SS code that taught him to fight to the bitter end. This one believed it, and lived it. He had a barely perceptible pulse, he was in shock, and yet he had the wild eyes of a fanatic. He had been shot through the chest more than once, and his legs were shattered. Obviously he was going to die, and he knew it. When the litter bearer kneeled down to give him a shot of morphine, the SS man reached around behind him and started to pull the litter bearer's combat knife out of its sheath on his belt. He planned to stab the litter bearer in the back with his own knife. Well, the other litter bearer was a tall lanky guy from Tennessee, and he had his helmet on. General Patton had said, "Don't buckle your helmet, because if a shell hits near you, the helmet strap, if buckled, could snap your neck." So all of our helmet straps dangled. He was standing there sort of half asleep because the litter bearers were absolutely exhausted. But when he saw this, he instantly whipped off his helmet by the strap and cracked the SS man's head with it. It sounded like somebody had dropped a melon, and he did it just in time to save his buddy's life. The tall Tennesseean calmly placed his helmet back on his head, looked at me, and asked me what to do. I said, "Put him over in the corner and let him go. There is nothing we can do for him." I was 3 feet away from this Nazi as his eyes glazed over, and I thought, "How could these people be so brainwashed as to die like this?" He might have been a good man if he'd not been born in Nazi Germany.

At another time in a little brick village schoolhouse near the town of Saarlautern on the Saar River in France an ambulance driver got out and said, "Doc, I've got a couple of real wildcats for you this time!" His ambulance had pulled up carrying a wounded American and a wounded German soldier. The driver said the two had been engaged in bitter fighting in the streets of Saarlautern and had shot each other at exactly the same time. The American had been down on the street and had been shot in the gut and was in bad shape but had survived. The German had been shot in the chest up in a window across the street. They were then placed in the same ambulance and continued their battle, throwing punches at one another until the morphine calmed them down. I operated on both of them in succession, and afterwards they were unknowingly placed in the same ward in beds right next to each another. When they woke the next day they were too weak to fight but stared at each other with bitter contempt. On the second day the GI offered the German a piece of gum, but the German rolled over and ignored the GI. By the third day the German accepted the GI's offer of gum, and they began speaking in little sentences of mixed English and German. Soon they were sharing snapshots of their families and girlfriends and laughing and showing off their wounds. They were shipped out on the same day and insisted on remaining together as they left our hospital in an ambulance going to a holding unit.

After the Bulge we set up our hospital in a bombed and shot-up schoolhouse in Asche, Germany, just over the border from France. We were billeted in a battered house about a quarter of a mile up the road that had the side blown out of it, but you could get to the second floor where there were a couple of beds. All we had was a GI bedroll and one thin blanket, and it was bitter cold. We put on everything we had to try to stay warm. I finally got to sleep around one in the morning when the sergeant came up and said, "Hate to wake you up, Major, but we need you." I was frozen and could hardly move out of bed. We got down the steps and walked back to the schoolhouse. My hands were so numb and stiff that they were useless. I washed up in nearly freezing water the best I could. Then I was able to get my gloves on. A soldier was prepared for surgery, asleep and draped, exposing a wound in the upper abdomen. I managed to make an incision in the belly where I wanted it, and once I got it open I put my hands in his belly and warmed them up. After my fingers got limber from the warmth of the patient's body, I was able to operate on him and others. He made an uneventful recovery and an unconscious contribution to his own surgery and those to follow. We continued to operate virtually without stopping for the next forty-eight hours. Such was our introduction to Germany.

The war ended on May 8, 1945. On May 10 my group was 30 kilometers east of Salzburg approaching the town of Ebensee on the south end of Lake Traun. We were driving along the lakeshore and continually passing bodies and emaciated and dying prisoners dressed in black and white striped prison uniforms. They were desperately and irrationally trying to get away as far as they could from this torture camp of horror. When we arrived the gates of the camp were wide open, and prisoners were hurrying out as fast as they could hobble, not caring about anything, even food or drink—they just wanted to get away from the camp. We were the first Americans in the camp. Most of the krauts had just left, and we thought we could see the dust of their vehicles in the distance. A few guards and the camp commandant did not get out. When I drove in I was told that the stronger prisoners had literally pulled the camp commandant apart while he was still alive; they just pulled him apart. They drowned the rest of the kraut guards in the German officers' swimming pool. It was a frenzy, and these poor skeletonized human beings still had rage in their souls. The prisoners had been worked in the salt mines, which have been there since long before Roman times. It wasn't an extermination camp per se, but they'd get all the work out of the prisoners that they could first, and when some couldn't work any more they would break their arms to keep the others working.

The Germans had built five long barracks buildings. They would put the weak prisoners in the first one. As they progressed into physical deterioration, they would be moved on to the last barracks, where they died, and if they didn't die, the Nazis didn't care. They kept over two thousand bodies, I estimated, in the storage room. This was a great big hangarlike structure from which they took the corpses to burn in the ovens. The bodies were stacked like cordwood, head to foot, 8 feet high and 6 feet long and about 8 feet wide. Then you couldn't believe it: on the wall were meat hooks where they had hung some of the prisoners that had remained alive, and there were scratchings under these hooks, bloody scratchings from their heels and their fingers as they struggled in their final torment for who knows how long.

When I entered that last barracks alone, I was appalled by what I saw. I was in there, I guess, for a couple of hours. I just sat there, dumbfounded. Soon I was in a deep depression. I looked at the faces. All these faces looked pretty much the same, and you could hardly differentiate them. They were completely emaciated, skeletonized, eyes sunken almost out of sight, noses just little bones. Their bodies were wasted so much that there was no odor; they didn't have enough fat left to break down and cause an odor. It was incomprehensible, the feeling this awful, evil morgue gave you. I would look at some face and stop and wonder where he had come from, what he had done in life, if he had had a family, friends, a job or profession, where he had lived, what his nationality had been, what he had believed in. It took me a day or so to get over this gruesome experience, and I had already seen many evil things before this. Now I realized I had witnessed what the Nazis had designated the "Final Solution."

Throughout the war I didn't turn to my Christian faith as fully as I have since then. Strange thing. During the war I really didn't commune with Jesus very much. I wouldn't say I was a good Christian. I didn't doubt. I never thought, "Why would God let this happen?" I know a lot of people did. But I was so occupied with the practical that I don't think I gave much time to religion or philosophy or theory. I just had a hard job to do, and my mind was totally consumed by it. I didn't actually stop to confront my emotions. I just ignored them. They say there are no atheists in foxholes; when things get sticky, you turn for help. There were times when I did too, and I got it. My prayers for help came spontaneously, and most seem to have been answered, maybe because they weren't about me.

It is amazing how much I remember about those days. When I entered the Army I was excited about the adventure of war, but my attitude changed when I saw how our boys were getting torn up.

When I recall the war, I cannot help remembering my good friend Jack Turnbull, who was a teammate on the Johns Hopkins 1932 Olympic lacrosse team. Jack was a wing commander in the Eighth Air Force and flew his required thirty-five missions in a B-17, but instead of returning home he volunteered for one more mission and was shot down and killed over Belgium. I also think of men like Colin Kelly, who dove his plane into a Japanese ship in the Philippines in 1941, and I heard of several instances of soldiers falling on hand grenades to save others around them. I am afraid people today do not understand what war is really like because it is glamorized in movies. War is the worst thing that can happen to mankind, and should be the last thing we allow to fulminate.

There are so many heroes from the war, including men and women who sacrificed their lives for others. Countless numbers will forever remain unknown to the public. The real heroes of World War II were all the combatants who served in the war, and especially those who deliberately and with forethought sacrificed their lives to save others and to advance the cause of victory for freedom.

EDA C. TEAGUE, R.N.

Brinklow, Maryland
44th General Hospital, U.S. Army Medical Corps

Eda Constance Teague was born in Colfax, Wisconsin, on May 11, 1920. In 1942 she graduated from Luther Hospital School of Nursing in Eau Claire, Wisconsin, and volunteered for the Army Nursing Corps. She was assigned to the 44th General Hospital and served two and a half years as a surgical nurse in Australia, New Guinea, and the Philippines. In 1947 she married her husband, Walter, who served as a mess officer with the 44th General Hospital during the war. They moved to Maryland in 1961, and Eda Teague briefly returned to nursing, working at the Walter Reed Army Hospital from 1969 until 1973. She and Walter have four children, eleven grandchildren, and one great-grandchild.

The following profile was based on an interview with Eda Teague, and on portions of her personal memoirs, which are reprinted here with permission.

I grew up in a small farming community in Wisconsin during the depression. I lived with my parents and fifteen brothers and sisters. We didn't have a radio, TV, computer, or health insurance. We were poor but didn't know it. We didn't have the news to tell us how bad off we were. "Poverty" was not a word in our vocabulary. In truth, we were rich in many ways. I sewed my own clothes and dreamed big dreams as any kid might dream today.

We were just coming out of the Depression, and jobs were scarce. There were jobs for women, but none like there are today. I had the opportunity to go to nursing school at the Luther Hospital in Eau Claire, Wisconsin. Back then nursing school required three full years of classes with no summer vacations. I had just graduated and passed my state board exams as a registered nurse when Pearl Harbor was bombed. At that time I was twenty-one years old and working as a surgical nurse at the Luther Hospital. I didn't learn of the attack until I arrived at work, because I didn't have a radio at home. The news was too stunning to believe. Until then the reports of the war overseas had trickled down from newspapers and radio. For my classmates and I, the names and places seemed far away. After the attack on Pearl Harbor, an enemy invasion of our western coastline seemed imminent.

After graduating, I remained at Luther Hospital. In the fall of 1942 an Army nurse recruiter came to our hospital asking for volunteers to join the 44th General Hospital for duty overseas. Five nurses from our graduating class, including myself, immediately volunteered. It was a spontaneous decision, and I am sure we all felt it was our patriotic duty to join. I never had any fear or apprehensions about enlisting.

The 44th General Hospital was organized at the University of Wisconsin School of Medicine as a fully equipped hospital with an accredited medical staff for surgery, medicine, radiology, and dentistry. The hospital was capable of serving a thousand patients at any one time, although the total number of patients often rose as high as fifteen hundred.

I received orders to report for duty on January 20, 1943, and reported to March Field Army Air Base in California just south of Los Angeles. I arrived with other nurses from schools and hospitals throughout Wisconsin. We were introduced to Army regulations and operating procedures. Naturally, the biggest difference between Army life and civilian life was the many regulations regarding conduct. We marched, did calisthenics, and learned how to address a superior officer. During the evenings groups of us gathered around the radios and listened to President Roosevelt's "Fireside Chats," becoming more and more committed to the American cause. Men of similar rank treated the nurses as equals. But the men never lost their habit, no matter what their rank, of extending to us the courtesies they extended to women in civilian life. I didn't mind this courtesy, and I thought it was nice.

The nurses were assigned to work in the base hospital treating patients. These were typical hospital cases, and none had been wounded in combat. We stayed at March Field for about three or four months, and during this time the Army was in the process of issuing the nurses new uniforms. Since they didn't know yet where we were going to be deployed, I eventually had a closet full of a variety of uniform styles and weights.

In early 1943 the entire 44th Hospital was assembled at Fort Sill, Oklahoma, for deployment overseas. The enlisted men assigned to our hospital were from all over the country, but all the nurses and doctors were from Wisconsin. We spent three months at Fort Sill performing more basic training tasks, which included running the obstacle course, 10-mile hikes, calisthenics, gas-mask drills, and more marching. We were housed in tarpaper-covered barracks, and in the midsummer months it was so hot we had to wrap ourselves in wet sheets to sleep at night. Our orders arrived, and the nurses and a few of the doctors were sent by train to Pittsburg, California. The train trip was wonderful. Our train was sidetracked for every other scheduled train along the way, which gave our officers plenty of opportunities to march us beside the train for exercise. We marched to the Mormon temple in Salt Lake City during one stop. Our route included a wonderful train ride along the Feather River in California.

We shipped out from San Francisco on the luxury ship USS *America,* which later was converted into a troopship and renamed the USS *West Point.* There were ninety-two nurses from our hospital on board and a few of our doctors in addition to five thousand troops plus the ship's crew. Talk about crowded! I shared the ship's tiny bridal suite with four other nurses. It took fourteen days to cross the Pacific Ocean, zigzagging to evade submarines most of the way.

We finally landed in Sydney, Australia, and spent a few days there until we were given orders to set up a hospital in New Guinea. Our doctors, enlisted men, and equipment were loaded on seven Liberty ships and sent ahead of the nurses. While en route to New Guinea, all the ships ran aground on the Bougainville Reef off the coast of Australia. It took twenty-four hours to rescue them, and consequently our orders were changed. The enlisted men and doctors were rescued and returned to Cairns, Australia, where they eventually established a hospital at Black River, a few miles out of Townsville. The nurses were sent to Brisbane to wait while the hospital was being set up. We lived in an isolated area outside the city limits of Brisbane, and we really had nothing to do but march, perform more calisthenics, and watch movies to kill the time. Several of us bought horses and rode through the Outback.

We eventually boarded a train and joined the hospital staff at Townsville and began treating war wounded. By the time these patients had reached us they were stabilized but still recovering from their wounds. We remained at Townsville for almost a year, treating American soldiers wounded by the fighting in New Guinea. The Navy had a separate hospital adjacent to ours for treating the wounded from the naval battle of the Coral Sea.

The 44th was scheduled to be in the initial landing force at Leyte in the Philippines. Our hospital in Townsville was closed, and the nurses were taken to Hollandia while all personnel and equipment were staged in New Guinea. At Hollandia we worked at the 54th Station Hospital. We worked long hours under very primitive conditions. Malaria, typhus, and hepatitis were the most common ailments that we dealt with, in addition to the battle injuries.

I wrote hundreds of letters during my time in the war, and it was very therapeutic for me to get out the emotions I was feeling inside. In a letter dated November, 24, 1944, I wrote:

This place has the most vicious bugs I have ever seen. Some little ones about $1/100$ of an inch bite like a rat. We have lots of rats here too. They are quite brave and they run through the tents all the time.

Nothing like having company anyway. I am anxious to get out of Guinea. We don't have such a hot place to live and it is going to be nice getting set up in our own hospital again. We are going north and expect to go into one of the Philippine islands as soon as they get the Japanese cleared out. I hope it's soon. I want to get this over with and get home. We never know where we're going or how long we are going to stay. You can't imagine what a strange life we lead. I guess "strange" is the only word for it. Anyway, it's different from anything at home. We just get on a boat or train and go. The boys over here are wonderful patients. It's a treat to do things for them. They do all they can for themselves, but they sure help a lot around the ward too. You should have seen the beautiful formation of planes that went over yesterday, about fifty of them. There's nothing nicer than planes flying in formation. The roar just shakes the ground. I like to watch the planes go over. It always impresses me so much. We have a wonderful Army over here.

The officers and Corpsmen of the 44th landed on Leyte in the Philippines on November 8, 1944. As they were landing, a kamikaze plane hit a large troopship in the same area, killing 135 men. The 44th rushed ashore and set up emergency ward tents and operating facilities. Those hurry-up-and-wait exercises that the troops had endured at Fort Sill for months finally paid off. It was a logistical marvel to see a five-hundred-bed hospital hit the beach and become operational within hours.

It didn't take long for us to realize that the Japanese had stripped the Philippine homeland of everything useful to their war effort, and we didn't see many of the native Filipinos because most had fled into the hills. The Japanese treated the Filipinos in an awful manner. When we returned to Leyte many years after the war, we were told stories of how the Japanese had forced the prisoners to dig their own graves before having their heads cut off or being shot. These "killing fields" where so many Filipinos were massacred are still tended today throughout Leyte amidst schoolyards and public buildings.

Within days after our landing the Japanese were driven from the village of Burauen 4 miles west of General MacArthur's headquarters. On November 15, 1944, the 44th moved off the beach and started taking patients at Burauen. Just as combat activity was reaching its peak on Leyte, the stream of patients steadily increased. The engineers had no time to establish water drainage systems around the ward tents, mess halls, and clinics, so the passageways between these tents became a quagmire. Pieces of wooden crates had to be placed under the legs of the folding metal beds to keep them from sinking into the mud, and cardboard cartons from ration boxes were laid beside the beds to keep the patients from stepping in the mud.

The 44th Hospital at Burauen was located about 400 yards from one of the best airfields the Japanese had built on Leyte. After its capture by American troops, the field became a base for the Fifth Air Force and was used for our P-51s, P-38s, and C-47 cargo planes. On December 6, 1944, two planes dropped approximately sixty Japanese paratroopers to recapture the airfield. All American personnel manning the airfield were killed, and all fighter planes were destroyed. By the next morning our perimeter guard and local infantry had retaliated and killed all but two of the Japanese paratroopers. The two wounded paratroopers were admitted to our hospital on the morning of December 7. Filipino informants warned us of the Japanese plan to send additional paratroopers to attack through the hospital perimeter in an effort to rescue the paratroopers. The hospital armed all enlisted and officer personnel to defend themselves. On December 10, Japanese troops attacked the west perimeter of the hospital. They immediately overran a 30-mm. machine-gun crew. For a period of nine hours the hospital personnel defended our facilities. When the attack was lifted, twenty-three Japanese were found dead in the area, and American troops had suffered only one dead and two injured medical officers.

The Japanese didn't respect the noncombatant status of our hospitals, so it was pointless to raise our red crosses anywhere. In fact, the Japanese used them for target practice. When the hospital was first established, Japanese snipers hid in the treetops and took potshots at the hospital staff at daybreak. Each morning our machine gunners guarding the hospital had to spray the tops of the trees to make sure there were no hidden snipers.

The nurses arrived at the hospital in Burauen three weeks after the hospital was attacked. Our living conditions on Leyte were awful. It was hot, and there was lots and lots of mud. We often worked long twelve-hour shifts. Our thousand-bed hospital was treating over fifteen hundred patients. Sometimes we didn't get our days off. When our patient count dropped below seven hundred, we worked eight-hour shifts. People who worked the night shift found it hard to sleep in the daytime because it was so hot. We slept on canvas cots, on the ground, and on the floor, if necessary. We slept under mosquito nets because the bugs were so bad. Often, patients who had just arrived from the front would dive for cover at the slightest noise and have to be cut free from the mosquito netting in which they had become entangled. Somehow I never felt tired from the lack of sleep. My busy schedule and my youth kept me going.

When we were off duty we talked about anything but the war and our patients. We had an officers' club at the hospital where we could go to relax. We had lots of movies, and we got to see them before they came out in the States. We were also cheered up whenever a celebrity would visit the hospital. Those who came by included Bob Hope, Irving Berlin, Jack Benny, Kay Kyser, Judith Anderson,

Eda Teague crosses a stream on the back of an ox belonging to local villagers near Burauen on Leyte Island in the Philippines in early 1945. Although she had waded across these same waters many times before, once she learned about the water's dangers, she knew that an ox was a wiser choice. The tropical climate posed numerous dangers to American service personnel, including schistosomiasis (blood flukes).

Danny Kaye, Joe E. Brown, and Phil Rizzuto. Their visits were a real lift for our patients as well as for us.

There were some local Filipinos who we paid to wash our clothes. They washed them in the streams, and since it was raining most of the time they built fires in their huts and strung our clothes over the flames to dry them out. Our clothes smelled terrible when we got them back, like they had been roasted and smoked for days. The food we ate was mostly from cans, and we didn't get any fresh food for a long time. Walter, my future husband, was the mess officer, and he went out to the ships anchored in the area and scrounged fresh foods from the ships' stores. We also scrounged the surrounding jungle for bananas and mangoes, if they could be found. We didn't have many luxury items during the war, and the PX on the base provided what we did have. On occasions the PX would sell hair curlers, which was a big treat to us. Walter also had a couple of guys working for him who were beauty operators, so we were able to get a decent haircut when we wanted. It was very important to keep our image up, and it made us feel good to look our best in an otherwise dreary situation.

People wonder if there were romances during the war. There were a few, but nothing that was ever anything serious. I don't think many of us were thinking much about the future. We lived for one day at a time, and we were working so hard we just didn't plan the future. When Walter and I met, we both had relationships back home. When the war ended we thought it was goodbye, but when things didn't work out in both of our situations, we were able to be together again.

The hospital remained at Burauen until May 1945. We were not informed about how close we were to the front lines. Except for seeing lots of our planes flying overhead and hearing the shells the artillery fired over our heads, I couldn't place any of the fighting. I never worried about our hospital being attacked again, but I did discover later on that we were in fact never more than 3 miles from the front lines.

During the early stages of the invasion our patient count consisted of about 80 percent battle casualties, and the remainder were illness-related cases. As the weeks wore on and the troops were exposed to the many tropical diseases prevalent on the island, we began treating as many illness cases as battle casualties. The tropical environment of the Pacific could be as deadly to our soldiers as the Japanese. The hospitals in the European theater treated combat wounds and the effects caused by bitter cold temperatures, while in the Pacific we had to treat combat wounds and many different types of tropical diseases. We treated everything from bullet wounds to jungle rot, dengue fever (called "break-bone fever" because of its painful side effects), malaria, dysentery, hookworm, and schistosomiasis (a parasitic disease caused by blood-fluke worms whose larvae are harbored by snails and infect humans who enter infected waters through the skin; the disease is characterized by a skin eruption at the site of entry, fever, diarrhea, and liver damage).

In a letter dated May 1945, I wrote about some of what we were experiencing on Leyte:

> We're really busy over in the hospital now—we've been admitting patients right and left. We have more patients now than we've ever had—they all come from islands up north. It's surprising how many are medical patients—I think we have more medical casualties than we do battle casualties. There are a million different kinds of diseases caused by snails and worms around these islands—the worst is called schistosomiasis—the boys know it as blood flukes—then of course there is hookworm—loads of it.

For some of the diseases we administered preventative measures, and the infantrymen in the field learned how to prevent illness as best they could. Every soldier was given a medication called Atabrine, which helped to prevent malaria. The side effect of Atabrine was that your skin turned yellow, and we affectionately called this an "Atabrine tan." This tan was like a badge for having served in the Pacific and usually lasted for about six months. We all took a series of typhus shots, too. Sulfa drugs and penicillin were the wonder drugs. Penicillin prevented many amputations, particularly if there was bone involvement. Some patients were given a penicillin shot once every four hours, around the clock, for weeks, and the needles were not small.

There was an affectionate bond between the soldiers and the nurses. When new patients arrived, we were often too busy taking care of them to do much talking, but as things settled down we could get acquainted with them. I was a friend to all my patients, and I couldn't help but get close to them in ways it is hard to describe. We were trained as hands-on nurses. Being a patient in those places was a pretty lonesome and painful experience, so we tried to be there for them. It meant that we often laughed and sometimes wept with our patients. When we couldn't give a patient medication for pain, we rubbed their backs, bathed them, and did everything we could to make them comfortable.

When I was off duty I didn't take their suffering home with me, because a nurse has to get used to working with pain and suffering. If you begin to feel too sorry for your patients, you can't do them any good. I did sympathize, but if I showed that I felt too sorry for them, then they would give up hope, too. I reminded myself often that I was there to help, to do a good job, and to make a difference. The fact that I felt needed in this capacity was what kept me going through the bad times. I was young then, and I suppose it was easier to deal with my emotions. But after a while it was impossible not to take what was happening around me personally.

We were on Leyte for a year, and that was a long time to witness such suffering. It got very depressing. Every nurse had to take turns treating patients who we knew were likely to die. We called this the "specialized" care shift, and you took care of just one patient. It was a very hard thing to do. I'm sure a lot of the men we "specialed" knew they weren't going to make it, but they never asked for much of anything. We didn't separate these men from the regular patients, and the other men were very supportive of those who were in the worst shape. One of the things that never failed to impress me was how the men helped themselves and each other the best they could. They didn't ask for any help if they could do things themselves.

The dying got all the care and affection we could possibly give them. They were the best patients I ever took care of. If the men were badly injured or ill, they didn't say too much, and maybe there wasn't much to say at those times anyway. The ones who could talk often told me about their homes and showed me pictures of their girlfriends, wives, and kids and talked about going home. I could not help but feel for these men. There were times I couldn't help but weep for the ones who had little hope of going home. At the moment when it was obvious a patient was near the end, I stayed with him and held his hand. Sometimes they were not conscious enough to speak, so just holding their hand was all they could understand.

I often remember one patient lost to typhus fever. His temperature was so very high, and he was so ill and in a lot of pain. He wanted to go home so badly. With the injured patients we could give medications for pain, but for those like my typhus patient there was often just nothing we could do. We finally got this one patient to a point that the doctor thought he was ready to go home. He was taken to the ship, but he died before he even left the island. That was the kind of thing I often had to deal with.

The men who came to our hospital hadn't been around women in a long time, and they were very sweet to us. When we nurses went to the open-air movies at night, we waited to enter until after dark because we couldn't go anywhere without all the men standing up and clapping at our arrival. Often a patient would run up and put his arm around me, but this affection was never abusive and always in good fun. They were all such wonderful patients.

I must admit that I hated the Japanese. We all hated them. After hearing what they had done to our hospital and reading the war news about their horrendous acts, it was hard not to hate them. We still treated Japanese wounded, because they were human beings. When a Japanese soldier was brought to us as a patient, he was no longer the enemy. I took care of a few Japanese soldiers, and they were very cooperative and very happy to be there. I don't feel any resentment towards the Japanese today. I think time has healed a lot of the wounds I once had.

When MacArthur moved from Leyte to Manila, we were given his abandoned headquarters, which consisted of several administrative buildings, a large club, and a mess hall on the beach. We finally had floors, concrete sidewalks, water towers, and wonderful showers. We were there when we received news that the atomic bomb had been dropped on Hiroshima. The news caused us to believe that the war would end soon, but we were so busy treating the sick and wounded that there was no sign that the war was ending for us. Days later, after the second atomic bomb had been dropped, it was announced that the war had ended.

It is hard to express how we felt when the end of the war was announced. The celebration in our area lasted far into the night. Many Navy ships were anchored in the harbor across from our tents, and they must have used up all their tracer ammunition that night. It was the best fireworks display I have ever witnessed. Transportation home became a real problem for our patients and personnel. Everyone wanted to be home for Christmas because no one wanted to spend a third consecutive Christmas away from home. I returned home days before Christmas in 1945.

It was my privilege and honor to have served as an Army nurse during the Second World War. I tried to give the best I was able to give, and my memories of those years are a mixture of emotions. I wouldn't have missed a minute of it, but I can't say I enjoyed anything in particular when there was so much pain and sadness around me. The joy that I remember of returning home was mixed with recollections of a time and place where friends were killed and patients died. This recollection will always bring pain. We mourned for the many dead, but we all had put our lives on the line, and we sincerely believed that they had not died in vain. We came home feeling like winners and felt we had done a good job, and the world seemed full of hope for the future.

I fear that people don't understand what happened during the Second World War. I don't think too many people know that women served as close to the front lines during the war as we did. I was ill a few times, but luckily I didn't get injured or sick. I am sure someone who lost their leg or was wounded somehow would have a different opinion of how the war affected them. We didn't talk about the war with our children because they grew up during that period of time when it was a taboo thing to talk about war. My daughter came home one day from college and said that the worst insult in the dormitory was to say, "Your mother wore combat boots." Well, I *did* wear combat boots, and she later told me she was proud to tell people that her mother did.

The soldiers who served in the war were the best, and there are a lot of real heroes out there who will forever remain unnamed. Credit should be given to the Corpsmen on all fronts whom I consider to be the unsung heroes of the war. They were always there to help us when needed and in other places risked their own lives helping to save the lives of soldiers in battle. I don't think we could have survived without them, and time has not tarnished my memory of their exceptional sense of duty to our patients.

I don't feel like much of a hero. For me the real heroes of the Second World War will always be those young men, some just boys actually, who gave their all for the cause of freedom. Their sense of duty, their love of country, and their undaunted courage will stand as a hallmark of service for all who cherish the American way of life.

ALFRED O. WARNER

Westminster, Maryland
29th Infantry Division, U.S. Army

Alfred Oden Warner was born in New Windsor, Maryland, on June 6, 1921. In 1938, following his sophomore year at New Windsor High School, he joined the Civilian Conservation Corps and found work as a cook. He enlisted in the Maryland National Guard in 1939 and was assigned to H Company, 115th Infantry Regiment, 29th Infantry Division. He participated in the Normandy D-Day landings and is a recipient of the Bronze Star for valor. After the war Warner worked as a mechanic until deciding to return to the Army as an artillery specialist with the 29th National Guard Division, where he remained until his retirement in 1971. He married his late wife, Hazel, in 1946 and has two children.

Things were tough when I was in high school, and jobs were hard to find, so I joined the CCC (Civilian Conservation Corps). I was trained as a cook and remained with the CCC for fifteen months before I decided I'd had enough of being a cook and quit. Six months later, in 1939, I joined the Maryland National Guard because I was broke and needed the money. I didn't know anyone in the Guard; it was just a job, and I was glad they took me. I spent two weeks at the armory in Westminster and then was sent to Fort Meade for basic training. I discovered that Guard life differed little from my previous work in the CCC except that daily Army life was stricter and more regimented. I was assigned to a mortar platoon, but we had no real weapons, just a sight for the mortars attached to a piece of rainspout acting as the tube. Before the war started, the 29th had few if any modern weapons, and most of these had been produced during or just after the First World War.

I remember hearing about the attack on Pearl Harbor, and I don't think I paid much attention to it. I had no clue where Pearl Harbor was, and I just said, "Shit," and went back to my business as usual. When I joined the Guard I was told I would only be in for a short time, but after the attack they told all of us we were stuck in the Army until the war was over, no matter what.

I was with my platoon practicing assembling a mortar when the lieutenant called my name and said I must report to the kitchen. I told him that I'd had KP duty the day before, but he said it didn't matter and that I was being assigned to the kitchen as a cook. I guess the Army discovered I had been a cook with the CCC and thought I could be of more use in the kitchen. I really didn't want to be a cook again, but I made the best of it for the next year or so while our kitchen traveled with the division on maneuvers all around the Southeast. One day I decided I'd had enough cooking; it wasn't the reason I had joined the Guard, and I made a complaint to the commanding officer. To my surprise, he said to me that if I didn't straighten up and get back to work, he was going to send my ass back to the infantry. The commander could have hardly known his transferring me back to the infantry was just what I wanted, and I made sure my attitude was just right to ensure he would. Two days later I rejoined the mortar platoon of H Company, 115th Infantry Regiment, and soon after we were given orders to pack up our equipment, and we boarded a transport headed for Europe.

My regiment was stationed in Oxford, England, and we began training again, but by now we had received new and modern equipment and we began to feel much more confident in our ability to fight. I knew we were being trained for an amphibious invasion, although we never were told when and where it would happen. In the late spring of 1944 the pace of our daily lives picked up. I began to feel as if something was going to happen soon. It was just a few more weeks until we boarded a ship and stood around crowded in the hold of a ship listening to General Eisenhower speak about the coming invasion of France. There was no doubt about it, then: it was my time to enter the war.

I didn't feel anything about going into combat. It really didn't dawn on me what was happening until I hit the water the next morning. The 29th Division was fresh and had yet to see combat during the war, so I think we were all confident the invasion would be a success. While crossing the channel most guys went about their normal routines playing crap games or cards, and there was little discussion of the invasion except perhaps I sensed a little excitement that we were finally going to do something besides the seemingly endless training we had endured over the previous two years in England. But no amount of training could have prepared us for the horror we were to witness the following morning.

On June 6, 1944, the morning of my twenty-third birthday, I woke up and joined those who were not too seasick to eat breakfast. Shortly after, we were assembled on the deck of the ship and I saw the beaches of Normandy, France, for the first time. There was a dense cloud of smoke hovering over the beaches, making visibility difficult, but I could hear the sound of guns and explosions in the distance. There were ships around us as far as the eye could see, and it was a scene I just can't describe in words. You wouldn't believe there were so many ships in existence unless you had been there to see them for yourself.

We slowly began our difficult climb down the side of the ship into the waiting landing craft alongside the ship. The water was rough, and getting everyone into the tossing landing craft was a precarious operation. As the boat shoved off and we began heading for the beach, the battleship *Texas* fired its big guns just over our shoulders. It was the loudest noise I had ever heard, and I could see the shells as they flew over our heads towards the beach. I don't think we had traveled more than a few hundred feet when I began to see the bodies of dead GIs floating in the water. Then there was a DUKW, an amphibious landing craft, just bobbing about in the water with no direction, and as we passed it I saw all of its crew and passengers were lying motionless, presumably dead. I don't recall being shocked at what I was seeing, as it all seemed surreal to me.

My platoon was part of the second wave to attack the beaches on D-Day, and we arrived at the beach at about seven in the morning. When the sound from the engine of our landing craft began to fade, the lieutenant ordered everyone up and ready to move forward. When the boat stopped, the front ramp fell into the water, and I followed the lieutenant into the water, which was up to my chest, and we must have been at least 75 yards from the beach. Artillery shells and bullets were landing all around, and it was then it dawned on me: someone was trying to kill me. I was scared as hell. I heard no talking as the platoon slowly waded forward through the water, each man holding a rifle, a BAR (Browning automatic rifle), or some other piece of equipment high above their head to keep it dry. Perhaps only a minute passed before we reached the beach, but it seemed like an eternity. My first glimpse of the beach was an unforgettable experience. It looked as if a morgue was operating on the beach, there were so many dead bodies just scattered around. There had been no time yet to remove the corpses, and worse were the detached pieces of bodies strewn randomly amongst the dead. The living men were running around or over the dead without a thought that they had once been human.

It's hard to explain exactly what I saw that morning. I don't think people today would believe what actually happened on those beaches during the early stages of the invasion. The movie *Saving Private Ryan* was as close as I have seen to recreating some of what I saw on the beaches, but there is always an element you find difficult to put into words. The only people who can truly understand were the ones who were there. What I saw on the beaches of Normandy was so terrible, I didn't really think about it then. I think I was numb to the whole experience until much later, after the war. Every man who was there had to move on and forget about it, or else I think a person would lose his mind looking at such images.

Surviving the initial invasion gave me a feeling of immortality: I had made it through the worst hell imaginable, and everything else would be easy after the beaches. It wasn't always so, but compared to the beaches I think anything else was tolerable.

I don't remember much about what I did during the next few hours, except I never saw anyone actually firing at us from close range, but there were some German prisoners on the beach. The platoon spent the remainder of the day waiting for the order to move forward until night fell and we were told to get some sleep. I was near a jeep, so I crawled under it for cover during the night, and when I woke the next morning I discovered my platoon had moved on without me. I ran up the bluff overlooking the beach, and the lieutenant grabbed me by the arm and proceeded to lecture me about having separated from the group. I explained how I had been sleeping under a jeep, and after a brief investigation it was discovered that everyone thought I had died, because the jeep I had slept under was full of mortar rounds. I was presumed dead because nobody could believe I would be so dumb as to remain under such an explosive arsenal during the numerous artillery barrages and air raids we experienced during the night. But I had, and had slept through them all like a baby.

My platoon was armed with six 81-mm. mortars, and our job was to support the infantry. Each mortar had a crew of four men: a gunner, a loader, and ammunition bearers. We fired smoke and high-explosive mortar rounds that weighed about 10 pounds. A charge was placed in the bottom of the mortar round and then dropped into the mortar tube, which had a pin on the bottom. The pin ignited the charge, and the size of the charge determined the range of the round. We could shoot about six rounds a minute, and the mortar was particularly deadly because it was silent before it landed, catching infantry in the open, and the blast was more lateral than upwards, expanding the lethal effectiveness of the weapon. A forward observer attached to the infantry would alert us to fire on a target, and we would fire a few rounds and then move quickly because it was easy for the Germans to locate our position and return the favor.

A couple of weeks after we landed, we were approaching Saint-Lô, and I remember we were ordered forward to set up for a fire mission. I was carrying the mortar base plate on my back, which weighed about 40 pounds, and as we were running up to our next position I jumped over a hedgerow and landed wrong, breaking my ankle. I was sent back to England, and as soon as I recovered after the New Year, I was sent back to my outfit and remained with them until the end of the war.

In between firing missions, I spent most of my time during the war sitting in a foxhole trying to stay warm, dry, and alive. Every day the platoon woke up and moved forward to dig another hole. My shovel rarely got the day off. To survive in combat, a person had to keep his head and ass low to keep from getting killed, and helping you was your foxhole buddy who watched your back and you watched his. Every man in the platoon felt like he could depend on everyone else in the group, and we all looked after each other. We lost friends during the war, but there was always another right beside you to take his place. My first foxhole buddy was a good friend, but he was killed just six weeks before the end of the war. When I saw friends get killed or wounded, I knew I had to put it out of my mind. Continuously thinking about the death and torment around you in combat could easily make a person lose his mind. I was able to keep such thoughts from affecting me then; it's now, after all these years, that I have thoughts about the friends I lost and I am saddened. I don't know why, after all these years, but it just happened that way. It helps to speak to other guys who served during the war, and we often make jokes about the things that otherwise would be very difficult to think about.

I guess a person can get used to anything, and combat is something you adjust to. I can best describe combat as organized confusion. I think we won the war by organized confusion. The little things sometimes made life more bearable: I always looked forward to a chocolate bar when I could get them. But the most important thing was to think about getting the job done so we could go home. Thoughts of returning home were what kept me, and probably every other man in uniform, going forward.

I had little fear during the war, but if I ever felt any, it was while looking at the German Tiger tanks. Even the destroyed ones made me shiver, they were so big and well armed with a big 88 gun. The German soldiers were good. They respected us, and I respected them. On the other hand I remember running into some of the Hitler Youth boys, and they were real bastards. They were young, but so arrogant and tough they seldom surrendered, and I don't think many made it home even after capture.

There are a few instances that stick in my mind when I think of the war. The first that comes to mind is the night we were ambushed soon after the D-Day landings. On the night of June 9 we were getting ready to bed down when all hell broke loose. We were sitting ducks for German tanks and machine gunners that had snuck up on us. We had not posted any guards to our rear, assuming any German attack would come from the front, but these Germans had been caught behind us. We lost a number of men killed and taken prisoner, and we had a rear guard from that night on, I can assure you. Another occasion was the time I saw eighteen hundred bombers fly overhead to bomb what we later discovered was the submarine bases in Brest. It was something you can never appreciate on film. I never would have imagined an army could have so many planes.

I recall a time when my lieutenant grabbed me and another guy, and we drove forward in his jeep to scout a place to set the platoon.

We drove for about five minutes until we reached a small clearing, where we got out of the jeep to walk ahead through the woods. We had not walked more than 20 yards from the jeep when an artillery round landed squarely on the jeep and blew it to hell. It gave us something to laugh about later, but you wonder sometimes what would have happened if we had sat there in the jeep a few minutes longer.

Perhaps the most memorable event I have always wondered about happened on a night when the platoon was in the rear on a break from the fighting. The platoon was relaxed, and some guys were drinking too much, as was often done to forget about things for a while, and one guy in the platoon got extremely drunk. He was normally a very friendly person, but for some reason he chose me and in a drunken stupor said, "Warner, I am going to go get a prisoner. Do you want to come with me?" I told him he was crazy and to go away. He kept urging me on until finally he got the message and left me alone. He came back two hours later with a prisoner on the end of his carbine. We had no idea where he had found the German, but from the look of horror on the prisoner's face we could tell the drunk GI had really shook him up. With the German by the arm he walked up to me and said, "Warner, you son of a bitch, I am going to shoot you!" He pointed the carbine at me and pulled the bolt back to put a round into the firing chamber. I didn't move. I froze from the shock of what was happening. Thankfully, someone grabbed the gun before he could pull the trigger, and another sergeant really worked him over for his stupid stunt. We never spoke of the event again, but all these years I sometimes wonder if he would have pulled the trigger.

There are so many thoughts I have about my experiences during the war, but I just don't know how to express them, and it's impossible to answer the question people ask me the most about D-Day, that begins with "What was it like . . . ?" There are no words to accurately describe what I saw.

I have very little to say about who were the real heroes of the Second World War. My heroes are the GIs we left behind when we all came home.

JAMES H. WILDERSON

Arbutus, Maryland
5th Ranger Battalion, U.S. Army

James Howard Wilderson was born in Elkridge, Maryland, on December 12, 1923. He is one of five Wilderson brothers who served in the armed forces during the Second World War, including Sam, who was killed when his B-17 disappeared on a raid over Germany. James Wilderson enlisted in the Army in 1942 and volunteered for the Army Rangers. He was assigned to the 5th Ranger Battalion, which "led the way" during the D-Day invasion of Normandy. He is a recipient of two Purple Hearts and two Bronze Stars for valor. After returning home he joined the accounting and credit department of the Sun Oil Company and retired from the Maryland Cup Corporation after a forty-year career. He married his wife, Beverly, in 1946, and they have four children, six grandchildren, and two great-grandchildren.

I graduated from Elkridge High School in June 1940, and because I was sixteen years old I could only find work as an office assistant for three Maryland senators in the legislature. After the session ended I was forced to find new work and wound up working in a machine shop, but with the rest of my family gradually entering the service I decided to go into Baltimore and enlist myself.

There were quite a few people at the enlistment office, but most were headed in another direction because they had been drafted. Since I was enlisting I was given a preference of which branch I wanted to join, and when I told the Army sergeant I wanted to enlist in the infantry, I don't think he believed I was serious. Three of my brothers were already in the service: Horace was in the Marines and was a veteran of the fighting on Guadalcanal; Dan was with the 35th Infantry Division and later fought at the Battle of the Bulge; Sam was a waist gunner on a B-17 in the Eighth Air Force, and he was later killed over Germany. My other two brothers joined after I did, with Bez serving in an antiaircraft unit in the Pacific and Stuart with a transportation unit in the Pacific. My parents were not too happy when I told them I had enlisted, but they knew my being drafted was inevitable, so enlisting was the best thing I could do.

The day before I left for the Army I went to visit some friends to say goodbye, and the next morning my father drove me to Baltimore to report for duty. I boarded a bus and was taken to the old B&O train station, and from there I traveled by train to Fort Meade, Maryland. I was full of wonder and excited to see what was going to happen. The first thing I remember when I arrived at Fort Meade was being herded into a room for a medical exam, receiving numerous injections into my arms. I then joined the line to receive a uniform, and my assumption about the Army carefully measuring each man individually to ensure that we all had properly fitted clothing was quickly foiled when I arrived at the counter and three or four guys just began throwing clothes at me. Half of what I received didn't fit, and when I asked the sergeant what I should do he said I needed to trade with the other men until I found the right size or take it to a tailor. The next day I boarded a train and was sent to Camp Breckinridge in Kentucky. I arrived in the middle of the night with snow on the ground, and the temperature was below zero. I was with a group of men dumped out onto the street, and a sergeant led us to our bunks. This was my warm welcome to the Army.

I was placed in a heavy-weapons company, and I thought the training was very thorough. I was introduced to all the weapons used by the infantry, and I participated in a lot of fieldwork between our academic classes. I enjoyed the Army life, but most of the guys

The Wilderson family, six of whom served during the Second World War. *Front row, third from left:* James Wilderson. *Back row, fourth from left:* Horace, a member of the 1st Marine Division who fought on Guadalcanal. *Back row, second from right:* Sam, who was killed when his B-17 was shot down over Germany. Standing next to him is Dan, a member of the 35th Infantry Division and a veteran of the Battle of the Bulge.

who had been drafted into the Army didn't share my enthusiasm. Before enlisting I had read about the Army Rangers, and during my first few weeks of training I inquired how I could apply for the Rangers, but nobody seemed to know anything about it. Then one day we were out in the field, and it was announced that the Rangers had arrived at our base and would interview any volunteer interested in joining. When I arrived back at camp I immediately ran to the battalion headquarters to inquire about how to join. I was given a very thorough physical exam and was interviewed by a captain of the Rangers. When he walked into the room I immediately noticed how clean and neat his uniform was. He had a distinctive short-cropped haircut and looked very fit. Before asking me any questions he explained at length how the Rangers were very intent on not accepting anyone they had the slightest doubt about being able to fit into their organization. He stated that if I was chosen to join the Rangers my chances of being killed were 50-50. I was not dissuaded from continuing, and the captain spent most of the next half an hour asking me to explain why I wanted to join a Ranger outfit despite the probability that I would be killed. I explained how my brothers had already entered the service and fought in various places, and how I wanted to do my part and I wasn't afraid and I would gladly accept the challenges the Rangers offered. At the end of the day I was called back to report to the captain and was elated to learn that I was one of only sixty-five men he had selected from the six hundred interviewed. Although the Rangers were an entirely volunteer outfit, being a member did not earn me any extra benefits except a great sense of personal pride in belonging to an elite group of men. My acceptance into the Rangers was possibly the greatest personal achievement of my life.

Soon after my acceptance my great excitement was dealt a heavy blow. While on guard duty one night a jeep pulled up to my position, and the sergeant of the guard handed me a telegram. I opened it and read the news that my brother, Sam, had been reported missing in action. The sergeant asked if anything was wrong, but I didn't say anything; I just handed him the telegram. He asked if I wanted to be relieved, and I accepted so I could call home, but I was not permitted to return home because I was getting ready to join the Rangers. At the time I didn't think too much about Sam's being missing in action because I thought it could have also meant he was still alive. I think being away from home had an effect of making it hard to accept that it had really happened. There was no one around to share my concern. My life just went on as it had before I learned of his being missing, and the whole episode sort of passed by me, and I only hoped he was still alive. When the war ended Sam was officially listed as killed in action, and they never found a single man from his B-17 crew. An ironic twist to Sam's disappearance was I remember reading about the raid in which he was killed a week after it happened. I found a newspaper article featuring the actor

Clark Gable, who had been an aerial photographer on the mission, and I remember being shocked when I read that forty B-17s had been shot down. I had no way of knowing that Sam had been on one of those planes.

A week later I was transferred to a Ranger school at Camp Forrest in Tennessee. It was a very rigorous experience, and we trained around the clock. The basic philosophy of our training was to overrun the enemy—to keep moving forward and not stop for anything, even to help our wounded comrades. We were told that when we held a position, retreat would never be an option and that we would prevail or most likely be killed trying. We learned how to endure combat conditions, and I was schooled in the idea that if everyone in the group followed our training, we were ensured success. Individuals who failed to live up to expectations, we were told, caused breakdowns, and any one failure could cause the entire group to fail. We were endlessly trained to perfect our assault, street-fighting, and hand-to-hand combat techniques. Our training exercises were very realistic and similar to combat situations, and I got banged up so much I didn't know if I was coming or going. We trained with live ammunition, and on a few occasions men were wounded but luckily not killed. Every minute of our training was conducted using a buddy system, ensuring no man was ever alone. The instructors made me feel like I was superior to any other soldier, and we all developed a tremendous amount of confidence in our abilities. We were never misled as to how well trained, intelligent, well armed, and experienced our enemy would be. But we were taught that if we implemented our training on the battlefield, we could overcome any adversary. I believed it, and they were right.

When we finished our training at Camp Forrest we transferred to Fort Pierce, Florida, in November of 1943 to conduct amphibious training. After three weeks of exercises we boarded a train and arrived at Fort Dix, New Jersey, on November 20. We weren't there too long before moving to Camp Kilmer, which was our staging area to be sent overseas. We spent a week at Camp Kilmer before shipping out for Europe.

We shipped out on January 8, 1944, from New York Harbor on the HMS *Mauritania*, a British liner whose 900-foot length placed her second only to the HMS *Queen Mary* in sheer size. We didn't get very far before a freighter slammed into our side, opening a large gash along the port side of the ship. Rumors ran wild that it was an act of sabotage, but it turned out to be just a careless accident. Two days later the damage was repaired, and we were on our way again.

The *Mauritania* traveled without escorts and zigzagged across the Atlantic Ocean to avoid German submarines. I killed time reading and walking on the decks along with the ten thousand other men on the ship. Many were too seasick to move, and they remained below the entire eight days in agony until we landed in Liverpool, England, on January 18, 1944.

We were camped in Leominster, England, and continued our training exercises at a more urgent pace. We were informed that we were going to spearhead an invasion of the Continent, but it all seemed so far away, and since we were strictly forbidden to talk about anything to anyone, the subject of going into the invasion headfirst never was an issue. In March we left Leominster for Scotland, where we began training with British Commandos. It was here they decided to lighten up our unit to improve mobility, and my machine-gun squad was converted to riflemen. I was very relieved to carry a small weapon because the thought of dragging a machine gun into battle was not appealing at all. We practiced numerous amphibious landings on fortified beaches, and one day they decided it would be fun to drop us off high in the Scottish hills with nothing more than a map and compass to help us find our way back. We eventually returned to Braunton, England, where we continued assault exercises on fortified positions, and our training included learning how to use steel ladders and ropes to scale bare cliffs. On June 1 we were ordered to assemble our gear, and it seemed like the entire countryside began a simultaneous movement towards the coast. The time for the invasion had come.

Trucks brought us near Weymouth Harbor, but we walked the last mile or so, and I remember groups of people standing along the roadside handing us coffee and donuts. When we reached the water I saw ships as far as my eyes could see into the distance, and it was an amazing spectacle to behold. We boarded the HMS *Prince Baudouin* and waited for the invasion for the next five days, spending our time receiving additional briefings about our mission and continuing to study small replicas of the invasion beaches. During the early evening of June 5 our ship's crew came to life, and we left port with all the other ships. I didn't get much rest that night because I was getting apprehensive about the invasion I was sure was to come the next morning.

At four-thirty in the morning on June 6 we were awakened and told to get our gear together. Those who could eat grabbed a little something before we headed up onto the deck and climbed into the assault landing craft. The water was very rough, and the landing craft bobbed and dipped alongside the ship. After loading we turned for shore, and the warships were firing at the beaches, and it seemed they were destroying everything. We passed under the bow of the battleship *Texas,* and her big guns were firing over us, creating a deafening noise. I saw several of our ships take direct hits from Germans shells exploding in huge fireballs over the ships.

Many of the men in our boat became sick from the violent motion caused by the rough water. Vomit bags were being filled at a fast pace, and a couple guys were filling up another soon after throwing one over the side. Seawater was filling the boat, so we bailed out the water with our helmets. During the 10 miles to shore I was standing in water up to my knees.

Daylight was breaking when I first saw the beach and the many other landing craft circling around trying to find an opening to the shore. Our coxswain managed to get us between two mines attached to steel I-beams, and we went right into the beach on the first pass. I looked to my right, and I saw men on PT boats using long poles with hooks to grab bodies floating in the water and pulling them aboard. I imagine most of the men floating in the water were already dead. We passed a dead pilot floating in the water, and for a moment I thought about my brother Sam.

As we neared the beach I could see nothing through the thick smoke that hung over the water and beaches. I could hear a lot of gunfire coming from the beach, and the noise made it hard to think about much other than what might happen once we landed and the ramp at the front of the boat fell down. I felt the landing craft slow, and the sergeant said we were close to the beach and motioned for us to check our gear one more time. The boat came to a stop, and the ramp was dropped into the water. We filed out, and I stepped off into water about waist deep, but we had it relatively better than the men who had been dumped into deep water and drowned that morning. We ran forward through a thick cloud of smoke, and I will never forget thinking someone had set the whole beach on fire. We came under a tremendous amount of rifle and machine-gun fire, and the ground around me was kicked high into the air from the impact of bullets. Artillery and rockets began to land, and we found cover behind the seawall until we found a way off the beach.

The first waves of regular infantry lost so many of their officers that they had difficulty regaining the initiative, but our smaller Ranger unit was able to retain its cohesiveness and advance according to plan. Our objective was to advance beyond the beach to a town named Vierville-sur-Mer and fight our way laterally along the beach until we met up with the 2nd Ranger Battalion, which had landed just north at Grandcamp. The combined actions of the Ranger battalions would secure a large chunk of beachhead so other larger units could be put ashore.

After we cleared the beaches we encountered a lot of mortar, small-arms, and grenade fire. We began to confront German infantry troops who were well entrenched in positions along the ridges above the beach and inland leading to Vierville-sur-Mer. Our mission briefings had instructed us not to take any prisoners on the first day, and whatever we saw, we shot. I didn't see any Germans trying to surrender, anyway. During the later parts of the war I fought German Nazi SS troops and elite paratrooper units who were less likely to surrender, but we always accepted German prisoners, and we were always reminded that it was our duty to do so.

As we reached the bluff above the beach, one guy in our company named Phillips, a real likable guy in the company, suddenly stopped. He turned to me and said he had to stop because he couldn't wait to relieve himself. He took a few steps back, and a shell landed between us, and he simply vanished in the explosion. I continued ahead, but it was a real awakening to me that this was the real thing and real people were dying.

I think it took me a while to fully appreciate the fact that men just a few feet away were determined to kill me. There was plenty of incoming fire, and of course I hoped it wouldn't hit me, but I had been trained so well under live-fire conditions, it seemed at times just another training exercise. I think I could say that my entire wartime experience in combat was spent dwelling on my own immediate surroundings and our mission objective, and I never worried about getting hit. Conversely, when I saw an enemy soldier fall to the ground, I was glad not to know if it was me or other members of my unit who had killed him. Infantry engagements involve many men firing at one target, and this helped me to rationalize killing because it was quite possible that any one of us could have fired the lethal shot. There was only one instance when I ran head on into a German soldier and it became a situation of whoever fired first would live, so there was at least one moment when I knew for sure I had killed. I didn't hate the Germans, but if any man had reason to it was me, because they had killed my brother. I never enjoyed killing, but I was glad to get rid of as many Germans as I could, if it meant getting the war over sooner.

By the time we had advanced through Vierville, darkness had begun to fall, and we were told to dig in for the night. A few of us settled in a barnyard, and I dug a hole between piles of manure and pulled a corrugated piece of tin over the hole to hide my head. I reflected on the day and felt very fortunate that we were advancing and not swimming in the ocean. I had thoughts of home, and I wondered how many more days the war would last, because I was in it until either the war or I was finished. I sat there listening all night for what might come at us out of the darkness. There was no sleeping, for my anxiety and the endless artillery exchanges made sure of that. Late in the evening I heard the sound of tanks approaching, and we had heard that just a few of ours had gotten ashore, so I thought we were going to get it for sure. We all waited until the sound got so close I thought they were going to run right over us. The tension was finally broken when the tanks emerged from the darkness and I saw they had big, beautiful white stars painted on the turrets.

In the morning we began our push on Grandcamp and found that the resistance had weakened because the Germans had begun to pull out during the night. After joining up with the 2nd Ranger Battalion on the third day, we were pulled from the line and brought back down to the beach—not for any rest, though, as we were given a new assignment to clear numerous bunkers along the beach that contained Germans who refused to surrender. The bunkers were made of concrete with walls 5 feet thick and housed defiant Germans who were heavily armed and ready for a fight. We advanced on each one and poured fire into the openings of the bunkers until our men could get close enough to drop grenades or explosives into the vents or gun openings. Most of the bunkers surrendered as soon as we began dropping charges on their heads, but many were blown up without anyone ever coming out alive.

Our missions during the remainder of the war involved conducting raids on heavily defended positions. A few weeks into the invasion we were given an assignment in Brest to destroy the large naval guns the Germans were using to wreak havoc on our advancing forces. The Germans had deployed SS and paratrooper units to protect the guns, and when my five-man scouting party was spotted we were lucky to escape alive. The next morning our company circled behind the German defensive positions, and we caught them sleeping. A fierce fight ensued, but we had the guns in our hands within thirty minutes.

There were some good times to be had in war, but even these presented some hidden dangers. We were approaching the Belgian town of Arlon and were ordered to halt our advance until the town was secured. About five of us decided to ignore this order and sneaked into Arlon that night to scout around for food. We found a bar occupied by some young women, and I think they were as pleased to see us as we were to see them. We stacked our weapons by the bar and had a great time drinking and dancing away the next few hours. When it began to get late, we said our goodbyes and retraced our steps out of town. Before we made it out we were greeted by a squad of Germans (who must have been upset that we were with their girls), and we had to shoot our way out of town and back to the company, luckily without casualties. The next morning our lieutenant was hot. He found out someone had ignored his orders and entered Arlon. He barked at us, demanding that the guilty men step forward, but for some reason none of us admitted to knowing anything about the issue.

My luck ran out in late November when I ignored an order to stay out of a bar after we passed through Arlon and I was caught along with three of my buddies by MPs. Our lieutenant, figuring he had caught the perpetrators of the previous delinquency, enjoyed punishing us by making us camp out in the cold rain while the rest of the company was put up in a dry and warm school building. We were further disgraced when the company found a supply of wine in the basement and they shouted drunken taunts at us from the school windows through the driving rain.

On December 3 the company endured its worst day while approaching the German town of Lauterbach. A long open field surrounded the town, forcing us to advance without cover, and the Germans were smart enough to allow us to get within yards of the town before they opened up with heavy machine-gun and rifle fire. Matters quickly worsened when Tiger tanks appeared from around buildings they had been hiding behind and began firing point blank at us. Within minutes half of the company was killed or wounded. I could only run forward and headed towards a German machine-gun nest about 100 yards ahead. The German machine guns fired at an incredible rate, but I never heard the bullets flying by me unless they hit something nearby. The machine gunner spotted me, and I knew I was hit because I saw a tracer round hit my rifle, and it was blown from my hands and landed on the ground smashed to pieces. Another round passed through my jacket front, narrowly missing me, and another round tore into the front of my helmet. The bullet missed me, but pieces of my shattered helmet were lodged deep in my head above my left eye.

I fell to the ground and found some cover in a shallow depression while the machine gunner continued to fire in my direction to finish me off. Blood was pouring down my face, and I could taste the blood in the back of my throat and coming from my nostrils. I reached up to feel my head, and my fingers went right into my skull. I felt no pain and I wasn't scared or panicked, but I knew I had to move quickly to safety to get help. I remember smelling smoke from the machine-gun rounds that were landing all around me. A medic who ran forward to help me was forced to turn back when the machine gunner fired on him, too. Lt. John Reville called out to me from the cellar of a house about 30 yards away, and he asked if I was OK. I told him I was hit and bleeding but able to move. He said for me to lie still until I could gather some composure to run for cover. I waited for the firing to stop, and then I ran as fast as I could towards the lieutenant and dove headfirst into the basement stairwell as machine-gun bullets ripped the cellar's wooden doorjamb apart. Other guys from my platoon grabbed me, and they told me later that when they tried talking to me all I could speak was gibberish. I was in a state of shock, and I don't remember much of what happened next until I arrived at a field hospital for surgery. Because the damage to my eye was extensive, I was flown back to England for additional treatment. The company took the town that day with little tank support, and we suffered heavy casualties.

It was a month before I was sent back to my unit, and I rejoined the company in the middle of the night. My welcome occurred the next morning when we attacked the German defensive Siegfried Line. Elements of other units had attempted an assault earlier, and they were torn to pieces. When we arrived, their dead bodies littered the ground. We lost a lot of men during our assault, especially in the heavily mined tank traps. E Company created a diversion to our right, successfully drawing the Germans away from our area and enabling us to smash through the Siegfried Line, opening the door for the waiting tank and infantry divisions to pour through. The costly assault led to a strange footnote to the mission when the graves registration unit began removing the bodies of our dead comrades and piling them on the back of a truck before we had had a chance to catch our breaths after the fighting. Some of our guys lost all composure and threatened to kill the men picking up the bodies. The scene became very heated, and fights were narrowly avoided when cooler heads prevailed. When we lost a man, it was as bad as watching a brother being killed, and perhaps the graves registration unit was just a place for some of us to vent our anger. Considering the types of missions we were conducting and the quality of soldiers we were facing, I thought our casualties were less than could be expected. By the end of 1944 I felt very lucky to have made it alive through so many bad days, and every day I lived I figured the better my chances were of making it home.

There were very few days we were not advancing and engaged in combat. When night came, we set up a perimeter and each man slept for an hour while his foxhole buddy stood watch. I remember times I was so tired I could barely keep my eyes open. Fatigue in combat plays very cruel tricks on your mind while on watch at night. You hear noises and see things that aren't there. The uncertainty and fear drain you even more, and at times you are overcome with the fear that you will fall asleep and wake up with the enemy in your face. Surviving the weather elements was another battle in itself. I was very fortunate to never get sick, and I attribute it to all the shots they pumped into us to keep us healthy. I didn't have any hot meals during the eleven months I was in combat but survived on the K rations I was given (and they were less than delicious). On one occasion we were given hot bean soup, and the whole company got the runs. Sergeant Cioffi had to take the pants from a dead German because he had messed his own pants so much.

I really don't know how I survived. I fought when it was as hot as the dickens, and I fought when it was freezing. It all becomes the same after a while: just another day of survival of the fittest, like a bunch of wild animals. I only saw one man in my outfit crack under the stresses of combat, and it was while we were on patrol, and we couldn't figure out why he kept circling around without actually advancing as he was supposed to. I think he had just chickened out, and the next day he was gone. I felt like he had let us down. If he didn't want to do his job, he should never have joined the Rangers, and he had been given plenty of chances to get out earlier, so he should have known better.

Our company entered the Buchenwald concentration camp soon after it was liberated, and I saw the atrocities the Germans had been committing. I saw piles of dead people all over the camp, and the so-called living were stacked together on shelves like lumber. The furnaces were still hot, and I saw bodies that were still burning inside. I am not sure what happened to me at that time. I looked at the scene around me, and it didn't affect me at all. We tried to help the kids by giving them chewing gum and candy or whatever we could until the Red Cross ordered us to stop because although we

The surviving men of F Company, 5th Ranger Battalion, after the war, excluding the few who were in hospitals recovering from their wounds. Wilderson is in the *back row, far right.*

meant well, what we were giving them after starving for so long could kill them.

I think I became immune to the death I witnessed during the war. When I first saw one of the men in my company die, I had a sick feeling about it. Later, I felt little emotion even when I saw friends of mine whose bodies were strewn in pieces all along the road. I can't remember the names of people I served with, but I can look at a picture of my company and tell you how some of them were killed like it happened yesterday. I recall two who were in a foxhole when it received a direct hit from an artillery shell, and we never found a single trace of evidence that either man had ever existed. I remember another kid who was our company runner who was a few feet in front of me when he stepped on a mine, and he was splattered all over me. I think a person's desire for self-preservation is an amazing motivation. It kept my mind clear of remorse while in combat. I managed to ignore these horrible things while they were happening, but I find myself thinking about these things in my softer and older age.

On February 23, 1945, we crossed the Saar River into Germany and advanced 9 miles through thick woods to cut the Irsch-Zerf road used by the Germans for supply and reinforcements. We established a square perimeter and began capturing walking German wounded returning from the front. The Germans began to shell our position heavily, and the entire wooded area was smashed to nothing. We were less than our full strength but managed to repel continuous frontal assaults by an entire regiment of the German 2nd Mountain Division. Our two-day mission stretched to nine until we were relieved on March 5. Interrogations of the prisoners revealed that the German commanders had known who we were and issued a directive to eliminate the 5th Ranger Battalion at all costs. We lost many men, but the number of dead and dying Germans in front of our positions was staggering. I had been slightly wounded again by shrapnel, but I suffered more from a concussion caused by the exploding shell.

I spent a few days in a field hospital and returned to the company while we were joining an American cavalry unit. We rode the backs of their tanks during the big breakthrough into the heart of Germany, chasing after what was left of the German Army for mile after mile until the order came for us to stop. We had reached the Danube River, and we began to prepare for an evening boat assault across the river. The Danube River was very wide and very swift, and during the day we watched the Germans fortify their positions on the opposite bank. Thankfully, word came that the war was over, and I think we narrowly escaped receiving a severe thrashing while trying to cross that river.

After the war our battalion was sent to Ried, Austria, and we spent the next month and a half just living. We commandeered a big limousine and a big comfortable house and managed to grab a German prisoner from the stockade and made him our chauffeur, and his mission each day was to find as much food and booze as he could for us. We really lived it up. We returned to Rosenheim, Germany, where we ran a prison camp and were on the lookout for individuals wanted for war crimes. Groups of people were brought to the camp, and we asked for their names and ID, and if they matched a name in a big book an intelligence officer had given us, we placed them under arrest. The German people were very nice to us. They didn't go out of their way to help us but were generally very polite.

Returning home was just like being on leave, and eventually the days turned into weeks, weeks into months, and life returned to normal.

I never thought there was one single group of people who earned the title of heroes. I don't care if you were in combat, in the Army, Air Force, Navy, or Marines, or were a supply person far behind the lines. Everyone, man or woman, who put on a uniform or built our equipment or went without at home during the Second World War was part of one big cooperative machine responsible for winning the war. If hero status is reserved for any one person, then it should be given to the men who died while fighting for freedom and our country. I hope they are never forgotten.

MYRON L. WOLFSON

Randallstown, Maryland
9th Infantry Division, U.S. Army

Myron Leonard "Mike" Wolfson was born in Baltimore, Maryland, on October 4, 1922. He attended Windsor Hill Elementary School and the Charlotte Hall Military Academy before enrolling in the University of Maryland. After completing reserve officer training school, he was commissioned in the Army as a second lieutenant and assigned to the 9th Infantry Division. He commanded an infantry platoon for three hundred consecutive days in combat and is a recipient of two Silver Stars, two Bronze Stars for valor, and the Purple Heart. After the war Wolfson graduated from the University of Maryland in 1948 and the University of Baltimore Law School in 1950, and he has practiced family law in Baltimore for over fifty years. He and his wife, Emily, were married in 1947, and they have two children and three grandchildren.

I was born in Baltimore, Maryland, on October 4, 1922, to Benjamin and Mimi Wolfson. I grew up in a neighborhood near Lake Ashburton and walked to Windsor Hill Elementary School until I turned fourteen and went to the Charlotte Hall Military Academy in Saint Marys County. The school has a rich military tradition since its founding in 1774, and it wasn't long after my arrival that I was trained to fire military weapons at silhouettes on the rifle range. We had officers from the Army who taught us military history and tactics, and although I was very young I was thoroughly indoctrinated into the military discipline. As for my attitude towards being a soldier, I wanted to follow in the footsteps of my father, who was a lieutenant in the First World War, and honestly I didn't really know anything else I wanted to do.

Upon graduation I enrolled in the University of Maryland and joined the Reserve Officers Training Corps. I completed the course in the summer of 1942, and I was sent to the infantry school at Fort Benning, Georgia, and when I graduated from the officer candidate school I was commissioned as a second lieutenant in the United States Army while retaining my reserve officer status. I was then sent to Camp Blanding, Florida, where I trained new troops in the basics of firing weapons. I made twenty-nine dollars a month teaching a variety of cursory lessons to the recruits aimed at introducing the general concepts of being a soldier until each class was divided and sent to particular outfits where they learned specific skills, whether it was for artillery, tanks, or infantry. The most important thing I could teach new soldiers was discipline. Skill in firearms is essential in combat, but nothing preceded the need to establish good discipline in soldiers.

In April of 1944 I was ordered to England without being assigned to any particular division. The morning before I left home I was standing on my front lawn talking with my father, and at the same moment we both discovered a four-leaf clover in the lawn. I kept those clovers in my wallet during the entire war, and I like to think they brought me luck a few times when I needed it.

I arrived in France about two weeks after the initial D-Day landings on the English destroyer HMS *Rapier*. I was fed well during my short stay on the *Rapier*, and there was plenty of whiskey on board to help me pass the time. I boarded an LCI (landing craft, infantry) and landed on Omaha Beach. My first sight were the dead bodies that still littered the beach, and to this day I cannot get the smell that emanated from their bodies out of my head. I was put onto a truck and was driven to the 9th Infantry Division headquarters in Carentan. I was at ease and not nervous about going into battle. It was a natural extension of all my years of military training.

When I arrived at the 9th Division I was the replacement for a lieutenant who had been killed in action the day before. I reported to the company captain, who we called "the Fox." When I first met him he was in a small house lying on a mattress next to a wall, and when I entered his room I saluted and introduced myself. He barely lifted his head while he informed me that I was to be placed in command of a platoon in Company F, 39th Battalion. Before he dismissed me he pointed in the direction my platoon was located and said I could find it "over there somewhere." That was all the captain ever said to me, and I think he figured I wouldn't be around much longer, so he didn't see the need for formalities.

On the way to the platoon I stopped into a field kitchen where the quartermaster came up to me and handed me a .45-cal. Thompson submachine gun with seven thirty-round magazines and a knife with brass knuckles. He suggested that I might need them and pointed over to a body lying on the side of the road, which was the body of the lieutenant I was replacing. I wrapped up the M1 carbine I had been issued and used the Thompson for most of my time in combat, except when my carbine came in handy when I was in the Harz Mountains.

I found the platoon dug in along a tree line and was welcomed by a sergeant by the name of Curry. It took everyone some time to get used to the new guy in charge, but after a few days of fighting, sleeping, and eating together we all got to know one another. They all were wonderful soldiers between the ages of eighteen and thirty-two, and they followed orders without hesitation.

Three rifle companies were in each battalion, and each company was comprised of three rifle platoons consisting of three squads. Each company was assigned a heavy-weapons platoon armed with mortars and .30-cal. machine guns. The primary task of the infantry was to advance and capture land and kill the enemy. We didn't see the big picture during the war. We didn't know or care to know exactly where we were at all times; it was just day after day of moving forward against the enemy. My platoon consisted of about forty men divided into three squads, with each squad assigned a sergeant as squad leader. It was my responsibility to lead the men under my command and to order them to do whatever it took to advance forward. When on patrol it was my responsibility to be up front leading the platoon forward.

I had to be constantly moving while in combat, so I couldn't carry too much stuff other than my weapons and basic survival gear. I always carried one grenade, a .45-cal. Colt automatic with four extra seven-round clips my father had given me before I was shipped overseas, and a .380 Walther automatic pistol I kept in my right shirt pocket. I also had a little pocketknife that came in handy opening C rations, a combination fork and spoon utensil I borrowed from a captured German, C rations, a canteen, a compass, a pipe and tobacco, a pair of binoculars, some extra clothes, and half a blanket. I carried most of this stuff in a green canvas musette bag, or "war bag," as we called it, that was designed to fit over the shoulder. Only when my platoon was relieved from the front line was I able to use my bedroll and extra blankets for added comfort.

In those days we didn't have compact little radios, so I had a radioman whose job it was to carry a large radio pack on his back. My initial radioman was named Carl, and he was from the southern Appalachian Mountains and was in effect my bodyguard. I wouldn't go to the bathroom without my bodyguard.

In each squad of my platoon, two men were armed with the Browning automatic rifle (BAR), which was essentially a small light machine gun, and the remainder of the squad was armed with the M1 semiautomatic rifle. The M1 rifle was a good, efficient, and very powerful .30-cal. rifle that held an eight-round clip. Being semiautomatic, the M1 rifle fired a single round every time the trigger was pulled, and it then automatically reloaded until the last was fired and the empty clip was ejected. The Thompson submachine gun I used fired rapidly, and while it wasn't a target pistol, it was accurate up to 100 yards, but I used it mostly at close range, and the impact the 230-grain .45-cal. rounds made on a target was very effective in close combat. I rarely permitted my troops to use captured German weapons, probably because I feared their sound would draw fire from other American GIs. On one occasion I relented after we had captured some Russians who had been conscripted into the German Army, and one of my men took a Russian machine gun. The next day he was advancing over a hill and ran into a German patrol and was killed when the Russian gun misfired. He had not known how to operate it properly, and I regret that I ever let him pick it up.

While in combat I was always on the move, and we fought continuously with just occasional rest. Every morning we woke up and went to work moving forward, and that was my typical day. There was no fun while in combat, and I felt exhausted all the time. I lived a very primitive life in battle, which included having to do my personal duties in the woods like a dog. I subsisted on C rations, which were slightly palatable canned rations of bacon, cheese, meat, crackers, and a variety of other items. Only once in a while when we were out on the front line for more than a day did we receive hot food. During a holiday, like Christmas, the cook would send up hot food for the guys. I had one little pleasure that consisted of some whiskey, English gin, or scotch rations we were given that helped to take the edge off the nerves.

Living at the front meant living in the ground under very difficult conditions. Anytime we stopped we began to dig holes, because your hole was the only protection you had from artillery, and your options were to live in a hole or die from shrapnel. Shells that landed in front of your position were deadly because the inertia of the shell would spread the shrapnel forward, so when a shell passed overhead I knew I was safe from at least that one. Deep snow also worked well in stopping a lot of shrapnel. In the winter it was very difficult to dig holes in the frozen ground, so we used blocks of TNT to loosen the earth so we could dig into the ground. I wouldn't stop for two minutes without starting to dig a hole. That's how I lived, and it helped me stay alive.

The weather was mild during our fighting in France, and into Belgium during the summer and fall it wasn't very cold until winter came, and then things were not so good. The Germans were a much more dangerous enemy than the cold, but the weather was something we had to endure. I wore all the clothes I could in layers to stay warm. Starting with underwear, I would layer as many pieces of my uniform as I could. While some men wore overcoats, I had lost mine, and it was so torn and shot full of holes I would have gladly thrown it away, anyway. I had no change of clothes or underwear, particularly in the winter. I had two pairs of socks, one of which I would wear until they became wet, and the other I wrapped around my waist to dry out. I got used to being dirty, I guess. I didn't wash or shave (the guys old enough had nice beards), and I lived like an animal in the ground. After the Battle of the Bulge during our advance towards the Roer River dams, I lived in houses in various villages during a good part of the winter, which made life much more comfortable.

We all accepted the fact that it was our duty to live in such miserable conditions, and to fight and die if necessary to win the war. I would be lying if I said I wasn't glad when it was all over and I went home. To the credit of my men, I saw many get killed, but not one ever complained of being sick in an attempt to find relief from the fighting.

We moved primarily during the daylight hours, and I didn't send patrols out at night very often, and little fighting was done after sundown. We were constantly on the advance, but in the rare situation when we were on the defensive, I would send out a reconnaissance patrol or establish a forward outpost with instructions to retreat back to join the rest of the platoon if fired upon. The heavy-weapons platoon would set up machine-gun positions for close support, and the mortar crews would presight their tubes so that if they heard any noises at night they could fire and know exactly where their rounds would land.

When we received orders to move forward we all knew guys were going to get killed, but we obeyed our orders no matter what; that's all there was to it. There was some sense of being all alone when you got up and moved against the enemy, but in reality we were moving abreast with the entire sector. Our advance was almost always accompanied by friendly artillery barrages booming overhead. We advanced, and if we were fired upon, we fired back. We had the advantage of having the Germans in retreat, and they had limited forces to delay our advance, but when they decided to stop and hold their ground, we had a significantly more difficult time moving forward.

We usually made contact with the enemy at long distances, and we didn't just walk across open fields into machine-gun fire. Instead, we always did something to soften their positions before we started our assault. We had a massive artillery advantage, and I could call a strike on the smallest target, if we so desired, and the German defenders would be forced to crouch down into their holes, run away, or die. Incoming mortar and artillery fire caused the most casualties within our ranks, and it was best to find cover as soon as you heard it approaching. On the other hand, when we came under small-arms fire we didn't run or hide because the key for any infantry to survive in combat is to return as much fire as possible when fired upon. An experienced group of infantrymen instinctively returned fire when fired upon, and our platoon delivered a tremendous amount of firepower that overwhelmed our German counterparts. We also had an advantage in having command of the air, and we never had to worry about German aircraft except when we crossed the Remagen Bridge, where it seemed like they had plenty around trying to blow the bridge before we could get across. We carried fluorescent-colored panels that we laid out in front of our lines so our planes would know where our positions ended so we wouldn't be bombed by accident.

The 9th Division was comprised of men who had fought in Africa and Sicily, and these men were our core of highly trained and experienced soldiers. There were no fools running around looking to get killed, but not a soul ever questioned my orders. It's easy to get killed in combat, and when men I knew died, I just walked on. There was nothing I could do to bring them back, and I got used to seeing death. Death became an everyday thing. In combat, men lose their sense of values about killing, being killed, or being sorry for their actions or the actions of others. It was always a matter of "better him than you," even when that "him" was my best friend lying dead next to me. Some men would wish for a wound in the leg after a while because they just got so tired of having to endure such stress and the horror of facing death every minute of every day. Combat is unreal, and even the best and bravest of men could lose their composure for a while. I had one or two men break up, and at the time I honestly couldn't have cared less if someone had shot them dead on the spot. But in combat, any man can be brave one day, a coward the next, and only those who have experienced the relentless stress of combat can understand why some men broke down.

I thought about the men I lost, and many of them I liked very much. I had seven platoon sergeants who were either killed or wounded during my time in combat, and often they were hit right next to me, practically. One sergeant who was named Curry died next to me. While in Belgium we took a position in very hilly country, and we camped at the base of a cliff where crevices in the rock allowed us to escape the German artillery. Some supplies arrived, and Curry went out to handle the distribution of the supplies, and a shell landed and killed him. He was an old soldier, regular Army from before the war, and had fought in Africa and Italy and had taught me many things. I didn't cry or weep. I was sorry he was killed, but I accepted it as something I had to endure and live through.

Our wounded were well taken care of by our medics, and many GIs owe their lives to the medics who I saw on numerous occasions run through heavy fire to attend to a wounded man. Those not too severely wounded were patched up and returned within days. Others were sent back to England, and I never saw them again. When a man was killed or wounded, a replacement showed up a short time later. Often I didn't even learn most of their names before some of them were killed, too. When replacements arrived I sat them down with the squad leaders, and they would get something to eat and drink, and then they joined the group and went forward. They weren't given any instructions, special treatment, or advice. The new men were immediately part of our team and were expected to perform.

I don't think I ever thought about hating the Germans. I didn't think of the Germans as people; they were just the enemy, and I killed them without anger. The German soldiers I fought against were regular German Wehrmacht troops, and I didn't see a great deal of difference between the Wehrmacht and the Nazi SS soldiers. The Germans had plenty of artillery and an excellent 81-mm. mortar very similar to ours, and they had a large quantity of tanks to support their infantry. Tanks had limited mobility and were restricted to roads and open fields and primarily fought other tanks. Nine times out of ten their tanks would sit at the edge of field and shoot it out with our tank destroyers, and I watched a number of noisy tank battles. The only times we had encounters with German tanks was when we just happened to be in their way, and we hid in holes or just got out of their way the best we could. If we had mines we laid them out in the road, and if one exploded under a tank it usually blew off a track, allowing us to get close enough to finish it off. If the crew didn't surrender we used bazookas and explosives to finish the tank.

One of the particularly distasteful jobs I had was leading a patrol through a German minefield. The most memorable occasions were at night and in the rain, which made it much more difficult to safely negotiate our way. The Germans were very good at laying minefields, and they used an antipersonnel mine that bounced into the air when triggered and exploded right about where your crotch is located. Typically, two patrols advanced through a minefield in single file with machine guns set up on either side to return fire if the patrols were fired upon.

The German infantry was well trained and equipped with good weapons and was always supported by artillery and mortars. The German 8-mm. light machine gun was the basis of their defense and attack tactics. The German infantry supported the machine gun by providing protection and transporting ammunition. The German riflemen were armed with single-action rifles, and the sergeant in their lead was armed with an automatic submachine gun. In the attack, the Germans established machine-gun positions to support the advancing riflemen, but mostly they were in defensive positions and would withdraw when we advanced or they were killed or taken prisoner.

We always took prisoners and never killed a prisoner except during the Battle of the Bulge, when we were ordered to the contrary; there were a few moments when we did not allow them to surrender, if that makes a difference. At all other times, when one guy threw his hands up and came forward, we made sure he was well protected so the others would see that surrendering was a safe way out of the war. As soon as one surrendered, many would throw down their guns and join in. There weren't too many heroes around when we surrounded a position and began to take prisoners. We didn't spend much time dealing with the prisoners; we basically lined them up and pointed in the direction they were to go. We never abused the prisoners but treated them like people, giving them food and water or whatever we could spare. Some of my men liked to scrounge for souvenirs, and I had to put a stop to one guy when I found he was removing the gold teeth from dead Germans. The only thing I had any interest in keeping was quality pistols, and I had a good collection by the end of the war.

In the Harz Mountains we captured a German, and at the time there was no way to send him to our rear, so I ordered him to pick up a couple cans of ammunition and pointed for him to walk ahead so I could keep an eye on him. It didn't surprise me that he dropped the cans and took off running as soon as it started to get dark, and I told my men to hold their fire and let him go. This could have been a disastrous decision, because a few moments later I heard some people speaking English and a GI came running out of a bunker who grabbed my arm and said, "My God, Lieutenant, I would have shot you if I hadn't heard you speaking English. I saw this German soldier run by a few seconds ago, and I thought you were another German."

By September we had advanced through Belgium and crossed the Meuse River, heading toward the German border a short distance further east. When we crossed into Germany we encountered strong resistance along the defensive position called the Siegfried Line. The line was composed of well-fortified positions and concrete bunkers surrounded by large concrete pyramids designed to prevent tanks from advancing. It took some time to advance through the line, and when we pressed into Germany, the resistance intensified considerably. The Germans were on their own soil, and they were determined to fight.

On September 13 we entered the Hurtgen Forest, and during the next three months the division suffered nearly 80 percent casualties. The Hurtgen Forest was 50 square miles of dense trees just south of the German city of Aachen. It had been planted at the order of the German military so that the Germans could take advantage of every hill and valley to defend against an invading army. The branches that hung low from neat rows of spruce and balsams created a natural obstacle, limiting our vision and mobility. It seemed I was always crouched over, ducking under the branches of the trees. The forest floor was absolutely clear of debris and vegetation, and the rains and snow turned the ground into knee-deep mud.

Somewhere in the Hurtgen Forest we captured a crossroads. I dug a hole under a huge beech tree, and just as I finished digging, we came under artillery fire. Sgt. Bill Leppard and I dove into the hole just as a shell hit the tree above us. Bill's foot was sticking out of the hole, and shrapnel hit it. I was on my stomach when the shell hit, and all my ammunition magazines were filled with shrapnel holes, and a tin of butter in my pocket was also shot full of holes. I had a few holes in my backside, too. It wasn't serious enough for me to miss any time on the line, but I was awarded the Purple Heart nonetheless.

We broke through the Hurtgen Forest and were fast approaching the Roer River when very strong resistance ground our advance to a halt. On the night of December 9 I was called to Lieutenant Colonel Gunn's command post and ordered to lead a portion of my platoon down the blacktop highway leading into the German town of D'Horn to conduct a reconnaissance mission for an attack planned for the next morning. I was instructed to find a railroad underpass just on the outskirts of D'Horn and to ascertain whether it had been destroyed and, if so, to clear a path wide enough for tanks and men. I gathered my men and a group of Engineers supplied with enough TNT to remove any obstacles we faced. We found the underpass intact. I decided to proceed beyond the underpass and entered D'Horn only to find it completely evacuated by the Germans. I found a comfortable home to wait out the night in until the battalion moved forward the next morning. Division history claims that when the battalion launched the attack the next morning, the lead elements found my men and me comfortably lounging around waiting for their arrival. That part is true, but what they fail to mention is that these troops made their entrance into D'Horn by tossing a grenade into the room we were occupying, killing two of my men. Somehow I walked out of the room without a scratch.

A short time after this, Sergeant Bill Leppard had the opportunity to save my life. Bill was also from Baltimore, and we stayed good friends after the war until his death recently. I was leading a patrol up a sunken road, and as I turned a bend in the road, a German officer appeared and began pointing his finger and shouting at me in alarm. A second German walked from behind the officer armed with a submachine gun, and I lifted my carbine to fire, but it jammed and didn't fire. I was in a real spot until Bill pushed me aside and shot and killed the German aiming the gun, undoubtedly saving my life. The officer ran back into a large concrete bunker, and it was some time before we managed to convince him and others to surrender by dropping grenades down the ventilation tubes.

The newly arrived 99th Infantry Division relieved the 9th Infantry Division, and we were sent back into Belgium for a break to get some much needed rest and relaxation. A few days later the Germans launched an attack through the area where the 99th was located, beginning what was to become known as the Battle of the Bulge. The inexperienced 99th Division was rolled over, and the Germans advanced quickly into Belgium. Many rear-echelon troops surrendered when they probably shouldn't have, compounding the success of the German attack. We didn't see the big picture and had no idea what was happening along the front. All we knew was that we were temporarily attached to the British Army and were moving north to take up defensive positions along the southern flank of the German offensive. We dug in along a ridge, and the Engineers laid a heavy minefield in front of our position. The Germans probed our lines often, but the experienced troops of the 9th Infantry wouldn't budge unless they were killed, so the Germans moved elsewhere to find weaker parts of the line. They dropped parachute troops behind our positions, and we killed every single one, but they didn't offer to surrender, either. We had heard that the Germans had killed about two hundred American prisoners in an open field, and in retaliation an order came down to not take any German prisoners, so we didn't.

We came under artillery fire often during the German offensive, and we discovered that a German tank was hidden nearby overlooking our position calling in artillery, so I gathered a patrol to resolve the situation. The snow was very deep, almost above our waists, and it took some time to reach the tank, which was about a mile away. Mines had been placed in front of the tank, so I circled around behind the tank, and we attacked from behind. I waited until the tank opened its turret hatch, and I had one of my men waiting to drop a grenade into the tank. The tank was destroyed, and we then quickly overran a bunker with six or seven Germans, and we took just one prisoner who we used to guide us back to our lines through their minefield.

A Belgian man who must have been in his late forties approached me a day or so later. He was dressed in his hunting outfit with bag and rifle, and we concluded that he was a member of the Belgian home guard and wanted to join us in fighting the Germans. He had little admiration for our tactics and became very upset when we began taking captured Germans prisoner again. He hung around with us for a few days before disappearing, and he often sat alone repeating the phrase *"Toujours, madame,"* meaning something like "Always, my wife." He had informed me that the Germans had killed his wife, and he wanted to avenge her death.

After the Battle of the Bulge there was really no great change in our advance, except perhaps we experienced a little more resistance when we began to fight our way back into Germany. We crossed the Roer River in early March and participated in the attack upon Bad Godesberg. Bad Godesberg was a resort town along the west side of the Rhine defended by elements of the German 3rd Parachute Division, a group we had tangled with on a previous occasion and that had proven their merit as soldiers. I remember the attack went well but that the Germans launched a tremendous barrage from "Nebelwerfers": multibarreled rocket launchers whose bombs made an eerie whine while in flight. We pushed the Germans to the far side of the town until all that remained was a well-fortified defensive position along a point extending into the Rhine River. Lieutenant Colonel Gunn thought the defenders would surrender if given terms, so I stepped forward when he asked for a volunteer to accompany an interpreter to speak with the commander of the German stronghold. I was instructed that if the Germans did not surrender their position by 4:20, an artillery barrage would be fired followed by an infantry assault.

I put my weapons aside and instructed my radioman and driver to do the same. We drove forward until we reached a German outpost, and I instructed my radioman and driver to stay put while the interpreter and I were escorted to the German who was in charge. We were led into the command bunker, and a German captain greeted me with a salute, which I returned. The captain was about 6 feet tall and dressed in a camouflage poncho. He spoke good English and offered me a drink, and as he poured I began to offer our terms for his surrender. The captain responded by urging that I understand the necessity for the German and American armies to unite to fight the Russians. I felt insulted at his remarks towards our Russian ally, and the conversation began to unravel until the captain held up his hands, shook his head, and made it clear he was not surrendering. The German captain said, "We are heavily armed, and I have four 88s aimed at all of your possible approach routes. Besides, it would be dishonorable for me to surrender." I responded by asking him to consider the lives of the many innocent civilians who were intermingled within his defensive positions, in the hope that this would give the captain an honorable reason to surrender. He offered to disengage but insisted on regrouping his forces in a different sector. I grabbed my interpreter by the arm and instructed him to take a message back to my radioman that the answer to our surrender offer was, simply, no. The interpreter exited the bunker, and I was left alone in the uncomfortable position of standing before a room full of heavily armed German paratroopers.

I began to lose hope of escaping alive if the captain decided to end the conversation abruptly. The moment was fast approaching when our artillery would start, and the time I stood staring back at the captain seemed like an eternity. Suddenly the captain looked at his holster and removed his pistol. I think my heart stopped, and I was sure this was the end for me. To my relief, the captain held out the pistol and handed it to me. He then spoke a few words in German instructing his men to drop their weapons and form two columns outside the bunker to begin a march towards the American lines. Things were going better than planned, and just then the artillery barrage began. The Germans became infuriated, and I ran from man to man urging them to stay down and not run for their weapons. I was outnumbered, and just as the Germans became unmanageable, members of my platoon came running up the road to help lead the prisoners away. I was very moved that my men had run forward under fire and against orders to rescue me from what would have been my certain death in just a few more moments.

The 9th Division was turned south and headed towards Remagen, where the last bridge across the Rhine River was still standing. The bridge was captured intact, and our battalion crossed the bridge the next day on March 7 amidst numerous other Allied divisions trying to get across the Rhine. The Germans were naturally very intent on destroying the bridge after their efforts to demolish it before we arrived failed. I crossed the Remagen Bridge under an intense artillery and air barrage, and I was nearly killed when a shell landed on the bridge, wounding or killing twelve men surrounding me, but I was unhurt. Most of the 9th Division crossed and established a bridgehead before the Remagen Bridge collapsed. But it wasn't long before pontoon bridges were built, and the flood of men continued across the Rhine.

Resistance continued to be stiff following the Rhine crossing, but gradually we began to encounter Volkssturm (civil defense) groups consisting of poorly equipped kids and old men who had been thrown into the line to slow our advance. These poor people were useless and posed little deterrence to our advance, and most were glad to surrender as soon as we came along.

By April we had entered the Harz Mountains. These are low rolling mountains in Germany very similar to the Allegheny Mountains here in the United States. During our advance into the mountains we discovered the Nordhausen concentration camp. The area around the camp was wooded, and the prisoners of Nordhausen had been used to cut timber and had constructed the roads surrounding the camp. When we liberated the camp, what I saw can hardly be described to someone who has never seen such a sight. I saw piles of naked dead, decayed, and dying people all over the camp. I thought I had become immune to seeing lots of dead people in war, but this was the first time I had seen row upon row of so many emaciated half-dead or dead and decaying bodies. I wasn't angry at what I saw, but it came as a shock to see something like this. We went into the nearby village and inquired if they had known what was happening at the camp. They all swore they hadn't known anything like this was happening, but I didn't believe a single one of them.

Our commanding officers ordered the able-bodied men to dig graves for the dead in the camp. We freed the prisoners from the camp, who were mostly Russian prisoners of war. They immediately ran for the village and began looting food and clothes, and we intervened when it appeared as though they were going to start killing some Germans. We herded the Russians back out of the village without anyone getting hurt, and we probably saved the village from complete destruction. We moved on, and the war continued, and my attitude didn't change a bit about anything, except it was just another example of what horrible things people can do to one another.

The war concluded a short time later, and my battalion was stationed in the German town of Titmoning located across the Salzach River from Salzburg, Austria. We had been ordered to occupy and defend an area that had been left unscathed from the war, and I lived in a beautiful medieval castle. The civilians were really no problem at all, but they weren't sorry about anything, except maybe sorry for losing the war. I found it less than amusing when they asked us why we were fighting the Germans when we should ally with Germany to fight the Russians.

The Russian were our allies, but I had some interesting situations with the Russians occur. A group of leaderless Russian soldiers arrived soon after the war ended, and they thought about moving into the castle I was occupying. I was forced to take their weapons and send them back across the Salzach River where they belonged. A week later a German woman came to us complaining that the Russians had returned and were in the town robbing, beating, and raping. I assembled a squad of men and went into the town and forced the Russians out once more, but this time we shot and killed two Russian soldiers who fired on us. I reported the incident to my commander, and the next day I received an order to stop the Russians from crossing the Salzach River. I couldn't think of any way of stopping them other than setting up a machine-gun post at either end of an open area on our side of the river. I sent a man to their side warning them against returning to our side, but when the Russians came again the next day, I gave the order to fire and killed them all. Generals on both sides wrote all kinds of letters saying I had done a terrible thing and was going to receive a court martial, but I never heard anything about the incident again.

As guys began collecting enough points to return home, the men I had fought with for almost a year began leaving, and it was difficult to say goodbye to friends I had served with in combat. I was eventually assigned to the division headquarters for a while before I too boarded a Liberty ship in Hamburg headed for New York City.

After returning home I was sent to Fort Meade and was separated from the active-duty Army. I was glad to be a civilian again and resumed life the best I could. I remained in the reserves and transferred to the 338th Counterintelligence Battalion based at Fort Meade, where I stayed until I retired as a lieutenant colonel in 1965.

The war took place a half a century ago, but I remember things as if they happened yesterday. The war went on for a long time and a lot of people died, and there were too many tragedies to record. I think about the war only occasionally, but I know that deep down inside, my experiences during the war have forever affected me. I don't fear or care about death, I don't cry when people die, and I just don't have the same normal feeling others have about death. It's nice that younger generations are learning about the war in recent movies, but I saw a show about the men who played soldiers in the movie *Saving Private Ryan,* and one actor made a comment about how he has an understanding of the fear we experienced during the war. He is just an actor and can't possibly know or understand the fear that only the men who have put on a uniform and walked into battle will know.

I was very lucky to have survived the many days I spent in combat and to be awarded a medal for my actions. I could tell a thousand stories and not even begin to fully express what it was like to serve in combat. It is something you just have to experience to understand completely. So many men performed heroic acts every day, and many went unnoticed or unreported. Awards were often issued in a very arbitrary and perhaps unfair manner. The historians or whoever had to write the news reports for the division would ask a commander to give them some stories for public relations reasons, and often just a very few were offered, and seldom were they described completely accurately. I would guess that for every one citation issued to a soldier, there were a dozen other incidents a soldier could have been awarded some kind of medal for. It was often just politics.

The real heroes of the Second World War were every dog-faced soldier who picked up a gun and went to the line every day. It is the infantry soldier who goes into battle who takes the most risks. He is forced to live, fight, and kill like an animal. The air support, artillery, and good direction from the generals all contributed to the victory, but it is the infantryman who wins the war. The infantrymen in any war are my heroes.

Target Hiroshima

The following is a speech delivered by Joseph D. Buscher in 1970 before members of a local service organization as part of ceremonies commemorating the twenty-fifth anniversary of the bombing of Hiroshima. Buscher, born in Silver Spring, Maryland, was well qualified to speak about the role of the 509th Bomb Group in the delivery of the atomic bombs on Japan. Having been elected before the war to the Montgomery County House of Delegates, he enlisted in the Army in 1942 and received a captain's commission before being assigned as a combat intelligence officer to the 393rd Squadron, 509th Bomb Group. After the war Buscher served as the special assistant attorney general for the Comptroller of the Treasury, and in 1949 he was appointed the special assistant attorney general for the State Roads Commission (State Highway Administration), a position he occupied until his retirement in 1971.

Ladies and gentlemen, I have been asked to talk on the atomic bomb. Even though I was with the atomic bomb project for over a year both in this country and at our overseas base, there is little I can say about the atomic bomb itself for two reasons: First, the principle of nuclear physics involved in the explosion and detonation of atomic energy is a question for scientists and physicists who are much more learned than myself. Second, much of the tactics employed in the dropping of the atomic bombs still remains top secret. I can give you nothing on the weight, size, or shape of the bomb, or the tactics used in the release of the bomb, or the distance above the earth at which the bomb detonated.

However, I can go into the training employed by our outfit, and into the group itself, which was unique in character. The 509th Bomb Group had its inception in Wendover, Utah, in September of 1944. At that time, one complete squadron, the 393rd, which was alerted to go overseas as a regular B-29 technical outfit, was ordered intact to Wendover. The reason we were so ordered was not made known to us. Upon arrival there, we were told that we would drop a new type of bomb, which if successful would hasten the conclusion of the war by at least one year. Around the 393rd Squadron the 509th Group developed. In addition to the tactical squadron, an air transport unit was formed, and an engineering unit, a military police unit, and a large ordnance outfit were developed. These in addition to several smaller units composed the 509th Group.

Our training at Wendover consisted of day and night flying at very high altitude, practicing certain tactics that were deemed necessary to successfully drop this new weapon. This intensive training, along with the administrative duties necessary to develop a tactical outfit, continued through the end of 1944.

On the 1st of January 1945, the tactical squadron was sent to the Caribbean theater and there based in Cuba, to further perfect tactics used in the employment of the bomb. Here, very long simulated combat missions were run. Those included nonstop flights to the Bahamas and back, nonstop flights to Norfolk and Washington, D.C., and simulated bombing runs being made on those cities, and all training there was carried on as nearly as possible to what we thought we would find in actual combat. We did not cancel training flights because of bad weather and in fact scheduled flights under adverse weather conditions for crew training. The average length of our missions in this area was thirteen to fifteen hours, which is the length of time required to fly from the Marianas to Japan.

On the first of March we returned to our base at Wendover, and there intensive training was conducted to determine the ballistics of this new bomb. By "ballistics" I mean actual time of fall and other information, which is important for the bomb to fall at the desired spot.

In April 1945 the group began its overseas movement, and by the end of June the group was set up at its base on the island of Tinian in the Marianas. When we arrived there, we found that our training was still incomplete, and between June and August we ran familiarization and training missions. These included actual bombing missions over such Jap-held islands as Truk and Marcus. Later we ran many actual demolition missions over Japan itself, dropping a special type of heavy demolition bomb from very high altitude. These, of course, were not atomic bombs, and the missions were run not only to destroy precision targets in Japan but also to familiarize the crew with actual combat conditions, including attacks of enemy fighter aircraft and enemy antiaircraft fire.

During all of this period while in the States, the Caribbean, and overseas, security was practiced to its highest degree. Not more than half a dozen officers or men of the entire group knew what their ultimate mission was to be. All personnel within the group were very carefully screened by the Department of Justice and military intelligence before being allowed to remain in the group. It might be noted that a number of the original tactical squadron and many of the replacements suited to do technical work in the ordnance squadron were rejected as a result of these investigations.

My particular job in this outfit was to assist in the preparation of missions; to brief the crews as to enemy targets and enemy defenses along the route and to interrogate the crews upon their return, and to disseminate the information to higher headquarters; and to fly missions occasionally with the crews as an observer.

We were a part of the Twentieth Air Force, whose headquarters were located on Guam, and to the best of my knowledge only a very few high-ranking officers of the Twentieth Air Force headquarters knew our mission.

On the 3rd of August of the last year of the war, we received top-secret field orders by officer carrier, which stated certain targets and their order of priority upon which we were to employ our secret weapon. We began intensive target study and briefing exercises. Each member of the crews, including the pilot, co-pilot, navigator, bombardier, and radio operator, was given a minimum of ten hours' target study on any of three targets that might have been hit on either of the atomic bomb missions. This meant each crew member received thirty hours of concentrated target information. When the course of study was completed, we required the crew members to draw from memory without the use of maps the entire route from our base in the Marianas to landfall at the proper place on the island of Japan, from thence to the various turning points, to the targets, and the route back to our base. For the ones who could not accomplish this, more target study was given. Then on August 5, Mariana time, we received the go-ahead for our first mission.

Final preparations were made and briefing completed, and at two-thirty in the morning of August 6, the first atomic bomb plane took off on its mission. Still the crews and the personnel of the group knew nothing of what the ultimate effect of the mission would be.

On the Hiroshima mission, two alternate targets were given, one being Nagasaki, and the other a city I cannot mention. On this mission, as in the second mission on Nagasaki, seven B-29s and their complete crews were involved. One B-29 and crew took off prior to the atomic bomb plane and landed at Iwo Jima, which is halfway, to stand in readiness in case the plane carrying the bomb should have mechanical failures and have to land there. Three other planes and crews took off one hour prior to the atomic bomb plane and circled Hiroshima, and the alternate targets, at a very high altitude and ascertained weather and wind velocity, so necessary to a successful bombing mission. Two planes accompanied the atomic bomb plane, and they carried cameras and other instruments and equipment employed in the drop. When the atomic bomb plane neared the coast of Japan, the weather ships over the various targets gave the weather information and the visibility, and it was then determined which targets would be attacked, and as a result of this, Hiroshima was selected as the first target.

One point of interest, I think, involves the placing of the powder charge in the atomic bomb by Captain (now Admiral) Parsons, the same person who invented the proximity fuse. Captain Parsons would not allow the bomb to be charged on the island of Tinian, realizing the terrific damage that would occur if something went amiss on this job, so he personally, while the plane was en route to the target, spent one hour and forty-five minutes working in the cold in the bomb bay of the airplane, placing the powder charge in the bomb. Many similar acts of individual heroism could be mentioned.

The results of the atomic explosion over Hiroshima I will not go into because you had access to many more newspapers and magazine articles than we did over there.

The second atomic bomb raid took place on the 9th of August and was conducted in a manner similar to the first. Shortly after that, as you know, Japan capitulated.

The successful dropping of the atomic bomb was not an Air Force project alone but required the joint cooperation of many civilian scientists, the Navy, the Army ground forces, and the Army air forces, and it was only because of that cooperation that the development and employment of the atomic bomb was made possible.

AFTERWORD

To the question "Who were the real heroes of the war?" there is an easy answer: the men who fought in combat. Almost three hundred thousand Americans died battle deaths. About a hundred thousand more died of disease and accidents, with some thirty-five thousand dying in aircraft crashes alone. All who survived combat were marked by it forever, even though most made successful transitions to civilian life.

While these men were the greatest heroes and suffered and sacrificed the most, honor must be paid to all who served in the forces. The average man or woman in uniform gave three years to his or her country. Most went overseas, often to places where heat or cold or disease or poor living conditions made daily life hard even for those who did not see action. During the war most regarded their time in the military as lost years—not in the sense of having been unnecessary, but as time taken from what should have been their normal progression through school and into the world of work and marriage. Generally their sweethearts, wives, and husbands back home or in another part of the war felt this way as well. This helps explain why the veterans astounded America by going to college, getting married, and starting families all at once instead of proceeding from stage to stage as civilians had done in peacetime. They were men and women in a hurry. They were the parents of the baby boom, but also the people who did so much to produce the economic boom that marked the postwar era.

Credit must be given to the members of Congress who produced the GI Bill in 1944, which made all this possible. Instead of voting to give veterans cash bonuses at some distant point in the future as after past wars, Congress enacted legislation that would provide them with immediate assistance: subsidies for trade school and college costs, guaranteed home mortgages and business loans, among other benefits. As a result, the war generation became by far the best educated and most productive America had ever seen. Great in war, it was great in peace as well.

The war generation was, and remains, stoic and self-effacing. When asked about what they underwent while in uniform, however courageous and self-sacrificing they may have been, veterans invariably shy away from the label "hero" and say that they were only doing their job. But even those in the safest jobs spent years serving their country, and those who fought endured what words can never fully describe. Still, words are all we have, and much can be learned from the men and women of the war generation, even if we can only dimly sense what they endured. I hope that this book will help people today appreciate the nobility of these modest men and women and the great debt we owe them for our freedom.

Time will not dim the glory of their deeds.

"Theirs Is the Highest and Purest Democracy"

The following is the invocation delivered by 5th Marine Division chaplain Lt. Roland B. Gittelsohn, U.S. Navy, at the dedication of the 5th Marine Division Cemetery on Iwo Jima on March 21, 1945.

Here before us lie the bodies of comrades and friends. Men who until yesterday or last week laughed with us, joked with us, trained with us. Men who were on the same ships as us, and went over the side with us as we prepared to hit the beaches of this island. It is not easy to do so. Some of us have buried our closest friends here. We saw these men killed before our very eyes. Any one of us might have died in their place. Indeed, some of us are alive and breathing this very moment only because men who lie here beneath us had the courage and the strength to give their lives for ours.

To speak in memory of such men is not easy. No, our poor power of speech can add nothing to what these men and other dead of our division who are not here have already done. All that we can even hope to do is follow their example. To show the same selfless courage in peace that they did in war. To swear by the grace of God and the stubborn strength and power of human will that their sons and ours shall never suffer these pains again. These men have done their job well. They have paid the ghastly price of freedom.

We dedicate ourselves, first, to live together in peace the way they fought together and are buried together in this war. Here lie men who loved America. Here lie officers and men, Negroes and whites, rich men and poor—together. Thus do we memorialize those who, having ceased living with us, now live within us. Thus do we consecrate ourselves, the living, to carry on the struggle they began. Too much pain and heartache has fertilized the earth on which we stand. We here solemnly swear: This shall not be in vain. Out of this, and from the suffering and sorrow of those who mourn this, will come, we promise, the birth of a new freedom for the sons of all men everywhere.

Saint-Laurent-sur-Mer

The haunting sound of taps told the battle monument story,
—Soldiers behind these walls rest in honored glory.
I was there to commemorate an Anniversary of war,
—How vivid it seemed as if in a dream my return to forty-four.
Here in this lovely memorial in Normandy by the sea,
—I looked on the graves of the soldiers as far as the eye could see.
Many beautiful flowers surround the graveside plots,
—But none seem more appropriate than the forget-me-nots.
The white crosses and stars were everywhere,
—Here in Saint-Laurent-sur-Mer.
Each has a poignant story to tell,
—They all hold a hero who passed through hell.
Could it be five decades ago?
—That thousands stormed the beaches below.
Like a western showdown at high noon,
—D-day was here on the sixth of June.
Europe waited in breathless anticipation,
—The mighty Allied armies and the joy of liberation.

Then came the start of Operation Overlord,
—With landings at Omaha, Utah, Gold, Juno and Sword.
On Omaha Beach in Normandy, France,
—H-hour began the first wave advance.
A fearful barrage of shells kept falling all around,
—Men died in the choppy water or died on the sandy ground.
Cursing and praying they drew their last breath,
—Courageously keeping a rendezvous with death.
Some were blown to pieces coming in on LSTs,
—Others with their legs torn off crawled forth on bloody knees.
There were so many bodies piled high on the beach,
—Many thought the high ground was a goal they could not reach.
Then out of the terrible fury of unrelenting battle,
—Men thundered to high ground like a wild stampede of cattle.

Now this ground is sacred where they found eternal rest,
—Beneath their cross or star they remain their Nation's best.
No sentries are needed here where guardian angels dwell,
—God took away their fear as he caught them where they fell.
Here in this marble orchard where seeds of valor were sown,
—You may find the noblest saints, some remain unknown.

The following poem was written by George Dewey Roberts Jr., of Mount Airy, Maryland, who during the Second World War served as a medic with the 175th Infantry Regiment, 29th Infantry Division, until he was transferred to the 184th General Hospital in England after being wounded by a shell explosion that ruptured his eardrums. He landed on Omaha Beach in Normandy on the afternoon of June 6, 1944, and witnessed the carnage that had been inflicted on the first waves of the 29th Infantry as it advanced inland against German defenses. Roberts wrote this poem in 1994 to commemorate the fiftieth anniversary of the D-Day invasion. In 1999 he returned to France and was honored by the French government for the poem, which is enshrined in the Allied D-Day Visitor's Center Museum in Saint-Lô.

"The poem was not for me," Roberts explained. "It was for the men who were killed on the beaches of Normandy and in the fields leading to Saint-Lô who are buried in the cemetery overlooking Omaha Beach. Without the victory in Normandy the Germans still could have won the war, and instead of the Stars and Stripes flying over the beaches of France you would still see the German swastika. I returned to France in 1999 to mark the fifty-fifth anniversary of the D-Day invasion, and I stood above Omaha Beach and looked over the 9,300 crosses and stars marking the graves of the Americans who had given their lives for freedom. It was very moving. When you think about the over 14,500 servicemen whose remains were returned to the States, the price was over 25,000 lives to take the 12 miles between the beaches and Saint-Lô. It is just staggering. What a horrible price we paid, but it had to be. We should never forget."

And when the harvest is gathered in Heaven's final edition,
—The Book of Life will show all the men who made this mission.
As I turned to leave a voice seemed to call after me,
—Please don't forget the price we paid to keep our country free.
They say man has no greater love than to give his life for others,
—It is true as I looked upon my sleeping brothers.
Humbly with my head bowed I said this little prayer:
—Dear God, bring multitudes to visit Saint-Laurent-sur-Mer.

George D. Roberts Jr.

The high price of liberating Western
Europe. German prisoners-of-war march
through a line of crosses on their way to dig
new graves in the Henri Chapelle Cemetery,
Belgium, March 1945. International News Photo
from author's collection.

INDEX

Page numbers in **bold** refer to photographs.